King John

ALSO BY MARC MORRIS

The Norman Conquest

A Great and Terrible King:

Edward I and the Forging of Britain

The Bigod Earls of Norfolk in the Thirteenth Century

Castle: A History of the Buildings that

Shaped Medieval Britain

King John

TREACHERY *and* TYRANNY
in MEDIEVAL ENGLAND:
The Road to Magna Carta

MARC MORRIS

PEGASUS BOOKS

NEW YORK LONDON

KING JOHN

Pegasus Books, Ltd.
148 West 37th Street, 13th Floor
New York, NY 10018

First Pegasus Books paperback edition November 2016
First Pegasus Books hardcover edition October 2015

ISBN: 978-1-68177-262-2

10 9 8 7 6 5 4 3

Printed in the United States of America
Distributed by Simon & Schuster
www.pegasusbooks.com

To William
my treasure

Contents

Acknowledgements

M y thanks as usual to all the experts who have taken the time to respond to my inquiries: Adrian Ailes, Nick Barratt, Paul Brand, David Carpenter, David Crouch, Rick Heiser, John Maddicott, David Morrison, Nigel Saul, Brendan Smith, Matthew Strickland, Paul Webster and Louise Wilkinson. I would especially like to acknowledge the kindness of Harriet Webster and her publisher at Boydell, Richard Barber, for allowing me to make use of her translations of Ralph of Coggeshall's chronicle and the Dunstable Annals ahead of publication. Thanks also to Nick Vincent for sending me transcripts of John's charters that have been collected and edited as part of the Angevin Acta project, and to Colin Veach for letting me have an advance copy of his excellent article on William de Briouze. I've enjoyed discussing King John on many occasions with Sophie Ambler, who lent me books and articles that would otherwise have been hard to obtain, and kept me informed of all the exciting research being carried out by the rest of the team at the Magna Carta Project. Once again I am enormously grateful to John Gillingham for reading the whole book in draft and informing me of its errors. Any that remain are all my own fault. At LAW I am indebted as ever to my agent, Julian Alexander, and his assistant, Ben Clark. The team at Hutchinson

– Sarah Rigby, Jocasta Hamilton, Stephanie Sweeney, Laura Deacon, and Najma Finlay – have been supportive and enthusiastic about this book from the first, and ensured that it was ready in time for the 800th anniversary of Magna Carta. My thanks to David Milner for his skilful copy-editing, Mary Chamberlain for her careful proof-reading, Jeff Edwards for drawing the maps and family tree, Charlotte Lippmann for her picture research and Alex Bell for compiling the index. Lastly, thanks and love to Cie, Peter and William for their support and patience, especially during the final months of writing. I look forward to spending more time with them now it is all done.

A Note on Money

In John's day (and indeed until the currency was decimalized in 1971), money in England was measured in pounds, shillings and pence: twelve pennies made a shilling, and twenty shillings made a pound. The only type of coin in circulation was the silver penny, so a pound was a weighty bag of 240 coins. The average income for a baron was about £200 per annum, and even a man who took home £20 a year would have been considered quite well-off. Money was also counted in marks, which were equivalent to 160 pennies, or two-thirds of a pound.

People being tortured during the reign of King John. A drawing by the thirteenth-century chronicler Matthew Paris.

List of Illustrations

E N G L A N D

Zwin

Calais • Ghent
Wissant • Gravelines
FLANDERS
Tournai
Lille •
Bouvines

N

Dieppe •
Barfleur • Arques
Cherbourg • Fécamp •
Bonneville
ROUEN
Radepont •
Bayeux • Montfort Gisors •
Caen • Vaudreuil Les Andelys
Falaise Evreux •
N O R M A N D Y PARIS •
Avranches • Verneuil •
Bonsmoulins • Brézolles
Dol • Alençon •
Seine

B R I T T A N Y Ballon • La Ferté-Bernard
M A I N E •
Le Mans •

Angers • Beaufort-en-Vallée
La Roche-au-Moine Tours • Loire
A N J O U •
Nantes • Saumur • Chinon B E R R Y
Fontevraud • TOURAINE
Loudun • Loches •
Vouvant • Mirebeau •
Mervent • Châteauroux •
P O I T O U Poitiers •
Niort • LA
Lusignan • MARCHE
La Rochelle •
Millescu
Oléron • Limoges •
Saintes • Chalus-Chabrol •
ANGOULEME LIMOUSIN
Angouleme •
Gironde
Bourg-sur-Mer •
Dordogne
Bordeaux • La Réole •
Garonne Marmande •
Montauban •
G A S C O N Y
Muret • Toulouse •

——— Frontier at time of
Treaty of Le Goulet (1200)

0   50   100 km

P y r e n e e s

France

England and Wales

N

SCOTLAND

Norham
Bamburgh
Alnwick
Newcastle
Corbridge
Carlisle
Durham
Barnard Castle
Richmond
Scarborough
Pickering
Hornby
Lancaster
Knaresborough
York
Pontefract
Isle of
Axholme
Humber
Tickhill
Liverpool
Peverel
Bolsover
Trent
Lincoln
Rhuddlan
Deganwy
Chester
Newark
Sleaford
The
Wash
Conwy
Dee
Nottingham
Belvoir
Oswestry
Mathrafal
Shrewsbury
Leicester
Stamford
King's Lynn
Norwich
Radnor
Fotheringhay
Aberystwyth
ENGLAND
Kenilworth
Ely
Framlingham
WALES
Worcester
Northampton
Bury St Edmunds
Brackley
Bedford
Hedingham
Llandovery
Hay
Coggeshall
Colchester
Brecon
Gloucester
Hertford
Pleshey
Abergavenny
Oxford
St Albans
Thames
Wallingford
Cardiff
Marlborough
Sonning
LONDON
Windsor
Dartford
Bristol
Reading
Staines
Kingston
Rochester
Sandwich
Ludgershall
Odiham
Guildford
Allington
Canterbury
Folkestone
Dover
Salisbury
Winchester
Sherborne
Southampton
Winchelsea
Shoreham
Wareham
Portsmouth
Corfe
Isle of Wight
Dartmouth

0   20   40   60 km

N

ULSTER

ULSTER

Carrickfergus

CONNACHT

LOUTH

MEATH

Trim

DUBLIN

LIMERICK

LEINSTER

Limerick

Kilkenny

Irish Sea

WATERFORD

Waterford

CORK

Cork

0   20   40   60 km

Ireland

Family Tree of King John

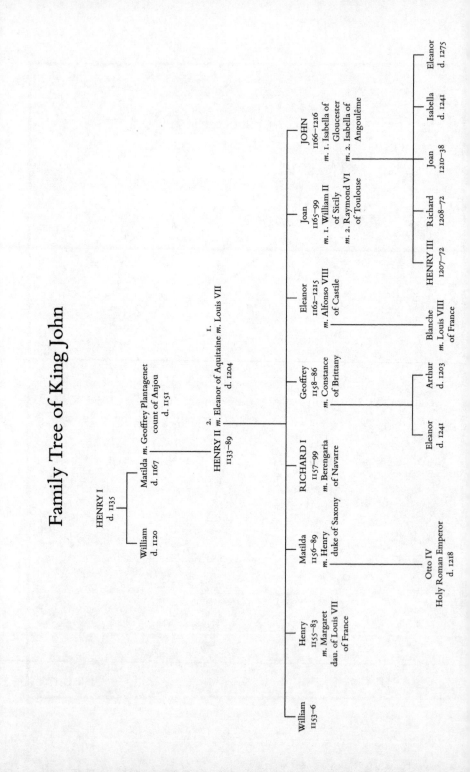

HENRY I
d. 1135

William
d. 1120

Matilda *m.* Geoffrey Plantagenet
d. 1167   count of Anjou
d. 1151

1.
HENRY II *m.* Eleanor of Aquitaine *m.* Louis VII
1133–89   d. 1204
2.

William
1153–6

Henry
1155–83
m. Margaret
dau. of Louis VII
of France

Matilda
1156–89
m. Henry
duke of Saxony

Otto IV
Holy Roman Emperor
d. 1218

RICHARD I
1157–99
m. Berengaria
of Navarre

Geoffrey
1158–86
m. Constance
of Brittany

Eleanor
d. 1241

Arthur
d. 1203

Eleanor
1162–1215
m. Alfonso VIII
of Castile

Blanche
m. Louis VIII
of France

Joan
1165–99
m. 1. William II
of Sicily
m. 2. Raymond VI
of Toulouse

JOHN
1166–1216
m. 1. Isabella of
Gloucester
m. 2. Isabella of
Angoulême

HENRY III
1207–72

Richard
1208–72

Joan
1210–38

Isabella
d. 1241

Eleanor
d. 1275

Introduction

In the summer of 1797 a group of workmen in Worcester
Cathedral caused a sensation, locally if not nationally, by
discovering the body of King John.

John's tomb had long stood in the middle of the cathedral's
choir, but the consensus view in 1797 was that it was empty.
Although the stone likeness (or effigy) on top dated from not
long after the king's death in 1216, the tomb chest had been
created in the sixteenth century in the style of more recent
burials (most notably Henry VIII's older brother, Arthur, who
died in 1502). It was known from the testimony of ancient
chronicles that John had been buried in the Lady Chapel, and
so it was assumed that, although his effigy had been moved
in Tudor times, his bones had been left undisturbed in their
original resting place.

The cathedral clergy found John's tomb a cause of 'much
annoyance', because its central position obstructed the approach
to the altar, and their plan was to move it to some more convenient part of the church. And so, on 17 July 1797, the workmen
set about dismantling it. They removed the effigy and the cracked
stone slab underneath, to discover that the chest had been parti-
tioned by two brick walls, and the sections in between filled with
builders' rubble. But when they removed the sides of the tomb
and cleared out the debris, the workmen, 'to their astonishment',
found a stone coffin. Immediately the dean and chapter of the
cathedral were convened, as well as some local worthies with
relevant expertise (the antiquarian Mr James Ross, and Mr
Sandford, 'an eminent surgeon of Worcester').

Inside the coffin they found 'the entire remains of King John'. His corpse had obviously decomposed somewhat in the course of nearly six centuries. Despite being embalmed, some parts had putrefied, and so 'a vast quantity of the dry skins of maggots were dispersed over the body'. Parts of the body had also been displaced, presumably when it was moved in the sixteenth century. A section of the left arm was found lying at an angle on the chest; the upper jaw was found near the elbow. But otherwise the king was arranged in exactly the same position as his effigy, and was similarly attired. He was dressed from head to foot in a robe of crimson damask (a rich fabric of wool woven with silk) and in his left hand – as on the effigy – he held a sword, in a scabbard, both badly decayed. Curiously, however, whereas on the effigy John wore a crown, his skull was wearing a coif, which the antiquarians took to be a monk's cowl, placed on the king's head after his death to help reduce his time in Purgatory. Measuring the body they found that John had been five foot six-and-a-half inches tall.

The experts might have continued their investigations further, but were prevented from doing so by a large number of people who had crowded into the cathedral to see the dead monarch. 'It is much to be regretted', explained the antiquarian Valentine Green in his published account of the exhumation, 'that the impatience of the multitude to view the royal remains, so unexpectedly found, should have become so ungovernable, as to make it necessary to close up the object of their curiosity.' He was not exaggerating. In the short time that the tomb was open, several bits of John's body were removed by souvenir hunters. His thumb bone was later recovered and can now be seen in the cathedral's own archives, along with some fragments of sandals and stocking, obtained at auction by Edward Elgar. Two of the king's teeth, stolen by a stationer's apprentice in 1797, were 'secretly treasured' until 1923, when they were handed over to the Worcester County Museum.[1]

★ ★ ★

It is easy to understand the excitement of the people of Worcester in 1797. King John is one of those characters from English history who has always exerted a hold on the public's imagination. Almost everyone, even if they know nothing else about the Middle Ages, must feel they know something about him. Unlike other famous medieval monarchs, this is not down to Shakespeare, whose *Life and Times of King John* is one of his worst (and hence least-performed) plays. We are introduced to John much earlier, as children, through the tales of Robin Hood. My own introduction to him, I'm sure, was Disney's *Robin Hood*, released in 1973 (the year I was born), in which the king, voiced by Peter Ustinov, is memorably portrayed by a scrawny lion, with a head too small for the crown he has pinched from his older brother, Richard the Lionheart.

As we will see, there is an element of truth in this story – John did at one point try to usurp the throne from Richard. But the association of John with Robin Hood is pure fiction. The tales of Robin Hood were not written down until the fifteenth century, and in their earliest versions they are said to take place during the time of 'King Edward'. It was not until the sixteenth century that a Scottish writer, John Mair, thought to relocate them to the reign of Richard the Lionheart. From that point, however, the association of John and Robin took firm root. The story was given an immense boost by Walter Scott in his 1820 novel, *Ivanhoe*, which became the basis for the celebrated 1938 Errol Flynn film, *The Adventures of Robin Hood*, itself the basis of the Disney animation.[2]

To get to the real King John, we have to look at the evidence from his own day – what was said about him by contemporary chroniclers, and what can be learned about him from official records. John's reign was a watershed moment in many important respects, including the amount of government archive. From the time of his accession in 1199, the king's chancery, or writing office, began to keep copies of the documents it produced by enrolling them, and these rolls have for the most part survived. (They are now housed in the National Archives at Kew.) As a result we have far more letters, charters, memoranda – in short, far more information – about John than we do for any of his predecessors. Most of the time we can see where he is, who he is with, and what is on his agenda.

Once he is king, that is. One of the problems with telling John's story is that he was the youngest of five brothers, and as such did not grow up expecting to inherit very much at all, let alone the most extensive dominion in Europe. There *is* evidence for John before his accession, but it is altogether more patchy. His life prior to that point has moments of high drama, but there are also long periods during which he almost completely disappears. For this reason, I decided to start my account a few years into his reign, and to look back to the earlier episodes in his life. Plotting the book in this way, it seemed to fall quite naturally into two themes or strands, with a turning point in 1203.

That, therefore, is where we find John at the beginning of Chapter One.

1

Under Attack

1203

In 1203 King John was the ruler of a vast international empire. Besides being king of England he was master of much of south Wales and lord of Ireland. He was also duke of Normandy, count of Anjou and duke of Aquitaine, meaning that he ruled all of what we would now regard as western France, from the English Channel to the Pyrenees. From north to south his authority extended 1,000 miles, and half that distance from east to west. Travellers could pass from the border of Scotland to the border of Spain without ever leaving his territories. Millions of people, speaking at least half a dozen different languages, were his subjects. By any measure, his was the most important and powerful dominion in Europe.[1]

But in the spring of 1203 it was a dominion under attack. John had a rival in the shape of the king of France, Philip II – or Philip Augustus, as he had been dubbed by an admiring contemporary chronicler. At thirty-seven Philip was just one year older than John, but he had been a king for much longer – twenty-three years to John's four. The kingdom he ruled was much smaller than the France of today, but since the start of his reign Philip had been consolidating and extending his power. He had, for example, completely transformed his capital at Paris, giving it new walls, paved streets and a palatial royal castle called the Louvre, expanding the city so that it was many times larger than it had been before. He had long nurtured similar plans to expand the size of his kingdom, and in 1203 he put them into action.[2]

Philip began his assault on John's empire a week after Easter, sailing down the River Loire into the heart of Anjou and seizing the castle at Saumur. At the same moment his allies in the region – John's rebellious subjects – successfully besieged several other castles and occupied the city of Le Mans. In this way John's enemies cut his empire in two, separating Normandy from the provinces further south. Normandy was Philip's main target, and he immediately moved his forces against it, quickly taking a string of major fortresses along its eastern frontier, some of which surrendered to him without a struggle.[3]

John himself was in Normandy at this time, moving between the castles on the frontier and the duchy's principal city, Rouen. According to one chronicler, messengers came to him with news of the invasion, saying 'the king of France has entered your lands as an enemy, has taken such-and-such castles, carried off their keepers ignominiously bound to their horses' tails, and disposes of your property at will, without anyone resisting him'. John's reaction, however, was reportedly one of blithe indifference. 'Let him do so,' he replied. 'Whatever he now seizes I will one day recover.'[4]

This is almost certainly inaccurate and unfair. The chronicler who reports these words, Roger of Wendover, was one of the king's harshest critics. He was a contemporary, in that he lived through John's reign, but he did not write his chronicle until after the reign was over. His account is extremely valuable, sometimes providing credible information that cannot be found elsewhere. But it also contains stories that are demonstrably false, and is shot through with hindsight and moral judgement. Describing John's behaviour at the time of Philip's attack, for instance, Wendover accuses him of 'incorrigible idleness', claiming that he feasted sumptuously every day and enjoyed a long lie-in every morning.[5]

In fact we can see from John's itinerary that during these weeks he was constantly on the move, and other sources state that his first reaction was to try to negotiate, offering the French king any sum of money to break off his attack. When this failed, he pinned his hopes on the intervention of the pope, who wrote to Philip in May, exhorting him to desist or face the Church's condemnation.[6] Then, in the middle of July, John tried to seize the military initiative. He succeeded in recovering a castle in central Normandy, Montfort-sur-Risle, whose lord had defected at the start of the crisis, and the following month he came close to retaking two other castles, Alençon and Brezolles, on the duchy's southern border, but in both cases he retreated on being told that a French army was approaching. Philip meanwhile convened a council of his own bishops and barons who collectively told the pope to mind his own business. Towards the end of August he resumed his offensive, marching his army down the River Seine to begin his assault on the greatest of all John's defences.[7]

Today Château Gaillard is a badly scarred ruin, set high on a rock above a bend in the Seine, about twenty miles south-east of Rouen. In 1203 it was a brand-new building, with pristine stone-work and regal interiors, the most technologically up-to-date fortress in Europe. It had been constructed just a few years earlier by John's older brother, and immediate predecessor, Richard the Lionheart. Richard had waged a long and inconclusive war against Philip Augustus along the Norman–French border, and Château Gaillard – literally, 'the Saucy Castle' – had been created as both a defence for Rouen and a forward base for future conquests. It was built at lightning speed between 1196 and 1198, and at the gargantuan cost of £12,000. (The mighty Dover Castle, built a decade earlier, had cost only half as much.) Richard's new fortress was nonetheless perfectly realized and, in his own immodest opinion, invincible. According to one contemporary, the king had boasted that he could hold it even if its walls were made out of butter.[8]

Philip was finally ready to put the Lionheart's bold claim to the test. Before he could assault Château Gaillard itself, however,

Les Andelys

N

River Seine

French pontoon

Fort

Isle of Andely

New Andely

Lake

Andely

Château Gaillard

Stockade

French trenches

0   100   200   300   400 m

he had to contend with the elaborate series of outer defences that Richard had constructed in the castle's shadow. At the foot of the rock, on a marsh formed by two small tributaries of the Seine, was a new fortified town. It was about a mile to the west of an existing settlement called Andely, and so became known as New Andely (or Little Andely). Opposite this new town, in the middle of the Seine itself, was a long, narrow island – the so-called Isle of Andely. Here Richard had created a crossing of the whole river by building bridges to the shore on either side, and to protect it he had given the island a fortress of its own: an octagonal tower, ringed with a double set of wooden palisades.[9]

Philip's first challenge was therefore to isolate Château Gaillard by taking these outer defences. The way in which he did so is described in great detail by his chaplain, William the Breton, who was an eyewitness.[10] Seeking to avoid the castle itself, the French king led his army up the left bank of the Seine, intending first to tackle the fortress on the Isle of Andely. The garrison there, hearing of his approach, had destroyed the bridge that linked the island to the left bank. But Philip had clearly anticipated such a move, for on their arrival his troops immediately set about creating a replacement crossing, requisitioning boats and barges to transport the necessary building materials into position. This itself was a perilous undertaking, because a little upstream from the island, directly under the walls of Château Gaillard, King Richard had planted a wooden stockade across the river, prohibiting all traffic beyond that point. To get his bridge-building supplies through this barrier, Philip had to send a team of swimmers out into the Seine, armed with axes, and have them hack out a breach. Contending with both the strong current and a shower of missiles from the castle above, these men sustained heavy casualties, but at length an opening was created wide enough for boats to pass. The rest of Philip's men began to construct an elaborate pontoon bridge, sufficiently strong and massive to bear the weight of his army, and fortified with two large towers. It was built not to the island, but right across the Seine to the opposite shore.

As soon as it was completed, the king led the bulk of his forces across to form a new camp on the river's eastern bank, directly menacing the new town of Andely, and leaving the garrison of the island cut off from both sides.

News of the attack on Andely had by now reached the ears of King John, who responded by returning to Rouen and devising a plan for the island's relief. Two separate forces would mount a daring night-time assault. The first, consisting of knights and mercenaries, would proceed along the left bank of the Seine and tackle the French soldiers who remained on that side of the river. The second would be a maritime force: a fleet of galleys, built by Richard to patrol and defend the Seine, together with other ships captained by pirates, would smash through the French pontoon, bringing supplies to the besieged garrison on the island.

The plan was put into immediate effect. The land army was not led by John, who remained in Rouen, but by William Marshal (or 'the Marshal', as contemporaries called him), a military veteran in his mid-fifties, who had plenty of experience executing such devious operations. Advancing along the left bank as agreed, his army fell upon the sleeping French camp in the pre-dawn darkness. Since most of those sleeping there were apparently merchants and other hangers-on rather than soldiers, it was an easy victory, with over 200 said to have been killed. Others tried to escape across the pontoon bridge in such numbers that it broke under the strain. The fleet, it seemed, would have no difficulty in completing the bridge's destruction.

Except that the fleet was nowhere to be seen. While the Marshal and his men had made their way along the river unopposed, the naval force had run into unexpected difficulties – John's scheme had failed to take into account the strength of the tide his oarsmen would have to contend with. In the meantime, the French who were camped on the opposite side of the river had been woken by the noise of the assault and the panicked arrival of their fugitive countrymen. Under the direction of William des Barres, a commander with no less experience than William Marshal, the rout was arrested. Hasty repairs were carried out to the bridge by torchlight, and, as soon as it was passable, des Barres led the French back across to confront their enemies. Surprised at this unexpected reversal, the Marshal's men were now defeated in their turn, with many killed or taken prisoner. The Marshal himself escaped.

The French, thinking the assault was over, recrossed the river, either to celebrate their victory or return to their beds. But a short while later the cry to arms again rang out around their camp: the mercenary fleet had been sighted. The fleet, if not quite so large as William the Breton would have us believe, was clearly a formidable fighting force; there can be little doubt that, had it arrived as planned – in tandem with the Marshal's army and under cover of darkness – the French lines would have been broken and the Isle of Andely resupplied. But, delayed as they were, the naval forces were deprived of the element of surprise, for by this point the sun was rising. By the time they reached the pontoon bridge, both banks of the river and the bridge itself were lined with French soldiers, and the ships sailed into a blizzard of arrows, stones and crossbow bolts. Some of them did crash into the pontoon, and their crews began desperately hacking at its timbers and cables. But the defenders engaged them in savage hand-to-hand combat, and the river ran red with blood. When two of the ships at the front of the fleet were sunk by a giant falling timber, the remainder retreated in confusion, back in the direction of Rouen. Two more ships were captured by the French as they fled.

Having beaten off their assailants, the French made an immediate attempt to take the island. According to William the Breton, this was achieved by a heroic individual who swam out to an undefended spot on its eastern side and threw firebombs at the wooden palisades surrounding the fortress. Very quickly the whole complex was engulfed in flames. Those members of the garrison who had taken refuge in the cellars of the tower perished; those who escaped were forced to surrender to their attackers. Seeing that the island had fallen, the citizens of New Andely abandoned the town and fled up the hill to seek refuge in Château Gaillard.

Philip occupied the deserted town and settled down to besiege his main target.

With the French in total control of both the Seine and the surrounding countryside, there was no question of attempting another relief operation. Instead John tried to lure Philip away by launching an assault on his allies. In early September he left Rouen with the remainder of his forces, heading in the direction of Brittany. The Bretons had been in rebellion against him since the previous autumn, and John now exacted his revenge, invading the duchy and laying it to waste. His mercenaries destroyed the city of Dol, burning down the cathedral and carrying off its relics.[11]

Philip, however, refused to be distracted. While John was busy harrying the Bretons, the French king's engineers were tightening their grip on Château Gaillard. Huge ditches were dug all the way round the castle on its landward side to prevent relief or escape. Along their length wooden forts were erected at regular intervals – seven in total, each surrounded by a ditch of its own, and filled with as many soldiers as it could hold. Philip himself, meanwhile, had left to attend to the siege of another of John's castles, Radepont, which he succeeded in taking in mid-September. Radepont lies just fifteen miles from Rouen.[12]

In early October, therefore, when John returned to his capital, it was to scenes of increasing chaos and despair. The city was said to be in flames at the time of his arrival (presumably due to an accident rather than enemy action) and the fire came close to destroying the ducal castle. This detail is provided by *The History of William Marshal*, a long biography of the famous warrior written in the 1220s, not long after his death. The *History* is one of our most valuable sources for John's reign but, like the chronicle of Roger of Wendover, it has to be used with caution. It was commissioned by the Marshal's family to defend his reputation, and at every turn seeks to disassociate him from King John. In its account of 1203, for example, it makes no mention at all of the Marshal's failed mission to relieve the Isle of Andely. It does, however, convey in vivid terms the growing desperateness of the situation in which the Marshal and his master found themselves that autumn.[13]

'Sire, listen to what I have to say,' says the Marshal after their return to Rouen. 'You haven't many friends.' The military situation, he explained, was becoming hopeless.

'Let any man who is afraid take flight!' replied the king. 'For I shall not flee this year.'

'I am well aware of that,' said the Marshal. 'I have not the slightest doubt about it. But you, sire, who are wise and powerful and of high birth, a man meant to govern us all, paid no attention to the first signs of discontent, and it would have been better for us all if you had.'[14]

This frank exchange made John predictably angry, and he shut himself away in his chamber. The next day he was nowhere to be found in the castle, and his men were annoyed to discover that he had slipped out of Rouen without them; they eventually caught up with him on the coast at Bonneville-sur-Touques, more than fifty miles away. For the rest of October, the king made similar rapid journeys around central and western Normandy, shoring up his remaining defences and doubtless trying to rally more support. But everywhere he went he was now dogged by fears of treachery. Returning to Rouen in November, he travelled by a deliberately indirect route; the main roads, he thought, were being watched by 'men who had no love for him'.[15]

Back in Rouen, John explained to his Norman followers that there was now only one solution: he must go to England, and persuade the barons there to come to Normandy's aid. Assuring his audience that this trip would be brief, he secretly sent his baggage on ahead to Bonneville. His own departure was equally furtive, for had become convinced that there was a plot among the Norman barons to hand him over to the king of France. With just a handful of trusted intimates, including William Marshal, John stole away from the city before daybreak. Travelling west by a circuitous route, he ultimately arrived at Barfleur, a port on the Cherbourg Peninsula, where a fleet to ferry him and his household across the Channel was waiting. The king sailed on 5 December. Most people, says the Marshal's biographer, suspected he would never return.[16]

2

The Family Empire

1120–1189

E ighty-three years earlier, almost to the day, another king
had set sail from Barfleur in the direction of England. This
was John's great-grandfather, Henry I.

Henry was the youngest son of William the Conqueror, and
both king of England and duke of Normandy – the two countries
had been yoked together by William's famous conquest of 1066.
Since that momentous event, royal crossings of the Channel had
become a matter of necessity and routine; William, for example,
had made the voyage at least nineteen times during his twenty-
one-year reign.[1] As this implies, it was not regarded as particularly
risky, and Henry on this occasion made it across without incident.
The king and his household set out from Barfleur at twilight on
25 November 1120, in calm and clear conditions, and arrived safe
and sound in England the next morning.

But it soon became apparent that one ship from the royal fleet
was missing. This was the so-called White Ship, a sleek new vessel
that had been offered to Henry by its owner just before his
departure, but which in the event had been left for the use of
the more youthful members of the court. These young men and
women had remained on shore as the rest of the royal entourage
embarked, partying with the ship's crew and becoming increasingly merry. When they finally put to sea it was late and dark,
and all of them were hopelessly drunk. Determined to overtake

the boats that had already left, they set out recklessly, and almost immediately struck a rock. The boat went down with the loss of all but one, who lived to tell the tale. Those who perished included many sons and daughters of the English aristocracy. They also included Henry I's son and heir, William.[2]

'No ship ever brought such misery to England', said one contemporary chronicler. When King Henry heard the news, says another, he fell to the ground, overcome with grief. It was not simply the loss of a child, devastating though that must have been – it was a dynastic catastrophe. Henry had fathered no fewer than twenty bastard children (the royal record), two of whom had also perished in the White Ship, but William had been his only legitimate son. The king, who had been a widower since the death of his queen, Matilda, two years earlier, wasted no time in trying to remedy the situation; barely a month later he married for a second time, taking a new young wife in the hope of producing a new male heir. But despite his best efforts, no more children were forthcoming. By the mid 1120s Henry was well into his fifties, and still without an obvious successor.[3]

And so the ageing king attempted to solve the problem in a different way, by fixing the succession on his only other legitimate child: his daughter, Matilda. Matilda had been married as a girl to the German emperor, but in 1125 she was newly widowed; Henry brought her back to England and lent on his leading men to accept her as his heir. The following year, to bolster Matilda's chances further, he arranged for her to be married to Geoffrey, son of the count of Anjou, a young man with the curious nickname 'Plantagenet'.* It was evidently Henry's hope that his daughter and her new husband would produce a son who would one day rule in his stead.[4]

---

* No one can say for certain why Geoffrey was called *Planta genista*, the Latin for 'broom plant'. None of his descendants used Plantagenet as a surname until it was adopted by Richard, duke of York, in 1460. But it remains a convenient and sometimes unavoidable way to describe the dynasty.[5]

And they did. In 1133 Matilda gave birth to her first child, and happily it was a boy, named Henry in honour of his royal grandfather. Young Henry would indeed grow up to inherit his grandfather's cross-Channel dominions, and much more besides. As King Henry II he would be the wonder of his age, greater in reputation than his grandfather: a successful warrior, a conscientious reformer, a maker of new laws and a builder of mighty castles. He would also be the father of King John.

But in 1133 all that lay in the distant future. In the meantime Henry had to obtain his inheritance, and that proved to be no easy task. Just two years after his birth his namesake grandfather died – his death famously said to have been caused by eating too many lampreys – and once the fearsome old king was gone his succession plan fell apart. Many of the barons who had sworn to support Matilda reneged on their oaths, and gave their support instead to her cousin, Stephen, who was crowned in December 1135, within days of Henry I's death. There followed a protracted period of civil war in England and Normandy as the supporters of each side slugged it out. For a few powerful men with flexible consciences and strong right arms it was a time of great opportunity; for everyone else it was a time of calamity and oppression. Contemporary authors complained of lawlessness, unlicensed castle-building and terrible unchecked violence. In the famous words of the Peterborough chronicler, 'men said openly that Christ and his saints slept'.[6]

Victory ultimately went to Matilda's party. In 1144 her husband Geoffrey, now count of Anjou, successfully wrested Normandy from Stephen's grasp, and five years later he granted it to his eldest son, the newly knighted Henry, just sixteen years old. At the start of 1153 Henry, now nineteen, invaded England, but with inconclusive results: the barons for the most part refrained from supporting either side, leading to a stalemate. It was only when Stephen's eldest son, Eustace, died that summer that the weary king agreed to recognize Henry as his heir. When Stephen himself died in October the following year, Henry peacefully succeeded him as king of England.[7]

Henry II, even at the start of his reign, was a much greater ruler than Stephen in every sense. Not only was he the undisputed ruler of both England and Normandy; he was also, since the death of his father in 1151, count of Anjou, which meant he ruled everything beyond Normandy's southern border to the valley of the Loire. Nor was that the limit of his power. In 1152 Henry had extended his rule even further, becoming the duke of Aquitaine, a vast territory that stretched from Anjou's southern border to the Pyrenees. He had obtained this massive windfall by marrying one of the most celebrated women in European history, Eleanor of Aquitaine.

The marriage of Henry and Eleanor has become the stuff of legend and romance, talked about and written about from their day until our own. For modern audiences, mention of their names together tends to evoke images from the 1968 film *The Lion in Winter*, in which Eleanor was played by Katharine Hepburn and Henry by Peter O'Toole. Picturing the real Henry is comparatively easy, thanks to several contemporary pen portraits which agree in their main details. He is described as being a little taller than average, red-haired, freckled and broad-chested, with a tendency to corpulence, despite constant exercise and a frugal diet. In Eleanor's case we are not so lucky: beyond describing her as beautiful, chroniclers give us no idea of her appearance. Nor do we have any physical remains to help us out. Both Henry and Eleanor were buried in Fontevraud Abbey in France, but their bones were lost when the abbey was sacked in the sixteenth century. We do still have the effigies that were originally placed on top of their tombs, and in Henry's case his likeness accords broadly with the descriptions provided by the chronicles. Eleanor's effigy, therefore, may also be an approximation of her likeness, but no more. The queen was over eighty when she died, yet her effigy clearly represents a much younger woman. It is best regarded as an idealised image of a queen rather than an attempt to portray an individual.[8]

Whatever her physical attributes, Eleanor's position as a great heiress made her irresistibly attractive. Probably born in 1122, she had suddenly inherited the duchy of Aquitaine in 1137 when her father, Duke William X, died unexpectedly while on pilgrimage, leaving no son to succeed him. Aquitaine was a mighty prize, covering perhaps a third of modern France, and so Eleanor became a highly desirable bride. Within a few months she was married to Louis, the son of the king of France, who one week later succeeded to the French throne as Louis VII. Their marriage, however, was not destined to last. Apart from being a similar age (Louis was about two years older) they appear to have had little in common, and when they went on crusade in 1147, malicious tongues whispered that Eleanor had seen rather too much of her uncle, Raymond of Antioch. Certainly by the time of their return from the east in 1149 the king and queen's marital problems were public knowledge, with even the pope encouraging them to start sleeping together again. The deciding factor was probably the fact that, after fifteen years of increasingly unhappy wedlock, they had produced two daughters but no sons. In March 1152 Louis had their union annulled.[9]

Eight weeks later, Eleanor married Henry. Although this marriage is often described as a love match in modern accounts, there is no reason to suppose that the motives of Eleanor's second husband were any less hard-nosed than those of her first. Aquitaine was still a great prize, and by marrying Eleanor Henry became its new duke. The question was whether he would be able to hang on to it. Henry was only nineteen at the time, but Eleanor was thirty. If her second marriage, like her first, failed to produce any sons, then Henry's claim to Aquitaine would last only for his own lifetime, and the duchy would pass to Eleanor's daughters, who remained in Louis' custody. The French king was not happy about his former wife's swift remarriage, but in divorcing her he was evidently prepared to gamble that no more children would be forthcoming.

Louis was set to be disappointed. Henry and Eleanor went on to have many children together – at least eight whose names are known to us. Their first child, born a year after their marriage, was a boy, named William in the long tradition of Aquitainian dukes, and three more boys followed by the end of the 1150s. Aquitaine was clearly going to pass to Henry's heirs.[10]

During these early years of his reign there was much else to keep Henry occupied. England and Normandy were both battered from years of civil war, and their great men had grown accustomed to doing as they liked in their own locales. Henry reversed this situation, restoring royal and ducal authority and taming the power of his magnates, sometimes destroying or confiscating their castles, and building new ones of his own such as Scarborough, Newcastle and Orford. A vigorous, intelligent and aggressive ruler, he moved like lightning across his vast demesnes as circumstances demanded, prompting some to comment that he must fly rather than travel by horse or ship. 'He was ever on his travels', wrote the cleric Walter Map, 'covering distances like a courier, and showing no mercy to his household.' And Henry's household was massive. Because of the sprawling empire he had assembled, he was the richest ruler in Europe, and in consequence he had the largest entourage. 'No such court like it has ever been heard of in the past,' said Walter, 'nor is likely to be feared again in the future.'[11]

This was the world into which John was born, probably around Christmas 1166 – or possibly 1167. The uncertainty arises because his birth occurred towards the end of the year, and because those few chroniclers who bothered to record it did so in lackadaisical terms. As Henry and Eleanor's eighth or ninth child – and, as it turned out, their last – John was not very important, at least from a political point of view. That much was made clear within a year or so of his arrival by the succession scheme devised by his father. Henry's plan, revealed in a peace treaty with Louis VII in 1169, was that on his death his extensive dominions would be divided. His firstborn son, William, had died as an infant, leaving a younger brother, Henry, born in 1155, as the eldest surviving child. Young Henry, it was envisaged, would inherit his father's patrimony – England, Normandy and Anjou. Aquitaine, which had been acquired by marriage, was to pass to the second surviving son, Richard, born in 1157, while a third son, Geoffrey, born in 1158, would receive the duchy of Brittany, which Henry II had obtained by force in 1166. But beyond that Henry had no more provinces to parcel out. For John there was, at present, no provision.[12]

There was very likely an element of prudence in this omission. The sons Henry had included in his planned division had all survived the perils of infancy and were entering adolescence and early manhood. John, by contrast, was still little more than a baby, and might well follow his eldest brother to an early grave. Yet John was also treated differently to his older siblings in another respect. As far as we can determine, it seems that Henry, Richard and Geoffrey, along with their older sisters, were raised in England. In 1160 the archbishop of Canterbury had written to Henry II, then on the Continent, suggesting that the king might consider returning to England at some point, since it would (among other things) enable him to see his children. As this implies, the older children did not get to spend much time with their father. They probably did, however, get to spend at least some time with their mother. Eleanor also had to travel, of course, but her constant childbearing in the 1150s and early 1160s must have meant her itinerary was less hectic than that of her husband, and her governmental duties seem to place her in England for most of this period. Certainly later in life Eleanor's older children were to demonstrate a closer attachment to her than to Henry.[13]

In John's case, however, matters were different. In 1168, now that Eleanor's childbearing days were over, Henry decided he could usefully redeploy her to govern Aquitaine. By this stage her older sons were sufficiently grown up to be learning the ropes of government. Henry and Geoffrey probably remained attached to their father's side; Richard, who was destined to rule Aquitaine, stayed with his mother and followed her south. But John had no such ropes to learn, and in any case was not old enough to accompany either of his parents as they executed their political responsibilities. Instead, he was left at Fontevraud Abbey in Anjou, to be raised by its community of nuns. He was not completely cut off from his family. His sister Joan, born in 1165 and thus a year or so older, was left at the abbey at the same time, and one of Henry's cousins, Matilda of Flanders, was a member of the community there. It is also possible that his mother could have made occasional visits – Poitiers is about a hundred miles from Fontevraud. Nevertheless, the permanent placement of John and Joan at the abbey suggests that both children probably saw a lot less of their mother than had been the case with their elder siblings.[14]

Harsh as this sounds as a childcare solution, there were good reasons for keeping toddlers in the safety of the cloister and away from the turbulent world of the court. In 1169, not long after her return to Aquitaine, Eleanor narrowly escaped an ambush by rebellious barons, in which her principal adviser, the earl of Salisbury, was killed. Then, in 1170, Henry committed the most notorious act of his reign by speaking the angry words that led four of his knights to murder the archbishop of Canterbury, Thomas Becket. The crime shocked all of Europe, and for a time Henry feared it would cost him his throne, as rival rulers urged the pope to excommunicate him and license their invasion of his lands. In the event the pope did neither, but the king remained a pariah until the spring of 1172, when papal legates finally absolved him as he knelt in penance outside the doors of Avranches Cathedral.[15]

Henry in fact remained in great danger, though he was slow to see it coming. Part of the problem was his increasingly strained relationship with his eldest son. The precise causes of their quarrel are now impossible to determine, but one factor was clearly the younger Henry's lack of independent power – the perennial complaint of heirs apparent down the ages. In 1170 the king had arranged for Henry to be crowned as an associate ruler – a common practice in France, but without precedent in England – from which point contemporaries referred to them as the Old King and the Young King. But it soon became evident that, despite his new title, the Young King had no real authority. He was given no lands of his own to manage, and hence had no independent income, while the membership of his household continued to be controlled by his father. Tellingly, the seal made for his use after 1170 depicts him without a sword. It is also possible that the young Henry harboured some resentment over the death of Thomas Becket, in whose household he had for a time been raised. It was certainly in revenge for Becket's death that the Young King claimed to be acting when he rose against his father in rebellion.[16]

The immediate cause of this rebellion, however, was the favour the Old King had shown to his youngest son. By 1172, it seems, Henry had become conscious of his initial failure to make any territorial provision for John. Within a decade or so, we find chroniclers referring to the boy as 'Lack-land' (Sans Terre), and suggesting that it was a nickname bestowed upon him by his father. True or not, towards the end of the year Henry set out to make good the deficiency, and arranged for John to be married to the daughter (and heir) of the count of Savoy. When the two rulers met in Limoges early in 1173, the count asked what lands his future son-in-law would bring to the marriage, and Henry responded, apparently spontaneously, that John would receive a trio of important castles in Anjou – Chinon, Loudun and Mirebeau. This proved too much for the Young King, who protested that his father had no right to make grants of land in Anjou without his agreement, and complained about his lack of power in general. When his protests and complaints were ignored, the Young King slipped away from his father's court at night, and rode to Paris to join Louis VII.[17]

Louis was a natural choice of ally for Henry II's disaffected offspring. Not only was he the Old King's main rival; he was also (and somewhat ironically) the Young King's father-in-law. Back in 1158 Louis and Henry had attempted to cement one of their periodic attempts at peace by arranging the betrothal of their infant children. Two years later, the young Henry, then aged four, had been married to Margaret, Louis' eldest daughter from his second marriage, then aged two. Neither the marriage nor the peace treaty was a great success, but it did draw the Young King into Louis' confidence, and make him a useful tool for French schemes against his father.[18]

Important as Louis was in encouraging the Young King's opposition, there is little doubt that the true instigator of the boy's rebellion was his mother. As soon as Henry II's back was turned, Eleanor of Aquitaine dispatched her other teenaged sons, the fifteen-year-old Richard and the fourteen-year-old Geoffrey, to join forces with their brother in Paris, while she herself rallied the barons of Poitou. This was an astonishing development. Contemporaries could (and did) note countless examples of sons rebelling against their fathers, but for a queen to rebel against her husband was unprecedented. Eleanor's reasons for doing so are necessarily speculative. Henry, who had just turned forty, had many mistresses throughout his career, so some commentators have supposed that the queen, now around fifty, was motivated by sexual jealousy. Others have suggested that Aquitaine itself was the key to the queen's displeasure, arguing that she and her Poitevin supporters had come to fear Henry's succession scheme, which made the duchy subordinate to the ruler of Normandy and England.[19]

Whatever the reason, by 1173 Eleanor of Aquitaine had reached the remarkable decision to rebel against her second husband in alliance with her first, and with her sons as co-conspirators. Nor was that the limit of the conspiracy. Right across Henry II's empire, others were ready to rise up against him. Nobles in England, Normandy and Anjou, still chafing at the losses they had suffered as a result of the king's masterful rule, rebelled in the hope of reversing them. Neighbouring rulers – the counts of Boulogne and Flanders, the king of Scotland – piled into the fray in expectation of territorial gain. It was a formidable, co-ordinated challenge on all fronts – the greatest crisis of Henry II's reign.

The Old King managed to ride out the storm. In part this was down to his superior resources: Henry was probably richer than all of his opponents put together, and he used his great wealth to recruit mercenaries in large numbers. In part it was due to his superior skills as a warrior and a politician. Henry knew when to sit tight and rely on trusted deputies, and when one of his legendary dashes would be decisive. In part it was down to luck. When his sons launched an attack on Normandy in the summer of 1173, their ally the count of Boulogne was killed by a crossbow bolt and the invasion collapsed; when the king of Scots invaded northern England the following summer, he was taken by surprise by loyalist forces and captured. In the latter case contemporaries saw divine providence at work, for the Scottish king was seized even as Henry was submitting to a penitential flogging by the monks of Canterbury for his role in the death of Thomas Becket. When the king returned to the Continent the following month the rebellion finally collapsed, and his remaining enemies sued for peace.[20]

Henry was for the most part magnanimous in victory. His eldest sons, if they did not achieve the autonomy they craved, were nevertheless appeased with larger allowances. The Young King was promised 15,000 pounds a year of Angevin money (about £4,000 sterling) and received two castles in Normandy. Richard was given two residences (apparently unfortified) in Poitou and half its annual revenues. Geoffrey received half the revenues of Brittany.[21]

But the biggest winner was the youngest son. In the first half of 1174, while the rebellion was still happening, John was removed from Fontevraud by his father and brought to England, to be raised thereafter in the royal household. Now seven years old, he had reached an age at which he would in any case have been expected to start learning the sort of skills that nuns did not normally teach, such as horsemanship and how to handle weapons. Moreover, once the rebellion was finally over, John was given a substantial endowment. It included the three castles in Anjou that had been the immediate cause of his brothers' rebellion, plus 1,000 Angevin pounds a year. In addition he received a similar sum from Normandy's revenues and two of the duchy's castles, while in England he was granted even greater gifts: the castle and county of Nottingham, the castle and lordship of Marlborough, and an annual payment of £1,000 sterling. Henry also reserved the right to grant to John any future English lands that might revert to the Crown on the death of their owners. All of these lands and revenues were at the expense of the Young King's inheritance. It did not amount to a province to call his own, but after 1174 John could no longer be said to lack land.[22]

By way of stark contrast, the big loser from the failed rebellion was Eleanor of Aquitaine. The queen had been captured in the autumn of 1173, reportedly disguised as a man, trying to reach her sons in Paris. Early in 1174 Henry escorted her to England, where she became his prisoner. For Eleanor there was to be no forgiveness. The following year the king tried to persuade the pope to have his marriage annulled, with the plan of forcing the queen into the abbey of Fontevraud as a nun. When the pope rejected this scheme, Henry settled for keeping her permanently confined, probably in the royal castle at Salisbury (now Old Sarum). In the meantime, he began to consort openly with his favourite mistress, Rosamund Clifford.[23]

How John might have reacted to his mother's imprisonment, given his apparently limited contact with her, is open to question. But Eleanor's older sons were clearly unhappy about her treatment: they, for instance, are also said to have objected vociferously to the planned divorce. That Henry, Richard and Geoffrey were close to their mother as children, or at least closer to her than to their father, is strongly implied by their willingness to join her in rebellion. By keeping Eleanor confined, however comfortably, the Old King was now effectively holding the queen hostage for her sons' good behaviour. It was an arrangement that might result in compliance, but one unlikely to foster genuine love or loyalty.[24]

Despite the obvious tensions between Henry II and his sons, they succeeded in co-operating in the years that followed. There was much work to be done in reversing the effects of the great rebellion. Henry himself devoted his efforts to England and Normandy, seizing and destroying the castles of former rebels; Richard and Geoffrey were dispatched to govern their respective provinces of Aquitaine and Brittany. For Henry the Young King there was less to do while his father remained in charge, so he devoted himself to the tournament circuit, winning many friends and admirers in the process. Periodically all three elder sons were recalled to attend their father's court at great festivals such as Easter and Christmas, and occasionally we also catch sight of John on such occasions. While they were able to work together in this way, the family proved to be unbeatable. In the summer of 1182, for instance, when Richard faced difficulty subduing a fresh rebellion in Aquitaine, his father came to his aid, along with Geoffrey and Henry the Young King, and together they easily brought the rebels to submission.[25]

Immediately after this, however, they again fell out, the source of contention once more the frustrations of the eldest son. Now twenty-seven, yet still without any meaningful power, the younger Henry approached his father in the autumn of 1182 and asked again for a portion of his inheritance – Normandy, or another territory 'from which he might be able to support knights in his service'. As in 1173, Henry II refused, with almost identical consequences: the Young King took himself off to the court of the French king.[26]

The difference on this occasion was that it was no longer the court of Louis VII. The old French king had suffered a stroke in the summer of 1179 and died the following year at the age of sixty. Into his place had stepped his fifteen-year-old son, Philip. From the moment of his birth, Philip – the future Philip Augustus – had carried a great weight of expectation on his shoulders. It had taken Louis three marriages and almost thirty years, but at last in August 1165 he had succeeded in fathering a son. The citizens of Paris had rung bells and lit bonfires in celebration, declaring 'By the grace of God there is born to us this night a king who shall be a hammer to the king of the English.' This was the reminiscence of a later chronicler, writing with the benefit of hindsight. Henry II for his part had endeavoured to cultivate good relations with Philip; by 1182 he and his sons had already intervened several times to assist the new French king in establishing his rule. But this initial help earned Henry little in the way of long-term gratitude. As Philip became his own man it became clear that his main policy would be to destroy the power of his Plantagenet neighbours.[27]

The Young King's trip to Paris in the autumn of 1182 turned out to be of only short duration. His father, worried that fresh filial disaffection could lead to another general revolt, quickly wooed him back with the promise of an increased allowance. At

Christmas the Old King celebrated by summoning all his sons to Caen for what the chroniclers describe as the greatest court of his reign, with more than 1,000 knights reportedly in attendance. During the festivities, however, the tensions within the family exploded. Henry II, perhaps in the hope of further mollifying the Young King, attempted to formalize the future relationship between his various dominions, and demanded that both Geoffrey and Richard do homage to their elder brother – that is, to kneel before him, place their hands within his hands, and promise to be 'his man'. Geoffrey obliged, but Richard refused: his older brother, he objected, was no better than he. Eventually Richard was won round, and agreed to go through with the ceremony, provided that his right to hold Aquitaine was guaranteed. But this was a guarantee that the Young King was unable to give because – as he now revealed – he was in league with the Aquitainian rebels whom they had collectively crushed the previous summer. Young Henry, it seems, was plotting to replace Richard.[28]

Henry II imperiously ordered his sons to swear peace to each other, and sent Geoffrey to arrange a conference with the rebels. But here the plot grew thicker still when Geoffrey, on meeting Richard's enemies, promptly joined them. Henry's court broke up in confusion. The Young King set out for Aquitaine to assist Geoffrey and the rebels, Richard to try to suppress them. Their father gave orders to raise an army and set out in pursuit.

A violent stand-off between the two sides followed, which lasted throughout the whole of the spring of 1183, and started to draw in the rulers of other regions, to the extent that it seemed certain to become a rerun of the great rebellion of ten years earlier. What stopped it escalating in this way was the sudden death of the Young King, who fell sick with dysentery while pillaging along the Dordogne, and died on 11 June. His father, who had suspected that reports of his son's illness were just another ruse, was reportedly struck down with grief when he discovered the truth. Whatever his faults, the Young King had been a popular figure, praised by contemporaries as the epitome of chivalry, and much loved by Henry II.[29]

At the same time, one less son might be seen to be a blessing, politically, for a king who seemed to have too many. The Young King had died without any children, so his death presented Henry with an opportunity to revise his plan for the succession. Richard, now the eldest surviving son, would take the place of his dead brother as heir to the patrimony – Anjou, Normandy and England. In return he would surrender Aquitaine to John, who would at last obtain a province of his own. Geoffrey, who had ended his rebellion in the summer, remained duke of Brittany, but was deprived from holding its castles.

But when Henry summoned his sons to Normandy in the autumn of 1183 to announce this plan, Richard made his feelings very clear. After obtaining a few days' grace to consult his advisers, he rode off at night back to his duchy, sending messengers to tell his father that he would never give it up. This might seem perverse: England, Normandy and Anjou together appear to constitute a greater prize than Aquitaine. But Richard had been linked with Aquitaine since his mother's return to the duchy in 1168. In 1172, at the age of fourteen, he had been formally invested as its duke, and since that time he had enjoyed – and, moreover, fought hard for – real political power. To accept his father's new scheme would mean giving up that power in exchange for the empty role his elder brother had found so frustrating.[30]

Since Richard was so well entrenched in Aquitaine, Henry's initial reaction was moderate: throughout the winter of 1183–4 he tried to win his son round with promises and reasoned argument. But eventually, faced with Richard's continued obstinacy, the king snapped, and angrily ordered John to seize the duchy by force. As in the case of Thomas Becket, it is debatable whether Henry really meant what he said, for John had no resources to attack Richard, nor did Henry lend him any. When the king crossed the Channel to England in June 1184, however, John did indeed invade Aquitaine, with the help of his brother Geoffrey. Since John was only seventeen years old and Geoffrey twenty-six, we may suspect the initiative lay with the elder brother. This was John's first political action, but Geoffrey had been playing these kinds of power games for many years. Contemporaries were aware of his skill in manipulating others, and condemned him for it. He was, said one, 'overflowing with words, smooth as oil, possessed, by his syrupy and persuasive eloquence, of the power of dissolving the apparently indissoluble, able to corrupt two kingdoms with his tongue, of tireless endeavour and a hypocrite in everything'. 'Geoffrey, that son of treachery,' said another, 'that son of iniquity.'[31]

The joint offensive of John and Geoffrey was not very effective, and Richard, rather than confronting his brothers head-on, responded by laying waste to Geoffrey's lands in Brittany. But when their father heard that his sons were once again at war he commanded them all to come to England. It is a mark of Henry's continuing authority that all three obeyed, but perhaps a mark of his desperation that, in advance of their arrival, he released their mother from captivity. Eleanor, now in her sixties, is known to have attended council meetings at the end of 1184, and so it may have been as a result of her influence that a public reconciliation between her sons was achieved that December. As subsequent events would show, nothing in reality had been settled regarding the succession, but Henry was apparently willing to leave Richard in possession of Aquitaine for now. That much was made clear from his sudden revival of a long-nurtured plan to make John king of Ireland.[32]

Ireland was the last significant addition to Henry II's sprawling empire. Before his accession it had largely avoided the successive waves of conquerors that had swept over the rest of the British Isles. Neither the Romans nor the Anglo-Saxons, nor even the Norman kings of England, had attempted to extend their power across the Irish Sea. The Vikings had settled there, but only in a handful of coastal towns. For the most part, Ireland remained what it had always been: a Celtic country, whose inhabitants, though they might trade with their English neighbours, owed no allegiance to England's kings.[33]

All this changed in the time of Henry II. The king had apparently contemplated a conquest of Ireland at the very start of his reign. Although he had been discouraged by his mother – and

was anyway soon distracted by more pressing concerns on the
Continent – he had been supported by the Church, who regarded
the Irish as a backwards and barbarous people, Christian only in
name, with reprehensible attitudes towards sex and marriage.
Divorce was available on demand, concubinage was commonplace,
and the line between bastardy and legitimacy so thin as to be
non-existent. Leaving the strictures of the Church aside, these
relaxed attitudes meant that Irish politics, based as they were on
rival dynasties, were wont to be turbulent. Ireland was a land of
many kings – as many kings as elsewhere there were earls, explained
one English observer – locked in a ceaseless round of competition. They competed in part for the distinction of being recognized
as the country's 'high-king', but this title was purely honorific,
and brought nothing in the way of administrative power. Power
in Ireland was based on tribute and military might.[34]

It was these turbulent politics that had ultimately drawn in
Henry II. In 1166 the king of Leinster, Dermot MacMurrough,
had been driven from his lands in south-east Ireland by his rival,
the king of Connacht. His first instinct was to seek help from his
powerful English neighbour, but Henry, preoccupied with affairs
in Aquitaine, was unenthusiastic. Instead, with Henry's licence,
Dermot turned to the Anglo-Norman lords of south Wales: men
who had long experience of fighting against Celtic foes by virtue
of living on a hostile frontier. In return for the promise of new
lands, some of these men crossed to Ireland with Dermot in 1167
and helped him recover part of his patrimony. Cutting-edge tech-
niques and technology – cavalry charges, crossbows and castles
– gave them the military advantage over the Irish, and their material
gains soon encouraged more adventurers to follow in their wake.
Eventually, in August 1170, they were joined by Richard fitz
Gilbert, known to posterity as 'Strongbow', a former earl who
had lost his title by supporting King Stephen. In return for
supporting Dermot he demanded the Irish king's daughter in
marriage, along with the right to succeed him after his death.
Thus when Dermot obligingly died the following year, it was fitz
Gilbert who had stepped into his shoes as Leinster's ruler.[35]

At this point Henry II had decided to intervene in person. It was one thing for his vassals to act as swords for hire and win new lands; quite another for one of them to set himself up as an independent power. In October 1171 the king sailed to Ireland, bringing with him his splendid court, and a large army, to overawe both the native Irish lords and the new English settlers. There was no fighting: Richard fitz Gilbert submitted at once and received Leinster back as a fief. Many Irish rulers also submitted to Henry, acknowledging him as their new overlord. The net effect of the king's intervention, however, was to leave Ireland in a state of limbo. The settlers would later complain that his action had robbed the conquest of its momentum, giving the Irish a chance to recover and fight back. After his departure in April 1172, the country entered into a state of almost constant war between the natives and the newcomers. Henry attempted to make peace with the Irish in 1175, but the English settlers had no interest in observing its terms. In Ireland, the castle-building, colonisation and conflict continued.[36]

It was against this background, perhaps in the hope of a fresh start, that Henry had earmarked Ireland as a suitable prospect for his youngest son. In 1177, in a council meeting at Oxford, he made extensive grants of Irish land to new settlers and had them recognize John as the country's future king. At that time John was only ten years old, so his interest in Ireland had to be upheld by deputies. Before his departure in 1172 Henry had granted the Irish kingdom of Meath to Hugh de Lacy, another baron from the Welsh borders, intending that he should act as a counterweight to Richard fitz Gilbert. But after fitz Gilbert's death in 1176, Hugh de Lacy himself had begun to seem too tall a poppy. When he married the daughter of the Irish king of Connacht, people began to speculate that he was scheming to take the kingship of Ireland for himself.[37]

The plan to send John to Ireland seems to have been shelved in 1183, when the death of the Young King prompted Henry II to think in terms of a more general reshuffle. Now that it had proved impossible to dislodge Richard from Aquitaine, however, the original plan was resumed. In the summer of 1184 Henry sent new officials to Ireland to prepare the ground for John's arrival. These preparations culminated on 31 March 1185 when the king knighted his son at Windsor Castle, the symbolic conferral of arms signifying that John, now aged eighteen, was old enough to wield power in his own right.[38] How enthusiastic he was about wielding power in Ireland is open to doubt. Two weeks earlier, during a council in London, he had reportedly begged his father to allow him to go to the Holy Land instead. Since the start of the year the patriarch of Jerusalem had been at Henry's court, trying to obtain military support for the beleaguered Christian communities in Palestine, and had identified John as a potential leader. But Henry had refused their imprecations. Within days of his knighting at Windsor John was dispatched into south Wales, where a company of 300 knights and an even larger force of soldiers and archers were waiting to accompany him across the Irish Sea. On 24 April they set sail from Milford Haven in a fleet of sixty ships, landing safely at Waterford at noon the following day.[39]

The expedition was an unqualified disaster. The contemporary chronicler Gerald of Wales, who travelled in John's company at Henry's request, explains how their mission was compromised from the moment they disembarked. The new arrivals were met at Waterford by a great number of Irish lords – those native leaders who had accepted English authority and come to welcome John as their new ruler. But, says Gerald, the newcomers treated these men with contempt and derision, even to the extent of pulling their beards, 'which the Irish wore full and long, according to the custom of their country'. Having been humiliated, these Irishmen withdrew their allegiance, and convinced others who had been contemplating submission to do the same. John, they told their fellow countrymen, was a mere boy, surrounded by others almost as young, who were interested only in juvenile pursuits. Under his leadership there was no hope of Ireland enjoying peace and security.[40]

To some extent, the behaviour of John's party was only to be expected. They had not come to Ireland to reach an accommodation with the natives – Henry II had abandoned that policy back in 1177. Gerald says that John also alienated the formerly loyalist Irish lords by granting out their lands to his own followers, and this is confirmed by his surviving charters. John's mistake lay not so much in provoking those whom he expected would be his enemies, as in simultaneously aggravating those whom he assumed would be his allies. The Anglo-Norman lords from south Wales who had founded the colony a generation earlier also weighed up their new lord's behaviour and found it wanting. Having goaded the native Irish into outright hostility, John and his coterie were said by Gerald to have spent most of their time in the towns on the coast, indulging in riotous living, leaving the settler communities of the interior to fend for themselves against Irish attacks. Gerald is doubtless exaggerating here; his bitterness at John's failure was personal, for he hailed from one of these same pioneering settler families. John's charters prove that he spent at least some time on the marches of his lordship, and Irish annalists report that he established three new castles to stake out claims to further territory. When the garrisons of these castles carried out raids into neighbouring Irish lands, however, they were defeated and slaughtered. Others among John's army reportedly deserted to the Irish side because he refused to pay them properly. By the end of the year, his forces were so depleted that he was forced to return to England.[41]

During John's absence in Ireland the struggle between his brothers Richard and Geoffrey had continued, with a fresh round of fighting in Anjou. At the root of their rivalry was Henry II's obstinate refusal, since the death of the Young King, to provide any clarity on the issue of the succession. Henry appears to have wanted to keep everyone in the dark, especially Richard, and to have encouraged the hopes of Geoffrey. Back in December 1183, for example, when Richard had been in open defiance over Aquitaine, Henry had reached a new agreement with Philip Augustus over the Vexin, a strip of territory on the Franco-

Norman frontier that had been in dispute for over a century. The two kings had agreed it would become the dowry of Philip's sister, Alice, and would pass to whichever of Henry's sons she married. The 'whichever' was highly significant, because Alice had already been betrothed for the past fifteen years to Richard. The new note of ambiguity implied that he might not inherit Normandy, and perhaps not England or Anjou either.⁴²

Soon after John's return from Ireland, however, the pendulum swung perceptibly in Richard's favour. In March 1186 Henry and Philip met to confirm the Vexin agreement, but this time it was specifically stated that Alice would marry Richard. Now it was Geoffrey's turn to take umbrage, since this seemed to indicate the decline of his own prospects. Like the Young King before him, he took off to Paris, where he began to plot with Philip. The French king obligingly bestowed upon him the title 'steward of France', an honour traditionally held by the rulers of Anjou, indicating that Geoffrey's thoughts were now bending in that direction.⁴³

As for John, Henry's intention was still very much to make him king of Ireland. The new pope, elected at the end of 1185, proved to be more enthusiastic about the plan than his predecessor, and had promised to send a gold crown with peacock feathers for the coronation ceremony. Then, in the summer of 1186, even more propitious news arrived. Hugh de Lacy, the tall poppy whom both John and Henry had regarded as an obstacle to their ambitions in Ireland, was dead, felled by a native Irish axe. On hearing this Henry was reportedly jubilant, and made immediate preparations for his son's return. A new expedition was hastily assembled at Chester and John was dispatched north to join it. He was waiting for a favourable wind to cross the Irish Sea when messengers arrived to tell him of another death. Geoffrey had been killed in a tournament in Paris on 19 August.

This startling news changed everything. At his father's command John returned south at once, sending a deputy across the Irish Sea in his stead. Ireland was suddenly a peripheral concern, the crown of peacock feathers redundant. New and much wider vistas now opened up to him. Geoffrey, not without Henry's encouragement, had been angling for a greater share of his father's inheritance. John now stepped naturally into that role. Geoffrey had died leaving two daughters but no sons; Richard was still unmarried and constantly engaged in the risky business of warfare. In the summer of 1186, John found himself in the exhilarating position of being a single heartbeat from the succession to all his father's dominions.[44]

The rivalry that this created between John and Richard was not immediately apparent, thanks to the precipitate action of Philip Augustus. Deprived of his leverage by the loss of Geoffrey, the French king demanded the surrender of Brittany and the dead duke's daughters, threatening war if Henry refused to comply. Talks during the autumn produced only a short truce, and in January 1187 Philip invaded the Vexin. Further talks in the spring led to a second truce until midsummer, at which point Philip invaded Berry, another contested region, east of Anjou. In the face of this new aggression, the fractious Plantagenets pulled together. John and Richard joined forces in Berry to hold the town of Châteauroux against Philip, and when the French king besieged them there, Henry marched to their relief. For a moment it looked as if the argument might be settled in the fields outside Châteauroux by a decisive battle, but in the event (as indeed happened on most occasions during the Middle Ages) neither side was truly ready to take such an enormous risk. Instead, after two weeks of protracted talks, a third truce was agreed, this time for two years.[45]

But as soon as the truce was sealed, dissension among the Plantagenets erupted once more, when Richard surprised everyone by riding back to Paris with Philip. 'Between the two of them,' wrote the well-informed courtier Roger of Howden, 'there grew up so great an affection that King Henry was much alarmed.' The fact that Howden, in describing this sudden affection, mentions that Philip and Richard shared the same bed has led some modern commentators to assume that they were having a homosexual affair, which was almost certainly not the case. Determining sexuality at a distance of 800 years is, of course, difficult, but 'sharing a bed' for medieval writers was a typical expression of friendship rather than erotic love. Richard's sexual preferences are probably better inferred by Howden's comment elsewhere that the men of Aquitaine disliked their duke because he abducted 'their wives, daughters and kins- women by force, and made them his concubines'.[46]

What alarmed Henry II in 1187 was not reports of his son sleeping with another man, but the political alliance this act implied. First the Young King, then Geoffrey, now Richard: Philip had beguiled one brother after another and turned them against their father. The likeliest explanation for this latest defection is that, during the final round of peace talks, Philip had played on Richard's fears that Henry was planning to cut him out of the succession, and aiming to pass England, Anjou and Normandy to John. Certainly this was the rumour that circulated among contemporary chroniclers, who were in no doubt about the balance of Henry's paternal affections. John was 'a son he loved and greatly trusted', said the biographer of William Marshal. 'The youngest son, John,' wrote William of Newburgh, 'he loved the most tenderly.' Richard, by contrast, had always been his mother's favourite, and events since 1183 had shown that there was little love lost between him and Henry. Soon after his visit to Paris, Richard raided his father's treasury at Chinon, using the proceeds to garrison his castles in Aquitaine. Such actions indicate the enormous distrust that existed between them.[47]

At length, by sending messengers to Richard with promises of redress, Henry induced him to return to his side; Richard admitted he had been led astray, and swore that in future he would remain faithful. But suspicion and ill will remained. Towards the end of the summer came the shocking news that the army of the crusader kingdom of Jerusalem had been wiped out in battle by Muslim forces led by the sultan Saladin. The Christian communities in the Holy Land, established nine decades earlier during the First Crusade, seemed to be on the point of extinction, and a few months later the people of western Europe heard the worst: Jerusalem itself had fallen. Richard responded at once, pledging to go on crusade by publicly taking the cross, much to the anger and alarm of his father, who saw that Richard's absence would delay any peace with Philip Augustus. As it was, by January 1188, the public mood was such that both Henry and Philip also felt obliged to take the cross. But now it was Richard's turn to be alarmed when Henry forbade John from doing the same. For what reason was John being held back, if not to usurp Richard's position?[48]

Despite the distrust, Henry and Richard were united in arms against Philip in August 1188, after fresh fighting broke out in Berry and along the Franco-Norman border. But, as before, the subsequent peace talks drew Richard and Philip into collaboration. In November, at Bonsmoulins in Normandy, they arrived together, and presented Henry with a proposal for peace. Philip would give up his recent territorial gains on two conditions: that Richard must marry Alice, and that Henry must make all his barons recognize Richard as his heir. When Henry refused, Richard took it as final confirmation of his long-nurtured fears. 'Now at last,' he said, 'I must believe what I had always thought was impossible.' So saying, Richard stunned his audience by turning to Philip and doing homage to the French king for Normandy, Anjou and Aquitaine.

It was the final break between father and son. Henry tried to woo Richard back as before, but without success. Attempts at further dialogue during the winter achieved nothing, and by the spring of 1189 both sides were readying themselves for war. At the end of May, at La Ferté-Bernard, not far from Le Mans, Richard and Philip repeated their demands for the marriage of Alice and the confirmation of the succession, adding that John must also take the cross and accompany Richard on crusade. John, for the most part invisible during these months, was still very much attached to his father's side.[49]

Henry again refused, at which point Philip and Richard launched their attack, seizing La Ferté-Bernard and a number of other castles nearby. Henry, who had retreated to Le Mans – his birthplace – was forced to flee as the city went up in flames, and came close to being captured by his attackers. The king at first headed north, towards the safety of Normandy, but only a few miles from the Norman border, to the consternation of his household, he decided to turn back in the direction of Anjou.

Henry was heading south to die. Although at fifty-six he was not particularly old, even by medieval standards, he was worn out from a lifetime in the saddle and the stresses of recent years. Already unwell the previous Christmas, his condition was no doubt made worse by the struggle against Richard during the spring. Now in the summer heat he fell ill again. By travelling on lesser roads and tracks he managed to reach Chinon, the castle of his Angevin ancestors, where he lay sick for a fortnight.

Meanwhile Richard and Philip were drawing ever closer, overrunning towns and castles in their path. When Tours capitulated on 3 July, Henry was obliged to rise from his bed to meet them, his attendants holding him upright on his horse as the terms of his surrender were dictated. In addition to agreeing to all of his adversaries' previous demands, Henry was now required to renew his allegiance to the French king, and pay him an indemnity of 20,000 marks. It was a humiliating end for a man who had been the greatest ruler in Christendom. As he leant forward to give Richard the required kiss of peace, says Gerald of Wales, Henry whispered in his son's ear, 'God grant that I may not die until I have had my revenge on you.'[50]

God was not nearly so generous. Too weak to ride, Henry was carried back to Chinon on a litter. As part of the terms of his surrender, the ailing king had agreed to receive back into his peace all those who had deserted him in recent weeks and joined forces with Richard and Philip. That night he asked to hear the list of their names, which his servants had been trying to keep from him. Henry insisted that they be read out, and received what several chroniclers believed to be the blow that killed him. 'Sire, so Jesus Christ help me,' said the vice chancellor, 'the first which is written down here is Lord John, your son.'[51]

3

Refusing to Rally

1204 – 1205

Five months into the siege of Château Gaillard, Philip Augustus' patience was starting to wear thin.

The French king had known from the outset that taking the mighty castle would be difficult. Its lofty position and ingenious design meant that any direct assault would probably prove futile. Nor was it likely that in this instance the garrison could be bribed into submission. Commanders of other castles, if they were landholders in Normandy, had sought to hold on to their lands by dint of a well-timed defection. But Château Gaillard had been entrusted to Roger de Lacy, a man who had no estates in Normandy at all, only in England, and thus every reason to maintain his allegiance to King John. The enormous effort Philip had made to blockade the castle, ringing it with ditches and towers, shows that from the first he was anticipating that it would be necessary to starve the defenders into submission. As his chaplain William the Breton commented, 'It is cruel hunger alone that conquers the invincible.'[1]

At the start of the siege the prospects for a starvation strategy had seemed excellent, for Lacy had made a strategic blunder in admitting the townspeople of Little Andely. There may have been a strong emotional and moral case for doing so, for many of them were the friends and relatives of the garrison, but Lacy belatedly realized that these 'useless mouths' – a multitude of perhaps 2,000 people – were quickly going to consume the castle's carefully stockpiled provisions. In an attempt to undo his error, he started sending them out in groups, and initially the French forces allowed them to pass through the siege lines to safety. At length, however, Philip himself learned what was happening, and called a halt to the exodus. When the final group was sent out from the castle, they were met with a hail of arrows; when they fled back in terror, they found the castle gates had been mercilessly barred against them. Appalling scenes followed that winter as these unfortunates were left to starve in the no-man's-land between the two lines, seeking shelter under rocks, and eating herbs, dogs and – eventually – each other.[2]

Besides being pleased with himself on this score, Philip must have been greatly encouraged in December by the departure of King John. Those who noted his stealthy flight from Normandy and concluded that he would never return seemed to have the evidence on their side. At some point during the winter, Philip intercepted a letter from John, intended for Roger de Lacy, thanking the constable for his stalwart service, but making it clear that he and the rest of the garrison at Château Gaillard could expect no relief in the foreseeable future.[3]

As time wore on, however, Philip's confidence in playing the long game must have started to ebb. Christmas came and went, and January too, but still Lacy and his men showed no signs of weakening. As winter turned to spring the likelihood of a relief force landing from England increased. Towards the end of February, the French king (who had not been present for the duration) returned to take personal command of the siege. He allowed the surviving wretches outside the castle to leave, and gave orders that they be fed (though the sudden consumption of food caused many of them to die). Philip could now afford to be compassionate, for he had decided to risk a direct assault.

The only direction from which such an attack could conceivably be mounted was the south-east, where the rock on which Château Gaillard stood was joined to higher ground by a narrow neck of land. King Richard had recognized this weakness and

Château Gaillard

N

Stockade

River Seine

Inner
Ward

Chapel

Middle
Ward

Outwork

0 10 20 30 40 50 m

built a large outwork facing that direction, completely separate from the main part of the castle. This was where Philip chose to strike. His men levelled and widened the ground so that a giant siege tower could be rolled towards the edge of the castle's outer ditch, and then attempted to fill the ditch so that the tower could be positioned right up against the walls. When this proved too time-consuming they descended into the ditch using ladders and began scaling the other side, intending to undermine the castle's foremost tower. It must have been a deadly business with heavy casualties, but eventually the French king's sappers managed to bring the tower down. As it collapsed it partially filled the ditch, making it easier for the attackers to storm the breach. The defenders, realizing that the outwork was lost, set fire to its buildings and withdrew into the castle's middle ward.

The French now faced a ditch of similar size and the prospect of sustaining further losses in trying to cross it, until one of them spotted a potential Achilles heel. Against the south-west wall of the castle, high above the Seine, stood a chapel. This was not part of the original design, but had been added on John's orders the previous year. By edging around the outside of the walls and standing on each other's shoulders, a small group of men managed to reach the chapel's window, which was unbarred and unguarded. Once inside what turned out to be a locked room, they beat on its door to make a racket. The defenders, startled to discover their enemies were already inside, panicked and fell back for a second time, once again firing the part of the castle they had abandoned. Safe within the chapel's vaulted chamber, the intruders waited for the flames to subside, then emerged to lower the main drawbridge, allowing the rest of the French army to enter.

Roger de Lacy and his men, reduced in number and now confined to the castle's innermost ward, could probably not have held out for very much longer. As it was, another design flaw (in this case Richard's) greatly reduced their chances. Instead of a drawbridge over the final ditch there was a solid span of stone, under which Philip's miners were able to shelter and work unimpeded. In desperation the defenders dug a mine of their own and confronted their attackers in underground combat, but the consequence of all the tunnelling was to weaken the walls above. After a few shots from the French king's catapult, the walls collapsed. Heroically, Lacy and his men fought on, even as their enemies swarmed around them, eventually to be dragged out by their ankles. Thus Château Gaillard was taken, on 6 March 1204, after one of the longest and most bitterly fought sieges in European history.

At that moment John was travelling in the Midlands, returning south from a visit to York. Since his arrival in England the previous December, he had made some preparations for his promised return to Normandy. He must have summoned a council of magnates and bishops almost immediately, for they had assembled in Oxford in the first week of January, and agreed to grant him financial aid and military service. In February he had sent messengers to his subjects in Ireland asking them for similar assistance. Beyond that, however, evidence of preparation for the king's return is thin. Towards the end of February some provisions, men and money were sent across the Channel, perhaps provoked by the news that Château Gaillard was now under direct assault. But John clearly believed that the castle would continue to hold out for many more weeks. On 6 March itself, the very day of its fall, he gave orders for beasts to be trapped in the New Forest and shipped to Normandy, so that he would be assured of good hunting when he eventually arrived.[4]

News of Château Gaillard's fall must therefore have been received with shock. A council was held in London at the end of March, at which it was decided to dispatch an embassy to Philip Augustus, in the hope of persuading him to accept a peace. The ambassadors were high-ranking, including the archbishop of Canterbury, the bishops of Norwich and Ely, and two senior earls (one of whom was William Marshal), as well as a visiting papal legate. But the talks that took place in mid-April were predictably fruitless, for Philip had no reason to negotiate. 'King Philip did not want peace,' wrote a contemporary chronicler, Ralph of Coggeshall, 'because he was sure that he would get possession of all the king's land in a short time, and so he always proposed something that was unacceptable, or something that was not possible, in the completion of the peace agreement.'[5]

As soon as the meeting was over, Philip proceeded with his invasion. Rouen was his ultimate objective, but the city was well defended with a triple ring of ditches, and its citizens steadfast in their attachment to the Plantagenet cause. The French king therefore led his army into western Normandy, to pick off easier targets. Falaise, the birthplace of William the Conqueror, resisted for a week, before the mercenaries holding it calculated that they would be better off switching sides. Caen, where the Conqueror lay buried, put up no resistance at all, because (in Ralph of Coggeshall's words) 'they had no one strong enough to defend them'. Philip's army quickly overran the Cherbourg Peninsula, taking Barfleur and Cherbourg itself. And so it continued across the rest of the duchy, as men flocked to make peace with the French king and secure favourable terms.[6]

Against this background of general collapse, the resolve in Rouen began to crack. On 1 June the city's military commander, Peter de Préaux, struck a temporary truce with Philip, agreeing to surrender if no help arrived from England within thirty days. Desperate messages had already been sent to John, telling him 'if he did not come to save his lands he would lose the lot of them'. The biographer of William Marshal says that John immediately ordered an army to assemble at Portsmouth, but was thwarted by the lackadaisical attitude of his barons. 'Many of those summoned delayed for too long, at a time when delay was not the order of the day.' The official record, however, shows no sign of any serious military preparations at this point. Word must have been carried back to Rouen, as Roger of Wendover says, that no assistance was to be expected, and that the citizens would have to fend for themselves. On 24 June, a week before the truce was set to expire, Peter de Préaux surrendered his command, and Philip rode through the gates of the city in triumph. With the fall of the duchy's capital, the remaining castles and towns of Normandy also submitted.[7]

Nor was it just Normandy. While Philip had been attending to the conquest of the duchy, his allies had been busy seizing John's lands further south. Here the signal for collapse had been the death of John's mother, Eleanor of Aquitaine, on 1 April. 'A noble queen, indeed, and a spirited and wealthy lady' (as a London chronicler described her in an obituary), Eleanor was interred at Fontevraud alongside Henry II. Released from captivity after Henry's death in 1189, she had gone on to play a pivotal role during the reigns of both her surviving sons, not least because she continued to command the personal loyalty of many southern magnates. But this vestigial attachment to the Angevin cause died with her. In the spring of 1204, the barons of Poitou deserted en masse to the king of France, and in August Philip made a triumphal entry into Poitiers. By the end of the summer, all that remained of John's huge continental inheritance was the southern part of Aquitaine, and even here his grip was becoming extremely tenuous. Everything else, apart a few embattled castles in Anjou, had been conquered.[8]

Contemporaries were well aware that these were momentous events. 'Since Duke William, who conquered the kingdom of the English,' wrote Ralph of Coggeshall, 'the kings of England have always been dukes of Normandy, up to the time of King John, who in the fifth year of his reign lost the duchy, together with many other lands overseas.' One hundred and thirty-nine years of joint rule, observed Ralph, counting inclusively from 1066 to 1204, had come to a sudden end.[9]

There is no doubt that, as a result of this ignominious loss, John felt an immense burden of shame and guilt. He had lost the continental lands of his ancestors. These were not, as English historians of past generations have sometimes pretended, peripheral territories, which England's kings were well to be rid of. They were, on the contrary, the heartlands of the Plantagenet Empire – the patrimony. There was a reason why Henry II had gone south to die at Chinon, and why he and Richard I were buried in an abbey beside the banks of the Loire: ancestrally, even emotionally, these lands were home.

This was also the attitude of many of the people surrounding King John. Like all medieval men and women of any importance, John was the head of a great household – in his case, the greatest household in the country, with a permanent staff of several hundred. The majority of them were menials: huntsmen, porters, carters, grooms, cooks, stable lads, laundresses, and so on. But there were also plenty of high-status individuals attendant on the king: knights, esquires and senior clerks. Knights could act as advisers and diplomats in peacetime, and form the core of the army during war; clerks performed religious devotions and acted as the royal secretariat. Above and beyond this, however, these high-status individuals were the king's intimate companions – his counsellors, even his friends. They were the people always on hand to offer support and advice.

In the years leading up to 1204, John's inner counsellors had become dominated by one particular set of men: military captains and clerks from Anjou and, specifically, the region around Tours. These men, having sided with John and followed him back to England, had lost everything in the course of the French conquest. As such they were fiercely loyal to the king, for being landless exiles left them wholly dependent on his goodwill, and always looking to him for reward, whether in the form of new lands, money or offices. They were also, like John, wholeheartedly committed to winning back the continental lands they had lost.[10]

But what was the attitude to the loss of the Angevin Empire beyond John and his intimate counsellors? What, for instance, did the barons – the great men of England, whose ancestors had crossed with the Conqueror – think? Here the picture is more mixed, and there is debate among historians today, just as there was no doubt debate in baronial halls at the time. In some cases, such families no longer had any links with Normandy, having divided their English and Norman estates between different branches at some date before the disaster.[11] But in other cases, there were families who held substantial lands on both sides of the Channel right up to 1204, who were afterwards left nursing serious financial losses. (And even if the estates themselves were not hugely profitable, they might be considered important for reasons of sentiment or prestige.) William Marshal and his fellow negotiator, the earl of Leicester, had succeeded in striking a private deal with Philip Augustus during their pointless embassy in the spring of 1204; in exchange for a payment of 500 marks each, both were allowed to retain their Norman estates for a year and a day. If they wanted to retain them beyond that, they would have to do homage to Philip as Normandy's new ruler. To all the other Anglo-Norman barons, whose estates had simply been seized during the conquest, the French king gave the same ultimatum: do homage within twelve months, or lose your lands forever.[12]

Some of the barons apparently nurtured the hope that there might be a peaceful solution to their dilemma – a diplomatic formula that would enable them to recognize Philip as their lord in Normandy and John as their lord in England. According to the so-called 'Anonymous of Béthune', a chronicler with close links to the English court, a group of barons approached John soon after the fall of Normandy with just such a proposal, assuring the king that their hearts would still be with him, even if they did homage to Philip with their bodies. John, in response, said he would consider the matter with his counsellors, but unsurprisingly these intimate advisers took a dim view. Baldwin de Béthune, a former household knight who reportedly stood high in the king's esteem, had lost his lands in Normandy to the French as early as 1196. 'Were I in your place,' he said to John, 'if the hearts whose bodies were against me came into my hands, I would throw them down the privy.' At this, says the chronicler, there was much laughter, but the question could not have been answered more decisively: there was to be no more talk of serving two masters. The king was not about to let any of his barons pledge allegiance to a man who had deprived him of his patrimony. If they wanted to recover their lost lands, their only option was to join him in fighting for them.[13]

John faced another major problem besides the lukewarm support of his baronage. Mounting a war on the scale required to reverse the defeats of 1203–4 would require massive resources – not only equipment such as ships, siege engines, crossbow bolts and carts, but also mercenaries, sailors and horses, plus the vast quantities of food, drink and other supplies they would need whilst on campaign. It was an almost endless list, all of which ultimately boiled down to one thing: money. Knights might fight for free, according to the terms of their service; mercenaries, mariners and merchants ultimately expected to be paid.

In general terms, England's economy in the early thirteenth century was in robust health. A rising population – around 3 million and counting – meant rising prosperity. Growth was visibly strong, with new towns being founded throughout the country at a rapid rate. Indeed, the period between the Norman Conquest and the start of the thirteenth century had witnessed more urban foundation than any other period in English history; John himself would found Liverpool in 1207. Towns old and new were establishing weekly markets, as well as annual fairs, some of which attracted merchants from all over Europe. Travel between these places was becoming easier thanks to greater investment and innovation. More bridges were being built, and in stone rather than wood; horses were replacing oxen for haulage, increasing the speed at which goods could be transported; cartwheels were less likely to break because they were now clad in metal.[14]

The problem in 1204 was inflation. In the decades before John's reign prices had remained fairly stable, but since his accession in 1199 they had rocketed, more than doubling in the space of just five years. One reason for this must have been the run of bad harvests reported in several chronicles, which would have led to increases in the price of food. Another was a perceived drop in the quality of the coinage. England had always prided itself on its silver pennies, the weight and fineness of which had been fixed soon after the Norman Conquest (giving us the word sterling, from the Old English *steor*, meaning 'fixed'). But in John's reign the weight had become noticeably varied; in government documents we see references to both 'strong pennies' and 'weak pennies'. The official line, picked up by the chroniclers, was to blame criminals, who were shaving small amounts of silver off the king's coinage. So-called 'coin-clipping' was always a problem in the Middle Ages, and no doubt at a time when prices were already rising, more people were tempted to make their money go further by such methods. But what is true of individuals is also true of institutions, and it is impossible to dispel entirely the notion that John's government may for a time have encouraged its moneyers to mint underweight coins as a quick and easy way to get more money. Whatever the true cause, once people noticed the drop in quality, it would have made a bad situation much worse. Sellers would either have refused 'weak' pennies, or else demanded more of them, pushing up prices further. People who had been hoarding money, seeing the value of their savings plummet, would have tried to offload them quickly, increasing the amount of coin in circulation and contributing further still to the upward inflationary trend. Confidence in the coinage was in danger of collapse.

By the autumn of 1204 the situation had become so acute that John and his ministers felt compelled to act, and initiated a nationwide reform. The Crown normally recalled and reissued all the coin in circulation every generation or so, though usually with the aim of turning a profit. The only precedent for restoring confidence had been Henry I's brutal re-coinage of 1124, in which the king ordered not only the complete replacement of his currency, but the mutilation of all his moneyers, each of whom was condemned to lose his right hand and genitals. John's measures in 1204 were not nearly so draconian. On 9 November he simply announced that no one was to have substandard coins after 13 January the following year; anyone found in possession of such money after that date would have it bored through and confiscated for the king's own use. There is a strong possibility, in fact, that John's measures were not harsh enough. Although new, heavier coins began to be minted at the beginning of 1205, old ones were allowed to remain in circulation so long as they were no more than one-eighth lighter than the new standard. As a result it is possible that no more than half of the currency was actually replaced. The upheaval and unpopularity of a full re-coinage was thus avoided, but whether John's reform would be enough to restore confidence in sterling and stop the country's runaway inflation remained to be seen.[15]

By the start of 1205 John's woes were increasing. As Ralph of Coggeshall explains, all of England was disturbed at this point by the rumour that a French invasion was imminent. Philip Augustus was still attracting lots of new men to his banner, especially 'those who had lost great incomes in England'. During the previous autumn, John had seized the English estates of those barons who had chosen to remain in Normandy and pledge their allegiance to the French king. This was an entirely reasonable retaliatory move, and had given John a massive windfall of lands (the so-called 'Lands of the Normans') which he was able to use to reward his loyal followers. At the same time, however, it created an equally cold logic for the Normans themselves. In order to regain their lost English lands, their only hope was to join Philip in his projected conquest.[16]

Fearing this invasion, John summoned a council to London for the middle of January, and overhauled the country's security arrangements. It was already the case that all able-bodied men were expected to turn out in the kingdom's defence, but John now introduced ferocious new penalties for those who failed to do so: landed men were threatened with perpetual disinheritance, while landless ones were promised permanent servitude. The king also appointed new constables to every shire, and beneath them in every city and sub-district, whose job it would be to muster local forces 'against foreigners, or against any other disturbers of the peace'. As this telling line suggests, John feared internal subversion as much as French invasion. If Philip Augustus succeeded in landing troops in England and started winning territory, even those barons who had remained in England might decide to switch sides in the hope of regaining their Norman estates. Such fears may have haunted John for some time: according to Ralph of Coggeshall, the king had failed to raise an army in England in 1204 because he had 'suspicions of treachery among some of his men'. All those who attended the January council, therefore – earls, barons, bishops and abbots – were required to take an oath of loyalty, which was afterwards administered throughout the whole kingdom to every male over the age of twelve. Such oaths had been used by previous kings during times of crisis.[17]

Whom among his magnates did John suspect? One man who certainly came under a cloud at this moment was Ranulf, earl of Chester. Ranulf, born in 1170, was a similar age to the king, and may indeed have grown up alongside him, since as a teenager he had been a ward at the court of Henry II. But despite (or perhaps because of) such youthful proximity, the two men had apparently never seen eye to eye. Ranulf had been one of the greatest landowners in Normandy, and hence one of the greatest losers from the French conquest. But, unlike other magnates such as William Marshal, he had received no subsequent grants of compensation from the Lands of the Normans, nor any new lands at the time of John's accession – not even those he considered to be his by hereditary right. John, for his part, seems to have regarded Ranulf with suspicion because of his family connections. The earl had twice been married into the Breton nobility, and in the spring of 1203 his second wife's family had defected to Philip Augustus – a move that had prompted John to seize Ranulf's estates. That seizure was only temporary, and the earl soon satisfied John of his own good faith. But in the winter of 1204–5, he fell under suspicion for a second time. On 14 December the king again ordered that Ranulf's estates be confiscated, asserting on this occasion that the earl had allied himself to the Welsh.[18]

As before, Ranulf moved quickly to quell John's fears. He was back at court by the time of the January council and so presumably took the oath of loyalty: before the end of the month some of his confiscated lands had been restored.[19] But there is reason to think that in general this council was not a success, and that other magnates may have avoided taking the oath by failing to attend. One man who was almost certainly absent was Roger de Montbegon, for his lands, like those of Ranulf of Chester, had also been seized in December. Roger was also a northerner; his main castle was at Hornby in Lancashire, and his other estates were spread across Yorkshire, Nottinghamshire and Lincolnshire. Although he and Ranulf are the only two men named in the king's writ that December, they are unlikely to have been the only ones who fell under suspicion. If disaffection during John's reign had a geographical focus, it was the north.

The north of England, viewed from Westminster or Winchester, was a far-off place where they did things differently. As well as being geographically distant, it was also hard to reach, cut off by the wide estuary of the River Humber and the bogs of Yorkshire and Cheshire. It was culturally distinct, too, a legacy of extensive Viking settlement during the ninth and tenth centuries, and for the same reason it had remained to a large extent politically separate until the Norman Conquest.[20] Since then the Normans and afterwards the Angevins had done their best to counteract these tendencies by imposing their will on the north, but not without provoking political discontent. John himself had visited the north many times, making four separate trips in the first five years of his reign, and on each occasion extracting large sums of money. During his visit of 1201, for example, he fined the citizens of York £100 for failing to welcome him with sufficient honour, and (according to the northern chronicler Roger of Howden) had even gone digging for buried treasure at Corbridge – without success.[21]

Royal demands for money seem to have lain at the root of northern disaffection during the winter of 1204–5. Since the Norman Conquest, all those who held their lands directly from the king had been obliged to supply him with military service. If for some reason (illness, for example) they failed to do so, they had to make a payment instead called scutage (or 'shield money', from *scutum*, shield). Although it generated usefully large sums for the Crown, scutage had not been particularly onerous during the reigns of John's predecessors. Henry II had demanded it on only eight occasions in the course of his thirty-five-year reign, and Richard only four times during his decade in power. John, by contrast, had already demanded five scutages by the end of 1204 – one in every year apart from 1200. He had also levied it at a higher rate than his predecessors, and ahead of campaigns rather than afterwards. In 1204 he had collected scutage even though there had been no campaign at all that year. John had also adopted Richard's one-off experiment of imposing additional fines for the privilege of paying scutage, and made them a matter of routine, demanding heavy fines for every one of his five levies.[22]

John's awareness of growing discontent in the north is reflected in his expenditure during the latter half of 1204: castles were repaired at York, Tickhill and Carlisle, and their garrisons reinforced by additional crossbowmen. Then, in February 1205, in the wake of his less than satisfactory January council, the king himself set out for the north, despite the fact that England was experiencing one of the worst winters anyone could remember. (It was so cold, wrote Ralph of Coggeshall, that the Thames could be crossed on foot, and the frozen ground could not be ploughed.) For three days in early March John held court in York. On 6 March he showed favour to Ranulf of Chester, who had followed him north, granting the earl the lands he claimed by marriage in Yorkshire, and also pardoning some of his debts. Around the same time, the king settled matters with Roger de Montbegon, though in this case the treatment was more stick than carrot. Roger received back his confiscated lands, but it was noted that his castle at Hornby was being restored 'for as long as he serves the king well and faithfully', and that, in order to guarantee this good behaviour, Roger had been required to hand over four hostages.[23]

John returned south in time for a new great council which assembled in Oxford towards the end of March. This must have been summoned soon after the previous council had broken up, and in itself suggests that the earlier meeting had not gone as well as hoped. Now, in the wake of the king's visit to the north, there appears to have been greater consensus. All the earls and barons present swore that 'they would render him due obedience'.[24]

But this consensus came at the cost of political concessions. In the first place, John dropped his demand for scutage from three northern counties (Yorkshire, Lincolnshire and Northumberland). Secondly, and more notably, the king was obliged to swear an oath of his own. According to one chronicler, the magnates compelled John to promise 'that he would, by their counsel, maintain the rights of the kingdom inviolate, to the utmost of his power'. These brief words are laden with significance. John's barons had complained about their rights once or twice in the past, but the phrase 'rights of the kingdom' suggests that, on this occasion at least, they were demanding something more than simply the redress of their private grievances. Equally significant and novel is the magnates' demand that John should maintain those rights 'by their counsel'. The feeling among the baronage was clearly that the king was not listening to their advice, and was far too reliant on his intimate advisers – the foreigners who shared his desire to mount a reconquest in France. In return for their 'due obedience', the barons wanted a greater say in royal government.[25]

The re-establishment of political consensus came not a minute too soon, for French invasion plans had in the meantime been gathering pace. In February Philip Augustus had patched up a quarrel between two of his vassals, the count of Boulogne and the duke of Brabant, and persuaded them to spearhead an attack on England, promising that he would follow within a month of their landing. As soon the Oxford council was over, John moved south to Winchester and issued writs of military summons. It had been decided, the king explained, 'with the assent of the arch-bishops, bishops, earls, barons, and all our faithful men of England', to assemble a select force: one knight in every ten was to muster in London on 1 May, fully armed and equipped, 'prepared to go in our service wherever we should bid them, and to remain in our service in defence of our realm for as long as necessary'.[26]

John had in fact already decided that the best form of defence was attack. His plan was to mount a continental campaign of the kind that had failed to launch the previous year due to lack of magnate support. This time he began to assemble two separate forces on the south coast: a main one at Portsmouth, where a decade earlier Richard I had established a royal naval base, and a supplementary force at Dartmouth, to be captained by his bastard son, Geoffrey (who steps unheralded on to the stage at this moment). Most chroniclers believed, probably correctly, that the object of these military preparations was Poitou, and that the king's plan was to attack Philip Augustus from the south. It is just possible, however, that John intended a two-pronged attack, and that the Portsmouth force was intended for Normandy. Ralph of Coggeshall reports that those French knights who were stationed in Normandy became terrified at the prospect of an English invasion and withdrew from the castles and towns along the coast.

Throughout April and into May, John concentrated all his energy and resources into equipping these two forces. At every major port in southern England, and in Ireland too, the fleet of galleys built by his brother – reduced in number from seventy to fifty as a result of its disastrous attempt to relieve the Isle of Andely – was repaired and refitted, at a total cost of almost £1,000. Hundreds of other ships were seized, in some cases as early as February, and pressed into royal service. Thousands of sailors were assembled at Portsmouth, and vast quantities of bacon and venison were carted there to feed them, along with all manner of military paraphernalia: defensive hurdles, crossbow bolts, nails for horseshoes. 'Oh what a huge sum of money, what piles of supplies, what endless costs were incurred,' said Ralph of Coggeshall, 'making ready and getting together the ships, stockpiling the foodstuffs and the weapons of war.'[27]

At some point soon into these preparations, John postponed the muster of his land forces, and moved it from London to Northampton. Crossbowmen from castles all over England had been ordered there in their hundreds. Prisoners had been pardoned, officially as a pious act for the soul of the king's dear departed mother, in reality to swell the amount of available manpower. John himself arrived in Northampton on 21 May and five days later marched his host south to meet the fleet at Portsmouth. The quaysides must have been crammed with sailors, the Solent filled with ships. One chronicler, Gervase of Canterbury, prosaically reports that the fleet contained 1,500 vessels. 'They say that never had so many ships sailed into any English port to cross the Channel,' wrote Ralph of Coggeshall, 'and that never had such a large army of stalwart knights been assembled in England, all of whom were keen and eager to go on expedition with the king.'[28]

It was around this point, however, that John received some scandalous news about the man who was supposed to be the most stalwart knight of all. William Marshal, knowing that his year and a day was almost up, had quietly crossed the Channel and done homage to Philip Augustus for his lands in Normandy. Soon afterwards he appeared before John in person and a tremendous row ensued. It is described at length in *The History of William Marshal*, which tries its utmost to justify an act that obviously did great damage to its hero's reputation. According to the *History*, the Marshal had been sent to France on a secret peace mission by John himself, and had obtained the king's prior permission to do homage to Philip, only to find on his return that the king denied all of this. ('"By God," said the king, "I did nothing of the sort!"') It is a wholly unconvincing story, undermined by numerous errors, not least the author's attempt to pretend that Normandy was not yet fully conquered. Despite the *History*'s claims to the contrary, John had good reason to be furious.[29]

While he was waiting at Portsmouth harbour, says the *History*, the king decided to revisit the issue. Surrounded by his other barons, he sat down facing the sea, and summoned the Marshal before him to account for his behaviour. Again the earl insisted he had only been acting on John's orders, and again the king denied it. John then put the issue to the test. 'Here's what I want,' he said to the Marshal. 'You will come with me to Poitou, without delay, to fight the king of France, the man to whom you've done homage, to regain my inheritance.' When the Marshal replied that he could not do so, the king again became very angry, and demanded that the other barons present pass judgement on the earl. The barons, however, balked at this demand. 'By God's teeth!'

swore John, 'I can well see that none of my barons is with me in this matter … I shall have to consult with my bachelors,' and so saying, he led his household knights away to consult in private. They agreed that the Marshal's behaviour was inexcusable, but none of them was willing to take on the great warrior in a judicial duel. Seeing that neither his barons nor his bachelors was willing to give him the judgement he wanted, the king got up and went to dinner.[30]

Deeply irritating though it was, the situation with the Marshal did not deflect John from his wider purpose. Preparations for the great expedition continued. The assembled ships were shared out among the various nobles and loaded with food and weapons. But, as the day of departure approached, the Marshal again came before the king, accompanied by the archbishop of Canterbury, and this time told him to call the expedition off. The whole plan, they argued, was dangerous and misconceived. The French king's forces were more numerous than their own; they had no safe refuge overseas, and John's allies in Poitou were not to be trusted. Moreover, if the king and all his knights left England, the country would be exposed to exactly the kind of invasion they knew was being planned, and 'seeking to recover the land that had been lost, he would lose what he still had'. Such a risky military adventure, they further pointed out, was all the more hazardous in that John had no obvious heir – no surviving brothers, and as yet no legitimate children.[31]

It is clear that this opposition amounted to more than the Marshal. The archbishop of Canterbury, Hubert Walter, was not some hand-wringing pacifist, worried about the human cost of war, but a man of vast governmental and military experience. A creature of King Richard, Hubert had accompanied the Lionheart on crusade and fought with distinction in many battles. He had acted as Richard's chief minister, and was currently serving as John's chancellor. He was, in short, a lynchpin of royal government, an elder statesman who commanded the respect not only of the clergy but the baronage too. He and the Marshal had clearly not approached the king as isolated critics, but as representatives of the whole political class. The barons evidently believed that, when they had sworn to help John defend the kingdom, this did not amount to a pledge to follow him as far as Poitou. As *The History of William Marshal* says, 'many were displeased at the prospect'. The scale of the opposition is evident from the fact that the king was all but physically overpowered. John, says Ralph of Coggeshall, was not persuaded by their arguments, and not deterred until the Marshal and the archbishop declared that 'they would detain him violently, lest the whole kingdom be brought into confusion by his departure'.[32]

And that seems to be essentially what happened. Around 10 June, the king sailed from Portsmouth to Winchester, 'unwillingly' according to Gervase of Canterbury, 'weeping and wailing' in the words of Coggeshall. 'Overcome by the pressure of his advisers', he finally assented to their demands. A token force of knights and nobles would be sent to assist the king's Poitevin subjects, but John himself would remain in England, and the rest of the great fleet and army – assembled for so long, and at such great cost – would be disbanded. The troops themselves, especially the sailors, says Coggeshall, giving us a rare insight into opinion below the ranks of the baronage, thought it an abominable decision, and left cursing the archbishop and the king's other counsellors.[33]

Even then, John was not prepared to abandon his plan. After two days at Winchester he gave his advisers the slip and returned to Portsmouth, where he went on board ship with his own followers and put to sea. A rumour ran around the country that he had crossed the Channel, says Coggeshall, but in fact John had gone no further than the Isle of Wight. By this stage even his intimates were urging him to stay at home. And so, after sailing about aimlessly for a further two days, the king finally put in to Studland Bay in Dorset, his plans for reconquest once again defeated.[34]

4

A Pact From Hell

1189–1194

Henry II died on 6 July 1189 in his castle at Chinon, and from there his body was carried along the Loire to Fontevraud, where it was laid in the abbey church. A short time later his rebellious son Richard arrived, accompanied, in all probability, by his younger brother John, who had lately defected to Richard's camp. John's defection had undoubtedly been a heavy blow to Henry, possibly (as several chroniclers opined) the blow that finally killed him. It should, however, be remembered that the principal cause of the king's suffering during the final years of his life had been his long-running feud with Richard. According to two chroniclers, as Richard drew near to his father's corpse, blood flowed from the nose of the dead king, 'as if', said Roger of Howden, 'his spirit were angered by his approach'. If this was a scene familiar from Arthurian romances, it nevertheless indicated that some people held Richard responsible for Henry's death. Howden and others describe Richard as full of contrition at Fontevraud, weeping bitterly. *The History of William Marshal*, by contrast, claims he showed no emotion, standing silently at the head of the bier for a while, before turning to his servants, saying, 'Bury richly the king my father.'[1]

Despite the years of uncertainty caused by Henry's refusal to name his successor, there was no question about what would happen next. Richard had vindicated his right to his inheritance by force of arms, and now succeeded unopposed to all his father's possessions. At Fontevraud he made peace with the men who had stood loyally by Henry to the last, and then rode north to Normandy, where he was invested as duke on 20 July in Rouen Cathedral. Two days later he travelled to Gisors on the border with France to meet with Philip Augustus. The French king, lately his ally, automatically became a rival as Richard stepped into his father's shoes. In spite of this, and by postponing contentious issues (such as the Vexin), an accord was quickly reached. In return for a sizeable payment of 24,000 marks, Philip returned almost all the territories he had recently conquered with Richard's assistance, and recognized him as heir to all the Plantagenet dominions. Their conference over, Richard rode to Barfleur and sailed for England, where his mother, already released from her long captivity, was preparing for his coronation.[2]

What role would John play in this new regime? On the one hand he was clearly very important. Richard, still unmarried, lacked legitimate children; John, his only surviving brother, was his most obvious heir. As such John needed to be accommodated, and accorded appropriate wealth and status. Before his death Henry II had apparently granted him lands in both England and Normandy, and Richard proved willing to honour this bequest. Soon after his investiture as duke, he gave John the county of Mortain in western Normandy, and promised him £4,000 of land in England.[3]

On the other hand, Richard clearly did not trust his younger brother. That there was no great love lost between them might be implied by the manner of their crossing to England. Not only did they set sail from Barfleur in different ships (which could be viewed as nothing other than prudent), they also put into different English ports, Richard landing at Portsmouth to the jubilant reception laid on by his mother, while John disembarked at Dover without any recorded fanfare.[4]

More suggestive still of the suspicion that John continued to provoke was his sudden marriage. The match Henry II had originally brokered in 1173, by which John would have married the daughter of the count of Savoy, had come to nothing – within a year of the agreement the girl was dead. But in 1176 Henry had found his youngest son a fresh marital prospect in the form of Isabella, the eldest daughter of the earl of Gloucester. This was principally a means of increasing John's landed estate, and on the earl's death in 1183 the old king had duly seized his lands for John's future use. No marriage, however, had followed. By this point Henry was reviewing his options, having recently lost his eldest son and fallen out with his second. By the end of the same year, he had been openly floating the idea that John rather than Richard might be married to Philip Augustus' sister, Alice. As his sons died off, and the feud with Richard intensified, Henry had every reason for wanting to keep John's matrimonial options open.[5]

Richard, once he was in charge, wanted to shut them down. Within days of the brothers' return to England in 1189 John was married to Isabella, his long-term fiancée: their wedding took place at John's castle at Marlborough on 29 August. To be fair, John's thoughts on the matter are unknown; it may be that he accepted his bride with alacrity. Isabella, sadly, is a completely anonymous character, whose attractions apart from her extensive lands are unrecorded. She was, however, already around thirty years old in 1189, and thus likely to have been regarded as something of an old maid by her twenty-two-year-old groom. Later events certainly suggest that theirs was not a match made in heaven.[6]

The notion that John was married at Richard's insistence is reinforced by the similar treatment of their half-brother, Geoffrey, the most prominent of Henry II's several bastard children. Born around 1151 and raised honourably in the royal household, Geoffrey had been marked out for advancement in the Church, yet had shown a notable reluctance to commit to a clerical career. Elected as bishop of Lincoln in 1173, he eventually resigned the position rather than take holy orders. In September 1189 Richard compelled him to do so, appointing him as archbishop of York, despite the objections of the cathedral chapter and of Geoffrey himself. By forcing him into a tonsure, Richard ended any misplaced hopes his half-brother may have entertained with regard to the succession.[7]

The reason Richard was so keen to keep his brothers' ambitions in check was simple: he was determined to depart on crusade. After the fall of Jerusalem to Muslim forces in 1187, the Christian communities of the Holy Land had been reduced to a handful of coastal cities and isolated inland castles. The pressure on western princes to come to their rescue remained intense, and Richard, having taken the cross almost two years earlier, was anxious to waste no more time. On 3 September 1189 he was crowned in Westminster Abbey, and invested with all the powers and responsibilities of kingship. John played a part in the proceedings by carrying one of the ceremonial swords. Two weeks later, the new king held the first great council of his reign at Pipewell Abbey in Northamptonshire, and set about delegating those same powers and responsibilities to others, setting out the details of his regency scheme. In his absence England was to be ruled by two justiciars, the earl of Essex and the bishop of Durham, with the help of a number of less distinguished but more administratively experienced assistants. John, who might have expected some role in the running of government, however nominal, was not included.[8]

For three more months Richard busied himself in England, raising money for his expedition and attending to the kingdom's security. From Pipewell he went west to Worcester to make peace with the various rulers of Wales. (John, sent to besiege the castle at Carmarthen, made a separate deal that Richard refused to ratify.) In December he travelled to Canterbury to receive the king of Scots, William the Lion, and, in return for a generous payment, tore up the humiliating peace treaty that Henry II had imposed on William after his capture in 1174. From Canterbury Richard went directly to Dover and crossed the Channel, to begin making similar preparations for departure in his continental territories.[9]

Before leaving England, Richard had honoured his earlier promise to John by making him a massive grant of land. John had already received a lot of land soon after the coronation – most notably the earldom of Gloucester brought to him by his marriage to Isabella, but also seven other substantial lordships (Ludgershall, Marlborough, Peveril, Tickhill, Eye, Lancaster and Wallingford), as well as other manors and the profits of two royal forests. Together these estates brought John around £1,170 a year, a sizeable sum, but one which fell a long way short of the £4,000 he had been promised. At Canterbury Richard had therefore granted his younger brother six whole counties, namely Nottinghamshire, Derbyshire, Somerset, Dorset, Devon and Cornwall – a huge amount of territory, concentrated in the Midlands and the south-west, which brought his income comfortably above the required amount.

Some people subsequently criticized Richard for this grant. William of Newburgh commented that John seemed to have been given almost a third of England, and condemned Richard for his 'immoderate and improvident liberality'. Newburgh, however (like later historians who echoed his criticisms) wrote with the knowledge of how the story would end. A more charitable interpretation of Richard's actions would allow that he was simply fulfilling Henry II's last wishes. Moreover, the new king, in giving these lands to his younger brother, retained many of the castles within them. (John received the castles at Marlborough, Ludgershall, Peveril and Lancaster, but not, for example, those at Orford, Eye, Wallingford, Tickhill or Gloucester, all of which were reserved to the Crown.) John had been given a lot of land, but not the wherewithal to hold it in a fight.[10]

More legitimate criticism can be levelled at Richard over the person he *did* leave in charge. Around the time of his departure from England, one of his two newly appointed justiciars, the earl of Essex, died, and the king attempted to solve the problem by granting additional powers to his chancellor, William Longchamp. A clerk who had been in Richard's service for some time, Longchamp was clearly a man whose abilities the king held in high regard. Formerly the chancellor of Poitou, he had been promoted to the same position in England at the time of Richard's coronation, and elevated to become bishop of Ely a short time later. Longchamp's origins, however, were comparatively humble – he was a scion of a modest knightly family – and so his rapid rise inevitably excited envy and disapproval. According to the chronicler Richard of Devizes, who wrote a wonderfully opinionated account of these years, the new chancellor was 'a remarkable person, who made up for the shortness of his stature by his arrogance, counting on his lord's affection and presuming on his goodwill'.[11]

Whether his faults were real or maliciously invented, Longchamp plainly did not see eye to eye with the surviving justiciar, Hugh du Puiset, the bishop of Durham. By February reports of their malfunctioning relationship must have reached Richard in distant Aquitaine, for at that point he summoned both men to attend a council. When it convened in Normandy the following month the king announced that henceforth Longchamp, as well as continuing as chancellor, would be England's new *chief* justiciar; the bishop of Durham would be responsible only for those lands north of the Humber.

Also present in the same meeting at Richard's command were John and his half-brother Geoffrey. There is nothing to suggest that either had played any part in the disputes between the king's regents, but Richard revealed his growing distrust of the pair by taking an additional security measure, and making both of them swear to stay out of England for the next three years. In John's case, however, this provision was immediately diluted thanks to the intervention of Eleanor of Aquitaine. At their mother's request, Richard allowed that John could enter and leave England provided he had Longchamp's permission.[12]

Whether or not John returned to England after this meeting is unclear – his movements in 1190 are for the most part mysterious. But Longchamp recrossed the Channel at once and took immediate steps to tighten his grip on power. He began by orchestrating the downfall of the bishop of Durham, interfering in his jurisdiction north of the Humber and arresting him when he came to complain. The bishop protested to the king and regained his liberty, but not his office; in June Richard confirmed that Longchamp would have authority over the whole kingdom. In the meantime the chief justiciar had been further increasing his control by appointing his own men as sheriffs and as keepers of royal castles – replacing, in some cases, men who had paid handsomely to have these offices only the previous year. He also invested large sums improving the defences of key fortresses; almost £3,000 was spent on the Tower of London alone. Nor was it just in the secular sphere that Longchamp's pervasive influence was felt. At Richard's request the pope made him a papal legate, giving him unrivalled authority over the English Church. As top ecclesiastical positions fell vacant, they were similarly filled by the justiciar's friends and relatives. 'The laity at that time felt him to be a king, and more than a king,' wrote William of Newburgh, 'the clergy a pope and more than a pope. Indeed, both of them [felt him to be] an intolerable tyrant.'[13]

No one can have felt more aggrieved at Longchamp's overbearing behaviour than the king's younger brother. Apart from the fact that a low-born cleric had been left to determine whether he – an Angevin prince – should be allowed to enter or leave the kingdom, John must have perceived the justiciar's actions as a programme intended to keep him in his place. He had deliberately been left with only a few castles, but Longchamp contrived to make it fewer still, confiscating the castles of Bolsover and the Peak in Derbyshire. Moreover, the royal castles that the justiciar had chosen to repair and refortify were all located near to John's lands or those of his associates, as if in expectation of trouble. His associates were also marked out for special attention. His seneschal, John Marshal (brother of the more famous William), lost his job as sheriff of York and keeper of York Castle to Longchamp's own brother, Osbert. And William Marshal himself (who was closely aligned with John at this point, despite his biographer's later attempts to disguise it) also clashed with the justiciar, who for a time tried to deprive him of Gloucester Castle, even to the extent of laying siege to it.[14]

Complaints about Longchamp's behaviour were naturally sent

to Richard, but the king was becoming increasingly hard to reach. He and Philip Augustus had finally set out on their journey to the east in July 1190; in August they then sailed, independently, along the west coast of Italy, and by September both had arrived in Sicily. Richard's reception in Sicily, however, was a hostile one, and his men clashed violently with the locals. In the process of resolving this conflict, the king made an extraordinary decision – one which had major repercussions for politics in England.[15]

Had Richard arrived in Sicily twelve months earlier, he would have received a much warmer welcome, for back then his sister Joan had been married to the island's ruler, King William II. But William had died in November 1189, and the Sicilian crown had passed to his illegitimate cousin, Tancred of Lecce. Tancred's hold on power was tenuous and he had treated Joan with suspicion, withholding her widow's dower and keeping her in close confinement. This obviously did not bode well for good relations with Richard. According to Roger of Howden, an eyewitness, the English king sailed into Messina that September 'in such magnificence and to such a noise of trumpets and clarions that a tremor ran though all who were in the city'. This demonstration of power had some effect on Tancred, to the extent that he released Joan from captivity and delivered her to her brother's camp. But in the meantime the crusading army had begun fighting with the population of Messina, many of whom were Greek, and some of whom were Muslim. When a riot broke out in early October, Richard responded by taking the city by force. As an added security measure, he built a wooden castle on a nearby hill, to which he gave the unsubtle name of Mategriffon, or 'Kill the Greeks'.[16]

Tancred had no option but to negotiate with his unwelcome visitors. In return for peace he agreed to pay Richard 40,000 ounces of gold – half to compensate Joan for her lack of dower, and half in lieu of the ships and supplies his predecessor had promised to contribute to the crusade. As was common in such cases, the deal was to be sealed by a royal wedding. Richard, alas, had no legitimate sons for such purposes, but he did have a three-year-old nephew. The boy, named Arthur, was the only son of his late brother, Geoffrey. He had not been born at the time of Geoffrey's death in the summer of 1186 – indeed, he must have only just been conceived, for he did not make his appearance until 29 March the following year. Young Arthur was the obvious, not to say the only solution to his uncle's diplomatic needs, and it was duly agreed that he would marry one of Tancred's three daughters. At the same moment, Richard also announced that, in the event he should die with no sons of his own, Arthur would be his heir.[17]

This, to put it mildly, was explosive. Although everyone was aware of Arthur's existence in the autumn of 1190, he was as yet only a small child, who might not make it beyond the hazardous years of infancy. Richard, moreover, had done nothing thus far to discourage the notion that his successor, in default of any sons, would be his younger brother, John. On the contrary, he had done much to encourage it by his generous provision for John in England, and there is even evidence to suggest that, during their meeting in March 1190, he had named John as his default successor in Normandy. John, said William of Newburgh, 'expected to become the successor to the kingdom, should the king, perchance, not survive his laborious and perilous undertaking'.[18]

Quite what Richard hoped to achieve, therefore, by suddenly naming Arthur as his heir is a mystery. Possibly his only intention was to make his nephew a more attractive bridegroom in order to extract maximum advantage from Tancred. According to Newburgh, the news of Arthur's nomination was kept secret, and the only person informed in England was the justiciar, William Longchamp. But Longchamp, continues Newburgh, passed the message on to the king of Scots, hoping to secure his support for Arthur's claim if the need arose, and no doubt he did the same with others. Somehow, early in the new year 1191, the cat was let out of the bag, and John found out.[19]

At first, says Newburgh, he hid his indignation, but began secretly building up his own party of supporters. Presumably by this point, if not before, he had returned to England. As the tension mounted, a meeting between the two sides was arranged at Winchester on 24 March. According to Richard of Devizes, our only informant, the debate concerned 'the custody of certain castles, and the money granted to the count [of Mortain, i.e. John] by his brother at the Exchequer'. This makes it sound as if John had not received all the money he felt was his due, and was belatedly contesting the extent to which Longchamp had gained control of the most important royal castles. In any succession dispute, these fortresses would be crucial; they were, in William of Newburgh's well-turned phrase, 'the bones of the kingdom'. Whatever was said at Winchester, however, failed to defuse the situation. As Easter came and went, it was obvious that men were preparing for civil war. 'Certain nobles became busy', says Devizes. 'Castles were strengthened, towns were fortified, ditches were dug.' Letters were sent in secret, soliciting the support of powerful people against the justiciar. Meanwhile John was travelling about the country with a large following, and 'he did not prohibit or restrain his followers from calling him the king's heir'.[20]

At last, says Devizes, 'the lid came off the pot'. Shortly before midsummer (21 June), Longchamp demanded that the keeper of the royal castle at Lincoln, Gerard de Camville, surrender its custody and swear allegiance to him as regent. Camville, whose right to hold the castle had only recently been confirmed by Richard, refused the order and went instead to swear allegiance to John. On learning of this open defiance, the justiciar sent overseas for foreign mercenaries, and in the meantime took such troops as he could raise to lay siege to Lincoln. John in turn rose to defend Camville's right. Moving north, he quickly forced the surrender of the ill-prepared royal castles at nearby Tickhill and Nottingham, and he sent messengers to Longchamp, explaining (in the evocative words of Roger of Howden) that he would 'visit him with a rod of iron' if Camville was not immediately reinstated.[21]

At this moment, with England apparently on the brink of civil war, an emissary arrived from Richard. Walter of Coutances, archbishop of Rouen but an Englishman by birth, had followed the king as far as Sicily, but had been sent home in April, Richard having finally realized he needed to do something about Longchamp's growing unpopularity. He arrived in southern England on 27 June and hastened north to act as intermediary between the two hostile factions. Negotiations were evidently not easy. The justiciar, says Richard of Devizes, demanded that John give up the castles he had seized and stand trial for having broken his oath to stay out of the kingdom. John, on being told this, 'became unrecognizable in all his body. Wrath cut furrows across his forehead; his burning eyes shot sparks; rage darkened the ruddy colour of his face.' At length, however, both sides agreed to a day of mediation, which was fixed for 28 July at Winchester. Longchamp in the meantime raised the siege of Lincoln and returned to London.[22]

The chances of a peaceful settlement at Winchester must have seemed bleak. Both sides appealed to their supporters to turn out fully armed, and both sides had taken the additional precaution of raising troops from Wales. (John kept his concealed near the conference place, which was outside the city walls.) Nevertheless, a peace agreement was reached, the terms of which have survived. For the most part they favoured John. He agreed to give up Nottingham and Tickhill castles, but the men named as their new keepers were members of his affinity. He promised not to harbour outlaws in his lands, but this merely serves to highlight how independent his power had become. Meanwhile his supporter Gerard de Camville was reinstated as keeper of Lincoln Castle, and all new fortifications raised since Richard's departure were to be dismantled. Richard's absence, and the possibility he might not return, linger over the whole document; John was clearly trying to strengthen his hand against such an outcome. In this respect, he won a crucial point, not mentioned in the treaty, but emphasized by both Devizes and Newburgh. Longchamp also agreed to drop his support for Arthur, and to support John's right to the throne in the event of Richard's death.[23]

Good as it was for John, the deal achieved at Winchester had no clear winner. Whatever concessions had been wrung from the justiciar, he still remained in power, and he still had Richard's support: according to Richard of Devizes, the archbishop of Rouen had returned with the particular message from the king that his brother was to obey Longchamp.[24]

What upset the fragile peace in England was the return of John and Richard's half-brother Geoffrey. The archbishop-elect of York had finally had his consecration approved by the pope in May, and the ceremony took place in Tours in August. Possessed of his new authority, Geoffrey decided to disregard his oath not to cross the Channel, and asked for John's assistance. John was only too happy to pledge his help, but Longchamp, perceiving the threat to his own authority, gave orders that Geoffrey was to be arrested on sight. Thus when the new archbishop arrived at Dover on 14 September, he was immediately surrounded by soldiers. He managed to escape to the local priory, but after five days the soldiers entered in their mail shirts and dragged him out, banging his head on the pavement. Dressed in his episcopal robes and clinging to his cross, accompanied by a crowd of curious townspeople, Geoffrey was pushed and dragged up the hill to Dover Castle, to be detained at the pleasure of the castellan, who also happened to be Longchamp's brother-in-law.[25]

'The story', says Richard of Devizes, 'went through the country more quickly than the wind.' Geoffrey was seemingly a popular figure among the laity, respected as a soldier and a loyal son; the clergy, whatever they thought of his spiritual deficiencies, objected to his treatment on principle. Inevitably the news that soldiers had violated the sanctuary of a church and injured an archbishop evoked memories of Becket's martyrdom. The outrage was instant. The bishop of Lincoln excommunicated the castellan of Dover, and other bishops added their voices to the outcry. Longchamp, desperately trying to retrieve the situation, ordered Geoffrey's release and gave out that he had never ordered his detention, but to no avail: the country was up in arms.[26]

For John this was the opportunity he had been waiting for. During his earlier clash over Lincoln Castle he had attempted to pose as the champion of those unjustly oppressed by the justiciar's tyranny, claiming that 'he was no longer willing to bear in silence the desolation of his brother's possessions and his realm'. Now he struck up this same tune again with greater gusto. Rushing south from Lancaster to his castle at Marlborough, he sent letters to all the magnates. 'As you love God's honour, and the Church's, and the lord king's, and the realm's, and mine,' he began, 'be at Loddon Bridge on the Saturday next after Michaelmas, between Reading and Windsor, because, God willing, I will meet you there, so that we may deal with certain great and arduous matters concerning the lord king and the realm.'[27]

This meeting, which took place on 5 October, was well attended, with both bishops and barons turning up in large numbers. Longchamp, who had been summoned to account for his actions, advanced heavily armed from London and lurked at nearby Windsor. Walter de Coutances, the archbishop of Rouen and broker of the recent peace, explained to the assembled company how he had lost patience with the justiciar, who had thwarted all his efforts to help govern the realm, as King Richard had commanded. He now produced an additional letter from the king, authorizing him to remove Longchamp from office. The magnates and prelates unanimously agreed that this was the right way forward, and instructed the justiciar to come before them on Monday to hear this judgement.[28]

Longchamp did set out on Monday morning, but then apparently panicked, hearing the news that John was marching on London. In fact all John had done was send his baggage train to London ahead of him, but the justiciar mistook this as an attempt to seize the capital and set out in pursuit. At one point during the journey there was a skirmish between the two households, in the course of which one of John's knights was killed. Longchamp arrived back in London ahead of his rivals and tried to persuade the citizens to bar the gates against them. But the Londoners, stirred up by the recently-arrived Archbishop Geoffrey, refused the justiciar's request, calling him 'a disturber of the land and a traitor', at which point Longchamp and his followers fled to the Tower. When John and the barons arrived later that evening, the citizens came out to welcome them with lanterns and torches.[29]

The following day – Tuesday 8 October – the bells of St Paul's summoned the Londoners and the new arrivals to a second meeting, in which all spoke out against the justiciar. On the authority of the royal letters brought by Walter de Coutances, Longchamp was dismissed from office, and so too were all the friends and relatives he had appointed to positions of power. 'The whole assembly', said Richard of Devizes, 'declared Count John, the king's brother, supreme governor of the whole realm, and ordered that all castles should be turned over to whomever he wanted.' All present, beginning with John himself, renewed their oaths of fealty to Richard, but they also swore to obey John during his brother's absence, and to accept him as king should Richard not return.[30]

Longchamp, still ensconced in the Tower, reportedly fainted when he was told this news the following morning, and had to be revived by having cold water splashed in his face. He stubbornly refused to resign his offices or his castles, telling John's messengers, 'You have forgotten your still-living king.' At length, however, his followers persuaded him to submit to the superior power of his enemies, who had placed the Tower under siege. Thus, on Thursday 10 October, the justiciar emerged to be formally stripped of his offices before a great crowd that had assembled outside the city walls. Courageously, given his predicament, he maintained to the last that he was not resigning his duties, merely being deprived of them by force. After this he was escorted to Dover, one of the three royal castles he was permitted to retain, but shortly afterwards escaped across the Channel. The bishops, earls and barons, meanwhile, wrote a letter to the king, explaining what they had done.[31]

During the summer of 1191, Richard had been winning the victories that would make him a legend. In April he had finally left Sicily with a fleet of 200 ships and perhaps 17,000 men, and in May he had conquered the island of Cyprus. Arriving in the

Holy Land in June, he had captured the city of Acre in July, ending the siege that had begun there two years earlier. In August, after massacring 3,000 Muslim prisoners outside Acre's walls, he had set out further south, and in September he had defeated Saladin's army in battle at Arsuf. On 1 October he sent home a confident newsletter. 'With God's grace,' he wrote, 'we hope to recover the city of Jerusalem and the Holy Sepulchre within twenty days after Christmas, and then return to our own dominions.'[32]

But in the course of making these conquests, the king had fallen out with several of his allies, most notably Philip Augustus. For years Richard had been promising to marry Philip's sister, Alice, but during their stay on Sicily he had at last revealed that this had been a deception. Richard could never consent to marrying Alice, he explained, because she had been his father's mistress – indeed, she had borne Henry II a bastard son. This revelation was forced from Richard because he had made alternative wedding plans. To safeguard Aquitaine during his absence he had entered into an alliance with the king of Navarre, and promised to marry his daughter, Berengaria. She was escorted to Sicily in March by the elderly but indefatigable Eleanor of Aquitaine, and eventually married to Richard in May while the king was still in Cyprus.[33]

Although Richard did his best to placate Philip, paying him 10,000 marks in compensation, the French king had taken the humiliation deeply to heart. He departed from Sicily ahead of the English crusaders and sailed directly to the Holy Land. Once Richard had joined him there, the two of them had done nothing but quarrel, taking different sides in political disputes and arguing over the division of spoils. Eventually, on 22 July, Philip had announced he was leaving for home, claiming he was too ill to continue, and two weeks later he departed. To compound his humiliation, many of his men chose not to accompany him, and remained behind to follow Richard. By October the French king had reached Italy, and by Christmas he was back in France – 'safe and sound', according to Roger of Howden, 'and impudently boasting that he was going to devastate the lands of the king of England'.[34]

Philip's first action, on 20 January 1192, was to meet the seneschal of Normandy on the border with France. Presenting forged documents, he explained that Richard, in rejecting Alice, had relinquished his right to hold the Vexin, and demanded that both his sister and the long-contested territory be handed over. The seneschal and the other barons of Normandy told the French king, in so many words, to get lost, at which point Philip vowed angrily that he would take the Vexin by force. As a first step to making good this threat, he sent an invitation to John, promising to make him ruler of all Richard's continental lands if he would make an honest woman out of Alice.[35]

John, to general consternation, responded enthusiastically to this proposal, and made preparations to sail to France. The fact that he already had a wife was not much of a problem: his marriage to Isabella of Gloucester had been declared invalid by the archbishop of Canterbury immediately after its celebration in 1189 on grounds of consanguinity (both bride and groom were descendants of Henry I). John, presumably at Richard's insistence, had subsequently obtained a provisional dispensation from a visiting papal legate, but since then had not bothered to seek confirmation from the pope. The ties that bound him to Isabella were thus weak, and could easily be undone.[36]

John's eagerness to conspire with Philip Augustus at the start of 1192 is more surprising in view of his apparently strong position the previous autumn. During that period he had been the hero of the hour, a liberator who had delivered the realm from the tyranny of Longchamp, welcomed into London by jubilant crowds. But John's popularity may have been more apparent than real. Richard of Devizes reports that he had been made 'supreme governor of the whole realm' and handed custody of all the royal castles, but if this was ever agreed it had not been subsequently carried through.[37] William of Newburgh states, more credibly, that the magnates had delivered management of the kingdom to the archbishop of Rouen, Walter de Coutances. *The History of William Marshal* adds that the archbishop ruled well and wisely, following the advice of the barons, but shunning the counsels of John, 'since he could see well what John's intentions were'. If this is not entirely true – there is evidence to show that he was consulted on certain issues – there is good reason to think that by the beginning of 1192 John must have been feeling marginalized. He had, of course, been recognized as Richard's heir, should the king die without children of his own. But Richard was now married, and his wife had accompanied him to the Holy Land. Even as John fervently hoped for news of some fatal encounter in the sands of Palestine, he must have feared that the spring would bring letters from his brother announcing the birth of a son.[38]

What prevented John from pushing ahead and accepting Philip's enticing offer was the rapid intervention of his mother. 'Fearing that the light-minded youth might be going to attempt something', says Richard of Devizes, Eleanor of Aquitaine crossed the Channel from Normandy on 11 February. By assuring John that his possessions in England would be confiscated should he leave the kingdom, the former queen and the archbishop of Rouen induced him to stay put. Philip, meanwhile, failed to persuade the nobles of France to participate in his planned invasion of Normandy, there being few things more dishonourable than attacking the lands of an absent crusader.[39]

John was, however, quite capable of causing trouble by himself. Soon after this setback he seized control of two of the most important royal castles, Windsor and Wallingford, somehow convincing their keepers to surrender them and garrisoning them with his own men. The regents responded by summoning a council of magnates to London, intending to bring him to book. But, says Richard of Devizes, 'each one, fearing the count, wanted the question to be put by another mouth rather than by his own'. John's provocative behaviour was highlighting the almost impossible bind in which England's great men found themselves. If they were to uphold Richard's authority they ought not to tolerate its usurpation; but, on the other hand, if Richard died, John would surely become the next king, and punish those who had opposed him.[40]

As if to emphasize their dilemma, while the council was sitting in London news arrived of the return of William Longchamp. The former justiciar had never accepted the legitimacy of his deposition, and during his self-imposed exile he had been busy drumming up support for a comeback. The pope, who naturally objected to the overthrow of a papal legate, had authorized the excommunication of those who had ousted him. Roger of Howden believed that Longchamp had bribed Eleanor of Aquitaine into supporting his readmittance, and William of Newburgh asserted that he had been secretly communicating with John. Whatever the truth, the former justiciar landed at Dover in late March and demanded to be reinstated as the realm's rightful governor.[41]

At this the magnates' attitude towards John was instantly reversed. 'The man whom they had been going to judge a perjurer and an offender against his lord', as Richard of Devizes calls him, was seen as being the only hope of resisting the danger that lurked at Dover. The count himself, meanwhile, was staying at Wallingford Castle, 'laughing at their assemblies', and messengers were sent there to beg him to intervene. After letting them beg for a good long time, he came to London, and allowed himself to be flattered some more by the magnates in council. 'There was no mention of the castles', says Devizes; all the talk was now of removing Longchamp, and John relished the discomfort of his rivals. The former justiciar, he explained, had offered him £700 to remain neutral, and he really needed the money. The regents took the hint and paid him £500 from the Exchequer in return for his continued support, and then sent messengers to Longchamp, informing him of the outcome and commanding him to leave; Longchamp, realizing he had lost the bidding war, returned to the Continent. The whole episode had turned out so well for John it is hard not to suspect he had some hand in orchestrating it. Essentially it was a less dramatic rerun of the events of the previous autumn, John once again delivering the realm from its sometime oppressor, reminding the regents how much they were reliant on his power. In exchange for his services, he exacted more than just money. The council in London concluded its business by again swearing fealty to Richard, and to John as his heir.[42]

Richard had hoped to be back in England by this point, but his plan to be in Jerusalem within twenty days of Christmas 1191 had not come to pass. The crusaders had come close: on Christmas Day itself they were camped just twelve miles from the Holy City, but soon afterwards they were forced to admit that they did not have the manpower or resources to mount an effective siege. In January 1192 they had retired to the coastal town of Ascalon, where they had remained for the next four months.[43]

Soon after Easter (5 April) news reached Richard of the overthrow of William Longchamp the previous autumn; the messenger, presumably sent by Longchamp himself, reported that John was trying to take over the realm, and urged the king to return home. But Richard was undeterred; probably he had also received the reports sent by Walter of Coutances and his fellow regents explaining their reasons for ending the justiciar's regime and assuring him that his affairs were still in good order. In May the king embarked on a fresh military offensive, advancing twenty miles further south to assault the castle of Darum, which succumbed after a four-day siege. At the end of the month, however, a second messenger arrived, informing Richard that his brother was plotting with Philip Augustus. This intelligence, which presumably came from Walter of Coutances, was much more disconcerting, for Philip was capable of doing far greater damage. After agonizing for some time, Richard decided on one final roll of the dice, and agreed to support a second attempt to take Jerusalem. This time he came even closer, and may even have glimpsed the city from afar, but once again he decided in conference with the other crusade leaders that an assault would be impossible. On 4 July the crusading army, paralysed by divisions over strategy, withdrew to the coast and resumed negotiations with Saladin. At the start of September they agreed a truce that would last almost four years – time enough for Richard to settle his urgent affairs in the west. On 9 October the king set sail from the Holy Land, hopeful that before too long he would be able to return.

In the meantime, he had to contend with the problem of how to get home. Philip Augustus had spent the previous twelve months trying to detract from his own humiliation by blackening Richard's name across Europe, accusing him of trickery, treachery and even murder (in April the king-elect of Jerusalem had been killed in mysterious circumstances). As a result there was no obvious safe route for Richard to take. Whatever his plans were, they were dashed by storms that drove his ships into the Italian coast, north-east of Venice. The king and his companions became lost and entered the lands of Duke Leopold of Austria. Leopold, alas, was another crusader who had fallen out with Richard: the king's troops had contemptuously thrown down the duke's banner as they entered Acre, and the insult had prompted Leopold to abandon the crusade. Inevitably Richard's attempt to travel incognito through Austria failed, and he was arrested in a tavern outside Vienna just before Christmas 1192. By the start of the new year, all of Europe had learned that the king of England was a captive.[44]

In England itself the news was greeted for the most part with predictable alarm. Eleanor of Aquitaine was reportedly distressed to hear it; Walter of Coutances wrote of his 'grief of mind' at the misfortune, 'momentous beyond all conception, which has befallen our king'. Others sought to rationalize it as the judgement of God. The dean of St Paul's, Ralph of Diceto, opined Richard's capture was divine retribution for having rebelled against his father.[45]

In John's camp, by contrast, the mood was jubilant. If he had been hoping for Richard's death, captivity was the next best thing. Had not their great-grandfather, Henry I, captured his older brother, Robert Curthose, and kept him in prison for nearly thirty years? John's advisers assured him that the time was ripe to claim the kingdom. Philip Augustus, who had sent the happy news, repeated his offer of the previous year to make John lord of all Richard's lands on the Continent. He rushed to accept, and came out openly in rebellion. 'Setting at naught his fidelity to his brother,' said William of Newburgh, 'he most shamefully declared himself his enemy.'[46]

John now controlled enough royal castles to disregard the regents' earlier threats to dispossess him should he go abroad. Strengthening their garrisons, he hastened across the Channel at the end of January. He met first with the seneschal and barons of Normandy and offered to help them defend the duchy against the expected French attack, provided they accept him as their new lord. When they refused, he rode on to France and entered what Roger of Howden called 'a pact from hell' with Philip Augustus, doing homage to the French king for all Richard's lands, promising to marry Alice and agreeing to surrender the Vexin. In return Philip granted him the county of Artois, a territory he had lately annexed after the death of its previous ruler, the count of Flanders, on crusade. For the first time a king of France had a maritime coast from which to threaten England, and Philip and John now began to do just that, recruiting Flemish mercenaries and assembling an invasion fleet, with the intention of crossing to England at Easter.[47]

Back in England the regents had been busy responding to the crisis and anxiously awaiting news of Richard. By late January they would have known that the king's captor, Duke Leopold, was negotiating to hand him over to his overlord, the Holy Roman Emperor, Henry VI. Henry was another ruler who had been worked on by Philip Augustus after his return from the crusade; as Philip had passed through Italy the two of them had entered a secret alliance. The emperor's eagerness to obtain Richard, however, had less to do with any loyalty to his French ally, and more to do with the sizeable ransom he knew such a high-status prisoner could command. Henry was plagued by rebellion across his wide dominions, and desperately in need of extra funds. The regents in England dispatched two abbots to Germany to discover what his terms would be. In the meantime, they focused on preparing to defend the realm against the feared invasion. An oath of loyalty to Richard was administered across the whole kingdom; coastal towns were strengthened, and troops were raised to guard the shore.[48]

Despite these measures, at some point in the weeks that followed John managed to re-enter the country in secret. He brought with him some Flemish mercenaries and set about trying to rally more support, telling people that his brother was dead. Some believed him, but most remained loyal, including the king of Scots and the various princes of Wales. Having succeeded in raising some Welsh troops, who ravaged the area between Windsor and Kingston, John marched on London and demanded to be given the realm. The Londoners, however, had lately reaffirmed their allegiance to Richard, and together with the regents they rejected his demand. In anger John withdrew to his castles and began attacking his brother's estates.[49]

Now was the supreme test of the loyalty of the magnates, whose predicament had never been so stark. Remaining faithful to Richard would require them to start actively waging war against John, the man who might very easily become their new ruler if Richard failed to return. Shortly before Easter, as they debated what to do, a messenger arrived from the captive king in the shape of Roger of Thurnham, a household knight and former crusader. Thurnham would have been able to tell his audience in London what the two abbots they had sent to Germany were simultaneously hearing from Richard himself: that the king was fit and well, and that negotiations for his release were already in train. If he was privately anxious about John's treachery, he was publicly dismissive, saying, 'My brother John is not the man to seize any land by force, if anyone meets his attack with even the slightest resistance.' Thurnham had arrived in London with Richard's armour, probably a symbolic gesture intended to spur faithful men into military action.[50]

The regents responded accordingly. By this stage it must have been clear that the danger of invasion from Flanders had passed; a few foreign ships had attempted to make a landing but their crews had been captured by the coastal levies. John's forces, meanwhile, had been confined to two main castles – Windsor in the south and Tickhill in the north – and towards the end of March both were placed under siege. Royal financial records reveal that over 1,000 men were deployed at Windsor, while three shiploads of stone were sent up the Thames to provide ammunition for the siege engines. Even once these assaults were under way, however, there were still signs of hesitancy. One chronicler accused Walter of Coutances of laxity in prosecuting the siege of Windsor because he had relatives among the defenders. In the north some magnates refused to join in the attack on Tickhill, asserting that 'they were liegemen of Count John', a refusal that led the archbishop of York to brand them 'traitors to the king and the kingdom'. Yet while the king himself remained out of his kingdom, the conflict of loyalties continued.[51]

What eventually ended both sieges was the arrival in England on 20 April of another of Richard's crusading companions, Hubert Walter. Hubert had been sent from the king's side to begin his career as archbishop of Canterbury – his appointment being in part a reward for the strenuous efforts he had already made in trying to procure Richard's release. He also came to assist the regency government in the Herculean task of raising the king's ransom, the working figure for which was 100,000 marks. Such a colossal sum could not be accumulated while money was pouring from the treasury to pay for the assault against John's castles, nor could it be collected in full unless John would allow royal agents to enter his own lands. Despite the fact that both Windsor and Tickhill were reportedly on the verge of surrender, a truce was agreed until the autumn. John gave up Windsor and Wallingford to his mother, but was allowed to retain Tickhill and Nottingham.[52]

All John's hopes must have now been pinned on Philip Augustus, whose attack on Normandy had enjoyed much greater success. Although deterred from besieging Rouen by the bravado of its citizens, he had succeeded in taking several major strongholds along the Norman border. Having achieved all he could for the time being by military means, he now engaged in a diplomatic struggle with Richard's regents; as they laboured to raise money for the king's ransom, so he sought to ensure that his rival would be detained indefinitely. A meeting between the French king and the emperor was scheduled for 25 June, though in the event Richard himself managed to persuade Henry not to attend by agreeing to increase the ransom by a further 50,000 marks. (One of the remarkable aspects of Richard's captivity was the skill with which he was able to charm and win over his captors.) When Philip heard tell of this latest twist in early July, he sent a despairing message to his ally in England, saying, 'Look to yourself, the Devil is loosed!' John, fearing his brother's return was imminent, fled across the Channel and sought refuge at Philip's court.[53]

In fact Richard's release still waited on the raising of his ransom, a process that would take many months. The government in England strained every sinew, demanding a quarter of the wealth of the clergy and the laity in tax, stripping the altar plate from churches and confiscating the entire wool crop of the Cistercian monks. A separate exchequer was set up to process the money as it poured in, and the sacks of silver were stored in St Paul's Cathedral. In the meantime Philip Augustus tried to resurrect his scheme to invade England. Hoping to secure more powerful naval support, he allied with King Cnut VI of Denmark by marrying his daughter, Ingeborg. Alas for Philip (and even more so for Ingeborg), their wedding night in August was such a disaster that he tried, without success, to hand her back to the Danish ambassadors the very next morning. All the episode gained him was years of domestic grief and condemnation from the Church for refusing to recognize his new queen.[54]

Quite what Philip's relationship with John was like by this point is more difficult to ascertain, but theirs too was a marriage of convenience rather than any genuine affection. John, for his part, seems to have tried to conceal the fact that he had given permission for Richard's ransom to be collected on his English estates. Philip, according to the more dubious *History of William Marshal*, was 'completely dismissive' of his Angevin house guest and 'thought him a fool'. Certainly Richard had hopes of parting the pair, for at some stage in the autumn he sent an offer to his brother, promising to restore all his possessions if he would renew his allegiance. John accepted, and travelled to Normandy, but at that point the plan backfired. So low had John's reputation sunk that the royal agents keeping his castles refused to hand them over, even when they were shown Richard's written orders to do so. John returned enraged to Philip's court.[55]

By 20 December 1193 so much treasure had been shipped to Germany that Henry VI declared himself satisfied, and announced that Richard would be released on 17 January 1194. Then, shortly after Christmas, envoys arrived from John and Philip with a range of last-minute counter-offers, including £1,000 a month to keep Richard captive or £100,000 to hand him over. ('See how much they loved him!' said Roger of Howden acidly.) John had by now become utterly desperate: it was also around this point that he made a fresh treaty with Philip, agreeing to surrender huge portions of the Angevin Empire if the French king would recognize him as its ruler and help him obtain it. The emperor was sufficiently tempted by these new proposals to postpone Richard's release date and show him the letters from Philip and John, which reportedly caused the king to despair of ever being liberated. But when Henry convened the bishops and princes of the empire to discuss these new bids, they reproved him for trying to back out of his existing agreement. On 4 February 1194, Richard was freed.[56]

The news spelt the end for John. Back in England Hubert Walter, lately invested as archbishop of Canterbury and appointed as the new justiciar, declared him excommunicate. The regency government, having left John's garrisons unmolested during the winter despite the expiry of the earlier truce, now abandoned their pragmatic caution and renewed their attack on his castles.[57] Most had already surrendered by the time Richard landed in England on 13 March (news of his arrival reportedly caused one of John's supporters, the keeper of St Michael's Mount, to die of fright). Only at Nottingham did the defenders hold out until the king himself appeared outside the walls, eventually capitulating on 28 March. Three days later in a council held in the castle's great hall, Richard demanded judgement 'against Count John his brother, who, contrary to the fealty he had sworn him, had occupied his castles, laid waste his lands on both sides of the sea, and made a treaty against him with his enemy, the king of France'. John was given forty days to present himself, on pain of forfeiting any future claim to the kingdom.[58]

Richard then went south: on 17 April he was ceremoniously re-crowned in Winchester Cathedral, and on 12 May he crossed the Channel to Normandy. In the weeks since his liberation, John and Philip Augustus had once again invaded the duchy and captured yet more castles; when Richard arrived they were laying siege to Verneuil. According to *The History of William Marshal*, as the king was advancing to confront them, he stopped for the night in Lisieux, where he lodged in the house of his friend, the local archdeacon. Noting that his host was ill at ease, he quickly deduced what the problem was, saying, 'You've seen my brother John,' then adding, 'Let him come forward, and have no fear of me.' A short time later a trembling John appeared and fell at his brother's feet. It had been over four years since they had last seen one another face to face – John was now twenty-seven years old, Richard thirty-six – but the nature of their relationship remained unaltered. Raising his younger brother up by the hand, the king gave him a magnanimous kiss of peace. 'Have no fear, John, you are a child, and were left with bad guardians … Go and have something to eat,' Richard added, sending his brother away to dine on a freshly caught salmon.[59]

5

Stemming the Tide

1205–1206

John sailed into Studland Bay in Dorset on 16 June 1205, presumably still furious about the collapse of the great expedition that he had hoped would recover his lost continental territories. Perhaps to occupy himself as much as for any other reason, he headed west to Dartmouth, where the subsidiary force under the command of his bastard son Geoffrey was still preparing to leave for Poitou. Geoffrey probably put to sea on 22 June, for at that point the king headed inland to spend a fortnight at his favourite castles and hunting lodges in Dorset and Wiltshire. Whatever solace he found during this time must have been diminished by the news that on 23 June his great ancestral castle at Chinon had finally surrendered to the forces of Philip Augustus, meaning that his very last toehold of territory in Anjou had been lost.[1]

A few days later, however, John received a message that apparently brightened his mood. The archbishop of Canterbury, Hubert Walter – the man who, along with William Marshal, had done the most to frustrate his planned expedition – was dead. The cause of his death, according to Ralph of Coggeshall, was a growth near his groin that he had been too embarrassed to have treated. The king, according to Roger of Wendover, was delighted. 'By God's feet!' he cried. 'Now for the first time I am king and lord of England!' These are actually the words of the chronicler

Matthew Paris, writing twenty years later, who liked them so much he has John say them again on the death of another royal minister in 1213. Yet there can be little doubt that both Paris and Wendover were right to imagine that the king was genuinely pleased. Hubert had been Richard's choice as archbishop and chief justiciar. He had excommunicated John in 1194 and helped to crush his rebellion. John may have appointed him as chancellor at the start of his reign, but this was probably to reassure those who doubted the new king's competence rather than his own personal preference. As far as John was concerned, the archbishop's recent actions must have proved he was an impediment to progress. Now he was gone, the king stood a much better chance of getting his own way.[2]

Hubert had died on 13 July at his manor of Teynham in Kent, at which point John was in Buckinghamshire. But by 15 July the king had arrived in Canterbury, his haste a measure of his anxiety to ensure that the right man was elected as Hubert's replacement. In theory, and especially since Henry II's clash with Thomas Becket, cathedral clergy were free to choose their own bishops, but in reality bishops were too politically important for their appointment to be left to local democracy. Normally kings would find a way of making their wishes known in order to ensure that their preferred candidate was selected. 'We order you to hold a free election,' wrote Henry II to the monks of Winchester Cathedral in 1172, 'but we nevertheless forbid you to elect anyone except Richard, our clerk.' Six years into his reign, by similar if perhaps more subtle means, John had generally been successful in getting the bishops he wanted.[3]

The complicating factor at Canterbury was that it was an archbishopric: whoever was appointed to that particular role had authority not just over his own diocese but over almost all the other bishops in England. (The exceptions were the bishops of Carlisle and Durham, who answered to the archbishop of York.) These other bishops, not unreasonably, felt that they should have some say in choosing their superior, but the monks of Canterbury thought otherwise, and insisted that the right to choose a new archbishop belonged to them alone. Of course, such arguments would only arise on occasions when the bishops and the monks were unable to agree on a mutually acceptable candidate, but that was evidently the case in 1205: by the time John arrived in Canterbury, the two sides were already deadlocked. The only way forward was to put the long-standing dispute about who had the superior right to elect to the judgement of the pope. The king therefore asked the prior and monks to postpone the election until the end of November, by which time they could hope to have received a papal verdict. According to one of their number, the chronicler Gervase of Canterbury, he spoke kindly to the monks, 'and gave them some hope that they could have someone from their own church'.[4]

If this was indeed the case, it is an example of John being completely disingenuous, for he already had in mind a non-monastic candidate. John de Gray was a clerk who had served the king loyally since before his accession. He had acted as the keeper of the king's seal from 1198, and had been rewarded two years later by being appointed as bishop of Norwich. He was attached to his royal master, said Roger of Wendover, 'by a great intimacy, and was the only one among the prelates of England who knew his private affairs'. John now intended to advance him to the top position in the English church, and to this end he secretly sent messengers of his own to Rome, hoping to persuade the pope to confirm his candidate, and so present the monks of Canterbury with a fait accompli.[5]

But, as Gervase of Canterbury explains, the monks got wind of the king's underhand scheme and responded with a little subterfuge of their own. With equal secrecy they elected their sub-prior, Reginald, and sent him to Rome with five companions. All of them had taken an oath not to reveal the nature of their business unless the pope was on the point of yielding to John's request, but in the event they acted more precipitately. As soon as they reached the Curia (or as soon as they were across the Channel, if we believe Roger of Wendover), Reginald was telling people that he had been elected as the new archbishop.

The king's agents in Rome and the bishops' representatives protested, and sent news of this unexpected development back to England.[6]

Travel between England and Rome took at least a month in the Middle Ages, and it was not until late November that the news reached John. He immediately returned to Canterbury at the start of December and demanded to know whether it was true that the monks had held an election in spite of their earlier promise not to do so. Evidently he spoke less kindly on this occasion than before: later papal letters suggest that the monks feared 'the loss of their property and danger to their persons'. In the face of the king's wrath they assured him that no election had taken place, and to placate him still further they dropped their appeal to Rome. John then rode to London to obtain a similar renunciation from the bishops, before returning to Canterbury a week later in the company of John de Gray, whom the monks obligingly elected as their new archbishop, and led ceremoniously into the cathedral to be seated on his archiepiscopal throne. Both the king and the bishops then sent letters to the pope, explaining that John de Gray had been elected 'for the honour and profit of the church of Canterbury, and the king, and the whole kingdom of England'.[7]

While his agents in Rome had been labouring to resolve his local difficulties in Canterbury, John's thoughts had rarely strayed from the greater, overriding problem of how to recover his lost lands in France. His immediate concern in 1205 was not with the northern territories of Normandy and Anjou, where everything had now been lost to the king of France, but the southern duchy of Aquitaine. In Poitou (the northern part of Aquitaine) the situation was extremely bad. The nobility there had deserted to Philip in August the previous year, and only the fortified seaport of La Rochelle continued to hold out. Meanwhile Gascony (the southern part of the duchy) had been all but taken over by Alfonso VIII, king of Castile, the greatest of the several kingdoms that made up medieval Spain. Back in 1177 Alfonso had married

John's sister, Eleanor, and it had been agreed that, after the death of her namesake mother, she would have Gascony as her dower. That at any rate was what the Castilian king claimed in the autumn of 1204, and set out to make good his claim by leading an army across the Pyrenees and occupying almost the whole region. Only a handful of towns – most notably Bordeaux – held out against this new onslaught; John wrote to thank the citizens for their good service at the end of April 1205. Throughout the rest of the year he remained in constant communication with his few remaining overseas subjects. In June, soon after the dispatch of his bastard son Geoffrey, he had sent another force of knights to Poitou under the captaincy of his half-brother William, earl of Salisbury (another of Henry II's bastards, to whom John seems to have been close), and in early October some Poitevin knights had come to visit him in England. According to Ralph of Coggeshall the king gave 28,000 marks to the brother of the archbishop of Bordeaux with which to raise a 30,000-man army. These figures look suspiciously high, but at the start of the new year 1206 arrangements were being made to ship large amounts of money to Poitou – royal letters mention sums totalling 2,500 marks.[8]

Money remained a major worry. Clearly an enormous amount had been wasted on the expedition of 1205 that had never sailed. (Royal records suggest a figure of around £2,200, but the true total was almost certainly a great deal higher.) To put together a similar force would require a sum of the same magnitude to be raised all over again. Added to this was the continuing problem of inflation. The partial re-coinage that John had carried out to combat rising prices during the winter of 1204–5 had been only partially successful: the rise in prices had been slowed down, but prices remained stubbornly high. Henry II and Richard had paid their mercenary knights a wage of eightpence a day, but John was having to offer three times as much (two shillings a day) to secure the same service. Such a steep hike meant that to mount an effective campaign more money than ever would have to be found, but doing so would be difficult. Immediately after the collapse of the 1205 expedition John had levied yet another payment in lieu of military service, or scutage, and this would eventually bring in a useful £4,000. But scutage had already proved politically contentious, particularly in the north of England, where opposition to the previous levy had led to its collection being abandoned earlier in the year. Moreover, the sums raised by scutage, while respectable, were not in themselves sufficient to fund a major campaign. Other sources of money would have to be exploited.[9]

In every county (or shire) in England, the king had a variety of agents who raised money on his behalf, the most important of whom was the sheriff (or shire reeve). Sheriffs raised money in a number of different ways: they collected rents from the king's own lands and the profits of justice from the county court, and they levied a tax known as 'sheriff's aid'. But however much a sheriff raised, he paid the king a lump sum, fixed by long tradition. Such fixed sums were known as 'farms' (from the Latin *firma*, 'fixed'), and the men who collected them were farmers. Thus the sheriff was a farmer responsible for collecting the county farm.

Traditionally, the biggest part of the county farm had come from the rents received from the king's own lands (the royal demesne). The problem by John's day was that the king's lands were nothing like as extensive as they had once been. Back in the time of Henry I, the royal demesne had been vast, but during the civil war between Stephen and Matilda it had been greatly depleted, as both sides gave away land to retain their supporters, while other magnates simply helped themselves to royal property. Henry II had arrested this trend and by the end of his reign had succeeded in clawing some land back, but Richard had quickly undone his father's work, selling or granting away lands to secure support for his crusade. ('I would sell London, if only I could find a buyer,' he is alleged to have quipped.) The drop in revenue was dramatic: at Henry's death in 1189 the county farms had been worth sixty per cent of their original value; by the time Richard died in 1199, so great were his alienations, the figure had fallen to just thirty-nine per cent.

On his return to England in 1194 Richard (or perhaps his new chief minister, Hubert Walter) had sought to increase the Crown's revenue by demanding that some sheriffs pay an additional sum, above the county farm, known as an 'increment'. This was tried in the case of nine counties, and although it succeeded in raising more cash, it proved highly unpopular. With less money coming in from Crown lands, the sheriffs had to find the extra money from other sources, increasing the amount they took in local taxes or judicial fines. John had maintained these increments, but he increasingly found that sheriffs were unable, or unwilling, to pay them in full.[10]

And so, in the autumn of 1204, John (or, again, perhaps Hubert Walter) had tried a new experiment. In the majority of counties, the king demanded not only the traditional farm, but all the money that the sheriff had raised above and beyond it.[11] At a time of rapidly rising prices, this was a sensible expedient. Many private landlords had by this date abandoned the practice of leasing out their estates for a fixed sum, and had instead begun to manage their lands directly, thereby netting all the surpluses that a farmer would have pocketed. At the same time, pocketing the profits of a county was what made the office of sheriff attractive. In introducing a system that made the sheriff simply a custodian of the Crown's lands, the government clearly found it difficult (or felt it risky) to retain the services of powerful and well-connected men, many of whom were replaced in their posts at this moment with local men who possessed less political clout. Nevertheless, in financial terms, John's experiment was a success. For the first six years of his reign the county farms had brought in an average of £4,000 a year, but in 1205 that total rose to over £5,000, and thereafter it was maintained at an average of £5,725 a year.

Important as this increase was, the revenue raised by the sheriffs amounted to only around fifteen to twenty per cent of all royal income in any given year. One simple way in which the king could raise additional sums of money was to sell offices. The office of sheriff, for example, was frequently sold to the highest

bidder. Sometimes a man close to the king would buy a sheriffdom with the intention of recouping his investment, and more
besides, from the shire in question. In 1201, for example, William
de Stuteville (one of the northern barons who had refused to
besiege Tickhill in 1193, saying he was John's liegeman) had
bought the sheriffdom of Yorkshire for £1,113. In other cases,
men of a particular shire might collectively offer the king a large
sum of money to have their own choice of sheriff, precisely to
escape the harsher financial regime that a voracious outsider
would invariably try to impose. Thus in 1205 Thomas de Moulton
became the new sheriff of Lincoln with the backing of the local
gentry in return for a payment to the king of 500 marks and
five palfreys.[12]

It was not just sheriffdoms that were sold. 'Everything was put
up for sale', commented Roger of Howden of the great auction
at the start of Richard's reign. 'Offices, lordships, earldoms, sheriffdoms, castles, towns, lands, the lot.' John may not have been
quite so eager to sell, especially after 1204,[13] but he was always
willing to strike a deal if the price was right. When Hubert Walter
died in 1205 the king needed to find not only a new archbishop
but also a new chancellor. In October that year the latter post
was filled by Walter de Gray, nephew of the bishop of Norwich,
a young man whose qualifications for the role were almost non-
existent, but who was sufficiently confident of the money he
would be able to make that he agreed to pay the king 5,000
marks for the privilege.

If offices could be sold, so too could justice. This is not quite
as negative as it sounds. Henry II had greatly extended the reach
of royal justice, sending his judges on regular tours around the
country to hear cases, and introducing standard civil pleas that
could be initiated by the purchase of an inexpensive writ. These
moves were extremely popular, though they did nothing for the
king's coffers, because the small sums charged went to the chancellor (which was one of the reasons the post was so lucrative).[14]

But not all justice was routine, nor could all of it be delegated.
Men who held their lands directly from the king (tenants-in-

chief, which generally meant the barons) had no choice but to have their cases heard in the king's own court, while others might choose to bring their case before the king in the hope of obtaining swift and decisive judgement. Wherever he was, the king would always have some judges with him, and would himself act as supreme judge when the necessity arose. There is plentiful evidence to indicate that John, like his father, knew the law well, consulted his judges on matters of controversy, and deferred to them on points of detail.

At this level, however, justice was inextricably mixed with politics. The king might refuse to hear the suit of an individual he disliked, for example, or he might delay a case for years on end rather than give judgement against a man whose support he needed. Consequently great men sought to grease the wheels of the system by offering large sums of money, often running into four figures. In 1200 William de Stuteville had offered John 3,000 marks to receive his 'right' in an inheritance dispute; his opponent, William of Mowbray, made a counter-offer of 2,000 marks 'to be treated justly according to the custom of England'. The beauty of this arrangement from the king's point of view was that he did not even have to demand such colossal sums – men would offer them freely, trying to outbid each other in the hope of obtaining a favourable verdict.[15]

Lastly, the king could raise large amounts of money on a regular basis in his capacity as a lord. Since the Norman Conquest, the kings of England had enjoyed an exceptional degree of control over the lives of their greatest subjects. If a tenant-in-chief died, for example, and his heir or heirs were underage, the king became their guardian, and they his wards; the king retained their estates until they came of age, and had the right to arrange their marriages as he saw fit. Similarly, if a tenant-in-chief died leaving a widow, the king had the right to find her a new husband. To modern ears these sound like outrageous infringements of individual freedom but, as in the case of justice, the lives of the baronage were bound up in politics. The king's greatest subjects held vast estates, and also castles – the raw instruments of political power.

The king could not afford to see these pass into the hands of his enemies through the unpredictable accidents of birth, death and marriage.[16]

These 'feudal' powers of the king had always offered an opportunity for profit. To enter into his inheritance, an heir had to pay a sum known as a 'relief'; in the case of underage heirs, the king retained not only their estates but also all the profits arising from them for the duration of the wardship. And there had always been a flourishing market at court for the marriages of both wards and widows. The king could reward his friends with the hand of a wealthy heiress or dowager, or simply sell the right to marry either to the highest bidder.[17]

Under the Angevins, however, the financial exploitation of these rights had increased dramatically. Henry II may have kept his demands moderate: on the nine occasions when he could have charged a relief for an earldom, for instance, he chose to do so only once. His sons, by contrast, showed no such moderation. At a time when the baronage felt that £100 was a reasonable figure, Richard had demanded reliefs of 500 marks and 1,000 marks. One northern baron, Eustace de Vescy, was charged 1,300 marks to have his inheritance, even though the Crown had enjoyed its profits during an eight-year wardship. John had set reliefs at a similar eye-watering level, typically charging 600 marks.[18] In the same way, proffers for the right to marry wards and widows had begun to rocket, so that they resembled the four-figure sums that were being offered for 'justice'. Widows could avoid remarriage if they wished, provided that they could keep up with the bidding. Thus in 1205 the estates of Alice Belet were seized when she refused to wed a man who had offered the king fifty marks and two palfreys for her hand; she regained possession when her father offered to pay 100 marks for her right to remain single. Amabilia, widow of the northern baron Hugh Bardolf, similarly beat off a £1,000 bid for her marriage by agreeing to pay the king 2,000 marks.[19]

By such expedients – fiscal, judicial and feudal – John and his immediate predecessors had pushed up their regular income, even though the amount of land they possessed had plummeted since the days of their Norman ancestors. Astute contemporaries were aware of the shift. 'One may marvel that Henry II and his sons, despite their many wars, nevertheless abounded in wealth', wrote Gerald of Wales. 'The reason is that they took care to augment their revenue from rents with casual income, and relied more on subsidiary than basic sources of profit.' The figures show that, since the loss of Normandy in 1204, John had been very successful augmenting his wealth in this way. In the opening years of his reign his income had averaged about £23,000 a year, but in 1205 and 1206 that average had risen to about £30,000 – a figure more than sufficient to fund a campaign to Poitou of the kind the king had in mind.[20]

The question that remained was whether John could muster the necessary political support, or whether he would end up repeating the humiliating scenes of the previous summer, when the baronage had refused to follow him. At the highest level, his position looked promising. Hubert Walter, the chief obstacle in 1205, lay dead and buried in Canterbury Cathedral. The new archbishop-elect, John de Gray, was the king's close confidant, and the new chancellor was Gray's nephew, Walter. As for John's other main opponent from the previous year, William Marshal, he was nothing like as removed from the king's inner circle as his biographer would have us believe. When John celebrated Christmas 1205 in Oxford, for example, the Marshal was there celebrating with him, as was the king's half-brother William, earl of Salisbury, along with Ranulf, earl of Chester, and the earls of Essex and Surrey. Clearly this was a king who could still command the support of his greatest men.[21]

The question was whether he could also command the support of the wider baronage. Soon after Christmas, in January 1206, John set out once again for the north of England. The main reason for this journey was a meeting with the king of Scots, about which we know nothing, but presumably arranged to ensure cordial relations would be maintained in the event that John did indeed leave the country. But while he was in the north John travelled widely, visiting his castles at Richmond, Carlisle, Lancaster and Chester, and during this tour he must have come face to face with many of his northern barons. The kind of pressure he could bring to bear on these men is well illustrated by the visit he paid in mid-February to his newly acquired castle at Knaresborough in North Yorkshire. For forty years down to 1203, Knaresborough had been in the possession of the aforementioned William de Stuteville, who had obtained it after its previous keeper had rebelled against Henry II in 1173. In 1203, however, William had died, and was soon followed to the grave by his underage son and heir – at which point John had pounced. In August 1205 he allowed the Stuteville inheritance to pass to William's brother, Nicholas, but in return he demanded a gargantuan relief of 10,000 marks. The point on this occasion was not to obtain payment, but the surrender of Knaresborough Castle, which the king retained as security for Nicholas' massive debt.[22] Knaresborough was one of the most strategically important fortresses in northern England; John immediately committed it to one of his most trusted military captains, Brian de Lisle, and began to invest large sums improving its defences. Part of his reason for visiting in February 1206 was presumably to see how this work was progressing. Precisely what Nicholas de Stuteville thought of this arrangement is hard to say, but in the short term it kept him obedient. When John mustered his forces for a new expedition to Poitou in the spring of 1206, Nicholas was one of the many northern barons who dutifully turned out.[23]

Advance preparations for the new campaign had been under way for some time. In London shipwrights had worked throughout the winter to build the king eight new transport ships, and in the early spring siege equipment was being manufactured in the forests of Sussex. The temporary wooden towers and galleries known as 'brattices' were already being shipped to the Channel Islands, which had been briefly lost to the French in 1204 but recovered by English forces the following year, and which obviously formed an important staging post on the sea route to Aquitaine.

In the last days of April, at which point John was in London, a flurry of writs showed that preparations were entering their final phase. On 29 April royal officials in Southampton were ordered to seize all the ships in neighbouring ports capable of carrying eight or more horses for a muster at Portsmouth on 20 May. When the king himself arrived on the Hampshire coast a few days in advance of this deadline, however, it was clear that not enough vessels had been found: on 19 May officials on the Channel Islands were ordered to send agents out into the southern shipping lanes 'who knew how to talk wisely and warmly to the steersmen and sailors, to move and induce them to come quickly into our service, and to assure them of our peace and goodwill and safe conduct'. By the end of the month more than 200 ships and some 2,100 sailors were assembled at Portsmouth, ready to transport the tonnes of supplies and thousands of soldiers that had been building up during the previous fortnight. On 28 May John crossed the Solent to the Isle of Wight, and at the start of June he set sail for Aquitaine.[24]

A week or so later, on 8 June, the king and his fleet put in to the great harbour of La Rochelle, to the relief of the locals who had held out so long and so loyally for this moment. Thanks to their efforts, bolstered by the troops and the money that the king had dispatched throughout the previous year, the military situation was not quite as desperate as it had been twelve months earlier. Towards the end of 1205 the town of Niort, forty miles inland to the east, had been recovered, and thereby become the new front line in the struggle against the supporters of Philip Augustus. John's first move was to advance in this direction, perhaps scattering any besieging forces, for he marched beyond Niort and a further fifteen miles towards Poitiers.[25]

Having relieved his subjects in Poitou, he turned his army south, consolidating his hold on the region around the town of Saintes before advancing further south into Gascony. Here too his local supporters had done much of the work ahead of his arrival. King Alfonso of Castile, having failed to take Bordeaux by siege, had by this stage withdrawn from Gascony altogether, reportedly complaining about the poverty of the region and the fickleness of its inhabitants; by the summer of 1206 the only remaining Spanish presence in the region was the garrison ensconced on the north bank of the Gironde at Bourg-sur-Mer, and these troops soon surrendered, apparently to local forces.[26]

John's army did, however, win one notable victory. Although Alfonso himself had returned home, he had enjoyed consider-able support from among the Gascon nobility, and these men had shut themselves up in Montauban, a fortified town on the duchy's eastern border. Montauban was a fortress famous in song and legend; Charlemagne, it was said, had failed to take it despite a siege that had lasted seven years. Contemporaries were impressed, therefore, when John's army succeeded in taking it in a matter of days. After a fortnight of bombardment by siege engines, explains Roger of Wendover, the castle fell to a direct assault, with English troops scaling the walls and fighting hand to hand until their enemies surrendered. John sent exultant letters back to England, naming the many nobles who had been taken prisoner and describing the prodigious spoils that had been seized.[27]

With resistance in Gascony at an end, the king retraced his steps northwards towards Niort, arriving there on or around 21 August. One week later, perhaps emboldened by his success in the south, he set out to try to win back some of the territory that had been lost to Philip Augustus. From Niort he marched his forces eighty miles east across Poitou to the border with Berry, and then almost double that distance west until he reached the border with Brittany. These manoeuvres persuaded the most powerful nobleman in the region, the viscount of Thouars, to renew his allegiance to John, a signal victory which spurred the king to try his luck further. In early September he advanced with his new ally into Anjou, and successfully forded the River Loire – a feat 'such as was never heard of in our time', according to a local chronicler. For a whole week he held court in Angers, home of his Angevin forefathers, before marching even further north in mid-September as far as the border with Maine.[28]

By this point, however, Philip Augustus had been stirred into action. No doubt alarmed by John's rapid success, the French king raised an army and marched towards Poitou. John, no doubt alarmed in turn, decided it was time to sound the retreat; over the course of the next three weeks he cautiously made his way back south, reaching Niort by 12 October. Caution, indeed, seems to have been the watchword on both sides. Philip advanced his army to the Poitevin border but no further; for the time being he had his hands full in Normandy and was content to allow John his recent gains. John, for his part, was not yet ready for a direct confrontation with his principal opponent. The aim of his present expedition had been to preserve his position in Aquitaine, and that objective had been achieved. Accordingly, on 26 October, a two-year truce was sealed. Both kings agreed to maintain the territorial and political status quo, and in the meantime to permit travellers and merchants to move freely between their dominions.[29]

With the truce in place, John returned to La Rochelle in early November, then moved to the adjacent Ile de Ré, from where he set sail in the middle of the month. After several weeks carefully negotiating the treacherous coast of Brittany, his fleet finally put into Portsmouth on 12 December. 'When he arrived home,' says *The History of William Marshal*, 'he was given a welcome by many who loved him and cherished him and paid him high honour as they greeted him.' The following day the sheriff of Hampshire was instructed to find 1,500 hens, 5,000 eggs, 20 oxen, 100 pigs and 100 sheep, the makings of what must have been the merriest Christmas feast at John's court for several years.[30]

6

Our Happy Success

1194–1202

In trying to usurp his brother's throne, John had done terrible
damage to his reputation. His failure in Ireland might have
been put down to youthful inexperience; his desertion of his
dying father explained as unfortunate timing. That men were
prepared to overlook these earlier mistakes is suggested by their
readiness to rally behind him in 1191 when he challenged the
rule of the justiciar William Longchamp. For a moment he had
been a popular hero, saving the realm from tyrannical oppression,
in return for which he had been recognized as Richard's rightful
heir. But John had gone on to overplay his hand and lost spec-
tacularly. No one could excuse the behaviour of a man who had
attempted to seize the kingdom of an imprisoned crusader. By
rebelling against Richard, said William of Newburgh, John had
simply succeeded in 'heaping up endless curses on his own
perfidious head'. He was a 'mad-headed youth' who had broken
'the laws of nature', and become 'nature's enemy'.[1]

The damage to his position was equally catastrophic. Within
days of Richard's release from captivity the regency government
had stripped John of all his lands and titles in both England and
Normandy; Richard, although he subsequently accepted his
brother's submission, refused to reverse this verdict. Apart from
his title 'lord of Ireland', which appears to have been a empty
designation by this point, John had lost everything. His household

was deliberately broken up, and those of his followers who had supported his rebellion found themselves similarly deprived of their lands and property.[2]

Had John also lost his position as heir apparent? In the period 1191–2 the political community in England had repeatedly sworn to recognize him as Richard's successor. In March 1194, after his brother's return, John had been warned he would lose all claim to the kingdom if he did not submit within forty days – a deadline he had failed to meet. Nothing official was subsequently said to clarify the issue. Richard's last known statement on the matter, back in 1190, was that his nephew, Arthur of Brittany, should succeed him. Whether or not that was still his wish is unknown. Richard, now freed from captivity and able to resume conjugal relations with his queen, probably hoped that in due course he would be succeeded by a son of his own. Whatever the king's intentions were, John's position with regard to the throne must have seemed very weak in 1194, his future – beyond perhaps a role in Ireland – in grave doubt.[3]

The only hope of recovery lay in faithful service. Richard's overriding concern from the spring of 1194 was the recovery of the lands that had been lost during his captivity to Philip Augustus. John, of course, had been the French king's willing co-conspirator in seizing these lands, and he was able to score an immediate success by returning to Evreux – a town given to him by Philip – and slaughtering the garrison before they realized he had switched sides. Whether this did anything to improve his standing with Richard is unclear, but it compounded his reputation for treachery in France, and provoked an angry response from Philip, who sacked the town in revenge. Late in the summer, while Richard was winning back territory in Touraine and Aquitaine, John was left in Normandy to besiege the French forces occupying Vaudreuil. Philip, beaten by Richard in the south, rushed north to vent his fury on John for a second time, falling on his camp at dawn and forcing him to flee, with the loss of most of his infantry and siege equipment.[4]

Despite its apparently limited results, John's military service impressed contemporaries – William of Newburgh commends him for fighting against Philip 'faithfully and valiantly' – and eventually caused Richard to soften his stance. In 1195, according to Roger of Howden, the king 'forgave his brother John all the wrath and displeasure he felt towards him', and restored some of his lands and titles: the county of Mortain, the earldom of Gloucester and the honour of Eye in Suffolk were all handed back, and John was also promised an annual payment of £2,000. He did not, however, regain custody of any of his castles. Richard's trust in his younger brother clearly still had its limits.[5]

With regard to the succession, too, John's position improved, largely due to Richard's botched attempt to tighten his grip on Brittany. The Angevins regarded Brittany as a dependency, but the duchy had been left to go its own way since the death of Henry II; in 1196 Richard tried to reassert this traditional mastery by obtaining custody of its young duke, Arthur. His plan miscarried, however, when Arthur's mother, Constance, was kidnapped en route to the king's court by her estranged second husband. The nobles of Brittany, suspecting that this was a plot on Richard's part, refused to hand Arthur over, and appealed for help to Philip Augustus; Richard responded by invading Brittany and crushing all resistance, but failed to apprehend his nephew, who was successfully conveyed to the French king. Clearly there was no way Arthur could be groomed as Richard's heir if he was Philip's ally. Moreover, by 1196, it was looking increasingly unlikely that Richard was going to father a son. Two chroniclers accused him of being unfaithful to his queen and neglecting to sleep with her. If only by default, John was once again coming to be regarded as first in line. There was no public avowal of his position, as there had been during Richard's absence, but in private the king seems to have accepted the fact. Documents drawn up in the autumn of 1197 – one concerning the construction of Château Gaillard – show John guaranteeing to uphold his brother's agreements.[6]

And yet, despite his apparent rehabilitation, John's reputation was such that suspicion could easily be rekindled. Although he appears to have served Richard loyally during 1198, fighting against Philip Augustus when war re-erupted that autumn, relations between the two brothers collapsed early in 1199, when the French king wrote to Richard to inform him that John had once again defected. Whether there was any truth in this is impossible to determine. By this point Arthur had repudiated Philip and returned to Brittany, and the Bretons had returned to Richard's allegiance. John may well have been alarmed by these developments and sought to counter their implications by plotting with Philip. Roger of Howden dismissed the accusations as a piece of malicious invention on the French king's part, but admits that Richard believed what he was told and again deprived John of all his lands in both England and Normandy. Two other chroniclers report that John remained dispossessed and out of favour in the spring of 1199, right up to the moment when Richard was hit by a crossbow bolt.[7]

It happened in Aquitaine, at an obscure little castle called Châlus-Chabrol, about twenty miles south-east of Limoges. Rumour said Richard had gone there to claim some treasure that a peasant had ploughed up in a field, but the real reason was a rebellion by two of his leading vassals in the region, the viscount of Limoges and his half-brother, the count of Angoulême. By 1199 Richard was clearly winning the war against Philip Augustus; he had won back almost all the lost ground in Normandy, and held more territory along the Loire than at the start of his reign. But Philip had struck back by allying with these two southern nobles and encouraging them to revolt. The castle at Châlus belonged to the viscount of Limoges and Richard held it in little regard. He was besieging it when a lone crossbowman, reduced to using a frying pan as a shield, shot him in the shoulder. A surgeon managed to remove the bolt, but butchered the king's flesh so badly that the wound turned gangrenous. Eleven days later he was dead.[8]

The sudden death of the great warrior forced the question of who would succeed him. The debates men must have been having in private for years suddenly required urgent resolution. Who had the greater right: John or Arthur? *The History of William*

Marshal relates a splendid scene, clearly much improved with hindsight, in which the Marshal himself learns of Richard's death four days after the event. He was staying in the castle at Rouen, and about to go to bed, when the news arrived, prompting him to pull his boots back on and seek out the archbishop of Canterbury, Hubert Walter, who was lodged in the nearby priory. After exchanging words of grief, their conversation turned quickly to the succession. Hubert opined that Arthur had the greater right, while the Marshal argued that John was nearest in line. But the reality was that the legal merits of the two claims, being debatable, hardly mattered: fundamentally the question came down to personalities and politics. 'Arthur has treacherous advisers about him, and he is haughty and overbearing,' says the Marshal. 'If we call him to our side he will seek to do us harm and damage, for he does not like those in our realm.' This was the crux of the matter: whether those who lived under Plantagenet rule wanted to see it endure in its existing form, or some compromised, truncated version. The Marshal speaks as a representative of the Anglo-Norman baronage ('our side') who wished to preserve the empire as it was, and with it their own cross-Channel holdings. But there were others – traitors in William Marshal's view – who would have been more than happy to see that empire broken up: not only the nobles of Brittany, who had long resented Plantagenet overlordship, but also nobles in other regions who had come to resent the rule of Henry II and Richard. There was also, of course, Philip Augustus, who had already indicated his readiness to collaborate with Arthur and to help the Bretons achieve their aim of throwing off the Plantagenet yoke. In addition to all this, there was the simple factor of age: even if Arthur had possessed the willingness to defend Plantagenet power and resist Philip, he was only twelve years old at the time of Richard's death – no match for the experienced and wily French king. In these circumstances, for those who wished to keep things as they were, the only possible candidate was John. He may have made a poor showing of himself in the past, but he was a grown man, and was also 'one of us', who would be committed to maintaining the whole of his inheritance. In *The History of William Marshal* Hubert Walter eventually defers to the Marshal's judgement on the matter, but prophesies that John will be a disaster. 'This much I can tell you,' he says to the earl, 'you will never come to regret anything you did as much as what you're doing now.'[9]

With opinion divided across the Plantagenet dominions, the struggle between John and Arthur would be decided by how quickly they moved to secure the sinews of power: key castles, important towns, and treasuries. In this respect, one factor in particular counted in John's favour. According to Roger of Howden, Richard in his final days had named his brother as his heir. There is no way of knowing whether this was true, but it was certainly the case that those around the dying king – his household, comprised chiefly of Anglo-Norman barons – were firmly in favour of John. The same was true of his mother. Eleanor of Aquitaine was one of the few people who had been informed of the king's injury, and had rushed to Châlus to be with him when he died. Richard's condition had otherwise been kept secret, and messengers had raced to alert key personnel to an imminent change of leadership. William Marshal, for example, was staying in Rouen Castle because he had received orders to secure it three days before the king's death.[10]

The same messengers must have been sent speeding to locate John. The fact that he had fallen out with Richard just a few weeks earlier and withdrawn from his court may have made it difficult to do so. According to Howden he was in Normandy, but Howden may be giving us an airbrushed version of the truth, in keeping with his assertion that the two brothers had been reconciled before Richard met his end. Another source which provides a very detailed account of these days is *The Life of St Hugh*; its subject, the saintly Bishop Hugh of Lincoln, happened to be travelling to see Richard at this very moment, and was thus a key witness to the ensuing drama. According to Hugh's testimony, John was actually staying in Brittany at the time of Richard's death, keeping company with Arthur. If true (and there seems little reason to doubt it) this reinforces the suggestion that John may indeed have been plotting with his brother's enemies.[11]

Presumably John was informed in secret of his brother's fatal injury, made his excuses and departed. He must have been told to make straight for Chinon, the most important castle in Anjou, and the location of the county's treasury, for when he arrived there on the morning of 14 April his mother and his late brother's household were already waiting for him. They had come north from Châlus with Richard's body, and laid the dead king to rest at nearby Fontevraud alongside the bones of his father. John swore an oath to fulfil his brother's will faithfully – Richard had bequeathed a quarter of his treasure to his servants and the poor – and also promised to preserve the laws and customs of the people he would rule over, in return for which those present recognized him as his brother's successor.[12]

It remained to secure the rest of his dominions. From Chinon John headed north-west to the castle of Saumur, pausing en route at Fontevraud to visit his brother's tomb. By 18 April – Easter Sunday – he had reached the castle of Beaufort-en-Vallée, about fifteen miles east of Angers.[13]

At this point he realized he was in danger. While had been making his somewhat leisurely progress along the Loire, his enemies had been on the move. News of Richard's death must have broken at Arthur's court shortly after John's departure, and Constance of Brittany and the Breton nobles had immediately set out to advance Arthur's cause. By Easter Sunday they had already reached Angers, where they were met by a crowd of nobles from Anjou, Maine and Touraine, who all swore allegiance to Arthur as their new ruler.[14]

John was travelling with only a few attendants. Confrontation was out of the question; capture and indefinite imprisonment were a real possibility. His only hope was to outrun his enemies and reach Normandy before they caught up with him. On the morning of Easter Monday he set out at speed, covering fifty miles to reach Le Mans by nightfall. During his stay in the city, however, he realized that his situation had not improved. By now he must have known that Philip Augustus had invaded Normandy, seizing the town and county of Evreux, and was advancing in the direction of Le Mans. Fearing a trap, John stole away from the city in secret the next morning, disappearing into the pre-dawn darkness. In so doing he managed to escape the pincer just before it closed: a few hours later Arthur and his army attacked and occupied Le Mans, and a short while later they were joined there by the French king, who recognized Arthur's right to Anjou, Maine and Touraine in return for his homage. Apart from a handful of castles along the Loire Valley, Anjou had been lost.[15]

Normandy, fortunately, was far more welcoming. The Norman nobility can have had no great love or respect for John, remembering how he had demanded their allegiance when Richard was in captivity and then declined to help defend the duchy against Philip Augustus when that allegiance was refused. Nevertheless, as William Marshal had already recognized, in the ongoing struggle against the French king, John was now their only candidate. On 25 April he was invested as duke in Rouen Cathedral. The archbishop of Rouen, Walter de Coutances, who had opposed John's attempts to seize power in England, performed the ceremony, placing a coronet worked with golden roses on the new duke's head.[16]

England was evidently in John's thoughts at this time. News of Richard's death had arrived there by Easter and provoked outbreaks of opportunistic lawlessness. Ralph of Coggeshall reports that the magnates began 'ravaging like hungry wolves'. Such reports must have reached John in Normandy, for immediately after his investiture as duke he sent Hubert Walter and William Marshal across the Channel to help keep the peace in England until he could come there in person. For the moment, having secured the support of the Normans, John was inclined to attempt the recovery of lost ground in Anjou. Both the Bretons and Philip Augustus had since withdrawn from Le Mans, and John now returned to punish the city for its earlier disloyalty, tearing down its walls and castle and imprisoning many of its leading citizens. He may perhaps have met up with his mother, for Eleanor had embarked on a similar punitive expedition, leading Richard's mercenaries on a ravaging campaign through the Angevin countryside, demonstrating to local lords the downside of resisting Plantagenet power. Soon afterwards, however, they went their separate ways, Eleanor heading south to secure Aquitaine, John turning north in the direction of England.[17]

Hubert Walter and William Marshal may have found the situation in England worse than anticipated. The period between the death of one king and the coronation of his replacement was a legal vacuum that always tempted some men to settle old scores with violence, but this was something rather more serious. According to Roger of Howden, Hubert's and William's first move had been to administer a general oath of loyalty to John, but there was clearly widespread resistance. All those who held castles, says Howden, both barons and bishops, began strengthening them with men, provisions and arms. The king's lieutenants responded by calling a meeting to Northampton, summoning 'those persons of whom they had the greatest doubts'. It was an impressive list: five out of the seven men Howden names are earls, and he adds that there were many others. Most of those named had helped to crush John's rebellion against Richard and had been rewarded for their loyalty; no doubt they now feared that the sudden change in leadership would bring a sudden reversal in their fortunes. The archbishop and the Marshal, together with the justiciar, Geoffrey fitz Peter, pledged their word that John would give each man his due if they would preserve their fealty and keep the peace. Satisfied with the guarantees of these upright individuals, the magnates complied.[18]

John's advance guard must also have been charged with making preparations for his coronation, which was scheduled to take place at Ascension (27 May). John himself landed on the Sussex coast just two days beforehand and hurried to London. The fact that he left it until the very last minute to cross the Channel shows how concerned he must have been about leaving the Continent while his lands there were still being menaced. Ralph of Coggeshall says he departed from Normandy in secret, presumably in the hope of keeping his absence concealed from his enemies.[19]

John's coronation was not unusual in being hastily arranged. Ever since 1066, when the Normans had introduced the notion that the ceremony itself made a man a king, contenders for the English crown had held their coronations at the earliest opportunity. They were still solemn and magnificent affairs, with as much pageantry as possible. Ralph of Coggeshall says that John's coronation was conducted with great pomp, and Gervase of Canterbury says 'in great glory', but sadly there is little else in the way of contemporary description.[20] Like all coronations since the Conquest it took place in Westminster Abbey, where John was first required to swear a threefold oath, promising to protect and honour the Church, to abolish bad laws and replace them with good ones, and to do good justice to his subjects.[21] Afterwards came the king-making moment itself, in which he was anointed on various parts of his body with holy oil. Custom decreed that the oil poured on his head had to remain there for a full seven days, so for the whole week that followed John wore a special coif, with straps tied under his chin, to hold it in place. The new king was then dressed in royal robes and crowned, with a crown so heavy that two earls had to help support it on his head, before finally being seated on the throne while Mass was celebrated. Afterwards the king and his nobles walked the short distance to Westminster Hall for the coronation banquet. Twenty-one fat oxen from Worcestershire and 2,000 yards of table linen had been purchased for the occasion. William Marshal and Geoffrey fitz Peter, who had been officially recognized as earls that day by being girded with their swords of office, served at the king's table. Archbishop Hubert, who had performed the coronation service, was appointed as chancellor.[22]

The only discordant note during this otherwise harmonious fanfare was sounded by ambassadors sent by the king of Scots, William the Lion. Almost half a century earlier, when he was just a small boy, William had inherited the earldom of Northumbria (it came to him via his grandfather, David I, who had extorted it from King Stephen). Henry II had subsequently compelled William to return it, but the Scottish king had never abandoned the hope of getting it back. It had prompted his disastrous decision to join the rebellion against Henry in 1173, and had remained a bone of contention with Richard I. Now, with Richard dead and John struggling to secure his inheritance, he saw a golden opportunity. He would agree to recognize John, if John agreed to cede Northumbria. Messengers had already been sent to convey this offer to John before his return to England, but the regents in England had prevented them from crossing the Channel. And so the Scottish ambassadors had returned on the day of the coronation with the same urgent question: would the new king restore Northumbria, or would William be forced to take it?

John responded by inviting William to come and discuss the matter in person at Northampton in ten days' time, and duly set off in that direction soon after his coronation, visiting the shrines at St Albans and Bury St Edmunds on the way. But after waiting at Northampton for several days he was met by more Scottish ambassadors, who explained that their king would not be coming. Instead they delivered a more precise threat. Northumbria must be returned at once, or else William would take it by force. John was given forty days to make his mind up, during which time the king of Scots would be raising an army.

The new king of England had no intention of surrendering Northumbria or of waiting forty days in order to defend it. He too was busy raising an army, but it was to fight a far more formidable opponent. Delegating the problem of protecting northern England to William de Stuteville, John set out in the direction of the south coast, leaving the Scottish envoys trailing in his wake. On 20 June, less than four weeks since his arrival, he set sail from Shoreham, taking with him what Ralph of Coggeshall describes as 'a mighty English host'.[23]

Normandy seems not to have suffered from any new assaults during John's absence. It probably helped that on 23 May, just two days before he had left for England, the leading nobles of

Poitou, rallied by his mother, had launched an attack on Tours, where Arthur of Brittany was known to be staying. This was unsuccessful in that Arthur escaped, but it did succeed in drawing the fire of Philip Augustus, who was forced to send some of his troops south. When John landed at Dieppe with his great English army on 20 June, he found the situation encouraging. A few days later a multitude of Norman knights and infantry flocked to Rouen to join their ranks. For the same reason, the French king decided to put out peace feelers, and so a truce was agreed, set to last a little under two months.[24]

During this truce John spent much of his time visiting the towns and castles along Normandy's southern and eastern borders, no doubt shoring up their defences against future attack. He also set about strengthening his position by securing an impressive list of allies. In the last year of his life Richard had assembled a formidable coalition against Philip Augustus, wooing to his side most of the counts and dukes who were notionally subject to the French king. John now succeeded in confirming these alliances. On 13 August the count of Flanders did homage to him in Rouen, along with many others (fifteen counts in total, according to a local chronicler). All of them swore an oath against King Philip.[25]

Thus by the time the truce expired on 16 August John was in a very strong position with regard to his rival. On that day the two kings travelled to the border to discuss their differences, meeting on a stretch of the Seine between Les Andelys and Vernon that had become the norm for such conferences since the completion of Château Gaillard.[26] After two days of communicating through intermediaries, they at last came face to face. John, says Howden, asked why Philip held him in such hatred, asserting that he had never done him any harm. Philip replied that John had taken possession of Normandy and other territories without first obtaining the necessary permission; he should have come to Philip first and done homage. He then outlined the territorial settlement he had in mind. John was to hand over the whole of the Vexin to Philip, and to relinquish his claim to

Anjou, Maine and Touraine, which rightly belonged to Arthur.

John had no hesitation in rejecting these demands. Philip's view of his rights as overlord, John might have pointed out, was over-exalted. The kings of France had always liked to think of the Plantagenets as their vassals, and Henry II had encouraged this belief by having his sons do homage from time to time. As king of England, however, Henry had long resisted the suggestion that he should do homage in person. Only once, in 1183, had he done so, at a time when his bargaining power was weak. The very fact that the kings of France came to negotiate with their Plantagenet neighbours on the frontier of their respective territories, sometimes on islands in the middle of the Seine (or once, in Richard's case, shouting from a boat) indicates that, from the Plantagenet point of view at least, this was a relationship of equals. John had readily done homage to Philip in 1193, but then he had been a desperate rebel; he had no intention of repeating the performance now he was king of England.[27]

As for Philip's demand that John surrender Anjou, Maine and Touraine to Arthur, these territories sat at the centre of John's continental dominions. To cede them would be to rip the heart out of the Angevin Empire, severing communication between its northern and southern parts. Fortunately, John did not have to entertain such outrageous proposals. He still had his mighty English army, bolstered by the military support of Normandy, and he also had his impressive array of allies from elsewhere in France. On 18 August, as talks with Philip Augustus broke up without agreement, the count of Boulogne joined John's alliance. The English king, says Gervase of Canterbury, 'made up his mind to resist the French king like a man, and to fight manfully for the peace of his country'.[28]

And so hostilities resumed. Philip may have struck the first blow, augmenting his existing gains in south-east Normandy by seizing the castle at Conches, but it quickly became clear that the momentum was with John. In the second week of September he advanced from southern Normandy into Maine, drawing the French king south. Around the middle of the month, Philip besieged and destroyed the castle at Ballon, a few miles north of Le Mans.[29]

It was at this moment that John received an unexpected visit from William des Roches. William was one of the most powerful barons in Maine and Anjou, thanks to his marriage to a rich heiress some ten years earlier. Now in his mid-forties, he had a strong track record of loyalty to the Plantagenets, remaining with Henry II up to his death and accompanying Richard on crusade. In April 1199, however, he had decided to back Arthur rather than John. His reasons for doing so are unknown. He may have felt, like other Angevin nobles, that Arthur simply had the better claim. He must have been induced by a promise of increased power, for Arthur had immediately appointed him as seneschal of Anjou. But by September William had come to rue this decision. His specific reason, reported by several chroniclers, was Philip's behaviour at the siege of Ballon; William argued that the castle ought to have been handed over to Arthur, but the French king had haughtily dismissed his objections and burnt it to the ground. Behind this, his broader reason must surely have been that by September John was clearly winning the war. During the summer all the other powerful men in France had given him their backing, and he was now advancing confidently into Arthur's supposed area of authority. William must have feared that he was going to end up with nothing. And so, with the two armies not far apart, he secretly slipped away from Philip's side and came at night to John's camp. In the course of a personal interview with the king, he explained that he was ready to defect. But that was not all. He also assured John that, if he promised to act on his advice, he would arrange to bring in Arthur and his mother Constance. John's rival for power was ready to submit.[30]

John readily agreed. On 18 September he promised, in writing, to abide by whatever peace terms William arranged between himself and his 'very dear nephew, Arthur'. Then, emboldened by the prospect of success, he went on the offensive, surprising Philip Augustus as he was laying siege to the castle of Lavardin, twenty-five miles north-west of Le Mans.[31] Philip retreated into the city, but Le Mans, thanks to John's destruction of its walls and castle earlier in the year, was no longer defensible. With his enemies still in pursuit, the French king fled once again, this time withdrawing from Maine altogether. At some point before his departure he had agreed to place Arthur and his mother in the keeping of William des Roches, wrongly assuming that the seneschal of Anjou was still on his side. On 22 September William, who had been left in charge of Le Mans, welcomed John into the city and presented him with his nephew, just as he had promised. This was a moment of triumph. John, barely a fortnight into his campaign, had driven the king of France from the field, and – much more importantly – obtained the submission of Arthur.[32]

And yet it was only a fleeting moment, for within just a few hours John's victory was undone. As Roger of Howden explains, on the same day that Arthur submitted at Le Mans, he was warned that his uncle 'intended to take him and throw him in prison'. In the case of other rulers, such a warning would have been hard to believe. John, after all, had sworn to abide by the counsel of William des Roches, and had agreed (according to *The History of William Marshal*) that he, William and Arthur 'would all be good friends'; the letters issued by the king himself use phrases like 'firmly promised' and 'in good faith'. But John's catalogue of earlier betrayals clearly limited the value of such promises, and made rumours of impending treachery seem all too credible. The night after his submission, Arthur slipped away from his uncle's court, along with his mother and many others, and fled to Angers, which was still being held by his supporters. John, who had moved south to Chinon, rushed back to Le Mans, but the horse had already bolted. A week later he went south again, this time to Saumur, perhaps trying to intercept Arthur or prevent him moving eastward along the Loire, but if so without success. Arthur managed to travel from Angers to Tours, where he was received once more by Philip Augustus.[33]

Having let his nephew slip through his fingers, and with no other obvious enemies to fight, John returned to Normandy in the second week of October. Soon afterwards, at the urgings of a papal legate, both sides agreed to a truce that would last until early January. John must have been kicking himself at having so carelessly dropped his trump card. Ralph of Diceto commented that, in losing Arthur, the king had acted 'less than cautiously', and others appear to have arrived at similar negative conclusions. During the truce, many of the French nobles who had sworn oaths to fight with John took the cross and prepared to go on crusade. Had they been exasperated by his ineptitude, or perhaps shocked by his alleged plan to betray his nephew and throw him into prison? Whatever their reasons, by Christmas John's coalition against Philip Augustus had completely collapsed.[34]

This collapse was reflected in the peace terms that were agreed when the two kings met in January. In contrast to his determination not to give ground the previous year, John now made considerable territorial concessions, ceding to Philip all of the Vexin as well as all the towns and castles the French king had seized in south-east Normandy in the wake of Richard's death. Philip in return promised to stop supporting Arthur's claim, and induced Arthur himself to do the same; John was recognized as the rightful heir to Anjou, Maine and Touraine. Significantly, however, John accepted that he ought to do homage to Philip for these territories, as well as for Normandy, admitting the French king's superior lordship in a way that he and his ancestors had previously sought to resist. In recognition of this new dependency, he took the unprecedented step of promising to pay a relief of 20,000 marks.

Despite these substantial concessions, John may have thought that the deal he had achieved was a good one. He and Philip reportedly stood talking for a long time and embraced each other warmly. Others certainly thought it was a good deal, and welcomed the prospect of an end to seven years of almost continuous conflict. Ralph of Coggeshall commented that John 'was a lover of peace, who intended to live a tranquil life free from wars, understanding how many enemies of the kingdom he faced, and what great misfortunes had befallen his father and brothers and all the kingdom from such frequent wars'. Gervase of Canterbury was similarly pleased. By acting manfully, he thought, John had cowed his opponents, and 'by prudence more than war he had obtained peace everywhere'. But Gervase also noted that not everyone was impressed by the king's performance. Some people, 'malevolent and envious', were calling him 'Softsword'. In other words, the monks commended John's peace; the military men thought he ought to have put up more of a fight.[35]

The peace drawn up in January 1200 was for the moment agreed only in principle. To seal it permanently, and to give Philip's territorial gains the appearance of a freely conceded gift, there was to be a royal wedding. Philip's eldest son Louis would marry John's niece, Blanche – the daughter of his sister Eleanor and her husband, Alfonso VIII of Castile. This meant that the bride would have to be fetched from Spain, and so a further five-month truce was put in place to enable this. Eleanor of Aquitaine, by this point in her mid-seventies, set out across the Pyrenees to collect her granddaughter.[36]

John in the meantime crossed the Channel to England, arriving in Portsmouth at the end of February. To the dismay of Ralph of Coggeshall, he immediately proved that peace could be as expensive as war by imposing a heavy tax to raise his 20,000-mark relief. As Coggeshall explained, this new demand, coming as it did after the scutage to finance the previous year's military campaign, 'very much weakened the people of the land'. John also intended during this visit to deal with the king of Scots. Despite his earlier threats, William the Lion had not raised an army or attempted to take Northumbria. John summoned him to York and travelled there in expectation of a meeting at the end of March. By this stage, however, William's courage had completely deserted him. The confrontational stance he had adopted in 1199 had been based on the assumption that the new king of England would be distracted by his problems on the Continent; there is some evidence to suggest he was acting in concert with Philip Augustus. But now that John and Philip had all but settled their differences, William was isolated, and must have feared retribution. Claiming that John's assurance of safe conduct was inadequate, he again declined to appear.[37]

The Scottish king's repeated failure to present himself must have angered John, but not as much as the appearance at York of several Cistercian abbots, who had been summoned to the city to discuss their contribution to the recent tax. The Cistercians had always been exempt from taxation, but when they pointed this out and refused to pay, the king exploded. In 'anger and fury', according to Ralph of Coggeshall, he ordered his sheriffs to persecute the Cistercians by all possible means, and to take no action against those who harmed them. The abbots complained about these 'cruel edicts' to the archbishop of Canterbury, who in turn 'freely rebuked the king for such great cruelty, denouncing him as a persecutor of the holy Church'. But despite this and subsequent attempts to placate him, John refused to be pacified, and sailed for Normandy at the end of April, 'breathing fire and slaughter against the followers of Christ'.[38]

By the time John recrossed the Channel, his mother had returned from her trip to Spain, bringing with her the bride-to-be, Blanche of Castile. Eleanor was too exhausted to travel any further than Bordeaux, so it fell to the city's archbishop to escort Blanche on the final stage of her journey to Normandy, where she was at last delivered to her waiting uncle. On 18 May John and Philip met at the border and the terms they had agreed in January were confirmed. Four days later, on an island in the middle of the Seine called Le Goulet, the peace was sealed. John did homage to Philip for his continental possessions, Arthur did homage to John for Brittany, and Blanche was married to Philip's son, Louis. The war of succession to the Angevin Empire was finally over.[39]

A fortnight after the peace was sealed, John set out south, to take possession of those territories that had spent the previous year resisting him: Maine, Anjou and Touraine. In expectation of continued resistance, he took no chances and advanced at the head of a large army, passing in turn through the cities of Le Mans, Angers and Tours. At Angers he stayed for four nights and took 150 hostages.[40]

In July he moved further south into Aquitaine. The great southern duchy had been secured for him the previous year by his mother, but only by making generous concessions to its leading nobles, granting them lands and castles in order to persuade them to stay loyal. Such was the way Aquitaine had to be governed, for ducal authority there had always been weak. Like his predecessors, John had little land of his own in the duchy and very few castles. To rule effectively it was necessary to work with the local aristocracy, sometimes appeasing them, sometimes playing them off against each other. Politics were thus naturally fractious, and rebellions more frequent than elsewhere in the Angevin Empire. It had been in Aquitaine that Richard had met his end, trying to suppress the rebellion of the viscount of Limoges and the count of Angoulême. As John prepared to advance into the duchy, he summoned both these men to come and do homage to him at Lusignan on 5 July. The choice of location was significant: the lord of Lusignan, Hugh le Brun, had been a rival of the count of Angoulême for many years, but lately they had agreed to bury the hatchet, and Hugh had agreed to marry the count's only daughter and heir.[41]

John had been giving much thought to his own marriage in recent months. As we have seen, his wedding to Isabella of Gloucester in 1189 was probably a forced affair, performed at Richard's insistence. With Richard gone, John was at last free to please himself. His intention to divorce Isabella must have been apparent from the very start of his reign, for she was not crowned with him in May 1199, and later that year he persuaded the bishops of Normandy to declare their marriage void. Other churchmen disapproved. The dean of St Paul's, Ralph of Diceto, thought that John had acted 'on the advice of evil men', and claimed that the king's actions had angered the pope. But John had good political reasons for wanting a divorce at this point, for he was recruiting allies against Philip Augustus, and was hoping to marry the daughter of the king of Portugal. In January 1200 Portuguese ambassadors had been received at his court.[42]

Whether John was still thinking about a Portuguese marriage

by the summer of 1200 is altogether more doubtful. His first reported act on reaching Aquitaine was to ask the local bishops to confirm his divorce, and on 10 July he did send ambassadors to Portugal. But the suspicion is that this last act was a smoke-screen to conceal his real intentions, for by this stage the king was secretly planning to marry elsewhere. In late July and early August, as he toured the south of the duchy, shock news arrived at court: the count of Angoulême had abducted his daughter from the custody of her fiancé, Hugh de Lusignan. According to *The History of William Marshal*, Hugh was travelling with John's court, and departed in anger, knowing that this was part of a plot. And he was undoubtedly right: on 24 August, John came to Angoulême and married the girl himself.[43]

According to Roger of Howden, the motivation was 'affection': the king had simply taken a fancy to the count's daughter and acted on impulse. This is, of course, possible, but not very likely. John's new wife – who, like his old wife, was named Isabella – was very young. Although he subsequently persuaded half a dozen bishops to attest that their union was legitimate, she may have been under the minimum age set by the Church, which was twelve; had she been any older, it is difficult to explain why she had not already been married to her betrothed, Hugh de Lusignan.[44]

The more likely (and, indeed, more charitable) explanation is that John married Isabella for political reasons. In 1200 Hugh de Lusignan was a man who was growing too powerful for comfort. One factor, for example, which had for a long time kept him and the count of Angoulême in check was their competition for the county of La Marche. But in the wake of Richard's death Hugh had obtained La Marche from Eleanor of Aquitaine (in one account, by kidnapping the queen and extorting it from her); at the start of 1200, John had been obliged to recognize Hugh's possession of the county as a fait accompli. Had his marriage to Isabella gone ahead as planned, Hugh would also have been set to inherit all of Angoulême. Together, these new acquisitions would have placed him in control of a huge power bloc, covering an area greater than Normandy, and cutting communication between the northern and southern parts of the Angevin Empire. By marrying Isabella, John had nipped this prospect in the bud, and secured Angoulême for himself. From a strategic point of view, this was a masterstroke.[45]

From a political point of view it was a disaster. 'This did not have a favourable outcome,' says *The History of William Marshal*, 'for the count of La Marche [i.e. Hugh de Lusignan] and his men left with anger in their hearts. They did not feel it was right that the girl had been abducted.' Not for the first time, John had sought to achieve desirable ends by resorting to under- hand methods, only to find that his scheme had backfired. It was perhaps unlikely that Hugh would have responded favourably to any candid, upfront suggestions that he break off an engagement which promised to increase his power so substantially, but in any case John made no attempt to placate him or offer anything by way of compensation. According to two contemporaries, the idea of marrying Isabella had been planted in the king's head by Philip Augustus. If that really was the case, then John ought to have been more circumspect, for the resulting ill will worked greatly to the French king's advantage.[46]

As soon as his wedding had been celebrated, John and Isabella set out in the direction of England. In early October they crossed the Channel and on 8 October they were both crowned in Westminster Abbey. (Ralph of Coggeshall, recording the event, charitably remarked that the new queen looked 'about twelve'.) Immediately after the ceremony, John summoned the king of Scots for a third time, sending a powerful delegation (one bishop, three earls and four barons) to give him the desired safe conduct. William must have realized he could put the matter off no longer; regardless of his claim to Northumbria, he held lands from the English king that he could not expect to retain if he failed to acknowledge John as his lord. The two kings met in Lincoln on 21 November. The following day, on top of a lofty hill outside the city, surrounded by a vast crowd of people from England, Scotland and Normandy, William did homage to John, kneeling before him and swearing eternal fidelity. William then raised the subject of Northumbria but discovered that, alas, John did not think much of his claim. The matter was postponed.[47]

A few days later, John also settled his row with the Cistercians. He had returned to England in no mood for compromise – on the day of Isabella's coronation he had increased their persecution by issuing more 'cruel edicts' – but at length his heart softened. The Cistercian abbots had gathered in Lincoln to seek his mercy at the suggestion of the archbishop of Canterbury who, after several days of patient cajoling, persuaded the king to grant them an audience. They fell down at his feet and begged forgiveness, and he, to their surprise, responded in kind, tearfully cancelling his earlier oppressions and promising in future to be their protector. He also proclaimed his wish to build a new Cistercian monastery for the good of his soul and the souls of his parents, where he intended one day to be buried.[48]

Thus, by Christmas, which was spent at Guildford, John could feel that all his major problems had been solved. His war against Philip Augustus and Arthur of Brittany was over, his succession to the Angevin Empire secure. His superiority to the king of Scots had been ritually established, and his rift with the Cistercians healed. He had divorced his older, unwanted first wife, and replaced her with a young, attractive and politically useful new queen. Soon into the new year 1201 he and Isabella set out on a tour of northern England.[49]

But in Poitou, the king's success was starting to unravel, precisely because of his second marriage. In the early months of 1201 Hugh de Lusignan, still chafing at his humiliation, rebelled against John's authority and began attacking the king's castles in Aquitaine. He was joined by his uncle, Geoffrey de Lusignan, a former crusader famous for his military prowess, and many other men besides. According to the Anonymous of Béthune, the whole nobility of Poitou was up in arms on account of what they regarded as the shabby treatment of Hugh. Eleanor of Aquitaine, who had retired to spend her final days at Fontevraud, sent panicked letters to her son in England, spelling out his deterio-rating fortunes.[50]

John, returning from his tour of the north, responded in the early spring, ordering his officials to seize the county of La Marche from Hugh de Lusignan. He also struck at Hugh's brother, Ralph, who held the county of Eu in Normandy, instructing his deputies in the duchy to seize all Ralph's territories. This was more controversial, because Ralph had seemingly not participated in his brother's rebellion; indeed, according to one chronicler, he was in John's service in England when the king ordered the attack on his estates. John was apparently bent on crushing the entire Lusignan clan, and not paying much attention to individual culpability. Shortly after Easter he ordered his English nobles to muster at Portsmouth in May, ready to engage his continental enemies.[51]

John's decision to wage indiscriminate war against Hugh and his family would have mattered less had he not recognized Philip Augustus as his overlord the previous year. As it was, his enemies were able to complain to the French king that they were being unjustly persecuted. Philip responded by acting as peacemaker, persuading the Lusignans to stop their attacks in Poitou, and arranging to meet John on the Norman–French border. The two kings renewed their commitment to the peace they had sealed twelve months earlier, and John ordered the restoration of Ralph de Lusignan's estates. Afterwards John accompanied Philip to Paris, where he was lodged in the royal palace and entertained lavishly (though laughed at after his departure, when it was discovered his men had drunk all the bad wines and left the good ones). In the course of this visit, John promised to give the Lusignans justice, and Philip agreed not to press the matter further.[52]

It soon became apparent, however, that John had a particularly rough form of justice in mind. Once he had returned to his own lands, he charged the Lusignans with treachery, and challenged them to a judicial duel. There was nothing illegal in this, but it was a decidedly old-fashioned way to proceed in an age that was increasingly reliant on settling such matters in court. John, moreover, set about ensuring his victory by recruiting the best fighting men he could find across all his dominions to act as his champions. This was effectively war by other means. Unsurprisingly the Lusignans refused to answer his summons, saying that they would only accept trial by their peers, and once again appealed to Philip Augustus.[53]

Philip intervened once more, and insisted that the Lusignans be given a fair hearing. John agreed, but began dragging his heels, refusing to set a date or to grant the Lusignans safe conduct. In the autumn Philip tried to apply some pressure, demanding that John guarantee his word by handing over the castles of Falaise, Arques and Château Gaillard. But since these were three of the most important fortresses in Normandy, John naturally refused, sending the archbishop of Canterbury to the French king's court to tender his excuses.[54]

By the start of 1202 patience was wearing thin on both sides. A conference was arranged for 25 March between the two kings, but they did not meet in person, communicating only through proxies. Philip insisted that John should come to Paris and stand trial for his contempt; John, perhaps belatedly realizing the negative connotations of his trip to Paris the previous year, countered that the dukes of Normandy had always been accustomed to meet the kings of France at the frontier. John was not being summoned as the duke of Normandy, replied Philip, but as the duke of Aquitaine and count of Anjou, territories for which he had lately done homage. And so their arguments went on from day to day, says Ralph of Coggeshall, and their hostility began to increase. The meeting apparently concluded with a climbdown by John, who promised to appear in Paris on 28 April to answer for his contempt, and to surrender two castles as security. But in the event he did neither, and so on that date Philip's court found against him. John was declared to be a contumacious vassal, and all his lands were deemed forfeit.[55]

At once Philip set about putting the sentence into effect, launching an attack on Normandy and taking Boutavant, one of the two castles John had promised as security, which he then razed to the ground. The French king had evidently been preparing his assault for many weeks in advance, for in the month that followed many other fortresses along the Norman border also fell. John lurked nearby but put up no resistance; only when Philip moved to besiege the castle at Radepont, ten miles south-east of Rouen, did his opponent move towards him, forcing him into a temporary retreat.[56]

By this point, the French king was ready to open up another front, using a pawn that had been out of play for over a year. In early July he had knighted Arthur of Brittany and betrothed him to his infant daughter, Mary. At the same time, he had invested Arthur with Anjou, Maine, Touraine and Aquitaine – all the territories that John was deemed to have forfeited, except Normandy, which Philip was determined to keep for himself. Arthur was now fifteen years of age, and his knighting signified that he was considered old enough to fight for his inheritance. The French king immediately sent him south with 200 knights to join forces with the Lusignans, to escalate the war against John in Aquitaine.[57]

When Arthur and his army met up with the Lusignans and their supporters in Tours towards the end of July, they had exciting news. Eleanor of Aquitaine, who was still regarded as one of the most important pieces on the board, had left Fontevraud, where she would obviously have been an easy target, and was heading in the direction of Poitiers. This was too good an opportunity to miss. Ignoring Arthur's suggestion that they wait for the troops he had summoned from Brittany, they set off at once, and caught up with Eleanor at Mirebeau, fifteen miles north of Poitiers. The queen and her household retreated into the castle, but managed to dispatch a messenger to her son, warning him that she was in imminent danger of being taken prisoner.[58]

John, knowing that Arthur had set out to meet the Lusignans, had already started to head in the same direction. He was at Le Mans when his mother's messenger reached him on 30 July. The situation must have seemed hopeless, for Mirebeau and Le Mans are almost a hundred miles apart, but John nevertheless set off at once. Taking a detachment of his army, he rode south at a gallop, covering the whole distance in under forty-eight hours.[59]

At dawn on 1 August the king and his knights fell upon their unsuspecting enemies. Arthur and the Lusignans had already taken the town of Mirebeau and occupied the outer ward of the castle, forcing Eleanor and her followers to retreat into the keep. They were enjoying a leisurely breakfast – Geoffrey de Lusignan was having pigeons – when the king's men rushed into the town, storming the one gate that had not been blocked. Fierce fighting followed in the streets – 'many a helmet was staved in', says *The History of William Marshal* – but in a short while John's troops were completely victorious. All of those who had been besieging his mother were taken prisoner, including Hugh de Lusignan, Geoffrey de Lusignan, and – most importantly – Arthur. Altogether, the king calculated that he and his men had captured half a dozen barons, 200 knights and innumerable infantry. It was a greater and more decisive victory than had ever been won by his father or brother. John sent a jubilant letter to his regents in England, describing his triumph in detail, and concluding with the words 'God be praised for our happy success!'[60]

7

King versus Pope

1207–1208

John had returned to England in December 1206 buoyed by the achievements of that year's continental campaign. The last Castilian garrisons had been driven from Aquitaine, and much booty had reportedly been captured; he had secured his hold on his wife's county of Angoulême and recovered the southern part of Poitou. Tantalizingly, he had led a sortie north into Anjou, and for a week had held court in Angers, his family's ancestral seat. Such was the good progress that the king and his magnates were able to celebrate during the Christmas immediately after his return.[1]

And yet John's success in 1206 merely emphasized how much work still needed to be done. His newly won laurels, whilst pleasing, were little ones, and he certainly could not afford to rest on them during the two-year truce that was now in place. It had taken him months of politicking and arm-twisting to raise an army to take to Poitou and the money to sustain it. If he was going to reconquer Normandy, Maine and Anjou, he was going to need to field much larger forces for a much longer period, and that would mean raising a great deal more cash. After John's loss of Normandy in 1204 it is possible to detect a new note of urgency in his government of England; from the start of 1207 it rose to an even sharper pitch.[2]

The king's first thought was to seek financial assistance from the clergy. The English Church was still leaderless in December 1206, because the controversy over who should be archbishop of Canterbury had continued. One year earlier, as we've seen, John had browbeaten the monks of Canterbury into accepting his preferred candidate, John de Gray, the bishop of Norwich, on learning that some of them had secretly elected one of their own number. But in May 1206, on the eve of his departure for Poitou, the king had received disappointing news from Rome. The pope, confronted by the conflicting claims and counterclaims from both sides, and perturbed by reports of royal coercion, had cancelled Gray's election and announced he would review the matter himself. A decision had been expected in the autumn, but so far there had been no news.[3]

At the start of 1207 John paid a short visit to Canterbury, perhaps rehearsing his case for cash with the local clergy. A few days later he travelled to London to meet a great council of magnates and prelates that had been summoned to assemble on 8 January, and put to them his plan. What he wanted, he explained to the bishops and abbots, was their permission to take a fixed portion of the income of every beneficed clergyman in the country. The bishops and abbots refused, possibly on the grounds that they had not been given time enough to consult, or that not enough of them were present; the king, after all, had not yet been back in the country for a month, so the council must have been called at short notice. A second council was summoned to meet in Oxford in four weeks' time.

The Oxford council was certainly well attended. Our best-informed source, the annalist at Waverley Abbey in Surrey, reports 'an infinite multitude of prelates and magnates'. When the demand for cash was put to the clergy for a second time, their answer was more decisive. 'The English Church', they replied, 'could by no means submit to a demand which had never been heard of in all previous ages.' According to the Waverley annalist, John then relented, 'having taken wiser counsel'.[4]

In fact, the king and his counsellors had in the meantime come up with an even more ambitious plan to tax everyone in the country, clergy and laity, from the highest earl or bishop to the poorest parson or peasant. This was not wholly unprecedented, but such general taxes were still sufficiently rare to be extremely controversial. The kings of Anglo-Saxon England had levied a tax known as the geld (or Danegeld, because they used it to pay off the Vikings and recruit Danish mercenaries), and it had continued to be levied after the Norman Conquest. But the geld had been eroded by exemptions. The Norman nobility had refused to pay it, and in consequence its yield had shrunk to the point at which it was outweighed by the unpopularity of collecting it. Henry II had levied it for the last time in 1162. Since then, general taxes had been sought only in extraordinary circumstances, and only with the consent of a great council. Henry had permitted the Church to collect three aids for the Holy Land, culminating in the Saladin Tithe of 1188, which demanded ten per cent of everyone's goods and revenue. A similar levy had been imposed by Richard I's regents in 1193 to raise his £100,000 ransom, the rate on that occasion set at an eye-watering twenty-five per cent. This tax must go a long way to explaining why chroniclers complained about the unheard-of amounts of money that were extracted during Richard's reign; it would also explain why, when the king tried to get a similar tax to fight Philip Augustus in 1197, he was refused. Taxation was regarded as tantamount to robbery, only to be granted in times of truly exceptional need.[5]

Seven years into his reign, John had already asked for taxes on two previous occasions. In 1200, he had sought an aid to pay his relief to Philip Augustus for inheriting the duchy of Normandy. Its yield is unknown, but was probably not great. Like the geld, it was levied on units of land rather than actual income, and as such failed to tap the country's true wealth. It was nevertheless unpopular. The Cistercians, as we have seen, protested against paying it and suffered months of persecution before finally winning their point. With altogether less success the king's half-brother, Archbishop Geoffrey of York, refused to allow his lands to be assessed and was deprived of them as a result until he relented. In 1203 John had imposed another tax, this time on the more dubious grounds that his military tenants in England had failed to support him in the fight for Normandy. This time the assessment was based on wealth, but only on revenues, not on goods. The scant impact it made on both royal records and contemporary chroniclers suggest it may have been even less successful, raising somewhere in the region of £7,000.[6]

At Oxford in February 1207 John demanded something far more ambitious: a tax to be assessed on both the income and the goods of every man. To justify this demand he referred to 'the defence of our realm and the recovery of our right'. Considering that Richard had failed to obtain consent to a similar demand during a time of war, John's attempt to get a tax at the start of a two-year truce was ambitious, even audacious. And yet, remarkably, the request was approved by the assembled magnates and prelates. The rate, probably negotiated, was set at one shilling in every mark, which equates to 7.5 per cent. Because a mark was worth just over thirteen shillings (13s 4d), contemporaries referred to it as the Thirteenth. According to the royal writ ordering the collection, it had been granted 'by common counsel, and with the assent of our council at Oxford'. According to Roger of Wendover, the king's request 'caused great murmuring among all, though they dared not contradict it'.[7]

The measures put in place to raise the tax were elaborate and unremitting. Assessment was made by specially appointed justices, who visited every town and parish within their particular county. Fourteen men, for example, were charged with the task in Lincolnshire. In each district, every local man had to appear before them and swear to the value of his rents and moveable goods; the justices made a record of the amount of tax due, which was then passed to the sheriff for collection. Penalties for evasion were harsh: those found guilty of making false declarations, or otherwise concealing their wealth, were to be cast into prison and have all their goods confiscated for the king's use.[8]

One magnate, in fact, did dare to contradict the demand made during the Oxford council. Archbishop Geoffrey of York, who had been dispossessed for opposing the tax of 1200, strongly objected to the new demand of 1207 and excommunicated the men who tried to levy it within his archdiocese. As on the previous occasion, John reacted by seizing his half-brother's lands and goods, prompting Geoffrey to appear before him. Perhaps remembering the successful histrionics of the Cistercian abbots in 1200, the archbishop fell at the king's feet to appeal for grace. John, however, simply responded in kind, falling at Geoffrey's feet, laughing and jeering, saying 'Look, my lord archbishop, even as you do, so do I!' Unable to gain redress, Geoffrey appealed to the pope and went into exile.[9]

By this point, the pope was not high on John's list of favourite people. Early in 1207, probably around the time of the Oxford council, news had arrived in England about the outcome of the Canterbury dispute. The pope, Innocent III, had finally heard the case in December. At his request fifteen Canterbury monks had come to Rome, as well as representatives of the English bishops and the king. Innocent had begun by rejecting the bishops' claim to have a say in the election of a new archbishop, confirming that this right belonged exclusively to the monks. This was a blow for John's cause, but when the pope called upon the monks to make their choice, he found that they were divided among themselves, some still supporting their sub-prior, Reginald, others now favouring the king's nominee, John de Gray. At this point Innocent intervened. Since they could not agree on either of the existing candidates, he proposed – or imposed, according to some sources – a third. The man the pope had in mind was Stephen Langton, a scholar of international reputation, lately summoned from Paris to Rome to become a cardinal, but by birth an Englishman who had begun his clerical career in York. The king's representatives objected to this development, but were powerless to prevent it going forward. The monks, probably after experiencing a certain amount of papal pressure, unanimously elected Langton. A few days before Christmas, Innocent wrote to John to inform him of the good news.[10]

The king was furious – 'exceedingly enraged', according to

Roger of Wendover, 'as much at the promotion of Stephen Langton as at the annulment of the election of the bishop of Norwich'. In response, he sent a hot-tempered letter back to the pope, making no attempt to disguise his displeasure. It was disgraceful, he said, that Innocent had cancelled John de Gray's election and appointed 'a man altogether unknown to him, who had been familiar for a long time with his declared enemies in the kingdom of France'. Moreover, apart from his particular objection to Langton, there was the general principle at stake, namely that the king of England ought to have a say in the appointment of the archbishop of Canterbury; between them, the pope and the monks of Canterbury had conspired to deny John that right. Reminding Innocent that England contributed more funds to the papal treasury than any other country north of the Alps, the king vowed that he would defend the rights of his Crown to the death, and declared he would not be deterred from his intention of making John de Gray his next archbishop. For good measure, he concluded with an outright threat, saying that he would cut all communication between England and Rome if the pope did not fall in line with his wishes.[11]

John's letter to Innocent was probably dispatched around mid-April, at which point the king was at Lambeth. For most of the rest of the spring, while contemplating his response, the king had been travelling between his hunting lodges in southern and midland England. Like almost all medieval monarchs, John was a keen huntsman. Hunting was the main leisure activity of the medieval upper classes: it kept them in shape; it enabled them to practise their horsemanship and hone their use of weapons; it also put food on the table. Even so, contemporary comment suggests that John was keener than most. The poet Bertran de Born contrasted the king's passion for 'pointers, greyhounds and hawks' with his apparent lack of martial prowess, while the Anonymous of Béthune said that he 'haunted woods and streams and greatly delighted in the pleasure of them'. John was not a great castle-builder, but his one original foundation was the tower he built at Odiham in Hampshire, substantial remains of which still survive. Begun in the first half of 1207, it was constructed, according to the Anonymous of Béthune, so the king could disport himself in the surrounding forests.[12]

The royal forest in which John hunted was not simply a reserve set aside for the king's enjoyment. It was also a highly developed sub-branch of government, almost a state within the state. The concept of a royal forest, governed by its own law, had been introduced to England by William the Conqueror. (The word 'forest', introduced at the same time, derives from the Latin *foris*, meaning 'outside' or 'apart'.) Forest law was extremely harsh. The penalty for taking a deer, established by the Conqueror, was blinding. It was also entirely arbitrary. 'The whole organization of the forests,' wrote Henry II's treasurer, Ralph fitz Nigel, 'and the punishment, financial and corporal, of forest offences, is outside the jurisdiction of the other courts, and solely dependent on the decision of the king, or of some officer specially appointed by him ... What is done in accordance with forest law is not called "just" without qualification, but "just, according to the forest law".'[13]

The simple solution, one might conclude, was to stay out of the royal forest; but for many people that was not an option. What had started after the Conquest as a royal hunting preserve had been massively extended during the twelfth century, chiefly by Henry II. Even as he was making the common law more accessible to his subjects, Henry was in this way extending his arbitrary power over them. By the end of his reign, the jurisdiction known as 'the Forest' did not apply only to the wooded or wasteland areas used for hunting, but to almost a third of all England. Land of any kind, arable or pasture, could be forest. Villages could be forest. All of Essex was forest.

Although Henry's love of hunting was almost as famous as that of his favourite son, he had not extended the scope of the Forest merely to extend his hunting rights; he had done so for financial gain. While savage corporal punishments could still be dished out – Richard I had increased the penalty for taking a deer to the loss of eyes *and* testicles – it was increasingly common for offenders to face fines. The forests were policed by a range of officials – foresters, verderers, regarders – ever vigilant for infringements, all under the ultimate control of the chief forester. During John's reign the chief forester was Hugh de Neville. Appointed by Richard in 1198, Hugh struck up a close working relationship with his new master after John's accession. Indeed, he became one of the king's most intimate companions, to judge from financial records that show the two of them gambling together from time to time.[14]

John's initial policy towards the Forest had been to raise money by selling exemptions, allowing men to turn forest land into arable (assarting) or simply declaring that certain areas were to be 'disafforested'. Hugh de Neville had been given a free hand to do this in 1203, when the king was in Normandy and in desperate need of ready cash, and extensive disafforestation had taken place the following year. But after his return to England in 1206, John changed tack, and decided it was time to exploit the Forest more efficiently without further diminishing its extent. Fines were raised from the Forest by periodically dispatching special itinerant justices, much like the regular justices the king sent round the country to hear common-law cases. There had been no such visitation, or eyre, since 1198, when Hugh de Neville had conducted one at the start of his term of office. But in the spring of 1207, while John was disporting himself in the forests of Hampshire, Northamptonshire and Dorset, a new eyre was launched by Hugh and his associates. They began in Cornwall, Devon, Hampshire, Northumberland, Rutland and Surrey. For the men of Cornwall this was a surprise, since in 1204 they had collectively given 2,200 marks and twenty palfreys to have their county disafforested. Hugh de Neville seems to have interpreted this as a temporary respite, for the eyre in Cornwall went ahead as normal and raised £325 in fines.[15]

The nature of the fines is recorded on the rolls of the Exchequer. Men were fined for hunting without the king's permission, or for attacking royal foresters. The foresters themselves were fined for laxity in carrying out their duties. A woman in Nottinghamshire paid 100 marks to recover land that had been confiscated because she had made a ditch without permission. The wide variety of offences was nothing new, but the eyre launched in 1207 was unquestionably more searching and more punitive than its predecessors. The total raised by Neville's previous eyre – which ran from 1198 to 1201, and was described by Roger of Howden as 'a torment to the men of the kingdom' – was £3,700. By the time the eyre launched in 1207 had finally run its course, it had raised £8,700.[16]

On 23 June 1207 John visited Odiham, either to initiate the building of his new castle there or to inspect its early progress. It must have been around this time that he received letters from Pope Innocent, sent from Rome four weeks earlier.[17]

The pope was not happy. He had not liked the tone of John's response. ('We wrote to you meekly and kindly, requesting and exhorting, but you wrote back to us insolently and impudently, as though threatening and expostulating.') Nor did he think much of the king's objections to the newly elected archbishop of Canterbury. John's claim that Stephen Langton had lived among his enemies and was 'unknown' to him was rejected as 'paltry'. If that really was the case, asked the pope, why had John written to Langton congratulating him on his promotion to the cardinalate? Innocent was similarly dismissive of the king's complaint about the lack of royal consent. Regardless of the procedural irregularities alleged by John's envoys, the fact was that the pope had plenary authority in this matter. Nothing could now impede Langton's advancement, and the king should not suppose otherwise. Matching threat with threat, Innocent concluded by warning John not 'to fight against God and the Church in this cause for which St Thomas [Becket], that glorious martyr and archbishop, recently shed his blood'.[18]

This letter gives us some insight into the character and motivations of Innocent III. Elected in January 1198, he had come to the papal throne at an exceptionally young age. His predecessors in recent decades had all been old men, appointed in their sixties, seventies and eighties, and thus had served for only a few years before their deaths. Innocent by contrast was thirty-seven or thirty-eight at the time of his election – three or four years younger than Richard I, whose rule had briefly overlapped with his own, and only six or seven years older than John. His early appointment to the most senior role in the Church gives some indication of how highly others thought of his abilities. A distinguished lawyer as well as an accomplished theologian, he was brilliant, quick-witted and abrasive, and came to power determined to assert papal authority to the full. The papacy had been asserting its supremacy on spiritual matters since the mid-eleventh century, at which point it had embraced the ideals of an earlier monastic reform movement. No pope, however, had pushed papal supremacy as hard as Innocent. He was, in his own words, 'less than God, but greater than Man, judge of all men and judged by none'. Having appointed Langton, he explained in his letter, 'we could not desist without loss of reputation or peril to our conscience'. Innocent was not a man for compromise.[19]

But nor was John. Aside from an Angevin temperament which made it unlikely that the king would back down, there was a clash of principles. The problem with Innocent's response was that it did not consider (or did not consider important) that, for John to desist, he would suffer a loss of reputation, and even peril to his own conscience. Part of the sacred oath that the king had sworn at his coronation was a promise, introduced by Henry II, to safeguard the rights of the Crown, and one of those rights was a say in the appointment of bishops.[20]

But by the time John received this letter, Innocent had already acted. On 17 June, without waiting for any further response from England, the pope personally consecrated Langton in the Italian city of Viterbo, fifty miles north of Rome. If his envoys travelled at lightning speed, it is just possible that news of this could have reached the king by 11 July. Equally there was enough in Innocent's letter for John to realize that this outcome was inevitable. Either way, on that date the king reacted, proclaiming that anyone who acknowledged Langton as archbishop would be considered a public enemy, and ordering two knights – Fulk de Cantilupe and Reginald of Cornhill, the sheriff of Kent – to expel the monks of Canterbury from England. Four days later these men, accompanied by a band of armed attendants, carried out their task. According to Wendover they entered the monastery with drawn swords, calling the monks traitors to the king and swearing that they would burn the monastery down if its occupants did not leave immediately. Thirteen monks lying in the infirmary were too sick to move, but the remaining sixty-four left at once, fleeing across the Channel to Flanders, where they found refuge at the abbey of St Bertin.[21]

John was back in Lambeth when he issued these orders, but by the time they were carried out he was en route to Winchester, perhaps to visit his queen, who was resident in Winchester Castle during the latter part of the year. The king's relationship with Isabella, the girl he had married seven summers earlier, is almost completely obscure. He was at least twenty years her senior, so their interests are unlikely to have overlapped, to begin with at any rate. After her coronation in October 1200 John had treated Isabella like the child she was, sometimes taking her with him on his travels, other times leaving her to stay at a favourite royal residence such as Marlborough, but certainly not entrusting her with any political power, and not even any land. This meant she was entirely reliant on the king's handouts, and royal financial records show she received a steady stream of necessities and luxury items. One of the men particularly concerned with attending to her needs was Reginald of Cornhill, the aforementioned sheriff of Kent. In 1207 he sent her, among other things, a gilded saddle and harness, three different-coloured hoods, a hundred yards of fine linen, two tablecloths, four towels, half an otter skin and a belt. Other entries show Isabella received clothes and equipment for her chaplains and payment for the keepers of her greyhounds.[22]

The financial records also suggest that, in one respect, the queen's domestic arrangements may have been unusual, in that she seems to have been lodged, at least for some of the time, in the same place as John's ex-wife. After their divorce in 1200 the king had continued to maintain Isabella of Gloucester, supplying her with goods and money on a scale that almost rivalled that of her replacement. Winchester Castle seems to have been her chief residence, and in 1205 and 1206 the expenses of the two Isabellas were recorded as if they were staying together under the same roof.

What this signifies about John's relationship with the two women is anyone's guess. It would take a considerable imaginative leap to suggest that he was keeping his former wife, now in her mid-forties, as a mistress, given that he had apparently not wanted to marry her in the first place. At the same time, the king's lack of legitimate children by 1207 suggests that he may not have been sleeping with his teenage queen, despite Wendover's scurrilous claim that John had idled in bed with her while Normandy was being lost. The king had several bastard children, such as Geoffrey, who led troops to Poitou in 1205, but they were all too old to have been fathered during his second marriage, and possibly even during his first. Gifts to women who might have been his mistresses do figure in royal financial accounts, but not until later in his reign. Despite what appears to have been an unusual ménage at Winchester, if we base our conclusions on evidence rather than hearsay, we have to entertain the alarming possibility that, during the early years of his marriage, John may have been both faithful and chaste.[23]

If the latter was ever the case, however, it was no longer so by 1207, for that year the queen became pregnant. She must have conceived at the start of the year, during the festivities at Winchester that had followed the king's jubilant return from France. At some point after March the older Isabella left Winchester for alternative lodgings at Sherborne, and as the time of the queen's confinement approached, John's visits to Winchester became more frequent. In July and August he interrupted his ceaseless round of hunting to pay four visits, and he was back there by the end of September, in time for the birth of the child that arrived on 1 October. To what must have been general rejoicing, it was a boy, christened Henry after his paternal grandfather. At last, at the age of forty, John had a legitimate heir. His dynasty was meant to continue. It was a sure sign of God's favour.[24]

Unfortunately John was still very much out of favour with God's principal representative on earth. Innocent III had reacted with surprising calmness when he had heard about the king's violent expulsion of the monks of Canterbury towards the end of August. True, he had immediately ordered the bishop of Rochester to excommunicate Reginald of Cornhill, Fulk de Cantilupe and all others who had carried out the attack on Church property. But when he wrote about John himself, the pope did so more in sorrow than in anger. With God as his witness, he explained that he really loved John, his 'very dear son in Christ', with the most sincere affection. Indeed, the affection he had shown to the king in the past was such that it had damaged papal relations with other princes (an allusion to Philip Augustus). And yet, despite this consistent love and kindness, John was ungrateful, and had followed foolish advice.

These remarks, written on 27 August, were addressed not to the king himself, but to the bishops of London, Worcester and Ely, a trio seemingly selected because they had acted as papal agents in the past and did not owe their advancement to John. They were instructed to visit the king and remonstrate with him, urging him to accept Stephen Langton as archbishop and to readmit the monks of Canterbury. If he refused to do so, they were to impose an interdict, which meant that there would be no church services. The English clergy would effectively go on strike.[25]

The three bishops cannot have received these instructions until the autumn, and probably did not approach John until 19 October, when all three can be placed in his company by their appearance as witnesses to a royal charter. The king, who had been in Westminster the previous week, was back in Winchester by this date, perhaps dandling his three-week-old son. According to the

Waverley annalist, the bishops approached him tearfully and on bended knee. According to Wendover, John reacted furiously, threatening to confiscate all the clergy's estates, and adding for good measure that he would send any Roman clergy in his realm back to their master with their noses slit and their eyes put out.[26]

Although Wendover has almost certainly sensationalized his account, there is no doubt that the king refused the bishops' request. It is also equally clear that, despite his refusal, the bishops chose not to impose the interdict. This may have been because they feared the consequences. Alternatively, it may have been because they, more so than Innocent, were better able to gauge the mood in England. By the autumn of 1207 John can hardly have been a popular ruler. His government was becoming ever more oppressive. The Forest eyre, as we have seen, had squeezed a great deal of money out of people of all ranks. The general tax known as the Thirteenth had squeezed a great deal more. By the time its yield had been checked at the end of September, it had brought in over £60,000.

Harvesting money on this scale was obviously unpopular. In Lincolnshire men had attempted to evade the tax by depositing their wealth in religious houses. In Warwickshire the evasion was such that the assessment had to be repeated in late May. Some men had refused to pay outright and suffered the harsh penalties threatened at the start of the year. The Exchequer rolls show several individuals imprisoned and others fined. Ruald fitz Alan was deprived of Richmond Castle for refusing to swear to the value of his goods and fined 200 marks. The abbot of Selby was fined forty marks and two palfreys for non-payment, and the monks of Furness lost two of their manors and some of their goods. As these examples imply, much of the resistance to the tax seems to have arisen in the north.[27]

And yet, when it came to choosing between the king and the pope, it seems that most people were on the side of the king. The annalist at Margam Abbey in south Wales, a source deeply hostile to John, nevertheless reports that, on this matter, all the laity favoured the king, and almost all the clergy. Whether because

John's propaganda was more effective, or because of historical precedent, it was clearly felt that the king ought to have a say – the final say, even – in who was archbishop of Canterbury. The archbishop was, after all, not simply a clergyman but a political figure of the foremost importance, whose estates put him on a par with the greatest magnates in the country.[28]

The fact that the Church held vast estates was an added incentive for a cash-hungry king to prolong the dispute. John had already deprived the archbishop of York of his lands in 1207 and driven him into exile before he did the same to the monks of Canterbury. He was also holding the estates of the bishop of Chichester, who had died in August, and those of the bishops of Exeter and Lincoln, both of whom had died the previous year, no doubt keeping their positions vacant as a way of demonstrating his mastery over the appointment process.[29] The bishops of London, Worcester and Ely, knowing the king far better than the pope did, must have realized that his threat to seize the lands of every clergyman in the country was unlikely to be an idle one. After their unsuccessful interview with John in October, they temporized by asking Innocent to clarify the nature of the interdict they were to impose. Did it apply to all religious communities? Did it apply to Wales?

The pope, responding on 19 November, indicated that he was starting to lose patience. He issued a short clarification of the terms of the interdict – yes, it applied to everyone, even the Welsh – and forbade any further delay. With it he dispatched a separate letter to the English bishops, chiding them for their inactivity ('It has come to our hearing that some of you have been tepid and remiss in the matter of the archbishop of Canterbury'), ordering them to put aside fear and to prepare themselves for persecution. He also attempted to open up a new front by addressing another letter to the nobles of England, telling them, 'You should regulate your loyalty to your earthly king so as never to offend your heavenly king.' In view of John's opposition to God, they should not give him their support. John's mind was sick, explained Innocent, and the pope was his doctor.

The king would one day be grateful to them all for administering his medicine, however bitter it seemed on the way down.[30]

Innocent's letters must have reached England shortly after Christmas 1207 or early in the new year of 1208. John had spent the days before Christmas inspecting his new castle at Odiham and celebrated the feast itself at nearby Windsor. It seems unlikely that any of the lay magnates he mixed with during the festive period would have remonstrated with him over his behaviour, but presumably at some point after receiving the pope's stern mandate the bishops of London, Worcester and Ely must have repeated their efforts to persuade the king to change his mind.[31]

To their surprise, perhaps, John now seemed inclined to do so. On 21 January he sent the three bishops a letter, indicating that he was willing to obey Innocent on the matter of Canterbury. Simultaneously, as a conciliatory gesture, he removed Reginald of Cornhill and Fulk de Cantilupe as custodians of the Canterbury lands and replaced them with less offensive agents. There was, however, a proviso. In return for John's compliance, the pope would have to undertake to preserve the king's 'rights, dignity and liberties'. In other words, John seems to have indicated that he would accept Stephen Langton, provided that he was given a cast-iron guarantee of his right to approve all future episcopal elections. His letter was witnessed by seven earls and three other leading barons, a clear display of magnate solidarity in riposte to Innocent's attempt to set the baronage against the king.[32]

Whether or not they passed this message on to the pope, the bishops were sufficiently encouraged to delay until they were joined in March by a papal emissary in the shape of Master Simon Langton, younger brother of the controversial archbishop. Master Simon, as his title suggests, was also a clerk and a scholar, and understood precisely what was at stake. When he appeared before the king at Winchester on 12 March, he made it clear that, when it came to the Canterbury election, there was no room for manoeuvre. 'When we spoke to him about safeguarding our dignity in this matter,' wrote John, 'he said he would not do anything about it unless we placed ourselves entirely at his mercy.' This was in a letter to the men of Kent, issued two days later, explaining why the negotiations had failed, and telling them to listen to Reginald of Cornhill's account of the meeting. The excommunicate sheriff was once again placed in charge of the Canterbury estates. The attempt to conciliate was over.[33]

On Sunday 23 March, in every church in England, the interdict was proclaimed. Henceforth there were to be no church services. Mass would not be performed. Marriages would not be celebrated in church. Confession would not be heard, except in the case of the dying. The dead could not be buried in consecrated ground. Church bells were rung for the last time that Sunday, and were not to be sounded again until the king surrendered.[34]

John had known this was coming and had made sure his retaliation was ready. The following morning, as the interdict began, his agents moved in to seize the goods and lands of every clergyman in the kingdom. In every parish four men were appointed to lock up and guard the Church's barns. At the same moment, the king appears to have let it be known that it was effectively open season on the clergy. 'Religious men and other ordained persons of any kind,' said Roger of Wendover, 'when found travelling on the road, were dragged from their horses, robbed and basely ill-treated by the king's followers, and no one would do them justice.' This sounds like typically sensational stuff from Wendover, but its essential truth is confirmed by a writ issued by John three weeks later, forbidding laymen from abusing clerics, on pain of being hanged from the nearest oak. That the king felt obliged to issue such strong counter-measures suggests that in the short term the clergy must have suffered many assaults at the hands of their lay neighbours.[35]

In the long term it was obviously impossible for the king to occupy and manage the lands of every churchman. After a short while many were able to strike a deal whereby they received their lands back in return for a fine – but only as custodians, allowed to take an agreed portion of the revenues for their sustenance and paying all the profits to the king. John also found a mischievous way to make even more money out of the clergy by seizing all their mistresses and girlfriends and holding them to ransom. Since clerics were supposed to be celibate there could be no official objection to this underhand move. Moralists had to reserve their criticism for those churchmen who rushed to pay for the release of their lovers.[36]

There is no sign that the laity were in any way bothered by the interdict or by the king's reprisals against the clergy. Some lay magnates, indeed, were given custody of confiscated Church land, and probably allowed to keep the profits for themselves.[37] Nevertheless, John may well have been troubled by Innocent's attempt to turn his nobility against him. At a time when men were already expressing their dissatisfaction about the general oppressiveness of his government, the idea that the pope might absolve them of their loyalty altogether must have been a disturbing one. According to Roger of Wendover, once the interdict had been imposed, the king was sufficiently worried that he sent out agents to those magnates of whom he was suspicious and demanded hostages from them in the form of their sons or nephews. At length they came to the home of a nobleman called William de Briouze and made this demand, but before he could answer, his wife, Matilda, responded on his behalf. 'I will not deliver up my sons to your lord, King John,' she told the royal messengers, 'because he basely murdered his nephew, Arthur, whom he ought to have taken care of honourably.'[38]

8

A Deed of Shame

1202–1203

The news that John had captured Arthur, the Lusignans and hundreds of their supporters spread rapidly from Mirebeau in all directions, bringing joy to the king's adherents and despair to his enemies. In Normandy those barons who had remained behind to resist the invasion of Philip Augustus were elated when the message arrived, and immediately sent it on to the French camp at Arques, where (as intended) it had the opposite effect. Ralph de Lusignan, hearing of the misfortune that had befallen his kinsmen, reportedly fell silent and had to have a lie-down in his tent. Philip became immensely angry, realizing that Arthur's capture meant his own campaign must come to an end. At once he called off his assault on the castle at Arques, and in his fury ordered his siege engines be smashed to pieces.[1]

John meanwhile was already heading northwards towards Normandy, taking with him his horde of high-status captives. By 10 August 1202, nine days after Mirebeau, he was at Falaise, and the mighty stone donjon built by his ancestor Henry I, which now became Arthur's prison. That same day he sent Hugh de Lusignan to Caen, another of Henry's great towers, ordering its constable to clear out any other prisoners being held there, and giving strict instructions to admit no one without the approval of his trusted henchman, Hugh de Neville. Dozens of less important prisoners were distributed in other castles throughout the duchy, and dozens more were sent across the Channel to be kept in castles all over England: Bristol, Wallingford, Corfe, Nottingham, Colchester, Pickering, Sherborne, Southampton, Marlborough, Portchester, Norwich, Carlisle, Peveril, Bamburgh, Oxford, Northampton, Windsor and Devizes. John had captured so many of his enemies that there were scarcely enough strongholds to contain them.[2]

Even before the king had reached Falaise, however, concerns were being raised about the way these prisoners were being treated. Roger of Wendover reports that when they left Mirebeau they were not only shackled and chained, but placed in carts, 'a new and unusual way of travelling'. Security was of course essential, but John, in the flush of his triumph, seems to have set out deliberately to humiliate his enemies, parading them through every town and village. 'When the king arrived at Chinon,' says *The History of William Marshal*, 'he kept his prisoners in such a horrible manner and in such abject confinement that it seemed an indignity and a disgrace to all those with him who witnessed his cruelty.'[3]

One person in particular who was concerned about this treatment was William des Roches. William, it will be recalled, was the man who had brokered a peace between John and Arthur in the autumn of 1199, negotiating secretly with the king and successfully bringing in his nephew. That peace had proved extremely short-lived, because Arthur had fled on hearing that his uncle intended to keep him in prison.[4] William, however, had stayed in the king's camp and kept his position as seneschal of Anjou. He was, in the opinion of contemporaries, a fine knight. He was also, according to more than one source, the true author of the victory at Mirebeau, advising John on how to mount the attack and fighting valiantly when it was carried out, on the understanding that the king would be similarly guided by his advice when it came to exploiting the final outcome. With this understanding in mind he had approached John afterwards to discuss the fate of the prisoners. According to *The History of William Marshal*, he began by reminding the king of the events of 1199, when he had delivered Arthur on condition that they should all be friends.[5]

John responded, not unreasonably, that a lot had happened since 1199, saying 'my nephew has done me much wrong'. But William persisted. In opposing his uncle, he suggested, Arthur had been the tool of others and had not been acting on his own account. If the king would let him take care of it, William was sure he could bring everything to a satisfactory conclusion. John, says the *History*, agreed to this, but then kept putting the matter off. William was asked to wait until they reached Chinon; at Chinon he was told to wait until Le Mans. By the time they arrived at Falaise, at which point Arthur was imprisoned in the castle, shackled with three sets of manacles, William must have concluded that he was being played for a fool, and that the king had no intention of heeding his advice or handing over his nephew. A few days later he left John's court and returned to his own estates.[6]

The king soon realized that des Roches had departed and appointed others to take over his role as governor of Anjou.[7] Given their reported exchanges, John may have anticipated this development and reckoned that it was a price worth paying to keep Arthur securely under lock and key. As far as the king was concerned, the only mistake he had made in 1199 was leaving his nephew unguarded. Clearly there was no way he was going to take that chance a second time.

In any case, John seemed to be on an unstoppable roll. Immediately after Mirebeau he had dispatched some of his troops on a punitive raid into Brittany, where they had ravaged the countryside and reduced several towns to ashes; by the time of William des Roches' desertion, the leading barons of Brittany were seeking safe conduct to come and negotiate. Meanwhile the king, having delivered his prisoners to Normandy, had returned south with similar hostile intent. In mid-August he burned down Le Mans as punishment for having earlier received his enemies. A few days later he pushed further south to Tours. Philip Augustus had installed a garrison there after his retreat from Normandy, and for a short time there was a violent struggle between these men and John's forces, until eventually the latter triumphed. Again the city was put to the torch. At the start of September the king struck west along the Loire until he came to Angers, which was similarly assaulted and occupied. Around the same time he received news from Poitou that one of his few remaining enemies, the viscount of Limoges, had been captured. On every front his military successes were multiplying.[8]

Satisfied that his affairs in Anjou were prospering, in late September John returned to Normandy. His precise reasons for doing so are obscure, but his appearance at Verneuil suggests that he was attending to the defences on the duchy's eastern frontier. Philip Augustus had taken many castles there in the course of his invasion during the summer, and although the French king had now withdrawn, there was as yet no talk of truce or peace.[9]

Towards the end of October, John discovered why. William des Roches and the nobles of Brittany, both angry over the continued detention of Arthur, had made common cause and were attacking the king's towns and castles. They were joined by lots of other nobles in Anjou, Maine and Touraine, who had been equally incensed by his destruction of their principal cities during the summer. John left Normandy and hastened south again,[10] but by the time he reached the Loire it was too late: des Roches and the Bretons had occupied Angers and the count of Amboise had taken Tours. Worse still for the king, he seems to have been unable to do anything to reverse these losses. For the first half of November he sat at Saumur and for the second half at Chinon. In the middle of the month he received the news that his favourite mercenary captain had been captured.[11]

It may have been at this juncture that John ordered the mutilation of Arthur. According to Ralph of Coggeshall, the king's advisers, seeing the scale of the disturbances that the Bretons were causing, and realizing that no reliable peace could be made with them, recommended that he give the order for Arthur to be blinded and castrated, their notion being that this would render the young duke unable to govern, and thus induce his supporters to submit. The story is well known because it was later taken up by the Tudor chronicler Holinshed, and from there by Shakespeare, who made it the dramatic hinge of his play *King John*. Coggeshall is, however, the only contemporary source, and so needs to be regarded with some caution. He continues his account by explaining that John, provoked by the ceaseless attacks of his enemies into a furious rage, gave the hateful order, and sent three of his servants to Falaise to carry it out. Two of them fled rather than have to do so, but the third eventually came to the castle, which was being kept by the king's chamberlain, Hubert de Burgh. When Hubert and his knights learned the nature of the newcomer's business they were moved to pity for Arthur, who in turn became aware of what was intended. At first he broke down in tears, but then leapt up and grappled with the man who had been sent to maim him. The knights managed to pull them apart, and Hubert ordered that the unwelcome visitor be ejected.

Hubert, says Coggeshall, then made a bold decision. Realizing that the order, if carried out, would cause terrible damage to John's reputation, he decided that Arthur would remain unharmed. The king, he was convinced, must have spoken in anger and would soon come to regret it. In the meantime, however, wishing to quell the rebellion of the Bretons, he pretended that the order had been obeyed, and let it be known that Arthur had died as a result of his injuries. Trumpets were blown in every castle and town to mark his passing, his clothes were donated to the local leper house, and it was announced that his body had been taken to the nearby abbey of St André for burial.

But – unsurprisingly – the news that Arthur had been killed failed to calm the Bretons, who raged with even greater fury than before, 'swearing that they would never stop fighting the king of England, who had dared to commit such a horrible crime against their lord, his own nephew'. And so, explains Coggeshall, after a fortnight or so, it was decided to proclaim that Arthur was in fact still alive and unharmed.[12]

Such is Coggeshall's story. If there is nothing in the way of contemporary evidence to corroborate it, nor is there anything to contradict it. Certain points of detail, such as the mention of the abbey of St André, suggest it was unlikely to simply have been invented by a chronicler in Essex. The original source, it has been suggested, may well have been Hubert de Burgh himself, since he is the person who emerges in the most positive light.[13]

Is the story, in general terms, credible? On the one hand, many people in the Middle Ages suffered such acts of mutilation. In England, as we've seen, you could lose your eyes and genitals for taking a deer in the royal Forest. Such punishments, however, were almost never applied to people of high status. Since the early eleventh century in France, and since the Norman Conquest in England, it had been morally and politically unacceptable for one nobleman to kill another who was at his mercy. Knights might die in battle, but usually their armour protected them until the fighting was over, and at that point the victors would take their defeated opponents prisoner. Sometimes they would release them in return for a ransom; other times they might detain them indefinitely. What they would not do was kill or maim them. Even kings with ferocious reputations respected this taboo. William the Conqueror, responsible for the deaths of countless thousands of ordinary Englishmen, ordered the execution of only one English earl, and suffered some opprobrium as a result. His son, Henry I, was scarcely less brutal. As well as ordering the mass castration of his moneyers, he is said to have disposed of a burgess of Rouen by throwing him off the top of a castle tower. Yet when Henry captured his elder brother and rival, Robert Curthose, he had no option other than to keep him captive, and Robert remained incarcerated until his death almost thirty years later.[14]

Detaining prisoners indefinitely was not a problem, provided you held the whip hand. A powerful ruler could be confident that a subject who surrendered a hostage would remain obedient simply in the hope of one day obtaining the hostage's release. John's difficulty in 1202 was that, in spite of his triumph at Mirebeau, his enemies were still very powerful. When the Bretons realized, as William des Roches had done, that John had no intention of releasing Arthur, they simply resumed their war against him. John had foreseen this possibility during the brief period of negotiations in August, when he had warned the Bretons 'not to do anything whereby evil may befall us or our nephew, Arthur'. His enemies had decided to take the risk that he was bluffing. It is not difficult to imagine how the king, enraged at their invasion of Anjou, yet powerless to contest it, might have decided to prove them wrong.[15]

The renewed rebellion of the Bretons may therefore have prompted John into ordering Arthur's mutilation, which may in turn have prompted Hubert de Burgh to announce that the duke was dead. If something of this kind did happen, however, it is clear, as Coggeshall says, that it failed to bring the Bretons to heel. In early December the king withdrew to Normandy, leaving Tours and Angers in the hands of his enemies.[16]

What is certain is that the renewed rebellion of the Bretons prompted John to take a gamble in completely the opposite direction. Much like the followers of Arthur, the followers of Hugh and Geoffrey de Lusignan had been seeking to intercede on behalf of their imprisoned masters since August. At that time, with his affairs going well, John had probably been disinclined to listen to them, but by the autumn his deteriorating fortunes had led him to negotiate in earnest. On 6 November he had given orders for Hugh de Lusignan to be released from his strict custody at Caen and brought to him at Saumur, heavily guarded, for talks with his brother, Ralph. Conditions of release must have been discussed, and by 23 December – at which point the king was in Caen to celebrate Christmas – castles had been surrendered to him and he was ready to receive their men as hostages. By the middle of January, the hostages must have been delivered, for at that point both Hugh and Geoffrey de Lusignan were freed.[17]

As the precautions imply, this was clearly a very risky move. John and the Lusignans had been bitter enemies ever since his decision to steal Hugh's fiancée and marry her himself. But since the capture of Arthur at Mirebeau, and because of his determination never to release him, John had made new enemies among the barons of Anjou, particularly William des Roches. He could not afford to be at war with so many men at once. The detention of Arthur, which ought to have ended the threat of his succession once and for all, was clearly paramount. It therefore followed that, in order to maintain a hard line with Arthur's supporters, the king would have to show leniency to the Lusignans. By granting them their freedom, and holding out the prospect that their recently surrendered castles and hostages might one day be restored, he hoped to be able to guarantee their faithful service. Once they were back in Poitou, they could attack his enemies in Anjou from the south, while he simultaneously advanced from Normandy in the north, and between them they would crush those who still entertained the hope that Arthur might one day be freed. The king's writs show that he was planning to advance from Argentan, close to Normandy's southern border, at the start of February.[18]

But before this happened, his plans suffered a massive setback. In mid-January John was in the vicinity of Argentan when he heard that his queen was in danger. Isabella was apparently at Chinon, in the midst of the king's enemies, much as his mother had been at Mirebeau six months earlier.[19] As on that occasion John set out immediately with a large army of knights and mercenaries, hoping to avert a disastrous capture. He had not even travelled as far as Le Mans, however, when the next hammer blow fell. Count Robert of Alençon, a Norman nobleman with whom he had dined earlier that same day, had defected. The town of Alençon, which the king had left just a few miles to his rear, had been occupied by French forces.

'Alas! Alack!' cried John, according to *The History of William Marshal*. 'What a cruel act of treachery! Robert has greatly wronged me!' The chronicler's account of his anger is borne out by the official record: months later, the king was dating his charters with the phrase 'the year when Count Robert betrayed us'. With a French garrison now cutting off his retreat, John was suddenly afraid to go further forward, fearing that his enemies would attack him on the road to Chinon. As it was, the situation was partially retrieved by the heroism of one of his knights, Peter de Préaux, who managed to reach Isabella at Chinon and deliver her safely to Le Mans. From there the king and his army managed to return to Normandy, avoiding Alençon by taking a circuitous route.[20]

The revolt of the count of Alençon was not quite the total disaster it could have been, in that neither Isabella nor John himself was captured. It did, however, spell the end for the king's plan of a combined offensive with the Lusignans against his enemies in Anjou. Alençon lies on the Norman frontier, controlling the main route south, and Count Robert had probably been expected to play a leading role in the campaign, to judge from *The History of William Marshal*'s comment that he had been given money by the king just days before his defection.[21]

With his military options shrinking fast, John made for Falaise, where Arthur was still being held. According to Roger of Wendover, the occasion for this visit was another volte-face in strategy. The king, says the chronicler, ordered his nephew to be brought into his presence and spoke to him kindly, promising him many honours if he would abandon Philip Augustus and recognize John, his uncle, as his lord. In other words, late in the day, Arthur was being offered the sort of deal advocated by William des Roches the previous summer – leniency in return for loyalty – evidently in the hope that, if he accepted, it would persuade des Roches, the Bretons and their increasing numerous followers to stand down.

But it was too late. Arthur, says Wendover, replied to his uncle's offer with indignation and threats. (Perhaps not surprising, if Coggeshall's story of the earlier attempt to mutilate him is true.) Whatever honours John had proposed were not enough; he, Arthur, was the rightful heir to the whole Angevin Empire, and unless his uncle resigned it all to him, he would never enjoy a moment's peace. At these words, the chronicler continues, the king was very troubled, and commanded that his nephew should be taken to Rouen and confined in the castle there. John's writs confirm that he did indeed make directly for Rouen at this point.[22] They also attest to the terrible nature of his anger. On 30 January, the day after his arrival at Falaise, and presumably after his reported exchanges with Arthur, the king sent letters to Hugh de Neville, who until recently had been guarding Hugh de Lusignan at Caen. Neville was ordered to cross the Channel to England, taking with him two other prisoners from Mirebeau, Warin de Craon and Maurice de Basuen, who were to be deposited in Corfe Castle. Five days later, after he had reached Rouen, John dispatched a barrage of writs to England, directed to the constables of eighteen castles, requiring them to send a further twenty-two named individuals to the same place, ignoring all previous orders about their custody. Finally, he wrote to the constable of Corfe 'that he should do what Thomas, clerk of our Chamber, and Hugh de Neville will tell him on the king's behalf concerning the prisoners that have been delivered to him'. The content of these orders, which could not be committed to writing, is revealed in a single line in the annals of Margam Abbey in south Wales: 'twenty-two of the noblest and strongest in arms were starved to death in Corfe Castle, so that not one of them escaped'.[23]

To kill men by starvation was clearly a cruel and unusual punishment; records of similar incidents are rare. According to Ralph of Coggeshall, Richard I had condemned one of the men who had supported John's rebellion against him to such a fate, after the man in question had tried to frustrate Richard's release from prison, and professed his unshakeable devotion to John's cause.[24] John's action in 1203 was clearly on a far greater scale, and seemingly provoked by the defiant rejection of his overtures to Arthur. The men John sent to Corfe, to judge from their surnames, were from Brittany and Anjou, so the king's intention, if it had any political dimension at all, was presumably to demonstrate to Arthur's supporters in those provinces the dreadful price of their continued disloyalty.

Loyalty to John was becoming an increasingly scarce commodity. Even within Normandy, disaffection was starting to spread. Few men, it is true, had followed the count of Alençon into revolt, and he in any case was a frontier lord whose family ties linked him to Arthur's supporters in Maine and Anjou.[25] But, at the same time, few men were rallying to their duke to help him defend his remaining territories. There were, no doubt, long-term reasons for this reluctance. No one in Normandy could have forgotten John's attempt to usurp Richard's place ten years earlier, and how he had refused to help defend the duchy against Philip Augustus. But there were also more immediate reasons for the king's unpopularity. As his vassals and allies in other regions had deserted him, John had become increasingly reliant on merce-naries, even to the extent of appointing such men to positions of public authority. On 4 December 1202, the day he had departed from Chinon and abandoned Anjou for Normandy, he had appointed one of his most notorious mercenary captains, Martin Algais, as seneschal of Gascony. Another mercenary captain of equal notoriety named Louvrecaire accompanied the king north, and was given safe conduct to bring his plunder into Normandy. When John withdrew to Rouen at the start of February, Louvrecaire and his routiers remained in Falaise, from where they proceeded to terrorize the interior of the duchy, living off the land like an army of occupation. Twenty-five years later, a letter written by a burgess of Caen recalled how these men 'violated the wives of knights and laymen, and carried off their goods … if they came across a man, they stole his horse or seized his plough, and said he should look to the king for compensation'. The peaceful, well-governed heartlands of Normandy, previously untouched by war, had been given over to freebooters.[26]

For all of February and most of March, John remained in Rouen or its immediate neighbourhood. Despised by his own subjects, he distrusted them in turn, and became increasingly reluctant to travel even within Normandy. On the few occasions when he did venture out of the capital, he went accompanied by a mercenary band, and moved along minor roads taking roundabout routes, always suspecting that around the next bend an ambush might be waiting. 'A man who does not know whom he has to fear', commented *The History of William Marshal*, 'is bound to fear everybody.'[27]

Every day, says the *History*, the king saw his duchy getting worse as the result of war, and the list of defections grew. By the middle of February, he had heard the worst from Poitou: the Lusignans, despite their promises, their hostages and their surrendered castles, were once again in rebellion. In March, leading rebels from Poitou, Maine, Anjou and Brittany travelled to Paris to swear allegiance to Philip Augustus, who was evidently preparing the ground for a major assault. Among the list of names we find both Geoffrey de Lusignan and William des Roches, who had fought on opposite sides at Mirebeau just eight months earlier. It is a remarkable testament to John's political ineptitude that he had driven these former enemies to unite against him in such a short space of time.[28]

It was during these dark and desperate days that Arthur was finally killed. The manner in which he met his end is shrouded in mystery, for few chroniclers knew anything in the way of details. Roger of Wendover and Matthew Paris, for instance, who would surely have relished telling a story that blackened John's reputation, could report very little. Wendover says simply that Arthur disappeared after he was taken to Rouen. He adds, however, that later a rumour ran around all of France that John had killed him with his own hand. That was indeed the story told by the French chronicler William the Breton, who relates how the king had taken his nephew out alone one night in a boat on the Seine, run him through with a sword and thrown the body into the river.[29]

The one other place that this story occurs is in the chronicle kept at Margam Abbey. According to its anonymous author, John killed his nephew 'after dinner on the Thursday before Easter, when he was drunk and possessed by the Devil'. Afterwards he tied a heavy stone to the body and dumped it into the Seine, where it was later found by a fisherman, and taken secretly for burial in a nearby priory.[30]

The existence of two similar stories, in which the king personally kills Arthur and dumps his body into the river, recorded by
writers living so far apart, might lead us to assume that they were
independent, and that therefore their content is broadly true. In
fact, the two stories almost certainly originate from a single source:
William de Briouze.

William de Briouze was one of John's greatest subjects, a
magnate whose pedigree stretched back as far as the Norman
Conquest and beyond. His ancestral estates were at Briouze in
Normandy, but the bulk of his fortune lay in England and Wales.
His lands in Wales explain why he features so prominently in
the annals of Margam, for the abbey lay within his lordship.
Towards the end of his life Briouze ended up in France at the
court of Philip Augustus, thus explaining how he came to the
attention of William the Breton.[31]

Briouze had been a close associate of Richard I, but he became
even closer to John. Present at the time of Richard's death at
Châlus in 1199, he was, according to the Margam annals, the key
figure in persuading the rest of the old king's followers to support
John as his successor. John was certainly very generous to Briouze
at the start of his reign, rewarding him richly with lands in
England, Wales and Ireland, and Briouze in consequence stuck
close to his new master: down to 1203 no layman witnessed more
royal charters. Briouze had been with John at Mirebeau and had
been personally responsible for capturing Arthur. He was still in
the king's company the following Easter, when Arthur is said to
have died. In short, if anyone was well placed to know the truth
about what happened to Arthur, it was William de Briouze.[32]

Whether or not he told the truth is another matter. The
striking thing about William the Breton's account is the extent
to which it exonerates Briouze and makes him a voice of concern
for Arthur's welfare. In this version of the story, once they had
arrived in Rouen, Briouze declares that he will be responsible
for Arthur no longer, hands him over to John safe and sound,
and then retires to his own estates. But this last part, at least, is
demonstrably not true. From his witnessing of royal documents

we can see that Briouze was present in Rouen the whole time.[33]

Since Briouze was clearly lying about his absence, there is no good reason to believe his claim that the king personally did away with his nephew when no one else was looking. It is more likely that the decision to kill Arthur was taken by John in consultation with his closest advisers, just as we are told had been the case when the earlier order had been given to mutilate him. One of those advisers was evidently William de Briouze. Other men who were with the king at this moment, revealed in the administrative sources, included his half-brother William Longsword, and Reginald of Cornhill, later to become the scourge of the monks of Canterbury. One person in particular who stands out from the list of names is Geoffrey fitz Peter, the justiciar of England, who suddenly appears in John's presence just before the time of Arthur's murder and then disappears soon afterwards. Geoffrey's duties as justiciar (in effect, the king's regent) ordinarily detained him in England; only on one previous occasion had he crossed the Channel to consult with John. His fleeting appearance in Rouen at Easter 1203 suggests he had been summoned there to approve some especially important piece of business.[34]

If the decision to end Arthur's life was taken in committee, who actually killed him, if not King John? A century later, when everybody involved was long dead, a Yorkshire chronicler called Walter of Guisborough named the murderer as Peter de Maulay. This testimony has been previously dismissed as too late to be trustworthy, but Maulay, who lived until 1241, later became a leading baron in Yorkshire, and his principal castle at Mulgrave lay not far from Guisborough Priory. He was certainly in John's employ by the spring of 1203, and rose rapidly in the king's service thereafter. In the absence of any other evidence, he would seem to be the likeliest culprit.[35]

Who killed Arthur cannot be said with absolute certainty. That he was dead by the middle of April 1203 is amply clear. On 16 April John sent a messenger to several of his leading supporters: Hubert de Burgh, now serving as constable of Chinon; Martin Algais, the mercenary seneschal of Gascony; the seneschals of

Anjou and Poitou; the archbishop of Bordeaux; and even his elderly mother, Eleanor of Aquitaine. All these people were instructed to give credence to what the messenger, John de Valerant, would tell them about the king's affairs, which were suddenly prospering. 'By the grace of God,' says the king, 'things are going better for us than he can tell you.' The letter was witnessed by William de Briouze.[36]

In fact, as all of his southern officials could have told him, it was already the beginning of the end. Even as these letters were being drafted, Philip Augustus and his allies were invading Anjou. In mid-April the French king sailed along the Loire and seized the castle at Saumur. William des Roches and the Bretons were already advancing from the west; by the end of the month they had taken Le Mans. John's rickety administration in the region collapsed completely, cutting him off from his officials further south.[37] Philip immediately swung his army north to begin seizing castles in eastern Normandy, finding in several cases that their disillusioned keepers were ready to surrender them without a fight. By the end of the summer he was drawing up his siege engines outside the walls of Château Gaillard.

To a large extent, therefore, the death of Arthur made no difference to the loss of the Angevin Empire. It was not known about in France or Brittany when the French king and his allies unleashed what was to be their final assault in the spring of 1203, and so cannot have been a trigger for war. Of course, once that war was under way, and rumours of Arthur's murder began to circulate, they no doubt added to the resolve of John's enemies. By the autumn of 1203 Philip clearly suspected that the disturbing stories he was hearing might be true: in a charter issued that October he referred to Arthur 'if he still lives'. By the spring of 1204, once Château Gaillard had fallen, he was convinced that they were fact. When John's envoys approached him in April in a desperate attempt to forestall his advance, he told them they could have peace only if Arthur was handed over to him alive. 'He was absolutely furious about Arthur's death', says Ralph of Coggeshall, and there is even some evidence to suggest the French king may have passed sentence against John *in absentia* in his court. But this was simply to add justification to a process that was inevitable and almost complete. A few weeks later and Normandy was conquered.[38]

If Arthur's fate ultimately made little difference to the loss of the empire, it nevertheless made a crucial difference to King John. In doing away with his nephew, John had broken one of society's fundamental taboos, with dire consequences for his reputation. The decision may have been taken in committee, behind closed doors, and the deed itself done in secret. But inevitably, once Arthur had disappeared, the rumours about him began to spread, and information leaked out. In the end, everyone must have heard what had happened to him, but if they were wise they did not speak of it. Those who were obliged to hand over hostages to the king after 1203 must have done so with trepidation, knowing what extremes he was capable of. That was apparently why, five years later, the wife of William de Briouze refused to surrender her sons to his agents. Her mistake was to say publicly what had hitherto only been whispered in private.

9

The Enemy Within?

1208–1210

Illiam de Briouze was acutely aware of the potentially disastrous consequences of his wife's incautious words. 'You have spoken like a foolish woman against our lord the king', he told her, before assuring the royal messengers that he was prepared to make amends to John for whatever offence he had caused. Such at least is the story told by Roger of Wendover. The messengers, continues the chronicler, returned to the king and told him all they had heard, at which John was predictably enraged, and sent knights to seize William and his family.[1]

As we shall see, there are good reasons for supposing that the essence of Wendover's story may be true. The king did indeed demand hostages from William de Briouze in the spring of 1208 and also sent agents in pursuit of his family. Moreover he persecuted William's wife, Matilda, with a malevolence which was exceptional even by his highly competitive standards. Where Wendover erred was in assuming that the demand for hostages was the cause of the rift between the two men. In fact their quarrel had begun several months earlier, and its roots lay in Ireland.

Ireland had been left in a state of limbo ever since the death of John's older brother Geoffrey. It was Geoffrey's death in the summer of 1186, rather than the failure of John's expedition to

Ireland the previous year, that had finally put paid to Henry II's plan for his youngest son to rule there as a king in his own right. Thereafter John became simply 'lord of Ireland', a less august title which always took second place to 'count of Mortain' in his charters. While Henry lived, John exercised no meaningful authority at all there, his acts always subject to review. After his father's death he enjoyed considerably greater power, rewarding several of his followers with Irish lordships, until his wings were again clipped in 1194 with the return of an angry Richard. By the time of his accession in 1199, Ireland had become the Wild West of the British Isles — an unruly frontier where men with the right talents could carve out new lordships at sword-point, chiefly at the expense of the natives, but also on occasion at the expense of each other.[2]

During the early years of his reign, when he was preoccupied with securing and defending his inheritance on the Continent, John had little time to think about Ireland. He relied on favourite magnates to uphold his interests there, granting them extensive territories to govern more or less as they pleased, though often setting them against one another to prevent any of them becoming too powerful. Grants of land at the expense of the Irish were a useful way to reward those men who were serving him in France.[3] Thus it was at the start of 1201 that he made such a grant to William de Briouze, giving him the former Irish kingdom of Limerick.[4]

Once his continental lands were lost, however, John began paying greater attention to the remaining parts of his empire, looking to see how they might contribute to his depleted coffers, and if they could be better administered. From that point on Ireland came under greater royal scrutiny and stricter management. In the second half of 1204, for example, the king ordered the construction of a new stone castle at Dublin, intending that it should be the future seat of royal government. At the same time he made Dublin the only place in Ireland where coins could be minted, forbidding the earlier practice whereby some magnates had minted their own, and introduced to Ireland the same legal and administrative forms that applied in England.[5]

William de Briouze was among those who immediately felt this change in the direction of royal policy, when on 2 November 1204 John ordered him to return the city of Limerick. This no doubt rankled with Briouze, but in this instance he could raise little objection, for the city had been not been included in the king's original grant, and he was only holding it at John's pleasure. Worse followed in April 1206, when the king ordered his justiciar in Ireland to begin 'shiring' the south-west of the country – that is, introducing the local government structures that had long been in use in England, with a view to increasing the Crown's authority. In establishing the boundary between the lordship of Limerick and the neighbouring lordship of Cork, the king ordered the confiscation of five territories that had previously belonged to Briouze.[6]

The justiciar, Meiler fitz Henry, set about tearing Briouze down to size with a certain relish. Meiler had been one of the first Anglo-Norman settlers in Ireland, and had played a leading role in wresting Limerick from the Irish more than thirty years earlier. A cousin of Gerald of Wales, he no doubt shared the chronicler's opinion that Briouze was a latecomer and an interloper – one of those men who, in Gerald's words, 'owed their position more to luck than ability, and their success to other people's endeavours rather than their own'. In the winter of 1206–7 Meiler launched an assault on Limerick and took the whole lordship by force.[7]

Briouze himself was not in Ireland when this attack was carried out. (As far as can be seen, his only visit to Limerick had been a flying visit to take possession of the lordship in 1201.) At the start of 1207 he was evidently still in England with John, and still very much in favour. On 12 February the king wrote to Meiler fitz Henry, explaining that Briouze ('who has served us well and laudably') had complained to him about the invasion of his lands, and instructing the justiciar to make amends.[8]

But in Ireland the fighting was already spreading in all directions. Briouze may not have been present in Limerick in person but he had powerful friends to defend his interests there. Around the time he had been granted the lordship he had married his daughter, Margaret, to Walter de Lacy. Walter was the eldest son of Hugh de Lacy, the early conquistador whose ambition and success had caused so much anxiety to both Henry II and John down to his death in 1186. Despite John's initial opposition Walter had succeeded to his father's lordship in Meath, as well as other lands in England, Wales and Normandy. After his marriage to Margaret, he and Briouze had come to a reciprocal arrangement, whereby he looked after the Briouze lands in Ireland and his father-in-law did the same for the Lacy estates in England and Wales.[9]

When the justiciar had attacked Limerick in 1207 Walter had upheld his end of the bargain and struck back hard: at one point he and his tenants in Meath had besieged Meiler in one of his own castles. Walter was joined in this struggle by his younger brother, Hugh de Lacy, who as recently as 1205 had been created earl of Ulster after John had fallen out with the previous holder of the title. And by February 1207 the two brothers had been joined by William Marshal. The Marshal was the greatest of all the Anglo-Norman landowners in Ireland, thanks to his marriage in 1189 to Isabella, daughter of Richard fitz Gilbert, the conqueror of Leinster. He too had suffered losses at Meiler's hands and had come to add his weight to the resistance. By the summer of 1207 what had begun as an attempt to increase royal authority had escalated into an all-out war between the justiciar and many of Ireland's major barons.[10]

Once it became clear that the situation in Ireland was spinning out of control, and that it could not be fixed simply by sending a few more crossbowmen across the Irish Sea, John ordered the leading figures on both sides to appear before him in England. Walter de Lacy did so early in the summer and was apparently reconciled; William Marshal and Meiler fitz Henry crossed in the autumn. In November all three men and many other barons from Ireland were present in a council at the royal manor of Woodstock, during which the king laid down the law about the way the country was to be governed in future. He also used the occasion to cut the Marshal down to size, persuading several of the earl's followers to desert him by making them new grants of land.[11]

It seems very likely that William de Briouze was also present at this meeting – he witnessed royal grants on other occasions both before and after that autumn. His relationship with John, however, was hitting the rocks. (The author of *The History of William Marshal* says that Briouze was 'badly embroiled' with the king at this time.) The likely cause was the behaviour of Briouze's seneschal in Limerick, Geoffrey Marsh: on 13 November, as soon as the council had ended, John gave orders for Geoffrey to be arrested, not only for various acts of war, but also for having ignored the summons to appear before him in England. To effect this arrest the king sent Meiler fitz Henry back to Ireland, and at the same time he actively forbade the Marshal and other magnates from leaving his court. His intention was that the justiciar should win the war while his opponents were detained in England.[12]

The Marshal dutifully complied, remaining at court throughout the winter, despite the fact that no one there dared to speak to him because he was out of favour. According to *The History of William Marshal*, John's behaviour during this time was despicable. At one point early in the new year he called the earl over to him and told him with a laugh that he had received news from Ireland: many of the Marshal's men had been killed in a clash with Meiler's forces. This was untrue, and in fact John was not in a position to know anything of the sort, since no ships had been able to cross the Irish Sea during the winter months. The earl, greatly troubled by the king's false report, nevertheless responded with calmness and courtesy, pointing out that the men in question had been the king's faithful subjects.[13]

William de Briouze appears to have coped less well in the face of similar royal provocation. On 5 December John granted part of the lordship of Limerick to Walter de Lacy, a move which was presumably intended to set Briouze and his son-in-law against each other. Briouze was at court until Christmas – he witnessed a royal charter on 26 December – but must have left soon thereafter. According to the well-informed annalist at Worcester Priory, the king suspected that he had ordered Geoffrey Marsh to seize the city of Limerick and other castles in Ireland, and summoned William to answer this charge. Briouze refused, and instead went to his lands in south Wales, where he began to fortify his castles.[14]

By 20 February, with news from Ireland still lacking, John had decided to deal with the situation there himself. On that date he wrote to all the mariners of the Welsh coast, forbidding them from crossing the Irish Sea for anyone else, and instructing them to be ready to transport him and his troops on 16 March. 'If you do otherwise,' his letters concluded, 'we will have your bodies hanged, and those of the owners of your ships, and all your possessions taken for our own use without compensation.'[15]

But before these preparations had been completed, news from Ireland finally arrived. The king's justiciar, Meiler fitz Henry, had been defeated. The men of William Marshal had appealed for help to the earl of Ulster, Hugh de Lacy, who had ridden to their relief. Meiler had been taken prisoner in the fighting and forced to conclude a humiliating peace with the Marshal's wife, Countess Isabella, handing over his son as a hostage.[16]

The defeat of his justiciar forced John into a climbdown. The planned expedition to Ireland was called off, and instead the king sought to come to terms with the magnates he had been detaining and harassing. William Marshal, having behaved with calm restraint throughout the crisis, was quickly received back into royal favour; Walter de Lacy was also rehabilitated, at least in part.[17] A question mark continued to hang over Lacy because of his close connection with William de Briouze, who at this stage was still out in the cold, defiantly holed up in his Welsh castles. Efforts were clearly made to persuade him to come in. On 17 March the sheriff of Gloucester, who had evidently invaded Briouze's lands on royal orders, was told to restore one of the manors he had seized. Two days later Walter de Lacy succeeded in bringing in Briouze's eldest son, also named William, as a hostage. Other friends and relatives were at court at this time, presumably trying to intercede for the older William and arrange terms for his surrender.[18] These efforts clearly failed. By the middle of April the sheriff of Gloucester was once again advancing into Wales, this time in concert with the sheriff of Shropshire, leading what amounted to a sizeable royal army to attack Briouze's lands.[19]

These attacks were enough to persuade the former favourite to submit. On 22 or 23 April, his friends and relatives (this time including his wife, Matilda) again appeared before the king to seek terms. By this point John had arrived in Gloucester, and a few days later, when he was at Hereford, Briouze came in. He agreed to surrender three of his Welsh castles – Hay, Brecon and Radnor – and to pay 1,000 marks to the sheriff of Gloucester to compensate him for the cost of the recent expedition. He also managed to secure the release of his eldest son, but only by handing over six other hostages, including two of his grandsons. It was hardly a heart-warming reconciliation, but it nonetheless meant that the two men were at peace – for the time being.[20]

One thing that makes John's quarrel with William de Briouze especially interesting is that, as well as the usual royal administrative records and chronicle accounts, we also have the king's own version of events. In the autumn of 1210, by which point their relationship had broken down irreparably, John issued an extraordinary public letter, in which he attempted to justify his decision to go against Briouze in the spring of 1208. Unsurprisingly, he chose not to talk about the proxy war in Ireland, nor about Briouze's attempt to start a revolt in the Welsh March. In John's account, the cause of contention was not political but financial. Briouze, the king explained, had owed him a great deal of money. In return for the grant of Limerick in 1201 he had agreed to pay 5,000 marks, and was also answerable for the rent of the city of Limerick. But, alas, despite being granted reasonable terms, Briouze had not paid off any of his debt, and ignored every deadline. In the end, in order to recover his money, John had been forced to foreclose. In the king's account, the decision to order the sheriff of Gloucester into Briouze's lands in south Wales is presented as a case of sending in the bailiffs to seize goods to the value. Similarly, when William afterwards surrendered castles and hostages, these were simply guarantees that he would in future keep up with his repayments.[21]

There is nothing in John's statement that is actually untrue. Briouze had entered into a large debt for Limerick and not made any attempt to pay it off. But this was not particularly unusual. Money promised for privileges or permissions was almost never paid up front. Men who offered hundreds or even thousands of pounds to have a certain piece of land, or to be sheriff of a particular county; women who offered similar sums for the wardship of their children, or for the right to marry where they chose – all expected to pay off these debts over a number of years. Moreover, some individuals, if they were sufficiently close to the king, or sufficiently powerful that he relied on their political support, might expect never to have to pay anything. William de Briouze seems to have been trading on precisely this assumption. After all, Henry II had taken a very relaxed attitude towards the debts of his magnates, and so too had Richard I.[22]

It was during John's reign that the time-honoured assumption that great men need not worry unduly about their debts to the Crown was disproved. A first sign of change came in 1201 with an amendment to the law, which allowed the king to seize land from a debtor if the land was connected to their debt. It was not until 1207, however, that we start to see this more aggressive attitude being applied in practice. The king's chief financial office, in existence since at least the time of Henry I, was the Exchequer – its name derived from the large chequered cloth, laid out on a table, upon which debts were computed using counters, rather like an abacus. It was here that royal officials and Crown debtors would come to render their accounts, subject to the searching examination of the so-called 'barons of the Exchequer'. From 1207 we can detect a new degree of rigour in the way these men treated magnate debts. Previously, for example, it had been hard for the Exchequer to be sure precisely how much a magnate owed, because debts were enrolled on a county-by-county basis, and great men invariably had estates scattered all over the country. From 1207, however, it became increasingly common for Exchequer officials to group all the debts of a particular magnate together, so that the extent of his liability could be seen in an instant. Roger de Montbegon, the northern baron who had fallen under suspicion in 1204 and surrendered hostages to the king in 1205, was among the first to have his debts treated in this way.[23]

Others actually had their debts called in. Thomas de Moulton had become sheriff of Lincoln in 1205 after promising to give the king 500 marks and five palfreys. But by the spring of 1208 he had fallen behind with his payments, and the Exchequer decided to come down hard on him. Deprived of office in May, he was later arrested on the king's orders and imprisoned in Rochester Castle, 'so that he may not leave until he has paid us everything he owes us, to the last penny'.[24] A similar unremitting attitude was in evidence during the summer of 1208 when John visited northern England. The bishop of Durham had died earlier in the year, and the king had apparently travelled north to ensure that the confiscated episcopal estates were being administered efficiently. This may explain why on leaving Durham he travelled west into Cumbria for an interview with Robert de Vieuxpont. Like William de Briouze, Vieuxpont was a dependable henchman who had served John loyally in Normandy down to his departure in 1203 and who had been richly rewarded as a result, receiving a barony in Cumbria, where he was investing considerable sums in rebuilding castles at Brougham and Brough. He had also been given wide-ranging responsibilities in the north, serving as sheriff of both Derby and Nottingham, and acting as custodian of the confiscated bishoprics of York and Durham. At some point in 1208, however, probably during the king's visit, he lost John's favour; later in the year, he was able to regain it by promising to pay 4,000 marks and surrendering a nephew as a hostage. As with both Briouze and Moulton, the official cause of the king's displeasure was debt: Vieuxpont and his deputies had apparently not paid as much into the Exchequer as had been expected. But it is tempting to suspect that, as with Briouze, there were other reasons. Vieuxpont had been keeper of Rouen Castle at the time of Arthur's disappearance.[25]

The essential point is that the workings of the Exchequer were far from being impartial or impersonal. In his self-defensive letter of 1210 John declared that Briouze's possessions had been seized 'according to the custom of England and the law of the Exchequer', as if to imply that these were automatic processes, the law following its due course. In fact the opposite was true: the law of the Exchequer, like the law of the Forest, was highly whimsical. The barons of the Exchequer might follow certain routines and procedures, and would always endeavour to maximize the Crown's revenue. But it was the king who ultimately controlled the collection of debt. He could tell the Exchequer to relax its demands or distrain an individual with particular harshness; he could choose to cancel a debt entirely or call it all in at once; he could require fines that were token or extortionate, and set repayment terms that were lenient or punitive. John had not only changed the law on debt to make the property of debtors vulnerable as never before; he had also decided from 1207–8 to enforce it ruthlessly, using fiscal measures as a way of exerting political control.[26]

In order to administer such control, the king required the right sort of personnel. If there was one person apart from John himself who was supplying the new and exacting tone in royal government, it was Peter des Roches. Peter was a native of Anjou (or, more specifically, the Touraine), a scion of the same knightly dynasty that had produced William des Roches. But whereas William had ultimately abandoned John because of his treatment of Arthur, Peter had remained in the king's service to become his most indispensable counsellor. Trained as a clerk in his youth, he had also picked up other useful skills along the way; according to Roger of Wendover he was more practised at besieging castles than preaching the word of God. Nonetheless, royal favour marked him out for ecclesiastical preferment, and in 1204 John nominated him as the new bishop of Winchester (in the face of opposition from some of the local clergy, which delayed his enthronement until 1206). From this point on he was clearly associated with the king's financial policies. 'The warrior of Winchester, up at the Exchequer / Keen on finance, slack at scripture', ran a contemporary satirical poem. It was, however, another financial institution, the Chamber, that des Roches made his own. The Chamber was the department of the royal household responsible for the king's personal finances. Unlike the Exchequer, which sat permanently at Westminster, it travelled with the king wherever he went, paying for his immediate needs, whether domestic (food, wine, clothes) or military (crossbows, mercenaries, siege engines). One of des Roches' innovations, carried through in the summer of 1207, had been to create new regional treasuries in castles such as Bristol, Corfe, Marlborough and Nottingham, where money could be stored and collected by the Chamber, bypassing the slower, more cumbersome processes of the Exchequer. It was the kind of hand-to-mouth, quasi-military system he had operated for the king on the Continent until the collapse of 1204.[27]

To run such a system required a more traditional type of sheriff. The earlier experiment of having 'custodian' sheriffs, carefully accounting for every penny of profit at the Exchequer, was largely abandoned during the financial year 1207–8. Instead, John began to appoint tough enforcers, allowing them once again to keep the profits of their office, provided they also kept order. Several of these men had previously served as military captains on the Continent. Hubert de Burgh, who had reportedly ignored the king's order to blind Arthur in 1202, had nevertheless been appointed as keeper of Chinon Castle, and had been captured in 1205 when the fortress finally fell to Philip Augustus. In 1207 John eventually got round to paying his ransom and the following year Hubert replaced Thomas de Moulton as sheriff of Lincoln. Another military captain and mercenary leader, Gerard d'Athée, had been commander of the garrison at Loches until that castle was taken in 1205. John brought him to England in the autumn of 1207 and appointed him as sheriff of Gloucester at the start of the following year, in which capacity he led the attacks on

William de Briouze. After Briouze's submission Athée was also appointed as sheriff of Hereford, making him the most powerful individual in the Welsh March. He took his name from Athée-sur-Cher, just outside Tours, and had close connections with that other man from the same region, Peter des Roches. A number of men, with the same connections of family and neighbourhood, followed in their wake. Later in 1208, one of Athée's relatives, Philip Marc, became sheriff of Nottingham and Derby, replacing Robert de Vieuxpont.[28]

If John was cracking down on debt as a way of exerting political control, it was still the case that he needed vast sums of money. The two-year truce he had agreed with Philip Augustus in 1206 was set to expire on 13 October, and John fully intended to be back in France to resume the military struggle. No sooner had he abandoned his plan to sail to Ireland in March 1208 than he was issuing new orders, instructing the men of all maritime districts to have their ships ready to sail from Portsmouth on 1 June. As before, any vessels that were not provided voluntarily were to be seized, and dire consequences were threatened for those who disobeyed. But despite these threats, the results were evidently disappointing, for when the king arrived in Portsmouth at the end of May no departure took place. It was probably at this stage, angry at the inadequacy of preparation, that he ordered severe reprisals against the men of the Cinque Ports. Gervase of Canterbury, well placed to know, describes how the king 'hanged some of them, and put others to the sword, imprisoned many, bound them in irons, and eventually released them only in return for pledges and money'. This last part, at least, can be verified, for the Cinque Ports did indeed make a fine of 1,000 marks for the king's goodwill. Fresh orders were given for a new muster in September, and throughout the summer, while John took himself off to northern England, his officials strained every sinew to find him the necessary fleet and crews. But, once again, his plans went awry. On 16 September, just five days before the muster date, the king suddenly ordered some of the ships at Portsmouth to redeploy.[29]

The reason was a fresh rebellion by William de Briouze. According to John's later propaganda letter – our only source – Briouze and two of his sons, William and Reginald, had gathered a large force of men and tried to retake Radnor, Brecon and Hay, the three castles he had surrendered to the king in April. Their attack was apparently well timed – the constables had gone to collect their salaries from their commander, Gerard d'Athée – but nevertheless unsuccessful. Having failed to take the castles they went on to attack the royal garrison in nearby Leominster, killing some of the crossbowmen and sergeants, wounding many others, and burning half the town to the ground.

Briouze's rebellion was a total failure. As soon as Gerard d'Athée heard the news he launched an immediate and overwhelming counteroffensive; within days Briouze's men were deserting him and pledging their allegiance to the king. Briouze himself was soon a fugitive, 'retreating from one place to the next', and by the end of September, barely a fortnight after his abortive attempt to recover his castles, he had run out of places to hide. Gathering up his wife, sons and his few remaining followers, he fled to Ireland.[30]

Briouze's short-lived revolt did not by itself unduly disrupt John's plans for France. When the news had broken he had ordered most of the ships to remain in Portsmouth and await his arrival. The unsuccessful rebellion did, however, set off a chain reaction of events elsewhere in Wales that would have far greater consequences. As soon as Briouze had revolted, John had given his lands in Brecon to another of his intimate counsellors, Peter fitz Herbert. Fitz Herbert had barely had time to take possession of his prize, however, before these lands came under attack from the Welsh.[31]

Beyond the marcher lordships that lay along its southern and eastern edges, Wales was still an independent, Celtic country. Like Ireland it had no single ruler, but a galaxy of petty kings and princes, all competing with one another as well as their Anglo-Norman neighbours. One of these princes, Gwenwynwyn of Powys, had long been a rival of William de Briouze, and saw in his opponent's fall the opportunity to expand his power. As soon as Briouze faltered, Gwenwynwyn moved into his lordship of Brecon, where he immediately came to blows with the new owner, Peter fitz Herbert.

It was this fresh contest in the March that caused John to abandon his plans for the Continent. On 29 September he gave permission to all his knights and bachelors to assist fitz Herbert in defending his lands. A day or so later he decided to follow in their wake, moving rapidly from Dorset towards the Welsh border. Confronted with a furious John and the forces he had been planning to lead into France, Gwenwynwyn quickly submitted, and appeared before the king at Shrewsbury on 8 October. The terms he received were terrible. In return for the king sparing his life and limbs, the prince was required to find twenty hostages, and obliged to remain in royal custody until all of them had been handed over. The hostages only bought Gwenwynwyn his liberty; all of his lands were confiscated.[32]

His expedition to France now dead in the water, John left the Welsh border and travelled along the Thames towards Westminster, arriving there in the last week of October. But during the rest of the autumn the fallout from the Briouze revolt continued. Just as the eclipse of Briouze had enticed Gwenwynwyn, so too the fall of Gwenwynwyn had created an irresistible temptation for his neighbour. Llywelyn, the prince of the northern region of Gwynedd, was easily the most successful of all the native rulers of Wales, thanks to a winning combination of military ability, pragmatism and luck. Having established his right to rule Gwynedd in the 1190s by fighting off rivals within his own family, he cemented his position by striking up a good relationship with John. At the start of his reign John had recognized Llywelyn's rights and taken him into his protection, and in 1205 the prince had been married to the king's illegitimate daughter, Joan. This was a singular honour for a Welsh ruler, and it had clearly marked Llywelyn out as John's favourite.[33]

But when, towards the end of 1208, the prince invaded Powys, lately vacated by Gwenwynwyn, he soon discovered that his father-in-law's favour had its limits. At first John seemed to take an indulgent line. On Christmas Day he sent a letter to Llywelyn, assuring him that he had forgiven the prince his recent trespasses, and continued to regard him with fatherly affection. One month later, however, the king was back at Shrewsbury, at the head of a large army, poised to invade Llywelyn's lands. Whether the prince had committed some new offence in the meantime, or whether John had simply been dissimulating at Christmas, is unclear. But Llywelyn, like Gwenwynwyn, rapidly submitted. The terms he received are unknown, but were clearly far better than imposed on his rival the previous October. Llywelyn was left at liberty, and in possession of all his lands, including his recent conquests.[34]

Thus, by the end of January 1209, Wales was finally settled, bringing to an end a turbulent five months. The king's plan to return to the Continent had been wrecked, but by the start of the new year it was apparent that his overseas subjects were coping in spite of his absence. When the truce with France had expired in October, Philip Augustus had launched an attack on John's ally, the viscount of Thouars, but soon into the campaign the French king had fallen ill and been forced to retire to Paris. Although his deputies continued the fighting, they made no substantial gains and the territorial status quo held. Philip was in any case distracted by problems elsewhere in France: a rebellion in Auvergne, and, in the Languedoc, the murder of a papal legate by Cathar heretics. The latter had led to pressure from the pope, who wanted him to crush the heretics by leading a crusade.[35]

By the start of 1209 it was the pope, rather than the king of France, who seemed to pose the greater threat to John's security. Innocent's reaction to the seizure of Church property carried out the previous year had been surprisingly muted. He was convinced that the interdict would soon persuade John to change his mind about the archbishop of Canterbury, and encouraged by the exchange of messengers that had continued throughout the summer. These negotiations, however, had petered out in the autumn, and by the new year the pope had realized that his strategy was not going to work: his adversary was quite content to let matters rest, and in the meantime enjoy the massive contribution that the Church's confiscated property was making to his revenues. On 12 January he dispatched an uncompromising letter to John, threatening him with excommunication. The king would be 'accursed and cut off from the community of the faithful' if he did not agree to the terms proposed the previous year. Innocent informed John that he had three months to comply, and made it clear that this was his final warning. 'Look, the bow is at full stretch', he wrote. 'Beloved son, avoid the arrow which turns not back!'[36]

The king had to take this escalation seriously. As we've seen, even before the interdict had been imposed, Innocent had written to the nobles of England, urging them to set aside their loyalty to John until he made peace with the Church. The king might have taken that less seriously had he not in the meantime had his plans disrupted by the rebellion of one of his greatest subjects – a man who was still at large in Ireland. How much easier it would be for others to justify such rebellion were he to be excommunicated. Moreover, the pope was already trying to persuade Philip Augustus to crush the Church's enemies in southern France by launching a crusade against them. If he suddenly licensed a similar attack on England, Philip, who had already planned to invade England in 1205, might need little persuading. Such considerations meant that Innocent's letter had to be answered, and John had to be seen to act. Accordingly, just before Easter, he reopened negotiations, and issued letters of safe conduct for Master Simon Langton, brother of the unwanted archbishop.[37]

A few days later, the king's attention was suddenly focused elsewhere. On 10 April he wrote to William the Lion, the king of Scots, asking for a meeting. This was somewhat unusual, because for many years John had shown little interest in attending to the concerns of his northern neighbour. Having obtained William's homage, very publicly, at Lincoln in 1200, John had repeatedly postponed or ignored the Scottish king's plea to hear his claim to Northumbria. In the intervening eight years they had met only twice, with inconclusive results.

In the spring of 1209, by contrast, John went out of his way to meet William. Previously the onus had been on the Scottish king to come south, for meetings at York, Lincoln or even Northampton. But when John wrote on 10 April he was already about to enter Yorkshire, and proposing to come as far north as Newcastle. The tone of his letter was friendly and accommodating. He rejoiced that William (who was in his mid-sixties) had recovered from his recent illness, and expressed a desire to conclude their long-running dispute. No wonder the Scottish king, in spite of his infirmities, responded eagerly. The two kings met at Newcastle a fortnight later, with unknown but apparently amicable results, and evidently some sort of settlement plan. William returned to Scotland and summoned a council of his leading subjects to approve it. They met on 24 May at Stirling, and dispatched a high-ranking embassy into England with their reply.

But when these ambassadors reached John's court they found him in a very different mood, thundering threats against the king of Scots and Scotland in general. What had changed? The answer seems to be that since their meeting in April John had discovered that William had allied, or attempted to ally, with Philip Augustus, just as he had tried to do at the start of John's reign. It seems very likely that John had suspected this was the case all along, and that his sudden desire to meet with William after Easter had in fact been an attempt to sniff out the conspiracy. If so, his suspicions had clearly been confirmed in the month that followed: the moment of truth may have come on 28 May, when the king, then at Arundel Castle in Sussex, paid half a mark to 'Fulcher, a secret messenger who came from overseas'.

The substance of the allegation is given further proof by John's reaction. According to Gervase of Canterbury, he demanded that William should surrender either his son, Alexander, or three castles on the Scottish border. When William refused, John threatened war, and summoned an army to invade. In the last week of July he marched north from Nottingham, leading what one contemporary called 'an innumerable army'. The Scottish king, who had been sending messages to play for time, assembled a force to resist the invasion at Roxburgh, but once again fell ill. When John drew up his host on the border at Norham at the start of August, William immediately submitted. He was forced to accept a humiliating peace, the outstanding feature of which was that it required him to hand over his two eldest daughters, Margaret and Isabella, to John's custody. Both girls were in their mid-teens and unmarried. John announced that he would marry Margaret to his own son, Henry, and find Isabella a husband of appropriate status from among the English nobility. The point was clearly for John to control the marriages, from which we can reasonably conclude that the plot he had uncovered involved one or other of the girls marrying Philip Augustus. As an additional security measure, William was obliged to hand over a further thirteen hostages, and promised to pay 15,000 marks within the next two years. This peace was imposed, according to one chronicler, 'against the will of the Scots'.[38]

Scotland may have been solved, but the problem of the pope remained. The talks proposed in March had come to nothing, but on 13 July, just days before setting out against the Scots, John had suddenly become earnest about reaching a settlement. He cannot have known by this date that, three weeks earlier, Innocent had authorized his excommunication at Stephen Langton's discretion. There may therefore be some truth in the comment of Gervase of Canterbury, who claims that the king's resumption of negotiations had been caused by murmurings in the ranks of his army about the perils of marching into battle against the Scots while England was under interdict. As everyone knew, it was God who determined the outcome of battles.[39]

Even as John was browbeating William the Lion into submission at Norham, therefore, his leading ministers were meeting with the pope's representatives at Dover, trying to hammer out an acceptable agreement. By 9 August they had drafted a set of terms. Stephen Langton was to be admitted to England and installed as archbishop of Canterbury; the monks of Canterbury, driven into exile in 1207, were to be allowed to return; and the Church as a whole was to be compensated for its financial losses, with the money paid by the end of the month.⁴⁰

Once the Scottish king had submitted, however, and with no dissenting soldiery in need of appeasement, John's enthusiasm for a settlement started to wane. When these terms were brought to him on his journey south from Scotland, he found them unsatisfactory, and immediately began to stall. On 23 August he wrote to the envoys at Dover, inviting them to come to Northampton for further talks. But the envoys doubted the value of his safe conducts, and feared they would be seized if they ventured inland. On 2 September they issued their ultimatum. The king must accept the terms as drafted by 23 September, or face excommunication a fortnight later.⁴¹

John's response was to take countermeasures of a kind never before witnessed in England. Although he no longer faced the pressing problem of desertion, his fear remained that if he was excommunicated Innocent might absolve his subjects from their loyalty, or even seek to sponsor an invasion. When he heard that the Church's sentence was imminent, he left the Midlands and went directly to Marlborough, his chief castle in southern England. From there on 13 September he wrote to Stephen Langton himself, inviting him to come to Dover for a personal interview. But this was merely a tactic to buy time for his actual response.

On the same day, dozens of other letters were dispatched to every sheriff in England, from Kent to Cumbria, advising them of his intention of taking a new general oath of loyalty. John had, of course, exacted such an oath before, in 1205, when he had been worried about a French invasion and internal dissension. When these anxieties returned to haunt him in 1209, however, he conceived of something bigger and altogether more powerful: a mass assembly, where his subjects would pledge their allegiance to him in person, against the backdrop of one of his most impressive castles. At the end of September, according to Gervase of Canterbury, 'all the men in England, rich and poor and middling, aged fifteen and upwards, came together at Marlborough on the king's orders, and there they swore fealty, both to the king and to his son, Henry'. The comments of other chroniclers indicate that John's summons actually applied only to freemen, and that some of them were permitted to take their oaths locally. But if Gervase was guilty of exaggerating, it was with good reason. Other evidence makes it clear that freemen came to Marlborough in vast numbers: thousands, and perhaps tens of thousands. The king seems to have required in particular the presence of townsmen, especially the men of London, almost all of whom are said to have attended. Later entries on the Exchequer rolls show that draconian fines were imposed for those who failed to do so.[42]

The reason for insisting on this mass migration was John's desire to forge a stronger bond with his subjects. Although Gervase speaks only of fealty – i.e. a promise of fidelity – other writers make it clear that the king additionally required those who came to Marlborough to do homage – to kneel down before him and declare that they were his men, regardless of the fact that they might not hold their lands from him (which was what an act of homage ordinarily implied). This, along with the pledge of allegiance to John's two-year-old son and heir, and the uniquely massive scale of the gathering, made the Oath of Marlborough an unprecedented event, and one which would never be repeated. It was a ceremonial, charismatic rejoinder to the spiritual authority of the pope; a reminder of the awesome, mystical power of the monarchy.[43]

A few days after this extraordinary spectacle, Stephen Langton arrived at Dover, as invited. The king, informed of his arrival, travelled to Kent, and stopped at Chilham Castle, not far from Canterbury, from where the two sides could easily communicate. But although they came physically close, no meeting took place. Gervase opined that John's mind had been changed by 'the tongues of evil detractors', but the truth was that on both sides, minds were already made up, and wedded to irreconcilable positions. The king wanted a guarantee of his rights and dignity, the pope required unconditional surrender. Having just taken elaborate steps to buttress his power, John saw no reason to compromise. He turned and left for London, leaving Langton to sail back to France, with inevitable consequences. One month later, the king was excommunicated.[44]

John successfully prevented an official proclamation of the sentence in England, but the news inevitably found its way across the Channel. It quickly became common knowledge – the subject, according to Roger of Wendover, of secret conversation everywhere. And yet, although it compounded the king's notoriety, the consequences of being cursed by the Church were far less disastrous than he had feared. There was no rebellion and no foreign invasion; the pope did not declare him deposed. The only immediate effect of his excommunication was the removal of the remaining members of the episcopate. In the final weeks of the year, the bishops of Bath, Lincoln, Rochester and Salisbury left the country, joining their colleagues from Worcester, Ely and London who had left at the start of the interdict. By Christmas, the only remaining bishop in England was 'the warrior of Winchester', Peter des Roches, singularly unperturbed by his master's pariah status. For John, of course, the departure of the other prelates had one very positive consequence, as their confiscated estates further swelled his revenues.[45]

To his critics John seemed all powerful, invulnerable. 'There was no one in the land who could resist his will in anything', said Gervase of Canterbury, commenting on the flight of the bishops. 'The king himself was the only power in the land, and feared neither God nor men.' Roger of Wendover, with more bitterness, observed that the laity seemed unperturbed by John's excommunication. When he celebrated Christmas at Windsor a few weeks later, 'all the nobles of England were present and conversing with him, notwithstanding the sentence under which he was bound'.[46]

But neither chronicler was entirely correct. There were several men who were *not* present at John's court that Christmas – men he had good reason to fear. One was William Marshal, who was in Ireland, having returned there soon after his reconciliation with the king in 1208, though not before being required to hand over one of his sons as a hostage.[47] Another was Walter de Lacy, who had also returned to Ireland, to join his brother Hugh, the earl of Ulster, who had never left. And, of course, there was William de Briouze, the cause of so much disruption during 1208, down but not out. He too was in Ireland, having fled there after his abortive rebellion that autumn.

In the aftermath of Briouze's revolt, the king had spent much time and energy imposing his will on England, Scotland and Wales. The king of Scots had surrendered his daughters to stave off invasion, and his son, Alexander, had done homage to John soon afterwards. The princes of Wales – those who had not been broken – had come to do homage to him en masse at Woodstock in mid-October 1209, just as men from all over England had done at Marlborough a fortnight earlier. In every part of mainland Britain, people had been forcefully and dramatically reminded of the extent of the king of England's power. Only in Ireland did men continue to resist him, convinced that they were beyond his reach.[48]

John had tried the soft approach. In the winter of 1208–9, not long after Briouze's flight, he had appointed a new justiciar of Ireland, replacing the discredited Meiler fitz Henry with John de Gray, the dependable bishop of Norwich (for whom it was a convenient posting, since the interdict did not extend across the Irish Sea). Gray had tried to apprehend Briouze, but discovered the fugitive and his family were being sheltered by their friends and relatives, first by William Marshal, later by Walter and Hugh de Lacy. Against these powerful magnates, the authority of the justiciar was no match, and they rejected his demands to hand over Briouze. The king himself, according to his own account, sent messages to them, reminding them of their fealty, and telling them they ought not to be harbouring his enemies. All he received was a procrastinating reply, saying that they would cease to shelter Briouze if he did not make amends by a certain date. The deadline came and went, but the promise was not kept.[49]

This was, it seems, more than just passive resistance. The Lacy brothers, at least, were actively plotting to bring John down. A letter survives from Philip Augustus, addressed to one of the brothers, referring to the war they were planning to wage against their king with the help of friends in both England and Ireland. It is unclear whether this plot was linked to the secret negotiations between Philip and the king of Scots that John discovered in the spring of 1209. It is also unclear whether or not John himself ever became aware of it. What is certain is that by the end of the year he had lost patience with his defiant Irish magnates and decided to deal with them in person. 'We could not tolerate their many outrages,' he explained in his letter, 'and assembled an army to go into Ireland.'[50]

Financial preparations for the campaign were already under way by the start of the new year. John had demanded another scutage in 1209 – the eighth of his reign – and by 1210 was busy calling it in, imposing exceptionally heavy fines on those who chose not to supply him with military service, and seizing the lands of those who could not pay. He also imposed an arbitrary tax, known as tallage, on all towns and royal manors, as well as the confiscated estates of the Church, again with exceptional results: Bristol and Colchester, for example, each paid 1,000 marks. During the first four months of the year the king tore around the country at his usual frantic pace, moving from Dorset to Durham and back in his quest for more cash. Another new regional treasury, operational by early February, was created at Northampton to collect it all, and in April its contents were transferred to Bristol. John arrived there in the middle of May, before proceeding through south Wales to reach the coast of Pembrokeshire at the end of the month, anxious to see what his millions of silver pennies had achieved.[51]

For once he was not disappointed. All the evidence suggests that the force that had been mustered near Haverford was massive. A surviving payroll reveals that there were more than 1,000 sergeants and crossbowmen, as well as 800 mounted knights. And these were merely the men who had agreed to serve for wages.

A great many more must have turned out to fulfil their customary military service to the king, swelling his army to many thousands. In anticipation of siege warfare, he had recruited miners, masons, ditchers and carpenters. Hundreds of tonnes of food and drink had been stockpiled to feed them, and hundreds more tonnes of grain to feed their horses. The total scale of the operation is perhaps best conveyed by the fact that John had 700 ships: a fleet equivalent in size to the one used by William the Conqueror to invade England in 1066.[52]

News of this inexorable military build-up found its way to Ireland and caused certain people to reconsider their positions. At some point in the spring William Marshal (whose first loyalty was always to himself) crossed to England and made his peace with the king, agreeing to join the expedition when it sailed. William de Briouze also sought safe conduct to come and treat for peace, but (according to John's account) once it was granted he went to Herefordshire and again tried to raise a revolt. When the king was on 'the shore of the Irish Sea at Pembroke', Briouze sought licence to negotiate for a second time, and drew near enough to communicate via intermediaries. He apparently offered the gargantuan sum of 40,000 marks to regain John's goodwill, to which the king replied that he 'knew well that this was beyond his capacity, but more within that of his wife'. John suggested that William should join his imminent expedition so they could discuss the matter with Matilda and reach an agreement. William, who clearly had a more realistic understanding about what John's coming to Ireland would entail, declined the invitation and withdrew to his refuge in Wales.[53]

The great armada sailed from Haverford on 19 June 1210 and landed near Waterford the following morning, just as its smaller predecessor had done when John had crossed to Ireland twenty-five years earlier. The king was immediately joined by his justiciar, John de Gray, leading a force of Irish friendlies, and other Irish lords who appeared to offer their submission. The royal army advanced through the Marshal lordship of Leinster, stopping at the Marshal's castle in Kilkenny, and arriving in Dublin by the end of the first week. There, on 28 June, messengers arrived from Walter de Lacy, offering their lord's submission and seeking to blame the situation on his brother, Hugh. John responded by banishing Walter, who may have left the country at that moment, and advancing into his lordship of Meath, seizing all his castles (including the mighty donjon at Trim) for the Crown, and confiscating all his lands, some of which were granted out to the king's followers.[54]

The remaining target was Hugh de Lacy, who was sheltering Matilda de Briouze and her family. When he realized that John was moving northwards into his territory, Hugh burnt some of his castles and retreated. The king pursued him, taking other castles with ease as their garrisons gave up without a fight. Eventually John arrived at Carrickfergus, the greatest and most impressive of all the Lacy strongholds, where the earl's diehard supporters had holed up in the hope of making a stand. The castle fell after a short siege and all inside were taken prisoner, but neither Hugh nor Matilda were among them. They had fled across the sea, first to the Isle of Man, where they were pursued by John's forces, and then quickly on to Galloway in south-west Scotland. The earl managed to evade capture, along with Briouze's son Reginald, and eventually made his way to France, where he was reunited with his exiled brother Walter.

But the rest of the fugitives were not so lucky. Matilda and her daughter Annora, together with William de Briouze the younger and his wife and children, were all arrested by Duncan of Carrick, a local Scottish lord, descended from a bastard line of Henry I and later richly rewarded for his service with lands in Ireland. His delighted second cousin dispatched two ships and a force of crossbowmen and sergeants to escort them back to Carrickfergus.[55]

Having driven the Lacy brothers into exile and captured most of the family of William de Briouze, John's main objectives in coming to Ireland had been achieved. He returned south to Dublin, taking more castles and receiving more submissions as he went, arriving in the capital on 18 August. One week later, and barely two months after his arrival, he sailed back across the Irish Sea to Wales.[56]

With him sailed his unfortunate captives, Matilda de Briouze and her family, who were taken to Bristol Castle and imprisoned. According to the Anonymous of Béthune, a very well-informed source for these events, Matilda was a formidable woman, well liked by everyone, who was not only beautiful but also valiant, vigorous and wise. As the wife of a marcher lord she had kept up the war against the Welsh and conquered much from them. On one occasion she had boasted to the count of Aumale that she owned more than 12,000 cows. In her negotiations with John, however, she seems to have veered between defiance and despair. According to the king's own account, she had initially offered him 40,000 marks to spare the lives of her husband, her family and herself, only to change her mind three days later. But by the time they were back in England she had changed her mind again, and upped her offer by 10,000 marks, agreeing that this extra amount would be paid immediately, and accepting that she and her family would remain in prison until the whole debt of 50,000 marks had been cleared. Having sealed this diabolical pact with the king, she sought permission to speak with her husband.

William de Briouze came in. While John had been in Ireland he had attempted to raise a revolt for the third time, but with pitifully feeble results. With his wife, son and grandchildren now held captive, he agreed to pay the fine as agreed, and was allowed to leave the court in order to begin raising the money. This was, of course, an utterly impossible task – 50,000 marks was a figure equivalent to John's ordinary annual revenue from the whole kingdom. After a while William managed to give his escort the slip and fled across the Channel to France.

When the king sent several leading magnates to tell Matilda what had happened, her old defiance returned. She replied curtly that she would pay nothing of the fine, since all she had left was twenty-four marks of silver, twenty-four gold coins and fifteen ounces of gold. 'So neither then nor afterwards did she, her husband, or anyone else on their behalf, pay me anything of the debt', said John, concluding his lengthy account of the whole sorry saga, hopeful that his subjects would share his indignation, and adding that he had ordered William de Briouze to be outlawed in every shire, 'according to the laws and custom of England'.

What he did not mention was the fate of William's indomitable wife. Matilda, along with her eldest son, William, was removed from Bristol and taken to another royal castle – some chroniclers say Windsor, others Corfe. All agree that once they were there, the two of them were starved to death. According to the Anonymous of Béthune:

> On the eleventh day the mother was found dead between her son's legs, still upright but leaning back against her son's chest as a dead woman. The son, who was also dead, sat upright, leaning against the wall as a dead man. So desperate was the mother that she had eaten her son's cheeks. When William de Briouze, who was in Paris, heard this news, he died soon afterwards, many asserting that it was through grief.[57]

10

Tyrannical Will

1210–1212

The horrific death of Matilda de Briouze and her eldest son clearly dealt a deeply damaging blow to John's already battered reputation. News of their starvation spread through the country in the autumn of 1210 and was eventually reported in almost every chronicle. The king's decision to put out his own version of events, 'so that there should be an authoritative statement of the truth', shows he was anxious to try to combat this negative public reaction. The fact that he felt it necessary to persuade seven earls and seven barons to add their seals to the bottom of the document serves only to illustrate how far his own credibility had collapsed.[1]

But if John was concerned about his popularity, it was only to a very limited degree, for his propaganda efforts were accompanied by no change in policy. Far from it. His expedition to Ireland in the summer, unlike his first youthful adventure there, had been a storming success. His enemies among the Anglo-Norman baronage had been driven into exile or compelled to accept humiliating new terms. New English laws and regulations had been introduced, and most of the native Irish had rushed to acknowledge him. A couple of chieftains, it is true, had refused to hand over their sons as hostages, but military pressure from the Dublin government would persuade one of them to change his mind before the end of the year. The campaign had left John vastly more powerful in Ireland than before. 'Many hoped that because of this victory the king would make amends for the bad deeds he had done towards the Church of God and would correct his errors', said Gervase of Canterbury. 'But', he added, 'a new anger inflamed him.'[2]

The first to feel the force of this anger were the Jews. They had arrived in England soon after the Norman Conquest, initially settling in London, then dispersing to other towns and cities in the decades that followed. In the second half of the twelfth century, after the Church had forbidden the practice to Christians, they cornered the market in moneylending. The Crown in particular found their services useful, and extended its protection to them, but at the price of exploitation. By the middle of Henry II's reign, all Jews were regarded as the king's property, liable to be tallaged whenever he felt the financial need. Royal protection, however, was worth having for a minority community, only a few thousand in number, living among a deeply anti-Semitic population. The crusading fervour whipped up at the start of Richard I's reign had led to violent attacks on the Jews in London on the day of his coronation, and pogroms against provincial Jewish communities in the months after his departure. These had culminated in March 1190, when the Jews of York, besieged in the city's castle, committed mass suicide rather than face death at the hands of the surrounding mob.[3]

John had begun his reign by extending his protection to the Jews, albeit at a hefty premium: in 1201 the community offered him 4,000 marks for a charter that guaranteed their right to 'go anywhere they wished with all their possessions, as our property'. Two years later, presumably after some infringement, he reminded the mayor of London that violence against 'his property' would not be tolerated. 'If we had given our peace to a dog,' he wrote, 'it ought to be inviolably observed.'[4]

But in 1207, when the king began to increase his demands for money across the board, he sought new ways to extract profit from his Jewish subjects. That year they were hit twice, first with a tallage of 4,000 marks, and secondly with a demand for one-tenth of the value of all their loans. How much this second measure raised is unknown, but its impact was felt not only by the Jews but also their Christian clients, some of whom suddenly found their debts were now owed to the Exchequer. This was also true of Christians who had run up debts to Jewish lenders who were long deceased, for on the death of a Jew his loans, like his other assets, automatically became the property of the king. Many such ancient debts had sat on the Exchequer's rolls for years, but from 1207 the king's officials suddenly began calling them in, demanding swift repayment on pain of disinheritance.[5]

In 1210 the king threw all restraint to the wind. Probably in September that year, immediately after his return from Ireland, he ordered the arrest of all Jews, male and female, along with all their financial records. The leading members of the community seem to have been summoned to Bristol and charged in the king's own presence with attempting to conceal the scale of their assets three years earlier, thus depriving him of revenue. The price of redeeming his good favour, their confiscated goods, and indeed their lives, was set devastatingly high: a tallage of £44,000 was demanded. Not all were able or willing to contribute, at least at first. Wendover tells the horror story of an unnamed Jew of Bristol who had a tooth knocked out every day until he agreed to pay up. Certainly several of the most prominent Jewish lenders were made to suffer: Isaac of Canterbury was hanged, and Isaac of Norwich regained the king's favour only after promising to pay 10,000 marks. Even the poorest Jews were required to find at least forty shillings each or else to leave the kingdom, a desperate option that many must have been forced to take. John's so-called 'Bristol tallage' dealt the Jewish community in England a blow so savage that it would take a generation to recover.[6]

It was not just the Jews. The king also came down hard on the Christian clergy in 1210, demanding money from both priests and monks. The Cistercians suffered particularly badly, for in the spring they had refused his request for an aid, relying on the exemption he had promised them at the start of his reign. On his return from Ireland John took his revenge, forbidding them from travelling overseas to their general chapter, and instructing his justices and foresters to persecute them without mercy until they paid up. The chronicles offer varying estimates as to how much he exacted in this way, but all agree it was a five-figure sum, and royal records show that some houses contributed as much as 1,000 marks each. Despite selling off their valuables, several communities were unable to raise enough funds to pay in full, and were forced to disband. Such was the fate, for a while at least, of the monks of Meaux Abbey in Yorkshire and Waverley Abbey in Surrey, the oldest Cistercian house in England. According to a chronicler in Norfolk, that autumn witnessed the unheard-of spectacle of Cistercians and Jews going together from door to door to beg for food.[7]

The Jews and the Cistercians may have suffered the most that autumn, but by this stage royal government was bearing down relentlessly on almost everyone. Take Jewish credit, for example. John had previously helped himself to ten per cent of Jewish loans, in addition to the loans he automatically inherited when Jews died. But after his arrest and imprisonment of the Jews in 1210, he simply seized *all* their loans for himself. Anyone who had borrowed money from their local lender suddenly found themselves faced with a demand for immediate repayment from the Exchequer.[8]

John's administration of justice was becoming similarly exacting and punitive. Previously there had been several ways of obtaining judgement in a royal court. Litigants could choose to have their cases heard before the king himself (*coram rege*), but there were alternatives. They could wait until his itinerant justices visited their own county, or bring their case before the same justices when they were sitting in Westminster, at the court known as the Bench. But in 1209 John had abruptly done away with these alternatives. In the spring of that year both the justices in eyre and the Bench were shut down; from that point on, all cases had to be heard before the king. This made life very awkward for the litigants, because John was a fast-moving monarch, and they were forced to follow him around the country. During his trip to Ireland in the summer of 1210, his court heard no cases at all.[9]

No justice, however, would have been preferable to the kind that was dished out in his absence. While John had been imposing his will in Ireland, England had been visited by a special eyre of so-called 'autumnal justices' (they actually operated in July and August), the purpose of which was purely fiscal. On their travels, these justices appear to have deliberately targeted the middling gentry – men beneath the level of the earls and barons, from whom it was clearly felt there was more money to be had. When these men appeared in court they were amerced for minor offences or technicalities. Of old the payment for such a 'trespass' was one mark, or half a mark, but these unfortunate individuals now found themselves being amerced for hundreds of marks at a time. On his return to England John subsequently reduced many of these sums, perhaps hoping that the victims would appreciate his clemency. But even if an amercement of 200 marks was reduced by half, it still represented a potentially crippling debt for a gentry family, perhaps equivalent to a whole year's income.[10]

But one did not even need to end up in court to be saddled with such a huge penalty. Merely by crossing the king in some indeterminable way and falling foul of his temper, it was possible to face financial ruin. This, it needs to be said, had been true in the case of kings before John's day. Henry II had once deprived a man of all his lands because he was angry with him about a hawk; another was deprived for refusing dinner to one of Henry's huntsmen. Yet the impression, from both the chroniclers and the official records, is that John indulged his whim in this way a great deal more often than any of his predecessors. With increasing frequency, men and women, great and small, were deprived of their lands simply because they had somehow incurred his displeasure. To recover it, and their estates, they would naturally need to offer large sums of money. And even if they managed to do so, they would invariably find that in the meantime the lands had been comprehensively asset-stripped by the king's custodians, all the moveable property, including animals, crops, furniture and clothes, confiscated, sold or spitefully destroyed.

Such was the general tenor of John's reign by the time of his return from Ireland in 1210: arbitrary, punitive, malicious, intolerable. Law, said the annalist at Waverley Abbey, had been replaced by 'tyrannical will'. John, opined another anonymous writer, was 'not a king, but a cruel tyrant'.[11]

One person who was unable to recover the king's goodwill in 1210 was his son-in-law, Llywelyn ap Iorwerth. While John had been in Ireland, the Welsh prince had risen in rebellion, probably acting in concert with William de Briouze, and made attacks across the border. The king's regents, Geoffrey fitz Peter and Peter des Roches, had acted quickly to contain this rising and indeed had driven Llywelyn back into Snowdonia. The earl of Chester, whose own lands had been ravaged during the revolt, occupied the prince's lands east of the River Conwy, and secured his hold by constructing three new castles.[12]

There was therefore no need for John to take direct action against Llywelyn after his return to England; it was in any case too late in the year to be leading armies into north-west Wales. What the king did do, however, was start to dismantle the overlordship of native Wales that his son-in-law had built with royal blessing during the previous decade. He began in September by giving aid to one of the prince's enemies in south Wales, Rhys Gryg, sending royal troops to help him recover the castle of Llandovery. Then, around the end of November, he took the larger step of rehabilitating Gwenwynwyn, the Welsh ruler he had comprehensively humiliated in 1208, restoring him to all his possessions in Powys. On every front, Llywelyn's achievements were being rolled back by his Welsh rivals or the king's henchmen. Gerard d'Athée, who had previously controlled most of south Wales and the March for the king, was probably dead by this date, but his role as sheriff of Gloucester had been filled by his nephew, Engelard de Cigogné, who kept up the cold war against Llywelyn by rebuilding the castle at Builth, formerly the property of William de Briouze.[13]

All these actions were clearly preparatory to a direct assault on the prince in the spring of 1211. According to the anonymous

Welsh chronicle known as the *Brut*, in that year Llywelyn 'made cruel attacks upon the English, and on that account King John became enraged, and formed a design of entirely divesting Llywelyn of his dominion'. The prince may perhaps have attempted to win back some of his lost territory in north Wales, and there must have been some incident in south Wales that drew the king to Abergavenny in March. But the truth was almost certainly that John needed no further provocation, and had been plotting Llywelyn's downfall since the moment of his rebellion the previous year. Unfortunately, the chancery rolls for 1210–11 are completely lacking, so John's plans, and even his movements, cannot be recovered in any detail. His financial records, however, confirm that in 1211 he was amassing material for a major campaign. An account from the bishopric of Durham, still in royal custody because of the interdict, shows that from that region alone the king obtained great quantities of food, tools and weapons: 204 quarters of wheat and 504 quarters of oats; 1,260 pitchforks, 240 spades, 160 picks and 100 axes; crossbows, crossbow bolts and four siege engines. All this material was carted to Chester, where in the middle of May the king mustered his forces, including Gwenwynwyn, Rhys Gryg and other Welshmen willing to participate in Llywelyn's downfall. 'He collected a vast army towards Gwynedd,' says the *Brut*, 'with the aim of utterly destroying it.'[14]

Despite the apparently extensive preparation, this campaign came close to disaster. From Chester John advanced his army along the north coast of Wales, through the region between the rivers Dee and Conwy known to the Welsh as the Perfeddwlad ('Middle Country'). But they found no enemy to resist them, for Llywelyn had withdrawn his people into Snowdonia, taking with them all their possessions, including the animals and foodstuffs that the invaders must have been hoping to seize. John's forces made it as far as Deganwy, an ancient hill fort high above the Conwy estuary, destroyed by Llywelyn in 1210 and hastily rebuilt in wood by the earl of Chester, but by that point food was running low. 'There the army was in so great a want of provisions', said the *Brut*, 'that an egg was sold for a penny and a half [about a day's wages for a soldier], and it was a delicious feast to dine on horseflesh'. Faced with the prospect of seeing his whole host starve to death, the king, 'after disgracefully losing many of his men and much property', withdrew in disarray.[15]

In John's discomfort, however, Llywelyn found only temporary respite. As soon as the king was back in England he began amassing even greater resources for a new offensive. By early July he was ready for a second attempt, 'his mind being more cruel and his army larger'. Setting out on this occasion from Oswestry in Shropshire, he marched back in the direction of Deganwy but this time kept going, crossing the wide waters of the Conwy and pressing on into Snowdonia to ravage the heartlands of Llywelyn's realm. Resistance was futile. When the bishop of Bangor refused to meet the king on the grounds that he was excommunicate, John directed his troops to burn the city and the bishop was seized in his own cathedral. Llywelyn, 'unable to bear the king's cruelty', sent his wife – John's daughter, Joan – to sue for peace.[16]

It was no doubt thanks to Joan's intercession that the prince managed to obtain a settlement that was, in comparative terms, favourable. In return for his submission his life was spared and he was allowed to remain at liberty. He was also left in possession of his lands in Snowdonia. Everything east of the Conwy – the Perfeddwlad – he was forced to surrender to the English Crown 'forever'. There was also a substantial price to be paid in animals and people. John demanded thirty hostages and a tribute of 20,000 cattle, as well as smaller quantities of horses, dogs and birds. All this was agreed when Llywelyn appeared before the king on 11 August. A few days later, John returned to England.[17]

He did so, said the *Brut*, 'victoriously, with extreme joy'. With the humbling of Llywelyn, opposition to royal authority within the British Isles, which had first begun to manifest in 1207, was finally at an end. The Scots had been bullied into submission in 1209; the magnates of Ireland, both native and Anglo-Norman, had been cowed by military force in 1210. Now, in the summer of 1211, every leader in Wales was ready to kneel at his feet. Soon after John's return from Snowdonia, he sent an army into south

Wales, comprised of those Welsh princes who had already submitted, and led by Falkes de Bréauté, seneschal of Cardiff, one of his most notorious mercenary captains. In short order they brought about the surrender of two remaining princes, Rhys and Owain ap Gruffudd, and seized most of their lands for the Crown. Falkes went on to secure his hold by building a castle at Aberystwyth, just as other workmen further north were constructing similar castles to cement John's power in Gwynedd. 'There was now no one in Ireland, Scotland or Wales who did not bow to his nod,' wrote the chronicler at Crowland Abbey, 'a situation which, as is well known, none of his predecessors had achieved.'

'He would thus have seemed successful and overflowing with promise for his successors,' added the same author, 'except that he had been despoiled of his foreign lands and subjected to the sentence of excommunication.'[18]

It was to these two problems that John now directed his attention. In the time since the pope's sentence had been served on him at the end of 1209 he had made some effort to get it lifted, sending a stream of envoys to Rome in the months that followed, and trying to reschedule the personal interview with Stephen Langton he had aborted during the autumn. This second initiative came to nothing: when John travelled to Dover in May 1210, just before his Irish campaign, it was the archbishop's turn to get cold feet, and he refused to cross the Channel. But the king's envoys at the Curia achieved more success, and by the spring of 1211 they had agreed a form of peace with the pope. As before, this required John to accept Langton, readmit the exiled clergy and make restitution for their losses. It also required him to swear a public oath to obey the pope unreservedly. On 14 April Innocent deputed two members of his household, Pandulf, a subdeacon, and Master Durand, a Templar, to take these terms to England, with full power to absolve the king if he accepted.[19]

Alas, by the time they arrived, John was busy invading Wales, and when they were finally granted an audience at the end of

August he was still flushed with victory. When the pope's representatives read out the terms of the peace before the king and his barons in a great council at Northampton, he rejected them entirely. The confrontational approach that Innocent had chosen to adopt in the letters brought by his legates can hardly have helped. 'Unless on this occasion you purpose to make amends to God and the Church,' the supreme pontiff concluded, 'we purpose to make heavy our hands against you, so that one who is unmoved by kindness may at least be changed by tribulation – though you might well fear that penitence will be too late after your downfall.' Here, at last, was an unequivocal threat of deposition. But John, having crushed all his enemies, felt he had nothing to fear.[20]

Far from being cowed by papal threats, the king was full of confidence. By this time he was no longer the only excommunicate ruler in Europe. In Germany, the new Holy Roman Emperor, Otto of Saxony, had been excommunicated by Innocent in November 1210, barely a year after the pope had crowned him. The same was true of Raymond, count of Toulouse, who had incurred the pope's anger by resisting his crusade against the Cathar heretics of southern France. Both these men happened to be related to John: Raymond, once married to the king's late sister Joan, was a brother-in-law; Otto, the son of John's older sister Matilda, was his nephew. Both, moreover, were natural allies in the struggle against the king of France. Philip Augustus had for years supported Otto's rival for the imperial title, Philip of Swabia, until the latter's death in 1208; he was also, at Innocent's urging, engaging in the crusade to crush Raymond of Toulouse. In his fellow excommunicates John had allies who could help him attack France from the south and east.[21]

What he lacked was allies in the north – the counts of Boulogne, Ponthieu, Bar, Louvain and Flanders, whom Richard had courted so assiduously, but who had deserted John en masse within months of his accession. In 1205 some of these men had been ready to join Philip Augustus in his planned invasion of England, but since that time John had been working to win them round, evidently with some success. In 1210 Philip demanded that several of these rulers swear an oath not to have any dealings with English agents. The French king was particularly concerned about the loyalty of the count of Boulogne, Renaud de Dammartin, yet, in trying to bind him more closely to France, he succeeded in pushing him into rebellion. In the autumn of 1211, Renaud was deprived of all his lands and driven into exile. The count committed himself to John's cause, and began actively to encourage his neighbours to do the same.[22]

By the end of the year 1211, therefore, the time was ripe for the king's long-postponed reconquest of his lost cross-Channel empire. The British Isles were subdued, and his list of allies on the Continent was growing. Thanks to his continued retention of the Church's property, his persecution of the Jews and the Cistercians, and his harassment of his subjects in general, money was in abundant supply. At some point after September 1211, he set out to squeeze even more, launching a new forest eyre that was sufficiently harsh and exacting as to make its predecessor seem benign by comparison. John had not sought a tax since his great experimental levy of 1207; his various expedients and extortions had meant there had been no need. At the start of his reign he had struggled to raise his annual income higher than £25,000. By 1211 it had soared to a figure well in excess of £100,000 – possibly more like £145,000, if the profits of the Jewish tallage are taken into account. This was enough to field a great army, and to assemble a mighty armada. By this date, if not before, the shipwrights of Romney and Winchelsea, under the direction of John's chief naval administrator William of Wrotham, were busy building twenty new galleys and thirty-four support vessels.[23]

While officials like Wrotham were making preparations for the coming campaign, the king himself spent the winter attending to affairs on England's borders. Shortly before Christmas he was at Hereford, probably in response to a revolt by some of the rulers of south Wales, who had ravaged the lowlands of Glamorgan and burned down the new royal castle at Aberystwyth.[24] Soon after Christmas, which was kept at Windsor, he set out towards Scotland, to meet William the Lion at Newcastle at the start of

February. Here there was no occasion for alarm, at least on John's part; it was probably William who had asked for the meeting, since during the previous twelve months he had been troubled by the unwelcome presence in northern Scotland of a pretender to his throne. He and John renewed their peace of 1209, adding new provisions about mutual protection clearly designed for the Scottish king's benefit. John did, however, use the occasion to emphasize the unequal nature of their relationship. Returning south at a leisurely pace, he took with him Alexander, William's thirteen-year-old son and heir, along with twelve other young Scottish nobles. For once these were not hostages but honoured guests: on 4 March, John knighted Alexander and his companions in a splendid ceremony at the hospital of Clerkenwell, just outside London. Nevertheless, in bestowing such honour, he was spelling out his mastery and Scotland's dependence. Three weeks later, when the king celebrated Easter at Cambridge, he staged a similar demonstration of soft power by playing host to his newly obedient son-in-law, Llywelyn.[25]

It was probably at Easter, or soon afterwards, that John issued the military summons for his French campaign. The writs themselves have not survived, but the muster was to take place at Nottingham on 20 May. In the preceding weeks his grand continental alliance came to fruition. Count Renaud of Boulogne had done sterling work, recruiting to the king's banner the counts of Bar, Limburg and Louvain. Renaud crossed to England in April, accompanied by Henry, brother of the emperor Otto. On Ascension Day – 3 May – the count did homage and fealty to John, and the following day the two of them entered into a solemn alliance. 'We wished these things to be done publicly,' the king explained in a letter to his ally, the vicomte of Thouars, 'so that our friends may rejoice, and our enemies be openly confounded.'[26]

But within a week or so of this diplomatic triumph, things began to go awry. On 15 May, five days before the intended muster, a messenger was dispatched to those earls, barons and knights who had turned out at Nottingham, evidently with orders to postpone. On 20 May itself, the sheriff of Hampshire was ordered to arrange for a wall to be speedily built around the harbour at Portsmouth to protect the king's new ships, presumably from French attack. Supplies that had been stockpiled in the town for the coming campaign were to be placed in storage until they were required.[27]

That there was resistance to the king's demand for military service is clear. On 21 May the sheriff of Essex was told that if the knight Ralph de Berners refused to serve overseas, his lands were to be given to his namesake nephew. Around the same time the earl of Hereford, Henry de Bohun, contested the extent of his service for the barony of Trowbridge in Wiltshire and had it confiscated as a result. That these were not isolated incidents is shown by the decision on 1 June to launch a countrywide inquest into all those who held land from the king in return for such service. The commissioners were required to work fast, and the results were with the Exchequer before the end of the month.[28]

But there was another reason for delaying. John had received an urgent appeal for help from William the Lion. The danger posed by the pretender, Guthrum MacWilliam, had apparently become critical; John was obviously warned that, if he did not honour the promise of mutual protection he had made in February, the peace of his northern border would be in jeopardy. On 3 June he made last-minute provision for his postponed campaign, ordering some of his siege engines to be shipped to Poitou. The next day he set out in the direction of Scotland, leading an army of Brabançon mercenaries.[29]

As John hastened northwards he was still thinking about how to deal with the refusal of service by his knights and barons. His solution was to demand military service from the towns. On 15 June writs were sent out to the citizens of thirty-nine cities and boroughs, instructing them to find specific numbers of men, armed and mounted, 'ready to cross over with us in our service'; all told a force of 820 was required. This was a startlingly novel experiment. Previously the only contribution that the towns had been required to make to military campaigns was the payment of tallage; now John was expecting them to provide troops to fight overseas, in order to make good the shortfall in service from his aristocracy. It may have been with this kind of contingency in mind that he had caused so many townsmen to do homage to him at Marlborough three years before.[30]

A fortnight after leaving London the king arrived in Cumbria, at which point the pace of his progress slowed. From the chronicle accounts it seems that he sent his Brabançon troops on into Scotland to assist in the hunt for MacWilliam, who was soon betrayed by his own men and handed over to the newly knighted Alexander for execution. On 26 June John left Carlisle, following the line of Hadrian's Wall to Hexham, and arriving at Durham two days later, where he expected to confer with William the Lion. But on this occasion, neither the Scottish king nor his son showed up.[31]

The reason for their non-appearance soon became apparent. That day John learned of a co-ordinated rebellion by all the princes of Wales. Llywelyn, last seen celebrating Easter with the king at Cambridge, had crossed the Conwy and reclaimed all the Perfeddwlad, except for the castles of Deganwy and Rhuddlan, which for the time were still holding out. All the other new castles that had been planted in north Wales were taken and destroyed, their garrisons either captured or decapitated. With the lord of Snowdon rose the other princes of Wales, among them Gwenwynwyn of Powys and Rhys Gryg, attacking the English castles and towns in their own territories. A year earlier these men had been Llywelyn's enemies, happy to participate in his reduction; a year on, they had become his sworn confederates, driven into alliance by the force of John's oppression.[32]

As soon as this news reached him the king sped south, covering the 150 miles between Durham and Nottingham in eight days. On 6 July he sent letters from Nottingham to Falkes de Bréauté in south Wales, seeking to know how many knights and sergeants would be necessary to crush the uprising in his region. At the same moment a messenger was sent to the earl of Chester at Rhuddlan, presumably with much the same message. Then, on

10 July, came John's considered response to the crisis. That day further letters were dispatched to sheriffs of thirty shires, commanding them to raise a great army of labourers, particularly carpenters and diggers, from the king's demesne lands and the Church lands in his custody: altogether, he required 8,430 men. John, in his fury, had determined to conquer Wales completely; these men would build the castles that would make that conquest permanent. It speaks volumes for the king's ambition that he demanded a workforce more than double the size of that employed by his grandson, Edward I, who would eventually effect this project some seventy years later.[33]

As this extraordinary request implies, the plan to lead an army to Poitou was now in tatters, and all the king's thoughts were now bent on crushing Wales. By 20 July a new muster had been announced. Knights and sergeants from all over England were ordered to be at Chester on 19 August. The king wrote to the constable of Scotland requesting 1,000 men from Galloway, and a further 200 knights were expected from Ireland. Markets were shut down by royal fiat to ensure that there would be enough food to keep the army supplied. Corn, flour, cheese, bacon and wine were sent to Chester, along with crossbows, quarrels and grindstones for sharpening swords.[34]

Soon after these orders went out, John learned that his commander in mid-Wales, Robert de Vieuxpont, was being closely besieged by the Welsh in his new castle at Mathrafal and in danger of being captured. In the last days of July the king tore around southern England, visiting Bristol and Winchester in quick succession, perhaps to plunder their treasuries to pay his troops, before rushing to the border. At the start of August he surprised his enemies with what the *Brut* calls 'a vast army', rescuing the garrison at Mathrafal and then destroying the castle.[35]

Robert de Vieuxpont celebrated his deliverance by hanging the son of one of his besiegers, surrendered as a hostage the previous year – a boy, the *Brut* noted sadly, 'not yet seven years old'. The king, not to be outdone, moved with his army to Nottingham, intending to lead them from there to Chester in a few days' time. On arrival at Nottingham Castle on 14 August, 'before he ate or drank', according to Roger of Wendover, he ordered the immediate execution of the hostages surrendered to him by Llywelyn – twenty-eight men, in Wendover's words, 'hung on the gibbet in revenge for the crimes of their countrymen'.[36]

It was immediately after this that John learned that his own life was in danger, because his barons were plotting to kill him.

11

The Hermit's Prophecy

1212–1213

As usual it is Roger of Wendover who tells the best version of the story. John, he says, was sitting down to dinner in Nottingham Castle, enjoying the meal he had postponed in order to hang his Welsh hostages, when a letter arrived from the king of Scots, warning him that there were traitors in his midst. Shortly afterwards, before the meal was finished, another letter arrived, this time from his daughter Joan, the wife of Llywelyn ap Iorwerth, with exactly the same message: if (in Wendover's words) 'the king persisted in the war which he had begun, he would either be slain by his own nobles, or delivered to his enemies for destruction'.[1]

Despite Wendover's dramatic flourishes, there is no doubt that something very like this happened. At least five other chroniclers report that soon after John arrived at Nottingham, he became aware of a plot against his life. All of them were also convinced that one of the reasons was that the king had been deposed by the pope. This was not in fact the case: Innocent, although he had made threats to that effect the previous summer, had refrained from imposing such a drastic sentence. But as far back as 1207, even before the interdict had been imposed, he had told the barons that they ought not to obey John for fear of offending God, and by 1212 this idea was sufficiently appealing that some of them were willing to encourage the belief that letters of deposition had indeed been published.[2]

News of the intended treason spread everywhere. The Crowland chronicler had heard that the king was to be expelled and another chosen in his place. The annalist at Dunstable Priory asserts the barons had decided upon the French magnate, Simon de Montfort, famed for his crusading exploits in the Holy Land and southern France (and father of the namesake son who later defied Henry III). Evil rumours ran around the whole kingdom, wrote the annalist at Bury St Edmunds. The royal treasury at Bristol had been raided by foreigners. Marlborough Castle had been pillaged and burned. The queen, who was staying there, had been raped, and her younger son Richard (born in 1208) had been killed, along with all his teachers and guards. None of these reports was true, but the sense of chaos that summer was fanned by real events. Crowland says that from town to town people began blowing horns, raising the hue and cry for no apparent reason, and fore-telling the coming of some greater calamity. On 12 July a terrible fire had ripped through London, the worst in its medieval history. Beginning on the south bank in Southwark, the flames leaped across the river, destroying London Bridge and eventually a large part of the city itself. Thousands are said to have perished. 'The whole kingdom was disturbed', says the Bury annalist. 'Everyone was afraid, fearing the fury of the king.'[3]

John's reaction to the news of the plot against him can be seen in his enrolled orders, which show that the substance of the chroniclers' reports was correct. On 16 August, two days after his arrival at Nottingham, he cancelled his plan to invade Wales, instructing those earls and barons who had mustered at Chester to return to their own parts. Having assembled men and supplies on a scale that contemporaries described as unprecedented, in the end all he was able to do was command eighteen galleys to raid the coast of north Wales and inflict as much damage as possible. On the same day he issued orders for the security of his son and heir, the four-year-old Henry; no one was to see the boy unless they were bearing special letters from the king himself.

John also attended to his own protection, sending letters to the mercenaries who had recently arrived in England from Flanders and Hainaut, urging them to come to him with all possible speed. 'He began to suspect everyone,' say the Crowland chronicler, 'and would go nowhere unless armed or accompanied by a great force of armed men.'[4]

What John wanted to know above all else was the identities of the plotters. According to Wendover, he dispatched messengers to demand hostages from all those whom he suspected might be involved, and two of them responded by running. The first, Robert fitz Walter, was described by the Anonymous of Béthune as 'one of the greatest men in England, and one of the most powerful'. It would in fact be fairer to describe him as a baron of the second rank, whose estates were mostly concentrated in Essex, though he did enjoy the unique distinction of having his own castle in London. A middle-aged man by 1212, fitz Walter had seemingly had little or no quarrel with John during the first decade of his reign. In 1203 he gained notoriety for surrendering Vaudreuil Castle in Normandy to the French without a fight, but the king had issued letters announcing that this had been done on his own orders. In 1206 he had fought alongside John in Poitou and in 1210 he had followed the king to Ireland. Thereafter, however, something had evidently gone badly wrong. The chroniclers offer at least three different explanations. Fitz Walter himself apparently put it about that John had seduced his daughter. The most one can say about this is that it was the kind of story that people were ready to believe. Wendover believed the rift had arisen after fitz Walter had quarrelled with the monks of Binham in Norfolk and placed their priory under siege, an outrageous act that had prompted the king to send troops against him. The Anonymous of Béthune reports that John threatened to hang fitz Walter's son-in-law when the latter killed a man in an argument over lodgings at Marlborough Castle.[5]

Any of these stories may be true, or perhaps none of them. What is more certain is that fitz Walter, in common with many others, had material grievances against the king involving land

and money. He had a tenuous hereditary claim to Hertford Castle, and had enjoyed custody for a few years until 1209, at which point John had taken it away from him. Towards the end of the following year, he had been similarly deprived of some of his maternal inheritance. Whatever the precise nature of his grievances, they were enough for him to take a leading role in the conspiracy to end the king's life. When John demanded hostages, fitz Walter gathered up his family and followers and fled across the Channel to France.[6]

The second fugitive, a northern baron named Eustace de Vescy, is even more of an enigma. Around forty years old in 1212, he had no discernible long-term grievances against the king, unless one credits the later story that John had seduced his wife. Like fitz Walter, he had served in Ireland, and acted on several occasions as an ambassador to the king of Scots. It was to Scotland that Vescy and his family fled when his treasonable intentions were discovered.[7]

Although fitz Walter and Vescy were the only baronial fugitives, they were clearly not the only barons involved in the plot. John's own list of suspects included Richard de Umfraville, lord of Redesdale in Northumbria, who had agreed within days to hand over his castle at Prudhoe and four of his sons, on the understanding that he would lose them all, along with his own life, if the case against him was proved. Another suspect was Earl David of Huntingdon, who was compelled to surrender his second son and his castle at Fotheringhay. It was probably also at this moment that the king demanded castles, lands and hostages from Richard de Clare, earl of Hertford, Richard de Lucy of Egremont and Hugh de Balliol, lord of Barnard Castle.[8]

All of these men were in one way or another connected. Richard de Clare and Robert fitz Walter, for instance, were cousins. Even more striking are the ties of neighbourhood in northern England. Vescy, Umfraville and Balliol all held lands in Northumberland, while Lucy's lands lay in Cumbria. There was also in several cases a strong connection with the king of Scots. Eustace de Vescy, now holed up north of the border, was married to one of William the Lion's illegitimate daughters. Another suspect, Earl David of Huntingdon, was William's younger brother. The Scottish king had, of course, long desired to be recognized as ruler of Northumberland, and had cultivated close links with its leading families. It is even possible that a similar connection might explain Robert fitz Walter's involvement, for his best friend and brother-in-arms, Saer de Quincy, was William's second cousin.[9]

Had the king of Scots been part of the conspiracy? It certainly seems convenient, in retrospect, that William should have demanded immediate military assistance in 1212 at precisely the moment John was preparing to depart for the Continent, and that a Welsh rising should have erupted while he was waiting on the Scottish border. That the Welsh had been in on the plot is beyond any doubt. Not only had Llywelyn been at John's court at Easter 1212, where he could easily have made contact with the English malcontents; his letters prove that by this point the Welsh prince had also entered into a formal alliance with Philip Augustus. The involvement of the French king is hardly surprising, for he had previously been in contact with Hugh and Walter de Lacy, talking of uprisings and invasions, before John had crossed to Ireland and driven both brothers into exile. This may indeed point to a connection between the plotters of 1209 and those of 1212, for in exile in France the Lacys had struck up a close relationship with Simon de Montfort, named (as we have seen) as the man who was to be John's replacement.[10]

The plot to topple John in 1212 was thus widespread and well co-ordinated. It stretched down to provincial knights such as Baldwin Tyrel, who jumped the gun and announced that the king had been killed on campaign in north Wales; such at any rate was the allegation later levelled against him. It infected the highest echelons of royal government, as shown by the senior Exchequer clerks who fled or suffered imprisonment on account of their complicity. One of them, Geoffrey of Norwich, was said to have read out a papal letter at the Exchequer, presumably a document advocating the king's overthrow. His fate was certainly to die in a royal dungeon as a result, even if he was not crushed under a cope of lead as later legend claimed.[11]

For a whole week John sat tight at Nottingham Castle, presumably awaiting the arrival of his foreign mercenaries with some anxiety. He then moved to the royal manor of Kingshaugh, also in Nottinghamshire, where he remained for a further five days. By the end of this period he had learned the identities of the plotters and drawn the obvious conclusion that the epicentre of disaffection lay in the north. As early as 20 August he had committed Northumberland to the joint custody of Philip of Oldcotes, a trusted soldier-administrator, and William de Warenne, the earl of Surrey, who first had to satisfy the king he had not been privy to the conspiracy. By 26 August these men had taken control of Eustace de Vescy's castle at Alnwick and garrisoned it with their own troops. Feeling slightly more secure, John set out for the north in person towards the end of the month, travelling as far as Durham by 3 September. Since those directly implicated in the plot had already fled, the purpose of this expedition was presumably to demonstrate to his remaining northern subjects that he was not to be easily cowed. As well as spending heavily on the foreign knights in his train, he also invested in the security of his northern castles. By the end of September, over £1,300 had been spent improving the defences at Durham, Norham, Scarborough, Bamburgh and Newcastle.[12]

It may have been on this excursion that the king encountered a man variously known as Peter of Wakefield or Peter of Pontefract. (John was at Pontefract on 29 and 30 August.) Peter was, according to chronicle reports, a hermit or ascetic blessed with the gift of prophecy, who had foretold that on Ascension Day the following year, the fourteenth anniversary of his coronation, John's rule would come to an end and the crown would pass to another. In the fevered climate of 1212 this idea had attained a wide circulation, and Peter found himself hauled before the king and invited to elaborate. According to Wendover all he was able to do was repeat his original prophecy. A later tradition, however, says that he urged the king to repent of his sins, and implies that he may even have spoken of Matilda de Briouze and Arthur. Either way Peter ended up being carted off for imprisonment in Corfe Castle to await the outcome of his prediction, with the inevitable result that more people than ever came to hear of his words and wonder whether they might prove to be true.[13]

That John should react to a conspiracy against him by cracking down on his opponents and ramping up his defences is, of course, entirely predictable. More surprising, perhaps, is that at the same time he started to conciliate, and began to address the roots of the disaffection that had driven men to imagine the end of his reign. At last the realization dawned that his government had been too harsh; that since his return from Ireland in 1210, if not since his return from Poitou in 1206, he had been pushing too hard, demanding too much, and offending too many. On 18 August, just two days after uncovering the plot, he wrote to all his sheriffs, telling them to proclaim that anyone who owed Jewish debts should come before him to have them relaxed. That this was his first reaction suggests that the king's abuse of Jewish credit must have been perceived as one of the main causes of contention. A month later, after his expedition to the north, he turned his attention to the royal forest, appointing two officials, not previously associated with such matters, to investigate the running of all the forests north of the River Trent. This reportedly led to recent forest exactions being abolished, and foresters being required to swear that future exactions would be kept at customary levels. 'The king began to have more consideration for his people', remarked the Crowland chronicler, noting these changes in policy, and praising the inquiry into the forest in particular as 'a deed of great and laudable memory'.[14]

As well as addressing general concerns, John felt the need to conciliate specific individuals. Relations with William Marshal had not been easy since the earl had sworn allegiance to Philip Augustus for his Norman estates; they had sunk to an all-time low after he had given shelter to the fugitive William de Briouze. By trimming his sails and abandoning his friends before the king's arrival in Ireland, the Marshal had avoided disinheritance, but had been compelled to surrender castles and hostages. Some of these hostages had been released after he served in the Welsh campaign of 1211, but not his eldest son. When the plot of 1212 was uncovered, John's first instinct had been to suspect that the Marshal must be involved, and he warned his naval commander at Chester to beware of attacks emanating from the earl's lands.[15]

William had, in fact, stayed loyal: at the time of the crisis he was helping the justiciar of Ireland suppress a native Irish revolt. When news of the plot reached him, the earl quickly realized that it was an opportunity to rebuild relations with the king. He persuaded the other barons of Ireland to swear a new oath of loyalty, and wrote to John offering to come to England and lend his support. The king was delighted, and sent back a long letter of thanks. He did not at present require William to come to England, and would rather he remained in Ireland to help the justiciar. Casually introducing the subject of the earl's son, as if he were being fostered at court rather than held hostage, he suggested that the boy should be handed over to one of the Marshal's men. Certainly William should not believe the rumour that John had been planning to send the boy to Poitou; he never had any intention of doing such a thing. (This was precisely what the king had done in the case of the tenants of Robert fitz Walter and Eustace de Vescy after their lords' flight.)[16]

One favour that John asked in return was that the Marshal and his fellow magnates in Ireland should draft and seal a letter, like the one recently drawn up by their counterparts in England – John helpfully enclosed a copy. This document, the text of which survives, was the king's propaganda fightback against the rumours that he had been deposed. The magnates who sealed it spoke of their 'heartfelt grief and astonishment' at recent reports that the pope was proposing to absolve them from their fealty to the king. John, they maintained, had simply stood up for his rights and dignity regarding the Church of Canterbury, and after delivering a short history lesson on this subject, declared that they were willing 'to live and die with the king', adhering to him faithfully as their liege lord.[17]

This was fighting talk, but it was intended to quell the stories about deposition rather than further antagonize the pope. When it came to his struggle with the Church, John was actually preparing for his greatest climbdown of all. In his recent letters William Marshal had recommended making peace with Innocent, and the king had written back inviting the earl and others to suggest a suitable formula. The events of the summer, the threats to himself and his family, and perhaps even the prophecy that his reign was shortly to end, had all spooked the king into submission. In November a fresh embassy was dispatched to Rome, carrying the message that John was ready to accept the terms proposed the previous year.[18]

John's propaganda offensive and his efforts to make his government more palatable apparently had little effect on his popularity that autumn. When he kept Christmas at Westminster, says Roger of Wendover, it was in the company of only a few knights. And so, at the start of 1213, the conciliation continued. Immediately in the new year the king set out once again towards the north of England. His progress was much more leisurely than it had been the previous summer, for this time he came not to present a martial face to his northern subjects but to lend them a sympathetic ear. The witness lists to his charters show that he was attended by many northern magnates, who evidently complained about the oppressiveness of their sheriffs. On 30 January, when he was at Fenwick in Northumberland, the king removed his notoriously harsh chief forester, Hugh de Neville, from the sheriffdom of Cumbria, and replaced him with Robert de Ros, a local lord, and the brother-in-law of Eustace de Vescy. Four weeks later, when he was back in southern England, the king similarly replaced the sheriffs of Yorkshire and Lincolnshire with local men, declaring in letters to the inhabitants of those counties that he had been moved by their complaints of extortion, and had appointed a four-man commission to investigate all the excesses that had been committed since his return from Ireland. Although these concessions were clearly focused on the north, the chroniclers suggest that this review of sheriffs was generally applied.

One measure which was certainly carried out across the whole kingdom was the abolition of increments above the county farm, introduced by Richard and extended by John. The new sheriffs appointed in 1213 thus had to exact less money than their oppressive predecessors.[19]

The reason for this new round of appeasement was to prepare for the relaunch of the continental campaign, cancelled the previous year because of the Welsh uprising. In spite of all his other worries, John remained firmly wedded to his grand plan of reconquest, so long in preparation, and of leading an army to Poitou to carve up France with his allies. As early as November 1212 he had given orders for ships to be seized for a muster on 25 March. On 28 January, at Bamburgh Castle, the furthest limit of his northern tour, he had written to Emperor Otto, promising to send him 9,000 marks and saying how much he was looking forward to receiving the counts of Holland and Boulogne in England, once he had made sure that the north was secure. By the end of February, the king clearly felt that this objective had been accomplished. Wales, too, was as secure as he could make it. Llywelyn was firmly entrenched in the north, but in south Wales the king's lieutenants had succeeded in regaining the upper hand. On 25 February, the same day he sent his letters of appeasement to the people of Yorkshire and Lincolnshire, John almost certainly issued the military summons for the coming campaign. A week later, back in London, he ordered every ship capable of carrying six or more horses to assemble at Portsmouth by 24 March, 'well manned with good and brave mariners, well armed, to go on our service and at our expense'.[20]

But if the king had been busy during the winter, so too had his enemies. In the autumn of 1212 Stephen Langton and the other exiled English bishops had travelled from France to Rome to lay their complaints about him before the pope. Innocent was sufficiently appalled by their account of the sufferings of the English clergy that he finally drew up letters declaring that John was deposed and committed them to Langton's keeping. Probably he was unaware of the king's change of heart, for the envoys dispatched from England in mid-November are unlikely to have reached Rome before Christmas, and Langton was reportedly back in France by January. Armed with his new letters, the archbishop approached Philip Augustus, who enthusiastically embraced the idea of leading a crusade to topple his English rival. By March, if not before, he was assembling the necessary ships for a cross-Channel invasion.[21]

News of these developments appears to have reached John around the time of his intended departure for Poitou and caused him to prevaricate. On 23 March, the day before his fleet was due to assemble, he suddenly issued orders to the keepers of all ports, telling them *not* to send their ships to Portsmouth. Two days later, he cancelled this cancellation, and told them to disregard his previous order: the muster at Portsmouth was back on. It was also apparent that the threat of invasion was not his only problem. On 24 March itself, the king issued fresh writs of military summons to his knights and barons, suggesting that once again many of them had failed to turn out.[22]

In the days that followed John's movements started to become frantic. At the end of March he hurried from Hampshire to London to seal an alliance with the count of Holland, who agreed to provide military support against a French invasion. By 4 April he was back at Portsmouth, but four days later he tore off again, this time to Rochester in Kent, perhaps to await the arrival of another foreign ally. It was almost certainly at Rochester on 14 April – Easter Sunday – that he finally accepted that he would have to abandon his plan to attack France and instead switch to a defensive campaign. By this stage he must have heard about the great council that Philip Augustus had held at Soissons six days earlier, in which the French king had made public his invasion plan, which involved installing his son Louis as England's new ruler. The French host had been ordered to assemble at Rouen on 21 April.[23]

This intelligence prompted John to take desperate measures. From Rochester on 14 April he dispatched extraordinary writs to his sheriffs, ordering them to assemble every ounce of available manpower – not just earls, barons and knights, but also all freemen, and even serfs: anyone, to quote the words of the writ, 'whomever they be, or by whatever tenure they hold, who ought to bear arms, or can procure them'. As they loved their king, themselves and their property, they were to come to Dover 'to defend our person, their persons, and the land of England'. None was to remain at home on pain of being branded a coward and condemned to perpetual servitude. The landed were to come with horses and arms, the landless to receive weapons and wages from the king. All markets were to be cancelled, and all merchants were to bring their wares to keep the army supplied. Everyone was to be at Dover by 21 April, to match the date of the French muster. It was perhaps the greatest mark of John's desperation that he hoped to raise his whole kingdom in arms at less than one week's notice.[24]

As these writs flew to the sheriffs, the king sped back to Hampshire, partly to round up those troops who had assembled at Winchester a month earlier in expectation of crossing to Poitou, but also to pay a flying visit to his fleet at Portsmouth. According to Roger of Wendover, John's ships were more numerous than Philip's, and in this he saw his best hope of thwarting the invasion, by engaging his enemies at sea, and drowning them before they landed. It was probably at this moment that he sent the fleet to raid the north French coast, where over the next few days they scored some notable victories, capturing and destroying ships in the mouth of the Seine, and attacking the towns of Fécamp and Dieppe, before returning to the Sussex port of Winchelsea. John himself was at Winchelsea in the final days of April, presumably to congratulate his captains on their success.[25]

From Sussex the king returned to Kent to discover the results of his emergency call to arms. The actual location of the muster was Barham Down, a hill between Dover and Canterbury; when John reached Canterbury on 4 May, he must have realized that his rallying cry had been almost too successful. A vast multitude had assembled, so great that it was impossible to keep it supplied. Those who had turned up without weapons were simply sent back home. Some of those who did have the necessary swords and shields were dispersed to other locations around the southeast coast – Wendover mentions Faversham and Ipswich. The rest remained with the king at Barham to await the feared attack. They included most of the earls and barons of England, as well as a force of 500 knights brought from Ireland by the justiciar, John de Gray. William Marshal had also crossed the Irish Sea in response to the crisis, and Ranulf of Chester had abandoned his struggle against Llywelyn to be present. But despite the high turnout, the mood was anxious and uncertain. Philip, it was said, had raised an army of 15,000 men. 'The heart of the people was wavering,' says the Crowland chronicler, 'as if men's courage had been dried up by fear and anticipation of the enemy whom they believed to be arriving on the next tide.' Many remembered with terror the words of Peter of Wakefield, who had warned that John would not rule beyond the coming feast of Ascension on 23 May.[26]

It was at this point, with the nation waiting nervously on the brink, that the king's envoys returned from Rome, bearing a letter from the pope. Innocent, after expending many words upbraiding the king for his deficiencies, indicated that he was prepared to accept the peace terms that had been drafted in 1211 – but only if the king had ratified them by 1 June.[27]

John rushed to grasp this offer of salvation. His envoys had travelled home in the company of the papal legate, Pandulf, who had stopped at Wissant on the French coast to await the king's reaction. For several days in early May messengers shuttled to and fro across the Channel in an effort to convince him that this time John really was in earnest. At last, on 13 May, Pandulf arrived in Dover, where he was immediately presented with royal letters accepting the terms of peace. Three English earls and the count of Boulogne swore on the king's soul that he would abide by them.[28]

This would have been enough to satisfy the conditions laid down by Innocent, but John had decided to go much further. Two days later, in the house of the Templars at Ewell near Dover, in the presence of the legate and a crowd of English magnates, he ceremoniously resigned his crown, and with it the kingdoms of England and Ireland, declaring that he wanted to receive them back as a vassal of the pope. This was, he explained, a spontaneous act, performed of his own free will, to atone for his sins and those of his ancestors, which would bind him and his successors forever. As a token of this obligation, he promised that he and his heirs would pay the papacy 1,000 marks a year.[29]

Some contemporaries were aghast at this surrender of sovereignty to a foreign power. 'To many,' said the Crowland chronicler, 'it seemed ignominious, and a monstrous yoke of servitude.' But Crowland himself considered that the king had acted wisely: he had been in a very tight spot, and there was probably no other way of evading the impending danger. Now that England was a papal fief, that chronicler was confident that no Christian prince would dare attack it. As soon as John had performed his homage, Pandulf hurried back across the Channel to break the news to Philip Augustus, who was told to stand down his forces on pain of being excommunicated himself.[30]

Having turned the tables on his enemies, John was in the mood to celebrate – and to prove once and for all that the prophecy about the end of his reign had been wrong. On Ascension Day he caused his tent to be set up in a field at Ewell, and proclaimed that everyone was welcome to spend the day with him. 'And a right joyous day it was,' says Crowland, 'the king taking his pleasure and making merry with the bishops and nobles who had come together at his call.' No doubt to the disappointment of his critics, John failed to choke on any chicken bones, and was still very much alive four days later, on the actual anniversary of his coronation. Those who had believed the predictions of Peter of Wakefield were left looking rather foolish. The following day, on the king's orders, Peter himself was removed from his prison at Corfe, dragged by horses to nearby Wareham and hanged. For good measure his son was hanged with him.[31]

Philip Augustus, meanwhile, had been predictably enraged to learn that papal backing for his projected invasion had been withdrawn at the last minute, and had decided to vent his anger and offset his losses by attacking his northern neighbour, the count of Flanders, who had refused to participate in the expedition. The count, Ferrand, having been non-committal for a long time, suddenly found he wanted to join John's alliance, and sent messengers to England in the hope of obtaining urgent military assistance. John received them on 25 May, two days after his party. On 28 May the English fleet, captained by his brother, the earl of Salisbury, and Renaud, count of Boulogne, set sail in the direction of Flanders, carrying 700 knights and numerous infantry.

Their plan was to land at the Flemish port of Zwin and march inland to link arms with Count Ferrand, but on arrival they discovered, to their surprise, the entire French fleet lying in anchor – 1,700 ships, laden with weapons and provisions, and almost completely unattended. Philip and his army were off foraging and besieging the town of Ghent, and had left their ships guarded by only a few sailors. In a short space of time the English forces had plundered and burned a hundred vessels, and sent a further 300 drifting back in the direction of England. It was a signal victory, on a scale that made the raids of the previous month look trivial by comparison, and which at a stroke removed any possibility of a French assault on England. Salisbury returned home a hero, laden with booty. 'Never before', said *The History of William Marshal*, 'had so much treasure come from France to England since the time of King Arthur.'[32]

12

Ready for Battle

1213–1214

John was determined to follow up his fortuitous naval victory at Zwin with an immediate attack on Philip Augustus. With the French king reeling from the loss of his fleet, it was the perfect moment for the king of England to put his long-planned European strategy into action. His allies in the Low Countries could keep Philip harassed and distracted in the north; John meanwhile could advance from his own territories in the south, where his position was stronger than ever. He and his existing southern ally, the count of Toulouse, had lately been joined by the king of Aragon, Peter II. The previous year Peter had fought alongside the other Christian princes of Spain at the Battle of Las Navas, and won what proved to be a decisive victory against their Muslim enemies. Now he was willing to cross the Pyrenees and help John bring about the ruin of his own most hated foe.[1]

But, as before, John's enthusiasm for an expedition to Poitou was not shared by most of his subjects. As early as 10 June, while he was still in Kent, the king was ordering knights to come to Portsmouth as soon as possible, and to follow him overseas if he had already left. In the event he passed straight through Portsmouth and headed for Corfe Castle, from where at the end of the month he was able to send his half-brother William back to Flanders with a subsidy of 20,000 marks for Count Ferrand. By this point, however, it must have been clear that very few knights were willing to cross the sea with John himself, for despite the king's anxiety to set sail, no departure took place.[2]

According to Roger of Wendover, the nobles refused to accompany John because he was still excommunicate, and this statement draws strong support from what the king did next. On 1 July he sent a powerful delegation across the Channel, headed by the archbishop of Dublin and the bishop of Norwich, with a message for the archbishop of Canterbury, Stephen Langton, and his fellow exiles, urging them to return to England as quickly as they could. Langton and his colleagues duly obliged, landing in Dover a week or so later and hastening to meet the king at Winchester. On 20 July, hearing of their approach, John came out of the city to meet them. In what was clearly a carefully contrived display of penance, he prostrated himself at the bishops' feet and tearfully begged them to show compassion to him and his kingdom. They responded by raising him up and leading him to the door of Winchester Cathedral, where they chanted the fiftieth psalm ('Have mercy on me, O God, [and] blot out my iniquity'). There, before a crowd of nobles, clergy and commoners, John was absolved. At the same moment, says Wendover, he swore on the Gospels that he would henceforth love and defend the Church and renew the good laws of his ancestors – a renewal, essentially, of his coronation oath. Langton then led the king inside the cathedral and celebrated Mass. Afterwards all the bishops and nobles joined John for a splendid and joyful feast.[3]

But in some cases the joy of the magnates, like the king's tears of contrition, must surely have been counterfeit. Among the crowd at Winchester were several men who until recently had been reckoned among John's most bitter enemies. Most notable were Robert fitz Walter and Eustace de Vescy, who had fled from England the previous year when their plot to kill the king had been unmasked. Fitz Walter, having escaped to France, had fallen in with the exiled English clergy, and convinced them that he and Vescy were being persecuted because they had championed the cause of the Church. When the pope had made his offer of absolution to John in February, one of its conditions had been

that the king had to readmit both men to England and grant
them his true peace. John had no option but to oblige, and fitz
Walter and Vescy had returned to England in July at the same
time as the bishops. The king had restored their confiscated estates
while he was at Winchester, but the absence of genuine reconciliation was obvious. On 27 May, the same day he had issued
letters of safe conduct for the two men, he also ordered the
demolition of Vescy's principal castle at Alnwick. (Fitz Walter's
fortress in London, Baynard's Castle, had already been destroyed
at the start of the year.)[4]

Despite the performances at Winchester, therefore, there was
still much rancour and ill will between John and some of his
leading subjects, and this became rapidly apparent in the days that
followed. As soon as the festivities were finished the king hurried
back to Corfe, intending to depart for the Continent immediately
now that his excommunication had been lifted. Yet again, however,
his magnates resisted, raising new objections. Some apparently
claimed that they had been impoverished by the frequency of
military service in recent years – the campaigns in Wales, Scotland
and Ireland, not to mention the long weeks they had already spent
in 1213 waiting around at Portsmouth and Canterbury. Others
went further still, asserting that the terms of their tenure did not
oblige them to serve in Poitou at all. This, according to Ralph of
Coggeshall, was the particular claim of the northern barons, a
group which must have included Eustace de Vescy.[5]

The king was naturally furious, and attempted to press ahead
with the campaign regardless. If Wendover is to be believed, he
may even have put to sea for a day or two, just as he had done
in 1205. As on that occasion, however, the failure of his barons
to follow him forced him to turn back. By the middle of August
his plan to go to Poitou had been abandoned. On 17 August he
wrote to the count of Toulouse, explaining that he had been
prevented from sailing by contrary winds, and a few days later
he sent letters to the mariners of Bristol, Wales, Ireland and the
Cinque Ports, instructing them to have their ships ready to depart
early in the new year.[6]

In the meantime John had one overriding desire, which was to take revenge on the men who had humiliated him. Towards the end of August he gathered together what Coggeshall calls 'a great force of knights' and set out for northern England, determined to terrorize its recalcitrant barons. News of his intention soon reached London, and the ears of Stephen Langton, who sped after the king and intercepted him at Northampton. The archbishop warned John that if he made war on his own subjects he would be breaking the oath to provide good government that he had sworn at the time of his absolution, and advised him to let the northern barons put their case in court. The king, says Wendover, angrily told Langton that this was none of his business, being a matter of secular politics, and continued his warlike advance. But the archbishop persisted in his pursuit, following the army as far as Nottingham, where he threatened to excommunicate everyone in it, apart from John, if they continued. This, according to Wendover, was enough to induce the king to abandon his plan, and to name a day for the northerners to have their hearing.[7]

John may have stopped short of harrying the lands of his opponents, but he nonetheless pressed on into the north, travelling as far as Durham with his military retinue, as if to demonstrate the kind of force he was capable of unleashing. He had, moreover, coercive powers at his disposal other than fire and sword. The Exchequer, with its carefully enrolled records of debt, was also a formidable weapon. Ever since resistance to military service in Poitou had reared its head in June, John had been leaning on individual knights and barons, offering to pardon their debts, or at least a portion of them, in return for a written promise to provide a guaranteed number of men. On 17 September, returning south from Durham, he stopped at Knaresborough in Yorkshire and struck just such a bargain with Hugh de Balliol, lord of Barnard Castle in Northumberland. During the previous year Balliol had been deprived of his castle, and all his other properties besides, which had then been restored to him that April. The likeliest reason for their initial confiscation is that he was suspected of being involved in the plot of 1212, and it seems as good as certain that he was among those northern lords who had refused to go to Poitou during the summer. But now, at Knaresborough, he agreed to provide John with two knights, at his own cost, to go wherever the king commanded. In return for this written undertaking, his debt to the Crown was reduced by the fairly meagre sum of eighty marks.[8]

Where no debts existed, of course, new ones could easily be created. Three days later, at Tickhill Castle in South Yorkshire, John imposed an even harsher deal on another northern magnate, John de Lacy. John was the son of Roger de Lacy, the hero of the siege of Château Gaillard. His father had died in October 1211, but thus far John had not received his inheritance, a massive estate comprised of five northern baronies, perhaps because he was underage. The king granted it to him at Tickhill, but imposed a colossal relief of 7,000 marks, the whole of which was to be repaid within just three years. The details of the agreement make it clear this was as much about royal fears of treachery as it was about raising money. Despite the size of the relief the king refused to hand over the Lacy castles at Pontefract and Donington to their new young lord, but nevertheless required him to pay for their garrisons. Lacy was also assured that, should he ever decide to join the king's enemies, he would lose all his lands forever.[9]

Perhaps the most striking thing about this deal is that it was by no means unique. By the autumn of 1213 John's income had fallen sharply from its six-figure peak.[10] During the previous year he had attempted to pacify his critics by reducing the demands of his sheriffs and foresters, and lately the peace he had made with the pope had obliged him to return all the Church's confiscated property. Yet the imminent prospect of a renewed assault on Philip Augustus meant his hunger for cash was greater than ever. Such was his need for both money and military service, and his desire to control particular individuals by threatening to call in their debts, that John began demanding such massive sums from his magnates almost as a matter of routine. During the summer of 1213, for example, Thomas de Moulton, who had previously been imprisoned in Rochester Castle for failing to pay his debts, promised 1,000 marks so that his new wife, a widow, could have custody of her daughters, while William fitz Alan offered 10,000 marks to inherit his father's medium-sized barony in Shropshire. From 1213 onwards, the king was exploiting his rights of lordship harder than ever, imposing the heaviest fines of his reign.[11]

The same day that John was at Tickhill (20 September) saw the arrival in England of another papal legate, Nicholas of Tusculum. The king had requested the presence of a legate back in May, at the time of his submission to the pope, and Innocent had been happy to oblige. Since John had made England a papal fief, he had been transformed from a pariah into the pope's most cherished son. From that moment on, Innocent's attitude towards John had become, and would remain, not merely supportive but indulgent. The king, for his part, was content to continue cultivating this response. A few days after welcoming Cardinal Nicholas in London, he repeated his submission to the pope in St Paul's Cathedral, presenting the legate with a charter sealed with gold to be preserved forever in the papal archives.

Nicholas had come to England to help repair relations between John and his senior clergy, lately returned from exile. By the time of his arrival they were already at loggerheads over the issue of the interdict, which still remained in force. The king wanted it to be lifted immediately, but the bishops wanted first to address the question of the damages they had suffered during the past five years. Back in May John had paid a token £8,000, and in July, at the time of his absolution, he had promised to make good all their losses by the following Easter, with a guaranteed 15,000 marks by Christmas. This seemed very reasonable to the newly arrived legate, who was following his master's instructions to be as helpful to the king as possible. The English bishops, however, set little store by such promises and guarantees, and stood their ground. The interdict would be lifted only once they had been compensated in full.[12]

Since agreement at this initial meeting proved impossible, a second council was summoned to meet in one month's time. When it convened at Wallingford at the start of November, there was still no resolution: John simply repeated his earlier offer, which the bishops again rejected as inadequate. What made the Wallingford council significant was not the ongoing dispute with the clergy, but the appearance of the northern barons who had refused to serve in Poitou; 1 November, it seems, was the date that had been set for their hearing. Happily, in this instance a reconciliation was achieved. Thanks, we are told, to the intervention of the legate, the archbishop of Canterbury, the other bishops and the other barons, the king gave the kiss of peace to the northerners, and accepted that they should enjoy the 'ancient liberties' he had sworn to uphold at the time of his absolution. On the same day, the king instructed the Exchequer not to enforce the agreements to provide military service he had been imposing on individual barons since the summer. It was probably also at this moment that John summoned a new council of knights and barons to meet him in Oxford in two weeks' time.[13]

This peace, however, did not last for more than a few days. Promises on both sides were not kept, says the Dunstable annalist, and certainly in the king's case we can see that this was true. On 4 November he ordered an inquiry into the damages of the Norfolk estates of Robert fitz Walter, suggesting he was trying to appease his principal opponent in East Anglia and part him from the northern barons. Then, on 7 November, John showed his true colours, instructing the sheriffs to cause all those knights who had been summoned to the council at Oxford to come armed, while ensuring that the barons came unarmed. Clearly the king was planning to end the dispute by force, or at least the threat of it. Presumably this council met on 15 November as ordered, for John was indeed in Oxford on that date. But presumably also his opponents, having learned of his bad faith, stayed away, and returned to their estates in the north.[14]

In his writs of summons to the Oxford meeting, the king had said that he wanted to speak with four knights from every county about 'the business of our kingdom'. Whatever this was, it no doubt included the preparations for the rescheduled expedition to Poitou. John intended to depart at the start of February 1214, and already his officials at Portsmouth were busy fitting out his fleet, converting ships to carry horses and amassing foodstuffs and armaments. The king was determined to press ahead, despite the continued opposition in northern England, and the dismal news from southern France. In September King Peter of Aragon had crossed the Pyrenees, expecting to join forces with John as planned, but in the event found only Raymond of Toulouse and his local allies. Together they had set out to besiege the town of Muret, just outside Toulouse, but had been engaged in battle by the crusading army of Simon de Montfort and obliterated. King Peter was killed during the fighting and Raymond forced to flee into exile. In December he arrived in England, penniless and power-less, now a liability rather than an asset. John was left more reliant than ever on his allies in the Low Countries. In January the count of Flanders crossed the Channel and did homage to him at Canterbury.[15]

The king was as impatient as ever to leave.[16] Over Christmas he had persuaded more men to promise military service by offering them better deals, reducing the number of knights they were required to provide in exchange for the reduction of their debts. When he arrived at Portsmouth towards the end of January, he found that he had an army that was tolerably large. Few earls had turned out, but most had sent substitutes to fight on their behalf. The king also had, in the words of Ralph of Coggeshall, 'a vast number of soldiers of lesser fortune', and 'a countless treasure of gold, silver and precious stones'. This was no exag-geration. In the previous weeks the king's castle treasuries had disgorged their long-hoarded contents, to supply a war chest of around 200,000 marks. And some of the northern barons, such as John de Lacy, heavily leant on the previous autumn, had also turned out. The hardcore among them, however, including Eustace de Vescy, had stayed at home, defiant and unpacified. The king had no choice but to depart without them. On 2 February he put to sea, taking with him his queen, Isabella, and their younger son, Richard. Bearing in mind the rumours of 1212, it must have seemed advisable not to leave both his sons in the same place.[17]

A little less than a fortnight later, after being delayed on the Isle of Wight for several days by adverse winds, John and his fleet sailed into La Rochelle. Having disembarked his troops on 15 February, he spent the next three weeks establishing control over the surrounding countryside, waiting to see which nobles would recognize his authority, and which ones would need reminding. The lord of nearby Millescu, just fifteen miles from La Rochelle, refused to do so, and as a result his castle was subjected to a two-day siege until it surrendered on 4 March. A few days later the king sent letters to every magnate in England announcing this minor triumph, along with the news that a total of twenty-six castles and fortifications had been recovered since his arrival. 'By the grace of God', he wrote, in separate letters dispatched the same day to the burgesses of every English town, 'we have already begun to expedite our affairs to the joy and gladness of our friends, and to the confusion of our enemies.'[18]

On 9 March John set out on a more major excursion, leading his army eastwards through his wife's county of Angoulême, and continuing into the region known as the Limousin. After three weeks he had travelled more than 200 miles and reached the town of La Souterraine on the frontier with the kingdom of France, where on Easter Sunday (30 March) he received the homage of the count of the Périgord. Four days later he entered the city of Limoges and received the reluctant submission of its viscount, Guy of Limoges, who swore loyalty to him as his 'natural lord … against all mortal men'. Guy promptly sent a terse letter to Philip Augustus, pointing out that he had previously done homage to the French king 'for the defence of my lands', but that John had been able to enter them with impunity, 'with so many men that I could not resist him, nor wait for your help'.[19]

This message probably reached Philip fairly quickly, for news of John's progress had prompted the French king to raise an army and make his way south. By April he had reached Châteauroux, close to the border with the Limousin: at one stage he was less than fifty miles away from John's forces. According to Philip's chaplain, William the Breton, his approach caused his opponent to scurry off southwards, but the truth was that John had already obtained all the submissions he wanted, and Philip had done nothing to stop him. During the following fortnight the English army retraced its steps in the direction of La Rochelle, and then marched south to assert John's authority in Gascony. Here they met a more pugnacious opponent in the shape of Simon de Montfort, who had destroyed the king's southern allies the previous September. John advanced up the River Garonne as far as La Réole, but when he sent troops further along the river to recover Marmande, Montfort and his army attacked them, provoking a speedy withdrawal. This was not the battle that the king had come to fight, and this marked the end of his advance into Gascony. By 22 April he was back at La Rochelle, planning his next move.[20]

As for Philip, he now faced perhaps the greatest dilemma of his reign to date. Around the same time that John had sailed from England, his half-brother, the earl of Salisbury, had left for the Low Countries, to marshal the coalition of counts and dukes that John had been constructing and subsidizing for the past three years. While the French king hovered at Châteauroux he must have received disturbing reports from northern France of the kind that eventually reached Roger of Wendover, who describes how Salisbury's forces ravaged Philip's territory in the cruellest manner, sparing not even the women and children. Towards the end of April, the king rose to the bait and made the momentous decision to divide his army. Several hundred knights and a few thousand infantry were to remain in the south under the command of his son and heir, Louis, in the hope of checking John's progress. The remainder followed Philip as he hurried north to resist his other foes.[21]

This was, of course, exactly the reaction John had been counting on. Having spent two months ensuring his lands in the south were secure, he was now ready to advance north into Anjou and recover the lost heartlands of his father's empire. With only a small French army to oppose him, the king could feel confident of success. Before he embarked upon it, however, there was one final matter to attend to in Poitou, and that was the Lusignan family, whose allegiance he had forfeited in 1200 by his fateful decision to marry Isabella of Angoulême. John appears to have agreed a truce with them very soon after his arrival, no doubt hoping that, as other southern lords submitted, the Lusignans would eventually be persuaded to do the same. But by the middle of May the truce had expired and the family remained defiant, and so at that point John marched his army to Mervent, forty miles north-east of La Rochelle, a castle which belonged to Geoffrey de Lusignan. 'Many might not believe it could be taken by assault', said the king in another newsletter to England, before describing how his troops had done it in the space of a single morning. From Mervent he moved a short distance to Vouvant, another of Geoffrey's castles, into which the lord and his sons had retreated, and for three days he subjected it to a relentless battering with his siege engines. He was about to order another direct attack when Geoffrey's nephew, Hugh de Lusignan, arrived.[22]

As the man who had been set to marry Isabella before John abducted her, Hugh de Lusignan had the greatest cause for ongoing resentment, yet during the previous weeks he had evidently entered into negotiations with the king and discussed the terms on which he and his family might submit. John was prepared to grant him large amounts of territory – all of Saintonge and the neighbouring isle of Oléron – until they could be replaced by other lands in Anjou once it had been recovered. To further sweeten the deal, the king offered the betrothal of his infant daughter Joan* to Hugh's namesake son, and conceded that she would be handed over immediately to the Lusignans' custody. It was the kind of generous compensation package that ought to

---

* Not be confused with his bastard daughter of the same name, the wife of Llywelyn ap Iorwerth.

have been proposed to the family fourteen years earlier, and it now succeeded in bringing them to heel. With Hugh's intervention, Geoffrey de Lusignan surrendered his castle at Vouvant and sought John's mercy. By this combination of stick and carrot, the king induced his former enemies, the most powerful barons in Poitou, to join his side. On 25 May Hugh and Geoffrey, together with Hugh's younger brother Ralph, did homage and fealty to him, and two days later the transfer of land was sealed. John sent jubilant letters back to England, describing his triumph and looking forward hopefully to the future. 'Now by the grace of God we have the opportunity to attack our main enemy, the king of France, beyond Poitou,' he wrote, 'and we tell you this that you may rejoice at our success.'[23]

John moved north immediately, his army now swelled by the Lusignans and their followers. His next target was Brittany, and in particular the city of Nantes, which controlled the lower reaches of the River Loire, and could thus open up a new supply route from England for the next phase of operations. After the 'disappearance' of Arthur in 1203, the nobles of Brittany had decided that the duchy should pass to his younger half-sister, Alice (the daughter of Arthur's mother, Constance, by her third marriage); in 1213 Philip Augustus had arranged for Alice to be married to his cousin, Peter of Dreux, who from that point had become Brittany's new duke. John was well placed to tempt Peter as he had done the Lusignans, for earlier dukes of Brittany had also been earls of Richmond, and the king now offered to restore this valuable inheritance. At the same time, he was able to threaten Peter, for besides bringing his queen and some of his children on campaign, John had also brought his niece, Eleanor – Arthur's younger sister. Eleanor had been captured with her brother at Mirebeau in 1202 and held captive in England ever since. Clearly she had a better claim to Brittany than anyone, and her presence in John's entourage implied that the king might be inclined to enforce it if the current duke refused to co-operate.[24]

In the event Peter was neither tempted nor cowed. When John's forces approached Nantes in early June, its French garrison rode out and attacked them. This proved to be a foolhardy move, for the king's army was superior in number and won an easy victory, capturing around twenty French knights, including Peter's brother, Robert. But despite this loss Nantes refused to surrender, and Peter rejected John's attempts to win him over. The capture of his brother, however, may have persuaded the duke to accept a truce, for the king was now content to leave Brittany and continue his advance. In the second week of June he moved eastwards along the Loire, taking much plunder as he went, and on 17 June he entered Angers, the chief city of his Angevin forefathers.[25]

This must have been a jubilant moment, at least for John and his supporters, but any celebration of victory would have been premature. Angers was easy to take because it had no defences – John had destroyed its walls and castle at the start of his reign in the struggle against Arthur. But this meant it was also impossible to hold: the king had recovered the city during his previous campaign in 1206, but abandoned it after only a week on learning of the approach of Philip Augustus. Until John's arrival in 1214, Angers was held by his sometime supporter, latterly his enemy, William des Roches, who had served as seneschal of Anjou since his defection to Philip in 1202. Knowing that he could not hope to defend the city against an assault, des Roches had withdrawn his forces to a more secure location. Ten miles to the south-west, on high ground above the north bank of the Loire, he had spent the intervening decade constructing a castle known as La Roche-au-Moine (today La Roche-aux-Moines, outside the town of Savennières). It was here that the seneschal left some of his men to reinforce the garrison, before riding off in search of help.

Determined to maintain the momentum of his campaign, John left Angers the day after his arrival and placed La Roche-au-Moine under siege. His mood was clearly confident. On 19 June, camped before the castle's walls, he ordered his officials in the south to send all his treasure up to the Loire, along with his wife and children. In spite of his failure to take Nantes, the king was moving his base of operations north to support his advance into

Anjou. His confidence must have been bolstered by the decision at this moment of at least one Norman magnate, possibly six, to seek guarantees of the king's goodwill against his arrival in Normandy. Clearly John was not alone in imagining that the total recovery of his lost empire was imminent.[26]

The same thought must have been weighing heavily upon the mind of Philip Augustus' son, Louis, left in the south to counter John's advance. Since his father's departure in April, Louis had apparently caused his opponent little trouble, his only reported activity an unsuccessful siege of one of Geoffrey de Lusignan's castles. At twenty-six years old, Louis did not lack either military experience or boldness, but he did lack manpower: according to every report, the forces under his command were fewer than those following John. As his enemy advanced into Anjou, however, the situation was becoming critical, and Louis realized that something must be done. He and his men had based themselves at Chinon, just over fifty miles east along the Loire Valley from La Roche-au-Moine. When he heard that John was besieging the castle (perhaps from William des Roches, who joined him at Chinon), he sent messengers to his father asking for instructions, and Philip replied that the siege should be raised. At the start of July, Louis and his army set out.[27]

By this point John had been besieging La Roche-au-Moine for almost a fortnight, his frustration clearly beginning to mount. According to William the Breton, he had ordered a gallows to be erected in view of the castle walls, and threatened to hang the garrison if they continued to resist. The defenders were apparently on the point of surrender when, on 2 July, the king was advised of Louis' approach, and informed by his scouts that the French army was significantly smaller than his own. John, says Roger of Wendover, was emboldened by this intelligence, and ordered his troops to ready themselves for battle.[28]

But the Lusignans, along with several other Poitevin barons, refused. According to Wendover they claimed they were ill-prepared for a pitched encounter. William the Breton suggests they were reluctant to fight Louis because he was the son of the

French king, and Philip was their ultimate overlord. It would be surprising if John, when he received their homage in May, had not obliged the Lusignans to swear loyalty to him 'against all mortal men', as he had done a month earlier in the case of Guy of Limoges, so there is much to be said for Wendover's description of their behaviour as treacherous. Whatever excuses they tendered, their refusal to obey the king at this crucial moment depleted his strength and caused his confidence to evaporate. 'In great annoyance', says Wendover, he ordered his army to abandon the siege of La Roche-au-Moine and retreat.[29]

As always in such circumstances, those on horseback were able to get away quickly. John's next datable appearance, five days later, is at Mauzé-sur-le-Mignon, over a hundred miles south of the Loire, only a short distance from La Rochelle. But such haste meant that the king had to abandon everything in his camp: his siege engines, pavilions, clothes, money and valuables, all of which were plundered by La Roche-au-Moine's garrison. It also meant abandoning his infantry, and the other slow-moving elements of his army, who were left to fend for themselves against Louis' troops, and who drowned in large numbers as they tried to escape across the river. Having killed as many of the fugitives as they could catch, the French army recovered all the territory in the region that John had lately invaded, reoccupying Angers and throwing down the new defences that the king had begun to construct.[30]

This was clearly a disaster, and John knew it. As soon as he reached La Rochelle on 9 July, he sent letters to his leading subjects in England. 'Know that we are safe and well,' he began, 'and that everything, by the grace of God, is prosperous and happy with us.' But the rest of the letter belied this upbeat opening, as the king all but begged those earls, barons and knights who had remained at home to join him in Poitou as quickly as possible. Those who did so, he promised, would earn his permanent gratitude, and anyone who suspected that he bore them any ill will could rest assured that their coming would remedy this.[31]

For John to reach out to the likes of Robert fitz Walter and Eustace de Vescy suggests that his situation was indeed desperate. But despite this rather craven appeal, the fact remained that all was not yet lost, for the war was not yet over. Even if his letter to England elicited no response, he still had adherents holding out in their castles on the Loire, and he could still hope to draw on the support of the barons of Poitou, who were summoned to a new muster at Niort on 27 July. Most of all, he still had his grand coalition of allies in the north, poised to attack Philip Augustus. It did not matter if John failed to recover any territory, so long as he could keep Louis occupied and the French forces divided. The earl of Salisbury could land a crushing blow on Philip Augustus that would render the recent setback at La Roche-au-Moine redundant.[32]

Four hundred miles away in Flanders, the king's half-brother was almost ready to commence his attack. Although he had been conducting raids into French territory throughout the spring, rallying all the members of the coalition for a major invasion had taken longer than anticipated, and at the start of July they were still awaiting the arrival of the Holy Roman Emperor, Otto IV. At last, however, Otto mustered his forces from the Rhineland and, around 23 July, linked arms with Salisbury and his companions at Valenciennes, about thirty miles south-east of Lille.[33]

The delay of his opponents had given Philip plenty of time to marshal all the military strength he could find to resist them. The problem, from the French king's point of view, was that it was still insufficient. Estimates of the size of medieval armies are always hazardous, but it seems clear that the combined forces of the coalition were bigger, possibly by as much as forty per cent. Philip therefore had good reason to be cautious as he marched his army northwards. William the Breton portrays him as eager for combat, but it may be that he was actually intending to shadow the movements of his enemies, hoping that they would eventually run into logistical difficulties and be forced to retire.

When the two armies unintentionally came within ten miles of each other on 26 July, the French king, then at Tournai, decided this was too close for comfort, and set out early the next morning for Lille, eighteen miles to the west.

It was probably around midday on 27 July, roughly halfway through this journey, that Philip was warned that his enemies were pursuing him and were about to attack. This was surprising, for it was a Sunday, a day when even the most devious medieval commanders usually tried to avoid bloodshed. It was also deeply alarming, for the French army was marching in a column several miles long, and was at that moment crossing a river by means of the bridge in the village of Bouvines. The warning gave Philip just enough time to avert what could have been a disastrous ambush. Those troops that had already crossed the bridge were recalled, and those that had not were able to array themselves. As a result, they turned the tables on their pursuers, who were themselves faced with the sudden difficulty of converting their own column into a line of battle.

What followed was one of the most decisive and momentous clashes in European history. William the Breton, who was an eyewitness, devoted many pages to describing the action. It was, he said, a melee so thick that the combatants scarcely had room to swing their weapons. The silk surcoats of the knights, emblazoned with their coats of arms, were cut to shreds, so that it became difficult to distinguish friend from foe. The day was searingly hot, and the clouds of dust kicked up by the two armies added to the sense of chaos. Everywhere across the field lay horses, dead or terribly maimed, having been targeted by knights seeking to unhorse and capture their opponents. Philip Augustus was brought down by the count of Boulogne but rescued by one of his household knights, while Otto reportedly had three of his mounts killed beneath him. The number of human casualties, given that there were also thousands of infantry involved, must have been huge. 'There was hardly anywhere', said William the Breton, 'that one did not find a body stretched out or a horse dying.'

Despite the confusion, it eventually became apparent that Philip's forces were having the best of the fighting. The coalition, because they had been forced into a hasty deployment, could not make use of all their troops, and their cavalry were too disorganized. 'I must tell you', says the Anonymous of Béthune, 'that they did not ride so well and in such an orderly manner as the French, and they became aware of it.' The duke of Brabant was the first to flee, and his departure seems to have triggered a general collapse. Otto decided to retreat, abandoning his army and his imperial banner. Others fought on doggedly against dwindling odds. The count of Boulogne was surrounded and captured, as was the count of Flanders. The earl of Salisbury was clubbed from his horse by a notorious fighting cleric, the bishop of Beauvais, with such force that it shattered his helmet. He too was taken prisoner.

The Battle of Bouvines was a historic turning point. It signalled Philip's God-given triumph over his rivals, and ensured the survival of the French monarchy. When news of their king's victory reached Paris, the students there are said to have danced for seven days; today Bouvines is recognized as being as important in the making of France as Hastings is in the making of England. At the same time, the battle signalled the end for Otto IV, who rapidly lost ground to his rival, Frederick II.

It also marked the end of the road for King John. In early August, as yet oblivious to what had happened, he was once again advancing rapidly northwards, skirting around Poitiers, perhaps planning to attack the city of Tours. But on 6 August his advance came to a sudden halt, suggesting that he had heard the disastrous news, and registered its catastrophic implications. The project to recover the lands of his ancestors, planned for so long, and for which he had governed England so relentlessly, was over – and, despite his massive expenditure, he had almost nothing to show for it. A few hours of bloody mayhem at Bouvines had confirmed that his loss of Normandy, Brittany and Anjou would be permanent. All he could hope for now was to salvage something from the campaign's wreckage by tightening his tenuous grip on his territories south of the Loire. In the last days of August Philip brought his army south and the two sides agreed to a two-week ceasefire. By 18 September they had agreed a five-year truce. In early October John returned to La Rochelle and took ship for England. He was not expecting a hero's welcome.[34]

13

Runnymede

1214–1215

The mood in England had not improved during John's absence. A few months before his departure the death of his long-serving justiciar, Geoffrey fitz Peter, had raised the question of who would act as regent while the king was overseas. John had procrastinated for as long as possible before eventually announcing on the day before he sailed that the post was to be filled by Peter des Roches. It was not a popular decision. The magnates, said Ralph of Coggeshall, muttered discontentedly that a foreigner had been raised above them. The bishop of Winchester was one of the principal architects of the king's oppressive regime, and governed the country no less harshly than his absent master. As a result, said the Waverley annalist, he succeeded in stirring up opposition.[1]

The greatest cause of unrest, however, had been contributed by John himself. On 26 May the king had written to des Roches from Poitou and ordered him to raise a scutage. The timing of this order was significant, for it was issued the day after John had received the homage and fealty of the Lusignans, a coup which left him feeling strong and confident. Since he seemed to have all the military support he needed, he evidently felt able to risk provoking the English barons who had refused to join him by demanding payment in lieu of service. This was as much about punishing the recalcitrant as it was about raising money. The new levy was set at the crippling high rate of three marks per knight's fee – the highest ever demanded.[2]

This demand had created great dissension. If no military service was owed in Poitou, as some barons asserted, it followed that no scutage was owed either. Many therefore had simply refused to pay, and in some cases des Roches had responded by ordering the sheriffs to seize their goods – both Eustace de Vescy and Robert fitz Walter were among those distrained in this way. Little wonder that when the king's campaign faltered at La Roche-au-Moine, his appeal to England for help fell on deaf ears. Once the campaign collapsed after the Battle of Bouvines, the dissension increased to the point where it seemed certain to become rebellion. On 16 August John had sent two agents back to England with secret instructions for the justiciar and more than twenty other trusted servants concerning 'the keeping of our castles and our person'. Several of these men were custodians of castles on the south coast, suggesting that the king was partly anxious about the possibility of invasion. But others were responsible for the security of the Midlands and the north. On 7 September, des Roches wrote to the sheriff of Northumberland, Philip of Oldcotes, instructing him to strengthen his castles as it seemed best 'according to the news that he hears'.[3]

It was doubtless for this reason that, when John returned to England on 13 October, he decided not to land at Portsmouth, his port of departure, and chose instead to put into Dartmouth in distant Devon. From there he moved quickly along the south coast to the safety of his castle at Corfe, before setting out again four days later, passing swiftly through Winchester and Reading, to arrive in London by 29 October. Securely ensconced in the Tower, he looked to the defence of his other castles, sending crossbowmen to Corfe, Windsor and Nottingham, and transferring 20,000 crossbow bolts to Marlborough.[4]

But despite the king's obvious fears, no immediate showdown took place. The barons, though furious about the scutage, were not yet up in arms. By this point some of those who had been distrained had been granted respite and had their goods restored.

Château Gaillard and the Isle of Andely as they appear today, and as they might have appeared during the siege of 1203–4.

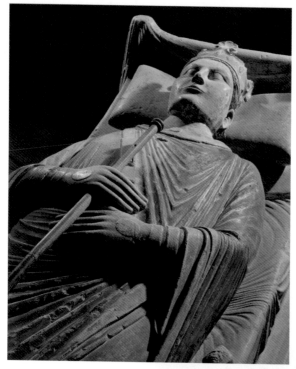

The tomb effigies of Henry II and Eleanor of Aquitaine at Fontevraud.

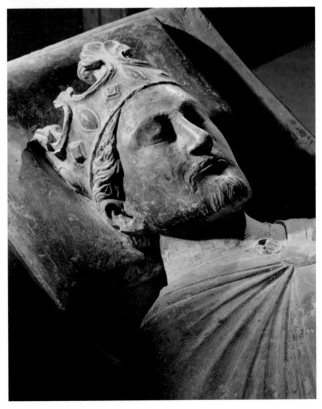

The tomb effigies of Richard I at Fontevraud and (top) William Marshal in the Temple Church, London.

A chamber inside Henry II's great tower at Dover Castle,
decorated and furnished in a late twelfth-century style.

Carrickfergus Castle in Ireland, besieged by John in 1210.

The ruins of Corfe Castle in Dorset, one of John's favourite residences.
Some people were entertained lavishly here. Others were starved to death.

A view of Runnymede, with Windsor Castle in the distance.

The seal-die of Robert Fitzwalter, one of John's leading opponents, who adopted the title 'Marshal of the Army of God'.

The great seal of King John, showing him crowned and enthroned.

Rochester Castle. The foremost corner of the keep was collapsed by John's miners in 1215, and later rebuilt with a round tower instead of a square one.

Medieval warfare, as depicted in the mid-thirteenth-century Maciejowski Bible.

John's tomb in Worcester Cathedral. The effigy was made about
fifteen years after the king's death, but the tomb chest is early Tudor.

Robert fitz Walter actually met with the king on 2 November, suggesting he was not yet regarded as an implacable opponent. Eustace de Vescy, by contrast, was viewed with a great deal more suspicion. Royal agents at the Curia were explaining to the pope how Vescy was stirring up trouble, obstructing the work of royal justices and plotting against the king. The pope's legate in England, Nicholas of Tusculum, had already issued writs denouncing such conspirators. The king clearly had to seize the initiative: win round the moderates and divide them from the diehards. By the end of October, if not before, he must have summoned a great council to London for the middle of November.[5]

As well as dealing with his barons, John also needed to settle with the Church. When he had left England in February the row with the clergy about the damages their estates had suffered during the interdict was still unresolved. They wanted compensation, and were determined that the interdict should not be raised until it had been received. At that point, however, the pope had intervened. Realizing that arguments about assessment could continue indefinitely, Innocent had decided that John should pay 100,000 marks, to be increased or reduced once all the evidence had been collected. In the spring, at the instance of the king's agents, he announced an even better deal, allowing that the interdict could be lifted once John had paid just 40,000 marks of this sum, with the remainder to be paid off in six-monthly instalments. Thus, on 1 July, Nicholas of Tusculum had been able to hold a great council in St Paul's Cathedral. As he explained to his audience, the king had already paid 27,000 marks in compensation, and the bishops of Norwich and Winchester (John's creatures, John de Gray and Peter des Roches) had agreed to stand security for the outstanding 13,000 marks. Declaring that the pope's terms had been satisfied, the legate announced that the interdict was over.[6]

For most people this would have constituted good news. Some among the laity, it is true, might not have been particularly bothered about their protracted exclusion from attending Mass, or even the ban on wedding services, since it was perfectly possible to get married without the Church's involvement. The ban on being buried in consecrated ground, on the other hand, is likely to have been more troubling, so there was doubtless relief that the bodies of those who had died since 1208 could now be dug up and reinterred according to a proper Christian rite. Across the country, for the first time in six years, the church bells rang out.[7]

For the clergy, however, the end of the interdict meant the loss of leverage on the issue of compensation. Senior churchmen had long suspected that, once the pope's sentence on England had been lifted, John's promises of future payment would count for nothing. This suspicion must have hardened into certainty once news arrived that the king's continental campaign had ended in disaster.

Although he had neither the inclination nor the resources to pay the clergy, John nevertheless wanted to placate them, lest they make common cause with the discontented barons. Since he could not offer them money, he had to offer them something else. The other main issue on which the king and his prelates had disagreed since their return from exile was the appointment of new bishops and abbots to replace those who had died during the interdict. This was, of course, always a contentious issue: it had been an argument over the election of a new archbishop of Canterbury that had led to John's rift with the pope. But since the king's submission to the papacy the polarities had been reversed. Innocent now wanted to oblige John, and had empowered Nicholas of Tusculum to make the necessary appointments, enjoining him very firmly to advance such men as would be useful to the Crown. The legate had been zealous in his execution of this mandate, touring the country throughout 1214, overruling the wishes of monastic and cathedral chapters, and promoting the king's preferred candidates.[8]

It was on this extremely sore point that John decided to appease his irate clergy. When his great council assembled in mid-November (at the Temple, the London base of the crusading order of the Knights Templar), the king set about buying off his senior clerics with a great number of individual grants. Some received long-coveted lands, others the rights of patronage over other churches. The quid pro quo (in one case explicitly stated in the terms of the grant) was that they would drop their claims for damages sustained during the interdict. In addition, John offered the Church as a whole a sweeping general concession: a charter, guaranteeing that in future the election to all cathedral and monastic churches would be free from royal interference. In this way the king quietened his clerical critics and drew a line under the issue of compensation.[9]

As the witness list to this charter reminds us, this was not just a council of churchmen. At least seven earls were present, along with many barons, some of whom were clearly by this stage thinking the same thought: if the Church could have a charter, why not the laity? The concept, after all, was hardly an original one. Most kings since the Norman Conquest had begun their reigns by issuing a charter around the time of their coronation, elaborating on the general promises of good governance contained in their coronation oath, and disowning the malpractices of their predecessors. John, for example, had issued a 'constitution' a few days after his accession in 1199, reducing and regulating the fees charged by his chancery, the cost of which had rocketed during the reign of his brother. Similar written promises and concessions had been issued at the start of their reigns by Henry II, Stephen and Henry I.[10]

At some stage in the period 1213–14 the coronation charter of Henry I had entered the political debate, though precisely when is unclear. Roger of Wendover claims that it was discovered by Stephen Langton and presented to the barons, secretly, as early as August 1213 – a scenario that most historians now reject as fanciful. All other sources suggest that Henry's charter did not become a talking point until the autumn of 1214. What seems certain is that it was discussed by some magnates prior to the great council at the Temple that November.[11]

What was it about this particular document, granted 114 years earlier by the king's great-grandfather, that the magnates felt was so valuable? It ran to only thirteen clauses, some of which were completely out of date, such as Henry's promise to pardon the debts of his predecessor, William Rufus, or his guarantee that knights should not have to pay geld, a tax that had not been levied for more than half a century. There were, nevertheless, several clauses that would have struck John's magnates as directly relevant to their own situation. Henry had promised, for example, not to arrange the marriage of the widow of a baron without her consent, or the marriage of an heiress without the consent of her relatives. He had also promised that when a baron died, his heir would pay a relief that was 'just and lawful'.[12]

Given the extent to which John had exploited his rights over widows, heiresses and reliefs, these words would have had particular appeal to many of the barons present at the November council, and none more so than Geoffrey de Mandeville, the young earl of Essex. Geoffrey was the son of the late justiciar, Geoffrey fitz Peter, but was clearly never going to enjoy the favour that had been shown to his father. According to one source (already noted in a different context), he had incurred the king's wrath by killing a man at Marlborough Castle. According to another, his first wife – a daughter of Robert fitz Walter – had been the victim of John's unwanted sexual advances. Whatever the reason, there was clearly no love lost between the two men, and the king had made this plain at the start of 1214, on the eve of his departure for Poitou, by forcing Geoffrey to marry his own ex-wife, Isabella of Gloucester, and charged him the princely sum of 20,000 marks for the privilege. Since Isabella's estates were worth about 800 marks a year, this was a deal that would have made sense only in the very long term; since Isabella was a middle-aged woman, well past the age of childbearing, it made no sense at all. John had nonetheless insisted that the marriage go ahead, and demanded that all of the money must be paid within ten months. When Geoffrey had inevitably failed to make the first instalment, Isabella's estates had been confiscated. Although they had lately been restored, the massive fine still stood, and the king's agents were busy exacting it from Geoffrey's lands. Never had John's exploitation of his powers of lordship been so brazen or so cynical.[13]

With this and countless other abuses of royal power in mind, the magnates in the November council produced the coronation charter of Henry I and demanded that the king reissue it. Clearly, it did not solve all their problems, for it said nothing about the related arguments concerning scutage and overseas military service, which continued to be the main bone of contention between the king and his barons. (This issue, said the Crowland chronicler, would have gone further, had it not been for the intervention of the papal legate.) But Henry's charter held out the tantalizing prospect of further reform, thanks to a catch-all statement in its opening clause, in which the king had promised to 'abolish all the evil customs by which the kingdom of England has been unjustly oppressed'. If the barons could get his great-grandson to repeat these words, they could fill in the details later. John, however, was too wily and astute not to realize the potentially limitless array of complaints this would allow. He therefore responded to the barons' request by postponing discussion of the charter until the new year. His own attitude to the debate may be surmised by the private letters he sent at this moment to the keepers of Nottingham and Scarborough castles, ordering the construction of siege engines.[14]

Thus the November meeting at the Temple broke up, with the clergy pacified but not the barons. John left London and went west to his hunting lodges in Dorset and Wiltshire, and the papal legate left for home. The barons also returned to their own parts, but at some point before Christmas they reconvened to plot their next move. According to Roger of Wendover, they assembled at the abbey of Bury St Edmunds in Suffolk, as if for prayer, and solemnly swore that, if the king did not confirm Henry's charter in the new year, they would make war on him, and seize his castles until he changed his mind. The Anonymous of Béthune tells a very similar story, without mentioning the meeting place, but naming several of the barons. Among those present, we are told, were Robert fitz Walter and Geoffrey de Mandeville, as well as the earl of Winchester, Saer de Quincy, and Gilbert de Clare, the earl of Hertford's son. All these men were closely connected by ties of kinship and neighbourhood; the fact that three of them were major landowners in East Anglia adds credence to Wendover's claim that they met at Bury. But the Anonymous also describes another group at this meeting: 'those they call the Northerners'. Again, he gives several names, among them Eustace de Vescy, William de Mowbray and Roger de Montbegon. By this stage, if not before, the two regional groups had joined forces.[15]

John, having spent Christmas in Worcester, was back in London at the start of the new year, in time for a second meeting at the Temple on 6 January. The barons were also there and, true to their word, they had arrived in arms. According to Roger of Wendover they demanded the confirmation of Henry I's charter, and also the laws of Henry I and Edward the Confessor, reminding the king of the oath he had sworn in Winchester at the time of his absolution, to restore ancient laws and liberties.[16]

Although Wendover may not be right about the particulars, the notion that the barons had started to expand their programme of reform accords with other available evidence. A copy of Henry I's charter with twelve additional clauses (the 'Unknown Charter' is its unhelpful modern name) may well have been produced at this moment. Some of its new clauses were simply refinements of the original provisions on relief, wardship and marriages. Others, however, were completely novel, and reflected the barons' most up-to-the-minute grievances. Scutage, for example, was to be capped at one mark a fee – to take more, the king would need to obtain the barons' consent. Military service would likewise be limited to England, Normandy and Brittany (no obligation, in other words, to fight in Poitou or Anjou, as John wanted). Three separate clauses aimed to reduce the size of the royal Forest and the severity of the Forest law, and another declared that debts to the Jews should not incur interest while an heir was underage. Some of these novel provisions may reflect the fact that the

Northerners were now adding their voice to the debate, but equally these were concerns shared by the aristocracy as a whole, regardless of which part of the kingdom they came from. The most striking clause in the document was its sweeping opening statement: 'King John concedes that he will not take a man without judgement, nor accept anything for doing justice, and will not do injustice.'[17]

In actual fact, John conceded nothing of the sort. The Unknown Charter is a draft document, probably prepared by the barons themselves, and certainly not an official grant made by the king. John's reaction to his opponents' demands was clearly to resist them. According to the later testimony of the barons themselves, he scorned their request, and tried to induce them to make a written promise 'never again to demand such liberties from him or his successors' – a scheme to which only Peter des Roches, Ranulf of Chester and William Brewer, another ardent royalist, were willing to consent. All the sources indicate that there was much heated argument over several days. The king, as before, sought a postponement, ostensibly so he could give such difficult and weighty business his full consideration. The magnates, however, were determined to resist this and pressed for an immediate answer. At length it was agreed that John would respond to all their demands at Easter. Reluctantly, the king allowed William Marshal, Stephen Langton and the bishop of Ely to guarantee his word on this. In the meantime, there would be a truce. John now feared an attack from the barons, said Wendover, and saw that they were ready for battle.[18]

And so the January meeting at the Temple, like its predecessor, broke up without resolution, and with a great deal of rancour. The king retired to Guildford for a week before heading for the south coast, and the magnates returned to their own parts. John immediately began preparing for war. In January and February additional troops were dispatched to the sheriffs of Nottingham and Northumberland, and across the kingdom money was spent improving the defences of royal castles. The barons, no doubt, were making similar military preparations, but what is more striking is their effort to rally people to their cause. According to the Crowland chronicler, the charter, previously discussed in secret, was now made public, and attracted widespread declarations of support. The king responded by sending messengers out into the shires 'to explain his business', and by trying to administer a new general oath of loyalty, requiring everyone to swear that they would stand with him against all men, and also against the charter. This demand went down so badly that it had to be abandoned, and John sent messengers to the pope, complaining that his subjects were ready to rise up against him contrary to their fealty. The barons sent envoys of their own to the Curia, protesting about the king's unjust exactions and tyranny.[19]

While the two sides were drawing up their battle lines, some men were still labouring to bring about a peaceful resolution to the crisis. Unfortunately the bishop of Ely, one of the three guarantors of John's good faith, died at the start of February, leaving the burden of negotiating to William Marshal and Stephen Langton. A proposed meeting between these men and the Northerners at Oxford on 22 February either failed to take place or else proved fruitless, but in March they came close to a breakthrough. At the start of the month the king returned to London and took up residence in the Tower. Then, on 4 March, he pulled what some modern historians regard as a diplomatic masterstroke by taking the cross, along with many of his followers. The pope had been pressing for a new crusade for some time, and this sudden show of commitment by John was bound to raise him even higher in Innocent's esteem. More importantly, the king's vow instantly gave him the legal benefit accorded to all crusaders, freeing him from all his secular obligations for three years, and placing his person and property under the Church's protection.[20]

The barons, says Crowland, viewed this as a cynical move, done 'not out of piety or for the love of Christ', but merely to deprive them of a decision. Nevertheless, John's strategy appears to have come close to success. In a later letter to the pope, the king explained how, having taken the cross, he had offered to abolish the evil customs of his and his brother's reigns, and to allow any that might have been introduced in the time of his father to be reviewed. That at least some of the barons accepted this proposal is suggested by a letter John sent to his chamberlain on 13 March, explaining that his 'business in England was over', and that he would therefore not be needing his subjects in Poitou to come to England as previously requested.[21]

Unfortunately some Poitevin troops had already arrived in Ireland by this point, and it seems that it was the barons' discovery that the king was importing foreigners that caused the fragile peace deal to collapse. In a subsequent exchange between the two sides, perhaps when John was at Oxford in early April, his messengers are said to have spoken so harshly to the barons on his behalf that they decided that this was the end of peaceful discussion. Their patience had run its course. 'Each returned in haste to his own lands,' says Crowland, 'in order to fortify his castles and to seek aid, and began to prepare horses and arms.'[22]

As Easter approached, therefore, and with it the date the king had set for his definitive answer to the barons' demands, few can have been expecting an amicable resolution. It had been agreed in January that they would meet at the end of Easter week in Northampton. In the days before, the Northerners assembled in arms at Stamford, forty miles to the north-east, and on the appointed day (26 April) they moved to Northampton itself. There they were joined by their confederates from East Anglia, including Robert fitz Walter and Geoffrey de Mandeville, and almost certainly by powerful men from other parts of the kingdom, such as the earl of Winchester, Saer de Quincy, and the earl of Hereford, Henry de Bohun. They were also joined by the bishop of Hereford, Giles de Briouze, the eldest surviving son of the man whom John had hounded to destruction, and whose mother and older brother had been starved to death in a royal dungeon.[23]

They were not joined by John. After leaving Oxford on 13 April the king had returned to London to celebrate Easter safely within the walls of the Tower. But when the time had come for him to head north for the promised rendezvous, he had instead ridden west to his palace at Clarendon and from there to his castle at Corfe, once again sending William Marshal and Stephen Langton to negotiate in his place. The Marshal and the archbishop met the barons near Brackley, midway between Northampton and Oxford. According to Roger of Wendover, the barons produced a schedule 'containing the laws and ancient customs of the kingdom'. We have no clue as to the contents of this document, but the barons' agenda had now clearly evolved far beyond their original request for a confirmation of the coronation charter of Henry I. A fortnight later, John would describe the barons' programme as 'the questions and articles they seek from us'. The barons declared that, unless the king immediately agreed to their demands and sealed them with his own seal, they would make war on him by seizing his castles.[24]

John was by this point advancing rapidly from Dorset towards Oxfordshire. By 30 April he had reached Wallingford, and it was probably there that he received his opponents' ultimatum. Wendover says he read their document with derision ('Why don't they ask for my kingdom as well?'), and there can be little doubt that this was the case. The king's response to the barons' threat of force was to match it. On arrival at Wallingford he ordered several lords of the Welsh March who had already mustered in Gloucester to assemble in arms at Cirencester and await further orders.[25]

It was at this moment, with typically dramatic timing, that messengers arrived from the pope. John had of course insisted on a three-month truce precisely in order to enable his envoys to make the round trip to Rome. Innocent's response to the crisis was predictably partisan. In separate letters to the barons, he utterly condemned their arrogant presumption and disloyalty, denounced any leagues and conspiracies they had formed, and threatened excommunication if they did not desist. He also sent letters to Stephen Langton and the other English bishops, upbraiding them for their failure to mediate and exhorting them to try harder to find a peaceful solution; some people, he told them, suspected that they were aiding the king's opponents. To John himself, by contrast, the pope used gentle words of fatherly advice. The king

was enjoined to treat his nobles kindly, and hear their just peti-
tions graciously, 'so they may know with rejoicing that through
divine grace [you] have had a change of heart'. Innocent also
proposed a form of peace, the text of which has not survived,
but which was presumably as one-sided as his letters, for John
indicated that he would be happy to accept it.[26]

The barons indicated that they would not. When they received
the news at Brackley that the king had refused to seal their
schedule, they formally renounced their homage and fealty, and
sent a messenger to the king to declare their defiance. The
messenger, a monk, found John at Reading on 5 May. The barons
in the meantime chose Robert fitz Walter as their military captain
and he adopted the title 'Marshal of the Army of God'. Raising
their standards, they marched back to Northampton, seized control
of the town, and laid siege to its royal castle. Their war against
the king had begun.[27]

John's immediate response to the barons' declaration was to
shore up his defences still further. He ordered several towns and
cities to strengthen their walls, and dispatched the earls of Salisbury,
Surrey and Pembroke to ensure that all royal castles were well
garrisoned and in an appropriate state of readiness. He meanwhile
rode rapidly from Reading to London, perhaps having heard
rumours that the mood in the capital was becoming dangerously
disaffected. On 9 May, lodged once again in the Temple, he issued
a charter confirming the city's privileges, and granting the citizens
the right in future to elect their own mayor.[28]

By such conciliation the king evidently still hoped he could
divide his opponents. The following day, having ridden to Windsor,
he issued letters for Geoffrey de Mandeville, proposing to review
the size of the earl's 20,000-mark fine, and also for Giles de
Briouze, who had been recently charged 9,000 marks for having
the lands of his late father. These offers were probably handed to
Stephen Langton, who had arrived at Windsor the previous day
with two or three other bishops in a last-ditch attempt to find
a peaceful solution. John indicated that he was willing to try
arbitration, and proposed that he and the barons should each

choose four individuals to settle the points at issue between them, with any outstanding controversies to be decided by the pope. In an effort to get his opponents to lay down their weapons, he added a last-minute proviso, based on the first clause of the Unknown Charter. If they agreed to the arbitration process, he would not in the meantime 'seize them or their men, nor dispossess them, nor go against them with force and arms, except according to the law of the realm or by judgement of their peers'.[29]

Within two days, however, the emptiness of this promise had been exposed. On 12 May the king ordered his sheriffs to begin seizing the lands of the men he now referred to as his 'enemies', and on 14 May he began to grant this property out to his own supporters. Possibly the barons had rejected his offer of arbitration, but two days is hardly enough time for even the fastest messengers to have ridden from Windsor to Northampton and then to have rejoined John at Wallingford. It is perhaps more likely that the king changed his mind because he suddenly felt surer of his strength. His letters indicate that he was anticipating the imminent arrival at Winchester of the Poitevin knights who had landed in Ireland a few weeks earlier, and a similar troop of knights was daily expected to arrive from Flanders. John felt able to start disseizing his enemies because he now had the force and arms to go against them.[30]

The barons, meanwhile, had been making slow progress with their siege of Northampton Castle. Not having any siege engines, they would probably have conceded, put them at a distinct disadvantage. Several of their number had already been killed, including Robert fitz Walter's standard-bearer, who had been shot in the head by a crossbow bolt. After a week or so, having achieved nothing, they moved twenty miles east to Bedford and took the castle there without a fight, thanks to the defection of its keeper, William de Beaumont. But this was only a minor victory, for Bedford was a far less important fortress than Northampton. Their threat to humble the king by seizing his castles was not off to an auspicious start.[31]

It was at this point that the rebels received exciting intelligence. A faction of Londoners was ready to help them, provided they moved fast. Bedford is almost sixty miles from the capital, but by setting off at once the barons managed to cover more than half that distance, arriving at Ware in Hertfordshire later that same day. They then, according to Roger of Wendover, rode through the night to reach London early in the morning on 17 May. It was a Sunday, and so they waited for the moment when most of the citizens were attending Mass. At that hour their accomplices within the city helped a small number of rebels to scale the walls, and they in turn were able to open the gates and admit those waiting outside. In this way London was taken by stealth. The barons quickly captured almost all the king's supporters and plundered their possessions; under fitz Walter's direction, the houses of the Jews were destroyed and their stones used to strengthen the city walls. Only the Tower and its small royalist garrison held out. But having manned the walls and stationed their own sentries on the gates, the barons were able to settle down to build siege engines.[32]

The fall of London was the tipping point. For John, it meant not only the ignominy and embarrassment of having lost his capital; far more damaging, it also meant the loss of his main treasury at Westminster, which must now have fallen into the hands of his enemies. Although some treasure was shut up in the Tower, this was small consolation since the king himself could no longer get to it. John was forced to turn to the regional treasuries that Peter des Roches had created in 1209, but these had been much depleted by the failed campaign of 1214. Nor could they be easily replenished, for the loss of London also meant the loss of the Exchequer and all its records. Regular royal finance collapsed, and the king was driven to the desperate expedient of pawning his prized collection of jewels. For a man who was reliant on mercenaries, this was a catastrophe.[33]

Perhaps even more important than all of this, the fall of London gave heart to the rebels. At a stroke they had gone from holding a single royal castle of little significance to controlling the principal city in the kingdom. According to Wendover, they now sent letters to all the other magnates, urging them 'to abandon a king who was perjured and warred against his own barons', at the same time threatening to regard all who did not join them as their enemies. Previously, says the Crowland chronicler, the rebels had mostly been young men, eager to make a name for themselves in war. But now fathers began to join sons, and uncles to join nephews; at this juncture, if not before, the earls of Hertford and Norfolk followed their heirs into rebellion. Such was the scale of the swing, in fact, that the chroniclers found it easier to list those who had *not* abandoned John's cause. William Marshal, Ranulf of Chester and William Longsword, the king's half-brother, are named among the remaining loyalists, along with the earls of Surrey, Derby and Arundel. Apart from them and a handful of lesser barons, said Ralph of Coggeshall, everyone else had gone over to the rebels. New risings broke out across the country. In the north a rebel army occupied Lincoln and laid siege to its royal castle. In Devon rebels who had recently been dispersed by John's Flemish mercenaries renewed their attacks and ravaged the king's manors. Shropshire was invaded by Llywelyn and the Welsh, and the king of Scots was also said to be in league with the barons. Even Philip Augustus had pledged his support and promised to send as much aid as he could supply.[34]

A week after London's fall, John accepted that he had no choice but to negotiate. On 25 May he issued letters of safe conduct for one of the baronial leaders, Saer de Quincy, to come and speak with him, and two days later similar protections were promised to those rebels who were coming with Stephen Langton to 'treat of peace'. The archbishop had by this point brokered a short truce, and John instructed his men to observe it. Very likely a meeting between the king and some of the barons took place near Windsor at the end of May or the beginning of June.[35]

John was undoubtedly playing for time, for his letters show that he was simultaneously trying to round up whatever military support was still available in England and obtain more troops from overseas. After his probable meeting with the barons in early

June he went to spend Whitsun at Winchester, where his Poitevin knights were stationed, and whilst there ordered one of his military captains to raise troops in Wales. Nevertheless, on 8 June, heading back in the direction of Windsor, he issued fresh letters of protection for the barons to meet with him 'to make and secure peace'.[36]

By 10 June John had reached Windsor Castle, the giant motte-and-bailey established by his ancestor William the Conqueror and extensively rebuilt in stone by Henry II. By the same date a party of barons had reached Staines, the place assigned in their letters of safe conduct. The two locations were both situated on the River Thames, six miles apart, with Windsor lying on the south bank and Staines on the north. Between them the river meandered through a low-lying landscape of islands and water meadows, the kind of neutral zone or no-man's-land in which medieval peace treaties were often negotiated. It was almost certainly here, at a point midway between Windsor and Staines, that the king and his opponents had met at the start of the month, and it was here that they met again on 10 June, in a meadow beside the Thames known as Runnymede.[37]

Ralph of Coggeshall evokes the memorable scene. At one end of the field, the giant royal pavilions; at the other, the smaller but more numerous tents of the barons. John's opponents, it seems, had turned out in far greater numbers than expected, bringing with them 'a multitude of famous knights, well armed in every respect'. Evidently they did not set much store by the king's promises of safe conduct. John presumably attended with a substantial bodyguard of his own, in case the parley turned into an ambush. Nevertheless, thanks to the mediation of Langton and the other bishops, swords remained sheathed, and the two sides started talking.[38]

The rebels began by presenting the king with their list of demands. They survive today in a unique document that begins with the words 'These are the articles which the barons seek', and is hence known to historians as the Articles of the Barons. John may have read many of them before, for their title recalls the 'questions and articles they seek from us' that he had rejected at the end of April. But new demands had clearly been added in the meantime, some of them in the three weeks since the fall of London. Altogether there were now forty-nine articles, almost double the number of demands that had appeared in the earlier Unknown Charter, and four times as many as featured in the coronation charter of Henry I.[39]

They amounted to a comprehensive indictment of the king's government. In the first place, they dealt with the key issues surrounding inheritance that had been the focus of Henry's coronation charter. The barons reiterated their demand for reliefs to return to their traditional levels; there were to be no more outrageous four- or five-figure sums, like the 7,000 marks charged to John de Lacy, or the 10,000 marks imposed on Nicholas de Stuteville (both of whom had by now joined the rebellion). In the case of underage heirs, no relief at all was to be charged once their wardship was over, and those who managed their estates in the meantime were to do so without running them into the ground. As before, heirs and heiresses were to be married with the consent of their relatives, and widows were not to be forced to remarry. Nor would a widow have to pay anything, after her husband's death, in order to have her dower and marriage portion.[40]

The Articles also incorporated and developed demands that had first been aired in the Unknown Charter. The earlier document, for instance, had proposed capping scutage at one mark per knight's fee, unless the king obtained consent to take more. Now it was simply stated that *all* scutages and aids required baronial consent – the king could take nothing unless prior permission was secured. The specific limits on military service were likewise replaced with the simpler statement that 'no one shall do greater service from a knight's fee than is due from it'. The Articles repeated the earlier demand that debts to the Jews were not to run at interest while an heir was underage, but added that the wife and children of a deceased debtor were to be provided for before his debts were settled. Lastly, the Unknown

Charter's demand for the reduction of the size of the royal Forest was repeated, but not its other clauses on the same subject. Instead, the Articles looked forward to a comprehensive review of the Forest, conducted by a dozen knights in every shire, that would lead to the amendment of all of its 'wicked customs'.[41]

With the partial exception of the review of the Forest, these demands reflected the grievances of barons and knights – those men who had initiated the struggle against the king during the previous winter. But since that time the barons had been trying to rally wider support, and this showed in the extent to which the Articles addressed the concerns of other social groups beyond the knightly class. This was most obvious in the case of demands that related to trade. Weights and measures for wine, corn and cloth were to be improved; merchants were to be permitted to travel freely, without paying 'evil tolls'; fish-weirs – an impediment to navigation – were to be removed from rivers throughout England, in particular the Thames and the Medway. The mention of the Thames strongly suggests that these new mercantile demands had been added after the barons' alliance with London a few weeks earlier. So too the clause added to the article about scutage which says 'the city of London shall have in full its ancient liberties and customs'.[42]

Many of the newer demands in the Articles were concerned with the activities of the king's local agents – the sheriffs and their underlings – and this of course was an aspect of royal oppression that bore down on everyone. One article insisted that the county farms should be returned to their customary levels; there were to be no more increments that would oblige the sheriffs to exact more. Increments had in fact already been abolished by John in 1213 as part of his attempt to placate the country in the wake of the plot on his life. The rebels now wanted to see this measure enshrined in law. Several other articles were concerned with stopping the sheriffs and their deputies from seizing people's property – corn, cattle, horses, carts and timber – for the king's use without offering payment. This sort of behaviour ('prise' was the medieval term for it) was likely to have escalated in 1215 as the king prepared for war and imported troops from overseas.[43] One article, obviously of recent origin, demanded that the king should remove the 'foreign knights, mercenaries, crossbowmen, routiers and sergeants who come with horses and arms to the detriment of the kingdom'. Another, clearly much longer in gestation, required the relations and followers of a particular foreigner, Gerard d'Athée, to be removed from office. Athée, the sheriff of Hereford who had been appointed to destroy William de Briouze, had been dead for several years, but his fellow émigrés from the Loire Valley were keeping his malevolent spirit alive as sheriffs and bailiffs elsewhere in England. They were unpopular, the Articles imply, because of their disregard for established English ways. In future, the king was to appoint sheriffs, bailiffs and judges, 'such as know the law of the land, and mean to observe it well'.[44]

It was on the subject of law and justice, above all, that the rebels' demands had expanded, and again this was largely a consequence of addressing the grievances of people other than the barons themselves. Some of the Articles were obviously formulated for the benefit of better-off individuals who were likely to be litigating in the king's own court. One took issue with John's perverse decision of 1209 to shut down the Bench at Westminster and suspend the work of his itinerant justices, thereby forcing litigants to follow him around the country in order to have their cases heard. In future, said the barons, such cases were to be heard in a fixed place – either Westminster or the county in which they originated. Other articles, however, were striking in their effort to be as socially inclusive as possible. When, for example, John's justices had begun imposing outrageous amercements in the summer of 1210, it had been a move aimed at the wealthier members of the gentry. But the Articles simply stated that amercements should be proportional to the degree of an offence for everyone, be they freemen, merchants or even peasants.[45]

Similarly inclusive were two demands, previously run together in the Unknown Charter, now separated to give them their due weight. The first, no doubt inspired by the vast proffers expected by the king in lawsuits involving men of baronial rank, was never-theless expressed as a general principle, 'that right be not sold or delayed or withheld'. The second built upon the king's earlier well-phrased but ill-kept promise not to attack or dispossess 'the barons and their men' during a period of arbitration. The Articles now expanded this into a permanent guarantee that 'the body of a freeman be not arrested or imprisoned or disseized or outlawed or exiled or in any way ruined … except by the judgement of his peers or by the law of the land'. The words call to mind in particular the fate of William de Briouze, a man of the highest rank, who had been disseized, outlawed, exiled and utterly ruined, and whose destruction the king had tried to justify as merely the due process of his Exchequer. The legal protection that Briouze had been denied was now demanded for the humblest freeman.[46]

The Articles of the Barons must have been put to John at Runnymede on 10 June, and he responded by sealing them. (It is his sealed copy that survives in the British Library.) This, however, was only an initial step, perhaps required of him by the barons as a guarantee of good faith, or to signify his willingness to take matters further.[47] What the barons wanted next − what they had wanted since the previous autumn − was a charter, issued by the king, in which their demands were converted into legally binding promises.

And so both sides remained at Runnymede to negotiate. Precisely who was involved in this bargaining process is unknown. We might guess that William Marshal was involved on the king's side, since he had featured so prominently in earlier exchanges between the two camps, and we might more tentatively suppose that Saer de Quincy was there on the side of the barons, since he was named in an earlier safe conduct. Probably for the majority of the time only a few individuals were involved. John's offer of arbitration in May had suggested each side should choose four men; had they chosen many more than that in June it would have made for an unworkably large committee, for there was a great deal to be debated.

Almost all of the Articles were to be preserved through their discussions in one form or another, but we can see each side adding new details, sometimes striving for greater precision, other times trying to avoid it. The barons scored a signal victory by nailing down the size of reliefs: in future, an earl or baron was to pay £100 to have his inheritance, a knight just a hundred shillings (£5). The king's men added provisos to certain clauses, allowing John a period of grace to correct his own errors, and postponing the correction of those committed by his predecessors. A lengthy new clause was added to explain precisely how the 'common counsel' now required for scutage or taxation was to be obtained. It was presumably the barons who insisted that *all* the king's tenants-in-chief had to be summoned on such occasions, not just the more important ones or the king's favourites. It was presumably John's negotiators who countered that the king's business had to proceed in these meetings, even if not all those summoned showed up.[48]

Although the identities of the negotiators are unknown, one individual who must have been involved in these discussions was Stephen Langton. It was once commonly supposed that the archbishop was the true author of the Articles, the barons obviously being too stupid and illiterate to have drafted such an elaborate programme. In fact, several of the Articles demonstrate that Langton can have played no part in their creation; in particular, the demand which forbade John from appealing to the pope. He was, however, clearly involved in the process of converting the Articles into a charter. His principal triumph was to insert a new clause at the beginning of the document, granting that the English Church should be free, and confirming the promise of free elections that the king had made the previous November.[49]

After five days of debate, the negotiators had made much progress, but there were still outstanding matters to be resolved. Perhaps the most contentious of all was the barons' scheme for enforcing the charter. The Articles had concluded by explaining that twenty-five barons were to be chosen to hold the king to account, any four of whom could confront him with reported breaches. If he failed to offer prompt redress, all twenty-five would compel him to do so by seizing his castles, lands and possessions. This was obviously controversial, though some on the barons' side apparently felt it did not go far enough, and demanded in addition the permanent surrender of the royal castles at Kenilworth, Nottingham, Scarborough and Northampton. That the debate was still ongoing after five days is suggested by the fact that the twenty-five barons had yet to be selected.[50]

At this point, however, the king himself intervened. John had been staying at Windsor for the duration of the talks, and it is not impossible he made further visits to Runnymede. Certainly he must have been aware of the progress of negotiations from one day to the next, and it seems that after five days he decided that there was no point in prolonging them any further. On 15 June he appeared at Runnymede and shut down the debate by sealing the charter, perhaps in an attempt to ensure that the names of the twenty-five enforcers were not included.[51]

This was, of course, the document that within a short space of time would be referred to as the Great Charter, or Magna Carta. (The term was first used in 1217.) We are all familiar with the scene, depicted in countless illustrated history books, of a scowling John, forced to seal it – or, in some versions, sign it – against his will, surrounded by a crowd of barons, their swords twitching by their sides. The reality seems to have been rather different. As the opening words of the charter make clear, the king issued it in the company of his own supporters, twenty-seven of whom are named, and described as 'our faithful men'.[52]

By sealing Magna Carta, John had batted the issue back into his opponents' camp. The barons now had to decide among themselves whether or not to accept it. They may have had to consult with colleagues who had remained in London to guard the city. Some probably wanted to hold out longer in the hope of obtaining even better terms – and, indeed, some additional concessions were wrung from the king in the days that followed. But on the content of the charter John stood his ground, and eventually his opponents had to accept that this was the best deal they were going to get. On 19 June the king returned to Runnymede, and the rebels renewed their homage and fealty. Peace was proclaimed, and all who were present swore to keep it inviolate.[53]

It would last only a matter of weeks.

14

Fire and Sword

1215–1216

'Know that, by the grace of God, a firm peace has been made between us and the barons and free men of our kingdom.' So began the letters that John dispatched to his officials all over England on 19 June, the day the rebels had renewed their homage at Runnymede. The problem, as several chroniclers realized, was that the peace was nothing like as firm as the king's writs pretended. Ralph of Coggeshall called it a 'sort of' peace (*quasi pax*) and the Crowland chronicler noted that it was incomplete. The barons were not so naive as to suppose that the struggle was over just because the king had issued Magna Carta. The charter, for all its later fame, was just a piece of parchment full of as yet unfulfilled promises. They had left London in order to negotiate, but they had by no means relinquished their grip on the capital. Nor were they going to do so, they made clear, until some of Magna Carta's specific conditions had been satisfied.[1]

A separate document, probably drawn up just before the peace, laid down what John would have to do before London was surrendered. In the first place, he had to set up the system that had been agreed for Magna Carta's enforcement, by making everyone in the kingdom swear to obey the twenty-five individuals mentioned in the charter's security clause. These men, not named in the charter itself, had presumably been chosen by the time the peace was proclaimed. Their names are known from later lists, and include such familiar figures as Robert fitz Walter, Geoffrey de Mandeville, Saer de Quincy and Eustace de Vescy. Altogether there were seven earls, three sons of earls, fourteen barons and the mayor of London. Without exception they were drawn from the ranks of the king's opponents.[2]

Secondly, John was required to 'return all the things which the earls and barons and other free men seek'. While most of Magna Carta was aimed at limiting royal power in the future – reliefs were to be at fixed levels, consent was to be obtained for taxation – several of the charter's latter clauses were concerned with correcting injustices that had been committed in the past. To a greater or lesser degree, all the king's opponents had personal or material grievances against him. They had been deprived of lands and castles, forced to accept exorbitant fines, or obliged to hand over hostages and charters as guarantees of good behaviour. In Magna Carta John had promised to put all this right. Any unjust dispossessions committed by the king himself were to be restored 'at once', and so too any hostages or charters. Unjust fines were to be likewise remitted immediately, or else referred to the judgement of 'the Twenty-Five'.[3]

In the short term, at least, John set about fulfilling these conditions. When the king wrote to his sheriffs, foresters and other officials on 19 June to announce the peace, he ordered them to administer the oath of obedience to the Twenty-Five, and informed them that twelve knights would soon be elected in each county to investigate 'evil customs', as provided in Magna Carta. These orders may have been issued in a somewhat dilatory fashion, and naturally the king did no more than the letter of his agreement required. He made no attempt to publicize the names of the Twenty-Five, and appears to have made scant effort to publish Magna Carta. Those copies of the charter that were drawn up in the days and weeks after it was first sealed appear to have been obtained largely at the initiative of the barons themselves or the archbishop of Canterbury. Only four of them survive today, but it may be that no more than thirteen official copies were ever produced.[4]

If John was dragging his feet in distributing Magna Carta, that was not the case when it came to correcting past wrongs. Both the king and the barons remained at Runnymede for several days after the peace had been agreed, and during that time many castles, lands, charters and hostages were restored. Robert fitz Walter re-obtained Hertford Castle, Richard de Clare received the town of Buckingham and John de Lacy secured the release of his brother, Roger. Altogether twelve of the committee of twenty-five received satisfaction on some old score or other, and many other barons obtained similar redress. At the same time John was seen to honour another promise he had made in Magna Carta when, on 23 June, he ordered the Flemish mercenaries he had brought to Dover to be sent home. As yet he appears to have taken no steps to dismiss from office any of the foreign sheriffs or constables mentioned by name in the charter, but he did remove his most unpopular alien adviser, Peter des Roches, from the post of justiciar, replacing him with the more acceptable Englishman, Hubert de Burgh.[5]

John was thus compliant with his obligations while he remained in the barons' company at Runnymede. Clearly not every long-standing grievance could be dealt with at once, and for this reason the agreement regarding London had given the king until mid-August to make all the necessary amends. Around 23 June the meeting finally broke up with both sides agreeing to meet again in three weeks' time to settle their outstanding differences.[6]

The suspicion must be, however, that John was complying with the barons at Runnymede only because he felt there was no other option. The chronicler Matthew Paris later painted a memorable picture of the king during the negotiations, publicly wearing a calm face and assuring everyone he was perfectly happy with the settlement, but privately raging like a madman, rolling his eyes and gnashing his teeth. Even if we reject this as a crude caricature, there can be little doubt that John had been dissimulating. After the meeting was over he headed west, first to Winchester then into Wiltshire, where he started to amass money and treasure in his castles at Marlborough and Devizes. On 2 July he ordered Geoffrey de Martigny, one of the foreigners proscribed in Magna Carta, to surrender Northampton Castle, but at the same time he instructed Geoffrey to come to his side with his knights and sergeants and all their equipment. The king may have been adhering to the letter of the charter but he was clearly ignoring its spirit.[7]

But if John was not respecting the peace agreement, neither were the barons. Suspicious of the king's intentions, they too remained in arms after leaving Runnymede by arranging tournaments in different parts of the country. A tournament scheduled for Stamford on 6 July was postponed by a week and moved to Staines because the barons who had returned to London feared an attack on the capital was imminent. Other barons, meanwhile, had returned to their own parts and were ignoring the peace settlement altogether. In some cases they expelled and attacked the royal messengers who came to try to restore the normal business of local government. In the north they simply renewed hostilities, pretending that they had not been present when the peace was agreed and laying waste to the king's woods and manors.[8]

Thus when the two sides reconvened in Oxford in mid-July there was much ill will and mutual recrimination. The barons no doubt complained that John had not dismissed all of his foreign castellans, for two more were deprived of office in the course of the meeting. They must also have pushed for the settlement of outstanding grievances – William de Lanvallei, one of the Twenty-Five, regained custody of Colchester Castle – and probably also the release of prisoners. Among those attending this conference were Llywelyn ap Iorwerth and the other Welsh princes, who very likely received back those hostages who had not been executed on the king's orders three years earlier.[9]

But not all the foreign castellans were dismissed, nor were all the grievances settled. John was no doubt determined to resist some of the more debatable claims being made against him, and moreover he had come to the meeting prepared to make demands of his own. Unable (or so he said) to attend on the first day, he had sent representatives to the barons 'to do for you what we ought to do for you, and to receive from you what you ought to do for us'. One thing that the king probably demanded, bearing in mind the recent attacks, was a statement recognizing that his traditional rights in the forest were not being respected and must be observed. Another was that the barons should put their seals to a written statement spelling out the conditions of their homage, including their obligation to defend him, his heirs and the rights of his realm. This the barons refused, and John had their refusal recorded and witnessed by the bishops. The king seems to have used the Oxford conference not so much to settle disputes as to shore up his ideological position. According to one chronicler he contradicted the peace that had been agreed at Runnymede, and the barons departed in indignation.[10]

After this meeting both sides started actively to prepare for the renewal of war. Across the country the barons began fortifying their castles (in some cases castles they had only just recovered) and in the north the plunder of royal estates and forests continued. It seems highly unlikely that any of the northern barons had attended the Oxford council. On its last day, 23 July, John had written to the magnates of Yorkshire telling them to surrender all the castles, lands, prisoners and property they had seized both before *and after* the peace of 19 June, and warning them that if they failed to do so by 15 August he would distrain them harshly. As for the king himself, he now renewed his efforts to obtain military support from overseas, secretly dispatching envoys and recruiting agents to Poitou, Flanders and even to the count of Brittany. It was probably also at this point that he sent messengers to the pope seeking to have Magna Carta annulled.[11]

It was the pope's intervention that delivered the fatal blow to the already fragile peace. As the well-informed Crowland chronicler explains, Stephen Langton and the other bishops, seeing that the country was sliding towards ruin, renewed their efforts to avert the crisis and persuaded both parties to agree to another round of arbitration. The plan was for John to come to Oxford and the barons to Brackley so that the bishops could mediate between the two camps. On the appointed day of 15 August, however, the barons gathered close to Oxford in great numbers, arrayed as if for battle, giving the king sufficient excuse to stay away. His envoys protested that he had done everything required of him according to the peace, but had received nothing in return except for 'grave injuries and enormous damages'. They also produced letters newly arrived from Rome.[12]

These were not, of course, a response to the request for annulment that John had made only a few weeks earlier, but a reply to royal letters that had been sent at the end of May. Innocent knew nothing of Magna Carta; all he knew was that the barons had rejected his proposed formula for peace and risen up against their royal lord – a papal vassal and a sworn crusader. He accordingly denounced them as 'worse than Saracens' for trying to depose a king who was pledged to succour the Holy Land, and at the same time accused Langton and the other bishops of complicity in this crime on account of their failure to oppose it. 'We excommunicate all such disturbers of the king and the kingdom of England', the pope thundered, and strictly commanded the English bishops to enforce this sentence on pain of being suspended from office.[13]

This uncompromising mandate provoked an intense debate among those present at Oxford, with royalists like Peter des Roches (to whom the letter had been addressed) pressing for the sentence to be published immediately, and Langton and the other bishops arguing for the matter to be delayed to allow further consultation with the pope. In the meantime the archbishop and his suffragans wanted to speak with John himself, but the king seemed to be slipping beyond their reach. It was now rumoured that he intended to leave the country, and was preparing to put to sea. After three days of discussion it was decided that the barons and bishops would reconvene at Runnymede in one week's time, with the hope that John could be brought back to the site and the spirit of their earlier agreement.[14]

But by the time the bishops reached him (probably at Wareham in Dorset) the king was already embarked and would not be

deterred from departing. To judge from the confused and contra-
dictory rumours about his voyage reported by Roger of Wendover,
John appears to have been deliberately mysterious about his
destination, and may perhaps have pretended that he was not
intending to return. All he was prepared to do was send some
of his own advisers back with the bishops. Around 22 August he
set sail, leaving his opponents with no idea as to where he had
gone.[15]

The bishops, no doubt highly bemused and frustrated, returned
to Runnymede to rendezvous with the barons and report the
king's departure. John's representatives protested to the meeting
on his behalf that the collapse of the peace had not been his
fault. The bishops, after much discussion, decided that they had
no choice but to publish the pope's sentence of excommunication, but did so without mentioning any names, merely repeating
Innocent's condemnation of 'disturbers of the king and the
kingdom'. According to the Crowland chronicler, many people
chose to interpret this as a condemnation of John himself. He
was the true disturber of the kingdom and for this reason had
gone into exile.

The barons were naturally quite pleased with this outcome.
'Not without pride', says the Crowland chronicler, they returned
to London and divided up amongst themselves those parts of the
kingdom that seemed to be in their power. Robert fitz Walter
was appointed to Northamptonshire, Geoffrey de Mandeville to
Essex, John de Lacy to Nottinghamshire and Yorkshire and Saer
de Quincy to Cambridgeshire and Huntingdonshire. As these and
other appointments suggest, the barons controlled most of
northern and eastern England. Each of them, says Crowland,
undertook to do justice in his region and keep the peace. This
arrangement, however, was only intended as a temporary measure.
Their long-term plan, now that John was gone, was to choose a
new lord in his place, and for this reason they sent letters to all
the other magnates, announcing that John had been deposed, and
summoning them to a council to elect a new king.[16]

Within a few days, however, the barons discovered their error.

Around 28 August John landed at Sandwich in Kent. He had spent the previous week securing the ports of the south coast and rounding up ships to add to his fleet. Now at last he was ready to reveal his carefully concealed hand. By the start of September he had moved to Dover, where some of his foreign troops had already arrived, and where many more were expected to join him by the end of the month. Also with him were Peter des Roches and the papal nuncio Pandulf. On 5 September, acting on the pope's earlier orders, they excommunicated the baronial leaders by name, along with the citizens of London. This amounted to a declaration of war.[17]

The news of the king's return and the discovery of his true intentions forced the barons to act fast. Having taken counsel with their supporters they appealed for help to Philip Augustus, urging him to send his eldest son and heir, Louis, to be crowned as John's replacement. Their plan, in other words, was the same as that proposed to Philip by the pope in 1213 – except that now, of course, it would have to proceed in the face of papal condemnation. Meanwhile, with Louis considering the offer and mustering his forces, the barons would have to buy themselves time by forestalling John's advance on London. The key to doing so would be Rochester Castle.[18]

Rochester was one of the most formidable and important fortresses in Britain. Its great tower, soaring to a height of 125 feet, was the tallest in Europe. The castle's importance lay in its location in the city of Rochester, situated on the road from London to Dover at the point where it crossed the wide tidal estuary of the River Medway. The Medway, as its name suggests, divided Kent in two from north to south. It was impossible for anyone to advance along this route if the castle was held against them. Since the fall of London in May both sides had recognized Rochester's crucial strategic significance, but neither had been able to obtain possession of it. By an agreement dating back to the days of Henry I, the castle was controlled by the archbishops of Canterbury. John had already made two attempts, in May and in August, to persuade Langton to hand it over, but on both occasions the archbishop had declined, endeavouring to stay neutral, and unwilling to hand such an obvious military advantage to the king. By early September, however, Robert fitz Walter was afraid that John might try to force the matter, and decided to take pre-emptive action. Around the middle of the month, he left London with a force of knights, sergeants and crossbowmen, and entered Rochester with the consent of its keeper, Reginald of Cornhill.[19]

The king was predictably furious when he learned of this development a day or so later. On 17 September he ordered the seizure of fitz Walter's lands, and sent Pandulf in pursuit of Langton, who was at that moment heading for Rome with the other English bishops for a general Church council. The nuncio caught up with the archbishop, either just before his departure or soon after he had crossed the Channel, and suspended him from office, citing Langton's failure to excommunicate the rebels and his dishonourable conduct relating to Rochester. John, like several chroniclers, clearly suspected that the archbishop had been secretly involved in the castle's surrender, and would later describe him on this score as 'a notorious and barefaced traitor'.[20]

The news that his enemies had left London and occupied Rochester prompted the king to advance inland towards them. On 20 September he moved from Dover to Canterbury and began to fortify the cathedral city against attack. When he was informed, however, that fitz Walter's forces were now just ten miles away at Ospringe, the prospect of an attack sent him scurrying back in the direction of the coast. To the derision of the Anonymous of Béthune, the rebels misread his flight as a hostile move and in turn withdrew to Rochester. Recovering his nerve, John retraced his steps to Canterbury and then advanced a further thirty-five miles westward, crossing the North Downs in order to arrive at the upper reaches of the Medway near Allington. It was probably at this point that he sent some of his forces up the river towards Rochester, intending that they should burn down the city's bridge, thus cutting off those inside the castle from their friends in London. This was unsuccessful: fitz Walter and his troops managed to beat off the attack and extinguish the flames, killing many of the king's men and forcing the remainder to flee.[21]

At the same time John received more bad news. A great storm that had raged across England on 26 September had destroyed several of the ships that had been transporting his Flemish troops across the Channel. Hundreds of their bodies were being washed up on the Suffolk coast. Nevertheless, some Flemish knights had avoided the disaster and found their way to him, and when the king returned to Canterbury on 5 October he discovered a great many more awaiting his arrival. Having taken their homages he ordered them to arms and set out at once towards Rochester, this time marching straight along the main road, determined on a direct assault.[22]

In the meantime Robert fitz Walter had returned to London, having handed Rochester over to another of the baronial leaders, William d'Albini. 'A man bold in spirit and tried in war', according to Roger of Wendover, Albini had been sent with a body of picked troops, variously estimated by the chroniclers to have been between 100 and 140 strong. They had apparently arrived at the castle on 11 October and been dismayed to discover it was ill-supplied with both weapons and provisions. There was little time to put this right, and they were able to add only what extra supplies they could find in the city. On 13 October John drew up his army outside the city walls and began his attack. Those manning the walls quickly realized that they could not hold them and fell back to the castle, chased through the streets by the king's men who had broken in through the gates. 'Many would gladly have fled back to London if they could', smirked the Anonymous of Béthune. They could not because John's troops had now made good on their earlier failure and destroyed the bridge across the Medway.[23]

Having cut off the defenders from any hope of relief, the king settled down to besiege them. To the disgust of Ralph of Coggeshall he allowed his men to occupy Rochester Cathedral, even to the extent of stabling their horses next to the high altar. Meanwhile in front of the castle his engineers erected five great stone-throwing machines and began to bombard the great tower day and night with missiles.[24]

Back in London, fitz Walter and the other barons were trying to round up enough troops to mount a relief operation. On 26 October, a fortnight into the siege, they set out in the direction of Rochester with an army of 700 knights. How they intended to cross the Medway is a mystery, but as it was they completed only half their journey. At Dartford they were warned that John's forces had grown greatly in number, and that he was making ready to attack them. The king had indeed been receiving more foreign mercenaries who were swarming all over Kent to find supplies to sustain the siege. Disheartened by this news, the would-be relief force rode back to London, leaving Albini and his men to their fate.[25]

Despite the odds the garrison at Rochester refused to surrender as October turned into November. From the outset John had envisaged that he might have to resort to undermining the castle's walls, and had ordered the smiths of Canterbury to work all hours to produce the necessary pickaxes. At some stage his men created a breach in the walls of the bailey, and forced the defenders to retreat into the great tower. The sappers then began to drive a mine under the tower itself. By 25 November it must have been nearing completion, as on that day the king demanded that Hubert de Burgh should quickly find him 'forty pigs, the fattest and least good for eating, to start a fire under the tower'. Soon afterwards the pig fat was used to burn away the wooden props supporting the mine, and the tower was partially collapsed, leaving a gaping hole in its southeast angle. Astonishingly, Albini and his men continued to resist, using the cross-wall that divided the tower in two as a desperate last line of defence. Finally, however, their own strength failed them, for the castle's meagre provisions had long since been exhausted, and the garrison had been reduced to eating the flesh of their own expensive warhorses. A day or so later, on 30 November, they surrendered, after enduring an assault that had lasted seven weeks. 'Living memory does not recall', said the Crowland chronicler, 'a siege so fiercely pressed and so staunchly resisted.'[26]

Because of the numerous casualties on his own side, and the

vast amount of money he had spent, John was in no mood to be merciful. In the days before the surrender Albini had sent out from the castle 'those who seemed less warlike', and the king had responded by cutting off their hands and feet. According to several chroniclers his intention after the fortress's fall was to hang all the remaining members of the garrison. Eventually the nobles in his own camp dissuaded him from doing so, arguing that this would trigger the revenge killing of any royalists who in future might fall into rebel hands. John contented himself with hanging just one of the defenders, a crossbowman who had been raised from boyhood in the royal household. The rest he sent to be imprisoned in various royal castles. William d'Albini was sent to Corfe.[27]

For the remaining barons this was a crushing blow. On hearing the news, says the Crowland chronicler, they were struck with panic, and either gathered in London or hid themselves in religious houses. After the fall of Rochester, one of the greatest castles in the kingdom, 'few were willing to trust in fortifications'. Their only remaining hope was that Louis would come swiftly to their rescue, but that still seemed to be a distant prospect. During the siege two of the rebel earls, Saer de Quincy and Henry de Bohun, had crossed to France to try to hasten his arrival, and in response Louis had dispatched 140 knights to England. This, however, was too small a force to make any meaningful difference, and after landing in Suffolk all they had done was join the barons in London. As for Louis himself, he was not expected to arrive in England before the middle of January.[28]

John, meanwhile, was ready to go on the rampage. From Rochester he made his way west to Winchester, then north to St Albans, where he held a council of war. As the St Albans chronicler Roger of Wendover explains, he decided with his military advisers to divide his forces in two. Half of them would remain in the south under the command of his half-brother, the earl of Salisbury, partly to keep the barons penned up in London, and partly to ravage the lands of the rebels in East Anglia. The other half would accompany the king, who was setting out to punish his enemies in the north.[29]

As well as wishing to revenge himself on the northern barons, John also wanted to vent his fury against the new king of Scots. The elderly William the Lion had died the previous December, having ruled Scotland for almost half a century, and had been succeeded by his son, Alexander, now sixteen years of age. Alexander had been quick to side with the English rebels in the hope of reversing the humiliations that had been inflicted on his father, and of making good his long-standing claim to Northumberland, Cumberland and Westmorland. The barons had been happy to oblige him on this score, and at some point in the autumn the council of twenty-five had ruled that these northern counties should be handed over. In October the new Scottish king had come south to take possession of his prize by laying siege to the border castle at Norham. On 22 October the Northumbrian rebels had done homage to him, and Eustace de Vescy had invested him with Northumbria using a special ceremonial staff.[30]

John set out for the north, said Wendover, 'intending to destroy everything that came in his way with fire and sword'. From St Albans he advanced rapidly to Nottingham, where he spent Christmas, in Crowland's words, 'not in the usual manner, but as one on the warpath'. Most of his army were Flemish mercenaries, and the king encouraged them to every excess, not only the destruction of his enemies' homes and the seizure of their goods, but also burning towns and setting fire to hedgerows. People of every rank and condition, says Wendover, were imprisoned and tortured until they paid heavy ransoms; one of the reasons John had embarked on this campaign was to enrich himself and his followers at his enemies' expense. Passing close to William d'Albini's castle at Belvoir, he persuaded its garrison to surrender by threatening to starve their lord to death if they refused. At Pontefract at the start of January he similarly induced John de Lacy to submit, along with another member of the Twenty-Five, Roger de Montbegon. Two days later he occupied York, where the terrified citizens offered £1,000 to be spared the depredations of his troops.[31]

Others fled in the face of his wrath. The barons of Yorkshire rode to Scotland and sought the protection of Alexander, doing homage to him in the chapter house of Melrose Abbey on 11 January 1216. The chronicler there records how these men had burnt their own estates and barns as they departed so as to deny any sustenance to John's army. According to the Anonymous of Béthune, the king had been ready to call a halt to his advance at Durham, but decided to continue when he learned that the king of Scots had burned Newcastle upon Tyne. Vowing to 'run the sandy little fox-cub into his earth', John marched all the way to the Scottish border, taking Berwick in mid-January and torturing its inhabitants for money. He then advanced into Scotland itself, burning the towns of Haddington and Dunbar and pillaging the abbey at Coldingham. After a week of destruction he left for England, setting fire to Berwick as he departed, reportedly putting the torch to his lodgings with his own hand.[32]

In southern England the other half of the king's army had been wreaking similar havoc. Ralph of Coggeshall, well placed to comment, describes how Poitevin mercenaries had harried their way through Essex, laying siege to Geoffrey de Mandeville's castle at Pleshey on Christmas Eve and stealing the horses from Coggeshall Abbey on New Year's Day. Across the whole of East Anglia they had ravaged the lands of the barons, stolen the valuables from churches and tortured people to get at their money. The barons themselves, meanwhile, had remained for the most part in London. The return of Saer de Quincy from France in early January, bringing with him forty-one ships full of French soldiers, must have boosted the rebels' morale, and at the end of the month they advanced into Essex to raise the siege of Colchester. But there was still no sign of Louis, who now let it be known that his coming was postponed until Easter. The presence of French knights in London also proved to be something of a double-edged sword when one of them accidentally killed Geoffrey de Mandeville in a tournament towards the end of February.[33]

By this point, says Ralph of Coggeshall, the king had been away in the north for so long that rumours of his death began to circulate. In March, however, John reappeared in the south, ready to prove that such reports had been greatly exaggerated. After reuniting the two halves of his army he marched them through East Anglia, targeting the homes of his enemies that were still holding out. The earl of Norfolk's mighty castle at Framlingham was surrendered by its garrison without a fight. Colchester, restored to William de Lanvallei the previous summer, resisted for only a few days, provoking accusations of treachery against the French knights who had been left to defend it. Castle Hedingham, the principal seat of the earl of Oxford, fell after the shortest of sieges, and the earl himself decided to seek the king's mercy. By the end of the month the eastern counties were completely subdued. At Hedingham, says Coggeshall, John distributed the spoils of the campaign among his mercenaries, so as to secure their services for an immediate attack on London.[34]

The rebels in London were still determined to resist. When they became aware of the king's intention, says Coggeshall, they opened all the gates to the city, ready to ride out and confront him if he came within ten leagues. John did in fact come within this distance, pausing at Enfield, twelve miles north of London, on the last day of March. But when some of his troops approached more closely, the barons launched a surprise attack, seriously wounding the Poitevin commander Savaric de Mauléon and killing many others. Around the same moment, the Londoners successfully beat off the ships that the king had sent up the Thames to blockade the city, capturing their mercenary crews or leaving them to drown. The result was that John withdrew to a safer distance, reaching Reading by 5 April.[35]

The truth was he had left it too late. The time to have attacked London had been in December, immediately after the fall of Rochester, when the barons' morale was at its lowest. Instead, John had taken the easier option of conducting a harrying campaign against his enemies. There were perhaps sound economic reasons for this decision. It had cost him a fortune to keep his mercenary army static for seven weeks before the walls of Rochester; by allowing them to plunder northern and eastern

England he had relieved some of this financial pressure. But strategically it had been a mistake. In the meantime several contingents of French troops had been able to reach London and the resolve of the rebels had grown stronger. For all the suffering and destruction the king had caused, the results of his ravaging had been more illusory than real. Many castles had been surrendered but most of the rebels had held out and gone into hiding. As soon as John had returned south they resumed their resistance. Alexander of Scotland attacked Carlisle at the end of February and in March the Northerners laid siege to York.[36]

The rebels were fighting more fiercely than ever because at last the arrival of Louis seemed to be imminent. Although he did not appear at Easter as promised, by that date (10 April) the extent of his military preparations on the opposite side of the Channel must have been obvious. At some point after Easter John responded by sending an embassy to Philip Augustus, headed by William Marshal and Peter des Roches, entreating the French king to prevent his son from sailing and reminding him of their five-year truce. Around the same time Philip and Louis were being warned of the dire spiritual consequences of attacking England by the papal legate, Guala Bicchieri, dispatched to the French court by Innocent III in an effort to save his crusade. Both these representations were rejected. John's ambassadors were simply turned away without a hearing. Guala by contrast was treated to a long justification of Louis' claim, and told bluntly that the papal overlordship of England was pretended. John had compromised his right to wear the English crown, the French maintained, by his treachery towards his brother Richard and his murder of his nephew, Arthur.[37]

While these futile attempts at diplomacy were taking place, John was preparing for the worst and trying to muster the strength to resist yet another invasion threat. It would, of course, be difficult to assemble the kind of huge land army he had summoned for the same purpose in 1213, since half his subjects were now at war with him. On 12 April, still at Reading, he made a desperate and wholly unsuccessful attempt to woo the men whose lands he had been plundering just a few weeks earlier, offering to make peace with Eustace de Vescy and others without financial penalty, assuring them 'what we desire from our barons is not so much their money as their good and faithful service'. Recognizing that this offer might not generate any results, John looked more hope-fully towards his naval resources. Two days later he sent letters to more than twenty coastal towns, commanding them to send every possible ship, crewed with the best mariners, to the mouth of the Thames as quickly as possible. His plan, explains Coggeshall, was to engage Louis' forces in a battle at sea and defeat them before they landed.[38]

According to the Anonymous of Béthune, it was a plan that had a good chance of succeeding, for Louis' ships were mostly small ones which would have been unable to defend themselves against John's much larger vessels. In the last week of April the king returned to Kent, and from the start of May he based himself on the coast at Folkestone, waiting for the first sighting of any French sails. At some point in the following fortnight his fleet moved to Dover, ready to repel the invaders massing on the other side of the Channel at Calais, Gravelines and Wissant. Some ships were sent to try to burn the French fleet while it was still anchored in these ports, in the hope of replicating the successful raid on Zwin in 1213. But this time the fortunes of war were reversed. On the night of 18 May a terrible storm blew up in the Channel and destroyed John's ships, overturning them or smashing them into each other, and scattering those that did not sink far and wide along the south coast. Any hope of repelling Louis at sea was lost.[39]

Louis quickly realized this was his chance and set sail at once, so soon that he almost fell foul of the same bad weather, which dispersed his ships and drove them in the wrong direction. On the morning of 21 May he landed at Stonar near Sandwich with only a small portion of his followers. John, who had gone inland to Canterbury to prepare for the reception of the papal legate, was quickly informed of the landing, but preferred to wait for Guala's arrival before he responded. It was not until the next day that the king arrived at Sandwich, just in time to see the remainder of Louis' fleet sailing into view. He immediately decided to risk all and fight them on the beaches: trumpets were sounded and his troops lined up ready for battle.[40]

But, with equal suddenness, John then changed his mind. His army was largely composed of foreigners who were serving him only for money; some of them had friends and relatives among the enemy force that was about to disembark. What if, in the thick of the fighting, they decided to switch sides? Such apparently was the fear of William Marshal, who, according to the Dunstable annalist, advised the king to retire. Other chroniclers, by contrast, blamed the decision on John's cowardice. The Anonymous of Béthune describes how the king rode off from Sandwich in secret, and had retreated a league in the direction of Dover before his troops realized he had deserted them. Despairing of his craven conduct, some of them nevertheless followed him as he withdrew along the south coast towards Winchester. Others felt that this was the final straw, and left his service for good.[41]

John's sudden departure allowed Louis to sweep all before him. With a force of knights that the Anonymous estimated to be 1,200 strong, he quickly secured Sandwich and then advanced to Canterbury, causing the citizens to submit and the papal legate to flee. He then marched to Rochester, taking back the crippled castle from its royalist garrison on the last day of May. On 2 June he entered London in triumph, to the general joy of its inhabitants, and was led into St Paul's Cathedral in a celebratory procession. On the following day he received the homage of Robert fitz Walter and the other rebel barons, assuring them that in return he would restore their 'good laws and lost inheritances'.[42]

Three days after his triumphant entry into London, Louis set out towards Winchester in pursuit of John. As he advanced the castles at Reigate, Guildford and Farnham submitted with little or no resistance, and by 14 June his army was drawing near to Winchester's walls. John was no longer within them, having fled further west as soon as he learned of Louis' approach. The city had been left in the hands of Savaric de Mauléon, who burned much of it down in a misguided attempt to frustrate the French advance, before deciding to retire to join the king. Winchester's defence was left to the garrisons of its two castles, which Louis pounded with his siege engines for ten days, until Savaric returned with the licence for them to surrender.[43]

It was now approaching the end of June, and John was at Corfe Castle, experiencing what must have been one of the lowest points in his life. His kingdom had been invaded, and almost all of the south-east had fallen to his foes. His capital had been occupied, along with the great cathedral cities of Canterbury and Winchester. Elsewhere across the country, all his recent gains were being undone as the rebels took heart from Louis' arrival. At the start of June, before abandoning Winchester, the king had dispatched a flurry of writs to his commanders in the Midlands and the north, telling them to hold their castles if they could, and if not to destroy them. Such desperate orders must have seemed to herald the beginning of the end. By this stage almost a third of his household knights had defected, and while Louis had been besieging Winchester, says Coggeshall, 'almost all the earls and barons came to him there, who had previously supported John'. The earls of Surrey and Arundel were prominent among the deserters, but the most devastating loss was surely the earl of Salisbury, the king's half-brother, who seems to have been one of the few men to whom John was genuinely close. It was later said that Salisbury bore a grudge because the king had seduced his countess, but the timing of his departure suggests that the truth was rather more prosaic. John's closest supporters were leaving him because his cause appeared to be lost.[44]

Having taken Winchester, however, Louis decided to abandon his pursuit. Rather than pushing on into Dorset to besiege John at Corfe, he led his army south-east to take the royal castle at Portchester, then struck north to attempt the same at Odiham. Why he acted in this way is unclear. The Anonymous of Béthune reveals that there were already tensions emerging between the newly arrived French nobles, who were hungry for reward in the form of lands and castles, and the English barons, who naturally felt that their own claims were superior. A more likely reason is that Louis realized that John would probably keep retreating and giving him the slip, and decided it would make better sense to tighten his grip on the territory he had already taken. In his dash to take London and Winchester he had bypassed several castles which were still defiantly holding out for the king. Odiham, despite being a relatively small fortress with a garrison of just thirteen men, resisted for a whole week, to the admiration of those besieging it. After its fall Louis returned to London, where he determined to tackle two far more prestigious targets. One division of his army was sent up the Thames to besiege Windsor. The remainder followed Louis back through Kent in the direction of the mighty castle at Dover.[45]

During all this time John had remained at Corfe, conveniently near to the coast in case Louis should change his mind, waiting to see how events would unfold. Eventually, once the French army had returned to London, the king emerged from his foxhole and headed north, moving swiftly to Bristol and Gloucester, before stopping at Hereford, where he remained during the last days of July. As this itinerary suggests, his hopes were now pinned on the west – and not just the west of England. Of his remaining supporters, the two greatest were William Marshal and Ranulf of Chester, both of whom had extensive lands in the March of Wales and, in the Marshal's case, in Ireland as well. John accordingly spent the next three weeks travelling up and down the Welsh border, visiting Shrewsbury, Whitchurch and Worcester, and shoring up what he thought would be his last line of defence. Letters issued on 19 August show that this is where he anticipated Louis or his forces would strike next.[46]

Louis was in fact at this point about as far from the Welsh border as he could possibly be, having spent the same three-week period outside the walls of Dover Castle, fruitlessly trying to force his way in. The mighty fortress, rebuilt by Henry II on a scale to rival the Tower of London and extensively added to by John himself, was being held by the redoubtable Hubert de Burgh with a sizeable royalist garrison. Like his father at Château Gaillard,

Louis had established huge siege works around the castle, 'erecting buildings around it', in the words of the Dunstable annalist, 'as if he were establishing a town'. He had also deployed his fleet to make sure the castle was cut off from the sea, and brought out his heaviest artillery. But despite this massive effort, and the relentless pounding of his siege engines, the defenders remained resolute, and meanwhile the waiting was taking its toll on his own army. Some of Louis' followers had already left for home even before the siege had started; now they began to desert in droves, said the Anonymous of Béthune, 'so that the host dwindled remarkably'. As well as having to contend with the hardship of the siege, the French forces in Kent and Sussex found themselves being constantly harassed and killed by a band of English bowmen based in the great forest of the Weald. Led by a former royal bailiff called William of Kensham (or 'Willikin of the Weald' as he became known), these prototype Robin Hoods were so successful that the king wrote to thank them for their efforts.[47]

Realizing that his opponent was being usefully detained in Kent, John decided to go on the offensive. At the start of September he rounded up his remaining forces and advanced down the valley of the Thames, apparently with the intention of raising the siege of Windsor. The French forces that had been sent to take the castle had enjoyed no more success than their colleagues at Dover, and were almost grateful for the distraction. The king himself came only as close as Sonning, seventeen miles to the west, but sent some of the Welsh archers he had recruited during the previous month to shoot into the enemy camp at night. When the French responded by readying themselves for battle, John took off at speed towards East Anglia. If, as some have suggested, this was a feigned flight, intended to draw off the besiegers, it was certainly a convincing one: the king and his army covered the hundred miles between Sonning and Cambridge in just three days.[48]

John had decided to head east for two reasons. Firstly, as Coggeshall explains, he had come to lay waste, once again, to the lands of the rebels. Soon after Louis' arrival in London, Robert fitz Walter and the other barons had marched into East Anglia to recover their estates and castles that the king had seized during the spring. John now moved swiftly from Cambridge to the border of Suffolk and Essex, visiting the earl of Oxford's castle at Hedingham and the earl of Hertford's castle at Clare, burning and destroying everywhere he went. His second reason for coming east was to try to apprehend the young king of Scots. In the course of the previous month Alexander had travelled from Cumbria to Kent to do homage to Louis, and John was apparently hopeful of intercepting him on his return journey.[49]

Shortly into his harrying campaign, however, the king discovered that the French army that had been besieging Windsor had indeed been pursuing him, and was about to descend on Cambridge. Forced once more to flee, he tore off towards the north, not resting until he had reached the border with Lincolnshire.[50] Burning the barns of religious houses, and even the crops still standing unharvested in the fields, he advanced towards Lincoln, where he succeeded in driving off the rebels who were besieging the city's castle, and pursued them into the inaccessible region known as the Isle of Axholme. But in so doing he seems to have missed his opportunity to intercept Alexander, who slipped past him and returned safely to Scotland. John moved back south along the Lincolnshire coast, burning all the while. 'Never had there been a time', lamented the local Crowland chronicler, 'when there had been such fires in the land.'[51]

Precisely what John's next move would have been is uncertain. The rebels who had been pursuing him had given up the chase after his flight from Cambridge and gone to join Louis, who was still besieging Dover. Although the king was heading south, he appears to have been planning a northern campaign. On 9 October he left Lincolnshire and went to King's Lynn in Norfolk, then one of the most prosperous ports in England, to arrange for supplies to be sent to several of his northern castles.[52]

At that point, however, John fell ill. Ralph of Coggeshall claims it was dysentery, and assumed it was caused by an excessive intake of food and drink; Roger of Wendover famously but unreliably describes a dish of peaches and new cider. More likely a body wracked by exhaustion was to blame: for the previous four weeks the forty-nine-year-old king had been travelling at a relentless pace, often riding more than thirty miles in the space of a single day.[53]

Two days after arriving at King's Lynn, despite his illness, he set out again, heading back in the direction of Lincolnshire. Still in a hurry, he decided to save time by taking a short cut across the great tidal estuary of the Wash, at the point where the River Wellstream merged with the sea. Disaster struck when parts of his baggage train, both men and packhorses, were sucked down into the treacherous sands. According to Coggeshall, the king lost all the precious items of his chapel, including his collection of holy relics. He may even have lost his crown and other regalia, since they do not figure in later royal inventories.[54]

Wracked with grief on account of this loss, John struggled to Swineshead Priory in Lincolnshire, then after two more days pushed on to the bishop of Lincoln's castle at Sleaford. There he was met by messengers from Dover with even worse news. Louis had undermined and partially collapsed the castle's main entrance. Hubert de Burgh and his men had prevented the French army storming the breach, but they could not hold out for much longer. A truce had been agreed to allow the defenders to seek the king's help, or else his permission to surrender.[55]

This news, says Coggeshall, caused John such distress that it brought on the return of his illness. An attempt to alleviate his condition by bleeding him seems to have made no difference, and on 15 October he wrote to the pope, describing how he was suffering from 'a grave and incurable infirmity'. The pope in question was not the formidable Innocent III, whose pontificate had done so much to shape the king's reign. Innocent had died on 16 July, to be replaced by Honorius III. John now addressed the new pontiff 'on bended knee', and committed his kingdom to the Church's protection, without which he could see no hope of saving the succession for his heirs.[56]

Having composed this letter, the king continued with his

desperate journey. Too ill to ride, he was carried in a litter from Sleaford a further twenty miles west to Newark, another castle confiscated from the bishop of Lincoln. It was probably there that he dictated his last will and testament, the original copy of which still survives. John began by assigning the administration of his affairs to thirteen of his faithful servants, including William Marshal, Ranulf of Chester, Peter des Roches and the papal legate, Guala. These men were to make amends to the Church for the damages and injuries he had inflicted, and to arrange for aid to be sent to the Holy Land. They were to help his sons obtain and defend their inheritance, and to ensure that his other faithful servants were rewarded. Lastly, they were to distribute money to religious houses and to the poor for the salvation of his soul.[57]

Had the imminent prospect of death and the danger to his soul brought any repentance? Eight days earlier, after the first onset of his illness at King's Lynn, John had given permission to Margaret, wife of Walter de Lacy, to found a religious house in Herefordshire in memory of her father, William de Briouze, her mother Matilda and her brother William.[58]

On the night of 18 October, a great gale howled through the town of Newark, with such intensity that the citizens feared that their houses would be destroyed. The abbot of Croxton must have been grateful to be safe within the walls of the castle. He had been summoned to the king's bedside because of his medical expertise, but by this point his patient was beyond saving. Instead he heard the dying man's confession, and administered the last rites.[59]

Conclusion

The morning after John's death his body was prepared for burial. His heart and intestines were removed and taken to be interred at Croxton Abbey, a macabre reward for the services of its abbot. The rest of the king's remains were embalmed and made ready for a longer journey. John had originally intended to be laid to rest at Beaulieu, the abbey he had founded in Hampshire towards the start of his reign after his reconciliation with the Cistercians. But Hampshire was now enemy territory, so the king had decided in his final days to bequeath his body to Worcester Cathedral. He may have had some attachment to St Wulfstan, who was also buried there, but in truth the options were extremely limited, and Worcester was probably selected because it was one of the few places where the royalist presence remained strong enough to guarantee the funeral would be secure. In death, as in life, John was escorted across the country by his foreign mercenaries.[1]

It would have taken several days to cover the hundred miles from Newark, so his supporters had time to assemble in Worcester. William Marshal was there, and his biographer describes how the bier was borne into the cathedral for a magnificent funeral service, 'such as befitted a king'. In one respect, however, the ceremony was notably lacking in regal splendour. Enough evidence exists to suppose that earlier kings had been buried wearing their crowns. Richard, for example, had been interred wearing the one he had used for his second coronation in 1194. John's funeral broke with this tradition, most likely because his crown or crowns had been lost in the

Wash a few days before, and there had been no time to make a replacement. Instead the king was buried with what remained of his regalia, including the linen coif that had been tied around his head at the time of his coronation to hold in place the holy oil used to anoint him. It was this that was mistaken for a monk's cowl when his tomb was opened centuries later. Tudor historians assumed it was intended to serve as 'a passport through the regions of Purgatory'.[2]

Certainly it must have crossed the minds of those who dressed John's body for his final journey that he was going to need all the help he could get. William Marshal was reportedly sad when he heard of the king's death, but he was clearly in the minority. The Crowland chronicler, in his short obituary notice, stated that John was 'little mourned'. Ralph of Coggeshall went much further. Once the king had passed away, he explained, many people had 'dreadful and fantastical visions' of him, the nature of which it was best not to write down. The implication is that John was suffering the torments of hell. 'Foul as it is,' wrote Matthew Paris in the 1230s, quoting a contemporary rhyme, 'hell itself is made fouler by the presence of King John.'[3]

There was no doubt that John's reign had been a disaster. He had come to the throne in 1199 as the ruler of a great empire, the most powerful prince in Europe. Yet within five years most of his continental inheritance had been lost, and now he was being buried in the midst of a bitter civil war. The Scots had occupied the north of England, the Welsh had overrun the southern March of Wales, eastern England was in the hands of the rebels, and all of the south-east had been invaded by the French. At the start of his life John had been dubbed 'Lack-land'. By the time of his death it seemed inevitable that the story was going to end the same way.

Was this because, as Coggeshall and others implied, John was a thoroughly bad man, or was he a victim of circumstance? The Crowland chronicler, who offers the most sympathetic view of the king's career, commented that John was 'a great prince, indeed, but an unlucky one', and others have since reviewed the evidence and reached a similar conclusion.[4] What, in the final analysis, is the fairest verdict on King John?

Even before his reign had started, John had been warned about the fate of bad kings. At Easter 1199, on the eve of his succession, he was treated to an impromptu lecture on the subject by Bishop Hugh of Lincoln. Hugh had come to France to speak with Richard, but arrived too late, and instead found himself at Fontevraud addressing the dead king's younger brother. Leading John to the entrance of the abbey church, the bishop showed him the sculpture of the Last Judgement above the door, and pointed out the kings being carried off to hell by demons. 'Fix your mind always on their howls and perpetual torment,' said Hugh, sternly. But John, quick-witted as he was, responded by noting that on the opposite side of the scene there were other kings being conducted joyously by angels towards heaven. 'My lord bishop,' he said, 'you should have shown us these, whom we intend to imitate, and whose company we desire to join.'[5]

But John's words, alas, were not matched by his actions, and over the next few days he shocked Hugh with his unseemly behaviour. During the service on Easter Sunday he hesitated in making his offering of gold coins at the altar, and admitted that a few days earlier he would probably have pocketed them. Then, when the bishop was delivering his sermon, John sent repeated messages telling him to hurry up so they could move on to breakfast. One week later, when John was in Rouen being invested as duke of Normandy, he was distracted by the applause and laughter of his cronies, and accidentally dropped the ceremonial lance that had just been conferred on him. The whole assembly saw this as a bad omen.[6]

Had these stories been written down by Hugh himself they would have been extremely valuable, for the bishop died in November 1200, not long after the events described, and without any knowledge of the disasters that were yet to come. Unfortunately, they were preserved for posterity by Hugh's biographer, Adam of Eynsham, who committed them to parchment in the early months of 1213, by which point the path that John had taken was all too apparent. The king had lost his continental territories and engaged in a struggle against the pope that had led to his excommunication and England's punishment by interdict. Adam was obviously writing with the advantage of hindsight. Having related the story of Hugh's lesson on the Last Judgement, he noted that it had taken place fourteen years ago, and lamented that in the meantime John appeared to have forgotten the bishop's valuable words of advice.[7]

And that, the argument runs, is the problem with using chronicle evidence to assess King John. Not only are the authors likely to adapt or improve their material based on their knowledge of how the story ends; they are also, as monks, bound to be prejudiced against John on account of his treatment of the Church. Some monastic chroniclers writing after the king's death portrayed him as an irreligious monster. According to Matthew Paris, John actually rejected Christianity, and at one stage tried to make England subject to the Muslim emir of north Africa. Such accusations, of course, have no basis in fact. John was not a notably pious king; his financial records show that he frequently gave alms to the poor to atone for having hunted or eaten meat on holy days. But they also show him spending money on vestments, altar cloths and crucifixes. On this score, at least, John was not nearly as bad as the later chroniclers made out.[8]

Similarly, the official records of John's reign can be deployed against the chroniclers' accusations of sloth. The king's itinerary, reconstructed from his chancery rolls, shows that he travelled at a relentless rate, sometimes riding more than thirty miles a day, and often remaining for only one or two nights in the same place before moving on. Wherever he went, moreover, John was constantly engaged in the business of government. Judicial records show that he frequently acted as judge, both in his own court and at the Exchequer, and that a steady stream of cases from other courts were marked for his attention. Historians who edited this material in the twentieth century came away greatly impressed by the king's energy, intelligence and attention to detail.[9]

It is the financial records, however, that have been most frequently mined to construct a case for John's defence. Some historians have argued that the king's loss of his continental inheritance in 1204 was inevitable, because at the time of his accession the Angevin Empire was already fatally overstretched, and too expensive to maintain. This argument obviously depends on an analysis of both John's financial resources and those of his rival, Philip Augustus, but the simple truth is that the records are not complete enough in either case to sustain such an analysis, however painstaking. John's defenders often point out that his rule coincided with a period of high inflation, meaning that he had to pay his knights two or three times as much as they had demanded during the reigns of his father and brother. But French records show that during the crucial period 1202–3 Philip was having to pay even more than John. It was for this reason that the most recent assessment of all the available financial evidence concluded that 'the causes for the loss of Normandy in 1204 must be sought elsewhere'.[10]

For contemporary observers there was one obvious and outstanding cause: the personality of King John. We do not have to believe Roger of Wendover, who accused John of incorrigible idleness and spending all morning in bed with his young queen. We might, however, give more credit to the author of *The History of William Marshal*, who was not a monk but a layman, and whose testimony reflected the views of the Marshal himself. In this author's opinion, the crucial factor in the loss of Normandy had been the change of rulers in 1199. The Normans, he explained, had once been grain but had lately become chaff, 'for since the death of King Richard they have no leadership'.[11]

John's reputation was already very badly tarnished at the time of his accession. His mistakes in Ireland, and even his last-minute desertion of his father, might easily have been forgiven; even the best medieval monarchs were criticized for the misadventures of their youth. It was, however, far less easy to excuse John's attempt to usurp the throne while Richard had been on crusade. This was treachery, pure and simple, and as such deeply damaging. The

Normans, in particular, must have regarded John with suspicion and loathing after his refusal to help defend the duchy in 1193. At that point they fought against both John and Philip Augustus, even though Richard was in prison. Ten years later, after the change in leadership, they were unwilling to resist Philip's invasion, even though John was present in person.

Besides his reputation for treachery, John lacked boldness. Richard, of course, had been as bold as a lion, and proved it time and again across Europe and the Holy Land; even his Muslim enemies told stories about his prowess.[12] No one, by way of sad contrast, ever told such stories about John. His elder brothers Henry and Geoffrey had been noted tourneyers, but there is no record of John ever having taken to the tournament field. This may have been because Henry II had forbidden it, especially after Geoffrey's death in 1186, but had John possessed a genuine appetite for such adventures he could have indulged it during Richard's reign. The likeliest explanation for his failure to do so is that physical combat held no real appeal. John had no problem with war, and throughout his career was keen to embark on military campaigns. He relished the prospect of conflict, so long as the odds were stacked entirely in his favour. Thus he was able to conduct successful sieges at Montauban, Carrickfergus and Rochester, relying on the supremacy of his artillery and infantry. Similarly in 1202 he accepted William des Roches' assurance that a surprise attack on Mirebeau would guarantee a total victory over his enemies.

As soon as the outcome seemed anything less than certain, however, the king preferred to cut and run. There was much truth in the remark attributed to Richard by Roger of Howden, 'my brother John is not a man to win lands for himself by force if there is anyone to put up a mere show of resistance'. Howden was dead by 1202, but his words proved prophetic. During his French campaign of 1206 John backed away from Philip Augustus, prompting accusations of cowardice. In 1214 he fled as Louis approached La Roche-au-Moine, even though the French prince apparently had a smaller force. In 1216, as Louis disembarked his troops in England, John once again rode off in the opposite direction without even bothering to sound a retreat. 'No man may ever trust him,' sang the troubadour Bertran de Born, 'for his heart is soft and cowardly.'[13] John's critics had dubbed him 'Soft-sword' at the start of his reign for his decision to make peace with Philip Augustus, and Gervase of Canterbury thought it unfair. By 1216, it was an epithet that John had earned many times over.

Being a poor warrior put John at a great disadvantage, which he managed to compound by being a poor politician. His most egregious mistake, in the eyes of contemporaries, was his marriage to Isabella of Angoulême, because of the gratuitous offence it caused to the Lusignans. 'This was the cause of the ignominy and war', said William Marshal's biographer, 'that led to the king losing his land.'[14] On many other occasions during his reign, John set about needlessly provoking people when he felt strong, then desperately trying to win them back when his confidence had evaporated. He goaded the Lusignans into rebellion, then tried to woo them again once his other allies had deserted. He victimized the Anglo-Norman lords of Ireland and the March of Wales, then sought their help when conspiracy threatened to topple him. He imposed a scutage of unparalleled severity on the English barons who refused to fight in Poitou, then cravenly sought their assistance when his military plans miscarried. He harried the Northerners, then looked for their support against a French invasion. John may well have been a genius when it came to devising new ways to extort money, but when it came to the fundamental skills of political management, he was clumsy and foolish.

He was also cruel. The Middle Ages, it might be countered, were a cruel time (though it is difficult to demonstrate convincingly that this is any less true of other ages, including our own). It might also be argued that, in the case of kings, it was better to be cruel than to be kind. One of Stephen's faults, according to his contemporary biographer, was his mildness in doing justice.[15] John, however, committed acts which were considered to be excessive even by the standards of his own day. One naturally thinks first of his nephew, Arthur, who was almost certainly killed on John's orders, if not by his own hand, in 1203. It was clearly regarded a notorious act at the time, and the French made it part of the case for trying to depose John in 1216. Yet Arthur was not the worst case, and it even proved possible to construct a defence. Shakespeare may have portrayed him as a vulnerable child, but in 1202 Arthur was fifteen years old and recently knighted by Philip Augustus, a ritual associated with entry into manhood. Roger of Wendover, no supporter of King John, rejected the French accusations of murder, putting words into the mouth of Innocent III. 'Arthur was no blameless victim', said the pope. 'He was captured at Mirebeau, a traitor to his lord and uncle to whom he had sworn homage and allegiance, and he could rightly be condemned without judgement to die even the most shameful of deaths.' Furtive as they were, John and his advisers no doubt took exactly this view in 1203, and Wendover's words suggest that at least some people in England thought that they had been justified in doing so.[16]

It was, however, impossible to make a similar case for the king's other victims. In a chivalrous age, when defeated enemies expected to be held in honourable captivity and eventually ransomed, John chose to starve people to death. His starvation of many of the knights taken at Mirebeau is well attested, as is his horrific treatment of Matilda and William de Briouze. Geoffrey of Norwich, the clerk involved in the plot of 1212, may have suffered the same fate, and on more than one occasion during the war of 1215 the king threatened to starve particular rebels.[17] This was about as cruel a death as could be devised. Richard, as we have seen, resorted to it on one occasion, to punish a man who had betrayed him. John used it repeatedly against anyone who fell into his clutches: knights, clerics and women.

It was the king's cruelty, said William Marshal's biographer, that cost him the support of the barons of Anjou, and the cruelty of his mercenaries that extinguished any vestigial support in Normandy.[18] Confined to England after the loss of these provinces, he governed the country with the feverish intensity that has drawn praise from some twentieth-century historians. Yet John's industry did not elicit the same response from contemporaries. On the contrary, they regarded his coming with dread, for it invariably left them worse off. The king's constant travelling and judging were means to the same end: raising money. Likewise, his military campaigns beyond England's borders were not perceived as great national triumphs, but as personal vendettas directed at particular enemies. His oppression of the Welsh and Scots, and also the Anglo-Norman magnates of Wales and Ireland, drove them into alliance with the barons of England, and eventually into conspiracy and open rebellion. The final result – Magna Carta – was thus a British document, as its clauses relating to the Celtic countries show.

Magna Carta was also a charge sheet directed squarely at John. It is often said in the king's defence that the charter was aimed not so much at him as the whole Angevin system. In fact the emphasis should be the other way round. Henry II, it is true, had greatly extended the scope of the royal Forest, and raised a lot of money from forest eyres. Richard had demanded more cash from the counties, especially after his release from captivity in 1194. These ancient grievances were brought to the table by the rebels in 1215 and informed Magna Carta. Yet they were nothing compared to the scale of the complaint raised against John, who had taken the exceptional measures of his predecessors and made them routine. Scutage went from being occasional to almost annual. Fines and reliefs were often charged at sums in excess of four figures. A comprehensive study of John's revenue concluded that his reign saw the greatest level of exploitation in England since the Norman Conquest.[19] The charter made allowances for John on some issues, giving him more time to deal with Forest or any unjust disseisins that had been made by his ancestors. But it gave him no such respite on amercements and hostages. Unable to inspire loyalty by other means, John had taken such coercive methods and made them standard procedure. In the opinion of the Melrose chronicler, probably writing very soon after Magna Carta had been sealed, the king 'had perverted the excellent institutions of the realm, mismanaged its laws and customs, and misgoverned his subjects. His inclination became law; he oppressed his own subjects; he placed over them foreign mercenary soldiers and put to death lawful heirs whom he had taken as hostages, while aliens seized their lands.'[20]

Melrose Abbey is in Scotland, and so was not directly affected by the interdict. Nevertheless, it might be objected that any monastic chronicler would be bound to take a negative view of an excommunicate ruler. The same sort of caveat can be raised against *The History of William Marshal*, for both the Marshal and his descendants had endured John's persecution and had axes to grind. It is more difficult, however, to dismiss the opinion of the Anonymous of Béthune. The Anonymous was writing for Robert of Béthune, a Flemish nobleman who had fought for the king towards the end of his reign and been well rewarded as a result. In this account, John is praised for his hospitality:

He spent lavishly, he gave plenty to eat, and did so generously and willingly. People never found the gate or the doors of John's hall barred against them, so that all who wanted to eat at his court could do so. At the three great feasts [Christmas, Easter and Whitsun] he gave robes aplenty to his knights. This was a good quality of his.

But, in the opinion of the Anonymous, this was about as much as could be entered in the credit column. His overall view of John was damning:

He was a very bad man, more cruel than all others. He lusted after beautiful women and because of this he shamed the high men of the land, for which reason he was greatly hated. Whenever he could he told lies rather than the truth. He set his barons against one another whenever possible, and was very happy when he saw hate between them. He hated and was jealous of all honourable men; it greatly displeased him when he saw anyone acting well. He was brim-full of evil qualities.[21]

Almost all of these charges can be supported by other evidence. John's readiness to lie, for example, is brought out vividly in *The History of William Marshal*, when the king, in an attempt to discomfort the Marshal, falsely maintains that the earl's men in Ireland have been killed. John's habit of pitting his magnates against each other is borne out by the numerous land disputes between baronial families that were allowed to fester, the king preferring to use the threat of disinheritance as a way of enforcing obedience. And John does appear to have found it very difficult to get along with his most powerful barons, the people the Anonymous probably intended by the phrase 'honourable men'. His closest companions were men of lesser rank, foreign exiles or mercenaries, always ready to do his bidding and easily dismissed if they in any way disappointed.

Since he seems to be correct on so many counts, it seems likely that the Anonymous may also be right in describing the king as a sexual predator. It has been claimed in the past that John's behaviour in the bedchamber was not really a problem, because mistresses and bastard children were no impediment to being a successful king.[22] The charge against John, however, is not that he led a debauched life, but that he targeted the wives and daughters of his leading barons. The evidence is naturally circumstantial – it is very hard to find conclusive proof on such private matters – but the accusation was made enough times by different authors citing specific examples (the daughter of Robert fitz Walter, the wives of Eustace de Vescy and William Longsword) for us to believe that the general allegation made by the Anonymous must have some basis in truth.

It was reportedly sexual attraction, rather than political calculation, that led John to marry Isabella of Angoulême. The couple certainly had regular marital relations during the latter half of their marriage, for Isabella had five children between 1207 and 1215. How much harmony there was in the marriage beyond this is a matter of speculation. Isabella has had few mentions in the preceding pages because very little is known about her activities. John allowed her no political role, nor even any role in the running of her own estates. Essentially he continued to treat his queen like a child, ensuring her needs were met and moving her from place to place as his needs required. Gervase of Canterbury claimed that at one point John imprisoned Isabella in Corfe Castle; the king certainly kept her under close guard during the final years of his reign, though this was probably for her own protection. The claims of other chroniclers that the king was infatuated with her occur only in the context of the dubious passages that describe him idling in bed while the Angevin Empire was lost. According to the Anonymous, John said to Isabella on one occasion, 'You hear, my lady, all that I have lost for you,' to which she replied, 'And I, my lord, have lost the best knight in the world for you' – a reference to her broken betrothal to Hugh de Lusignan. Undoubtedly the most suggestive evidence about Isabella's feelings for John was her behaviour after his death. In 1217 she returned to Angoulême, abandoning four of her five children, in order to marry Hugh de Lusignan's namesake son, with whom she went on to start a new life and a new family. The queen lived another twenty-nine years, during which time she enjoyed far greater control of her own destiny and inheritance, and so issued many charters. Not one of them contains a reference to John or to prayers for his soul.[23]

Perhaps the most clinching argument for the personal nature of John's failure and the loathing he inspired is the speed with which the situation in England was retrieved once he was gone. After the king's funeral at Worcester, William Marshal and the other royalists rode to Gloucester, where on 28 October 1216 John's eldest son was knighted and crowned as King Henry III – a circlet borrowed from his mother was placed on his head in lieu of anything better. The following day the Marshal was elected as his guardian and effectively became the kingdom's regent. A nine-year-old boy and a seventy-year-old man: the future seemed terribly bleak. Some of the Marshal's men talked about retreating across the Irish Sea, and the earl himself declared he would, if necessary, carry Henry on his shoulders from island to island, 'even if I have to beg my bread'. Meanwhile, on the other side of the country, the earl of Salisbury, who had already defected during the summer, was urging Hubert de Burgh to do the same and abandon the defence of Dover Castle. The cause of the new king, he maintained, was hopeless.[24]

But within a year the royalists achieved a remarkable turn-around. Henry's youth, and his innocence, actually proved to be a great advantage. It was much harder for the rebels, many of whom had been deprived of their hereditary lands by John, to justify continued resistance against his blameless son, and deny the boy his own birthright. The Marshal's age also proved to be an asset, for his experience and reputation lent the royalist govern-ment a credibility and trustworthiness it had never possessed while John had been in power. Despite his advanced years, the earl showed himself to be no slouch on the battlefield, exhibiting exactly the kind of grit that his late master had lacked. When Louis divided his forces in the spring of 1217 and sent half his army to join the rebel siege of Lincoln Castle, the Marshal seized his chance. On 20 May his forces fell upon the city of Lincoln, capturing many of the leading rebels, including Robert fitz Walter. The Marshal, leading the assault, almost forgot to don his helmet in all the excitement. The news caused Louis to break off his siege of Dover, with equally catastrophic results. In August Hubert de Burgh and his men sailed out from Dover and, in a great sea battle off Sandwich, destroyed the French fleet that was bringing reinforcements. The following month Louis agreed to make peace, resigned his claim to England and returned to France.[25]

Part of that peace was Magna Carta, now described as such to distinguish it from the new Charter of the Forest that was issued at the same moment. The regency government had revived the rebel manifesto a fortnight after Henry's coronation, publishing a modified version in the hope of wooing back some of their opponents. The clauses most damaging to the Crown – most particularly, the security clause that licensed the barons' use of military force against the king – had been removed, but most of the points of detail had been retained. In future, on a whole range of levels, the coercive power of the Crown would be curtailed. Fines would have to be proportionate, taxes would have to be consensual – the charter obtained its definitive form in a reissue of 1225, granted in return for a tax of £40,000.[26] Above all, future kings would have to rule within the law. This was the lasting legacy of King John. He lost the continental empire of his ancestors, and left England divided and ravaged by war. But his oppressions led to the creation of a document that ensured they would not be repeated, and which still symbolizes the rights of the subject against the power of a tyrant.

Magna Carta, 1215

A Translation

John, by the grace of God, king of England, lord of Ireland, duke of Normandy and Aquitaine, count of Anjou, to the archbishops, bishops, abbots, earls, barons, justiciars, foresters, sheriffs, stewards, servants and all his officials and faithful subjects greeting. Know that we, from reverence for God and for the salvation of our soul and those of all our ancestors and heirs, for the honour of God and the exaltation of Holy Church and the reform of our realm, on the advice of our reverend fathers, Stephen, archbishop of Canterbury, primate of all England and cardinal of the Holy Roman Church, Henry, archbishop of Dublin, William of London, Peter of Winchester, Jocelin of Bath and Glastonbury, Hugh of Lincoln, Walter of Worcester, William of Coventry and Benedict of Rochester, bishops, Master Pandulf, subdeacon and member of the household of the lord pope, Brother Aimeric, master of the knighthood of the Temple in England, and the noble men, William Marshal, earl of Pembroke, William, earl of Salisbury, William, earl of Warenne, William, earl of Arundel, Alan of Galloway, constable of Scotland, Warin fitz Gerold, Peter fitz Herbert, Hubert de Burgh, seneschal of Poitou, Hugh de Neville, Matthew fitz Herbert, Thomas Basset, Alan Basset, Philip d'Aubigny, Robert of Ropsley, John Marshal, John fitz Hugh and others, our faithful subjects:

1. In the first place have granted to God and by this our present charter have confirmed, for us and our heirs in perpetuity, that the English church shall be free, and shall have its rights undiminished and its liberties unimpaired: and we wish it thus observed, which is evident from the fact that of our own free will before the quarrel between us and our barons began, we conceded and confirmed by our charter freedom of elections, which is thought to be of the greatest necessity and importance to the English church, and obtained confirmation of this from the lord pope Innocent III, which we shall observe and wish our heirs to observe in good faith in perpetuity. We have also granted to all the free men of our realm for ourselves and our heirs for ever, all the liberties written below, to have and hold, them and their heirs from us and our heirs.

2. If any of our earls or barons, or others holding of us in chief by knight service shall die, and at his death his heir be of full age and owe relief, he shall have his inheritance on payment of the ancient relief, namely the heir or heirs of an earl £100 for a whole earl's barony, the heir or heirs of a baron £100 for a whole barony, the heir or heirs of a knight 100s. at most for a whole knight's fee; and anyone who owes less shall give less according to the ancient usage of fiefs.

3. If, however, the heir of any such person has been under age and in wardship, when he comes of age he shall have his inheritance without relief or fine.

4. The guardian of the land of such an heir who is under age shall not take from the land more than the reasonable revenues, customary dues and services, and that without destruction and waste of men or goods. And if we entrust the wardship of the land of such a one to a sheriff, or to any other who is answerable to us for its revenues, and he destroys or wastes the land in his charge, we will take amends of him, and the land shall be entrusted to two lawful and prudent men of that fief who will be answerable to us for the revenues or to him to whom we have assigned them. And if we give or sell to anyone the wardship of any such land and he

causes destruction or waste, he shall lose the wardship and it shall be transferred to two lawful and prudent men of the fief who shall be answerable to us as is aforesaid.

5. Moreover so long as the guardian has the wardship of the land, he shall maintain the houses, parks, preserves, fishponds, mills and the other things pertaining to the land from its revenues; and he shall restore to the heir when he comes of age all his land stocked with ploughs and wainage such as the agricultural season demands and the revenues of the estate can easily bear.

6. Heirs shall be given in marriage without disparagement, yet so that before a marriage is contracted it shall be made known to the heir's next of kin.

7. After her husband's death, a widow shall have her marriage portion and her inheritance at once and without any hindrance; nor shall she pay anything for her dower, her marriage portion, or her inheritance which she and her husband held on the day of her husband's death; and she may stay in her husband's house for forty days after his death, within which period her dower shall be assigned to her.

8. No widow shall be compelled to marry so long as she wishes to live without a husband, provided that she gives security that she will not marry without our consent if she holds of us, or without the consent of the lord of whom she holds, if she holds of another.

9. Neither we nor our bailiffs will seize any land or rent in payment of a debt so long as the chattels of the debtor are sufficient to repay the debt; nor shall the sureties of the debtor be distrained so long as the debtor himself is capable of paying the debt; and if the principal debtor defaults in the payment of the debt, having nothing wherewith to pay it, the sureties shall be answerable for the debt; and, if they wish, they may have the lands and revenues of the debtor until they have received satisfaction for the debt they paid on his behalf, unless the principal debtor shows that he has discharged his obligations to the sureties.

10. If anyone who has borrowed from the Jews any amount, great

or small, dies before the debt is repaid, it shall not carry interest unless the heir in under age, of whomsoever he holds; and if that debt falls into our hands, we will take nothing accept the principal sum specified in the bond.

11. And if a man dies owing a debt to the Jews, his wife may have her dower and pay nothing of that debt; and if he leaves children under age, their needs shall be met in a manner in keeping with the holding of the deceased; and the debts shall be paid out of the residue, saving the service due to the lords. Debts owing to others than Jews shall be dealt with likewise.

12. No scutage or aid shall be levied in our realm except by the common counsel of our realm, unless it is for the ransom of our person, the knighting of our eldest son or the first marriage of our eldest daughter; and for these only a reasonable aid is to be levied. Aids from the city of London are to be treated likewise.

13. And the city of London is to have all its ancient liberties and free customs both by land and water. Furthermore, we will and grant that all other cities, boroughs, towns and ports shall have all their liberties and free customs.

14. And to obtain the common council of the realm for the assessment of an aid (except in the three cases aforesaid) or a scutage, we will have archbishops, bishops, abbots, earls and greater barons summoned individually by our letters, and we shall also have summoned generally through our sheriffs and bailiffs all those who hold of us in chief, for a fixed date, with at least forty days' notice, and at a fixed place; and in all letters of the summons we will state the reason for the summons. And when the summons has thus been made, the business shall go forward on the day arranged according to the council of those present, even if not all those summoned have come.

15. Henceforth we will not grant anyone that he may take an aid from his free men except to ransom his person, to make his eldest son a knight and to marry his eldest daughter once; and for these purposes only a reasonable aid is to be levied.

16. No man shall be compelled to perform more service for a knight's fee or for any other free tenement that is due therefrom.

17. Common pleas shall not follow our court but shall be held in some fixed place.
18. Recognizances of novel disseisin, mort d'ancestor, and darrein presentment shall not be held elsewhere than in the court of the county in which they occur, and in this manner: we, or if we are out of the realm our chief justiciar, shall send two justices through each country four times a year who, with four knights of each county chosen by the county, shall hold the said assizes in the county court on the day and in the place of meeting of the county court.
19. And if the said assizes cannot all be held on the day of the county court, so many knights and freeholders of those present in the county court on that day shall remain behind as will suffice to make judgements, according to the amount of business to be done.
20. A free man shall not be amerced for a trivial offence, except in accordance with the degree of the offence; and for a serious offence he shall be amerced according to its gravity, saving his livelihood; and a merchant likewise, saving his merchandise; in the same way a villein shall be amerced saving his wainage; if they fall into our mercy. And none of the aforesaid amercements shall be imposed except by testimony of reputable men of the neighbourhood.
21. Earls and barons shall not be amerced except by their peers and only in accordance with the nature of the offence.
22. No clerk shall be amerced on his lay tenement except in the manner of the others aforesaid and without reference to the size of his ecclesiastical benefice.
23. No vill or man shall be forced to build bridges at river banks, except those who ought to do so by custom and law.
24. No sheriff, constable, coroners or others of our bailiffs may hold pleas of our Crown.
25. All shires, hundreds, wapentakes and ridings shall be at the ancient farm without any increment, except out demesne manors.
26. If anyone holding a lay fief of us dies and our sheriff or bailiff

shows our letters patent of summons for a debt which the deceased owed us, it shall be lawful for the sheriff or our bailiff to attach and list the chattels of the deceased found in lay fee to the value of that debt, by the view of lawful men, so that nothing is removed until the evident debt is paid to us, and the residue shall be relinquished to the executors to carry out the will of the deceased. And if he owes us nothing, all the chattels shall be accounted as the deceased's saving their reasonable shares to his wife and children.

27. If any free man dies intestate, his chattels are to be distributed by his nearest relations and friends, under supervision of the Church, saving to everyone the debts which the deceased owed him.

28. No constable or any other of our bailiffs shall take any man's corn or other chattels unless he pays cash for them at once or can delay payment with the agreement of the seller.

29. No constable is to compel any knight to give money for castle guard, if he is willing to perform that guard in his own person or by another reliable man, if for some good reason he is unable to do it himself; and if we take or send him on military service, he shall be excused the guard in proportion to the period of his service.

30. No sheriff or bailiff of ours or anyone else is to take horses or carts of any free man for carting without his agreement.

31. Neither we nor our bailiffs shall take other men's timber for castles or other work of ours, without the agreement of the owner.

32. We will not hold the lands of convicted felons for more than a year and a day, when the lands shall be returned to the lords of the fiefs.

33. Henceforth all fish-weirs shall be completely removed from the Thames and the Medway and throughout all England, except on the sea coast.

34. The writ called *praecipe* shall not, in future, be issued to anyone in respect of any holding whereby a free man may lose his court.

35. Let there be one measure of wine throughout our kingdom

and one measure of ale and one measure of corn, namely the London quarter, and one width of cloth whether dyed, russet or halberjet, namely two ells within the selvedges. Let it be the same with weights as with measures.

36. Henceforth nothing shall be given or taken for the writ of inquisition of life or limb, but it shall be given freely and not refused.

37. If anyone holds of us by fee-farm, by socage or by burgage, and holds land of someone else by knight service, we will not, by virtue of that fee-farm, socage or burgage, have wardship of his heir or of land of his that belongs to the fief of another; nor will we have custody of that fee-farm or socage or burgage unless such fee-farm owes knight service. We will not have custody of the heir or land of anyone who holds of another by knight service, by virtue of any petty sergeanty which he holds of us by the service of rendering to us knives or arrows or the like.

38. Henceforth no bailiff shall put anyone on trial by his own unsupported allegation, without bringing credible witnesses to the charge.

39. No free man shall be taken or imprisoned or disseised or outlawed or exiled or in any way ruined, nor will we go or send against him, except by the lawful judgement of his peers or by the law of the land.

40. To no one will we sell, to no one will we deny or delay right or justice.

41. All merchants are to be safe and secure in leaving and entering England, and in staying and travelling in England, both by land and by water, to buy and sell free from all maletotes by the ancient and rightful customs, except, in time of war, such as come from an enemy country. And if such are found in our land at the outbreak of war they shall be detained without damage to their persons or goods, until we or our chief justiciar know how the merchants of our land are treated in the enemy country; and if ours are safe there, the others shall be safe in our land.

42. Henceforth anyone, saving his allegiance due to us, may leave

our realm and return safe and secure by land and water, save for a short period in time of war on account of the general interest of the realm and excepting those imprisoned and outlawed according to the law of the land, and natives of an enemy country, and merchants, who shall be treated as aforesaid.

43. If anyone dies who holds of some escheat such as the honours of Wallingford, Nottingham, Boulogne or Lancaster, or of other escheats which are in our hands and are baronies, his heir shall not give any relief or do any service to us other than what he would have done to the baron if that barony had been in the baron's hands; and we shall hold it in the same manner as the baron held it.

44. Henceforth men who live outside the forest shall not come before our justices of the forest upon a general summons, unless they are impleaded or are sureties for any person or persons who are attached for forest offences.

45. We will not make justices, constables, sheriffs or bailiffs who do not know the law of the land and mean to observe it well.

46. All barons who have founded abbeys of which they have charters of the kings of England, or ancient tenure, shall have custody thereof during vacancies, as they ought to have.

47. All forests which have been afforested in our time shall be disafforested at once; and river banks which we have enclosed in our time shall be treated similarly.

48. All evil customs of forests and warrens, foresters and warreners, sheriffs and their servants, river banks and their wardens are to be investigated at once in every county by twelve sworn knights of the same county who are to be chosen by worthy men of the county, and within forty days of the inquiry they are to be abolished by them beyond recall, provided that we, or our justiciar, if we are not in England, first know of it.

49. We will restore at once all hostages and charters delivered to us by Englishmen as securities for peace or faithful service.

50. We will dismiss completely from their offices the relations of Gerard d'Athée that henceforth they shall have no office in

England, Engelard de Cigogné, Peter and Guy and Andrew de
Chanceaux, Guy de Cigogné, Geoffrey de Martigny with his
brothers, Philip Marc with his brothers and his nephew, Geoffrey,
and all their followers.

51. Immediately after concluding peace, we will remove from the
kingdom all alien knights, crossbowmen, sergeants and mercenary soldiers who have come with horses and arms to the hurt
of the realm.

52. If anyone has been disseised or deprived by us without lawful
judgement of his peers of lands, castles, liberties or his rights
we will restore them to him at once; and if any disagreement
arises on this, then let it be settled by the judgement of the
Twenty-Five barons referred to below in the security clause.
But for all those things of which anyone was disseised or
deprived without lawful judgement of his peers by King Henry
our father, or by King Richard our brother, which we hold
in our hand or which are held by others under our warranty,
we shall have respite for the usual crusader's term; excepting
those cases in which a plea was begun or inquest made on
our order before we took the cross; when, however, we return
from our pilgrimage, or if perhaps we do not undertake it, we
will at once do full justice in these matters.

53. We shall have the same respite, and in the same manner, in
doing justice on disafforesting or retaining those forests which
Henry our father or Richard our brother afforested, and
concerning custody of lands which are of the fee of another,
the which wardships we have hitherto by virtue of a fee held
of us by knight's service, and concerning abbeys founded on
fees other than our own, in which the lord of the fee claims
to have a right. And as soon as we return, or if we do not
undertake our pilgrimage, we will at once do full justice to
complainants in these matters.

54. No one shall be taken or imprisoned upon the appeal of a
woman for the death of anyone except her husband.

55. All fines which were made with us unjustly and contrary to
the law of the land, and all amercements imposed unjustly and

contrary to the law of the land, shall be completely remitted or else they shall be settled by the judgement of the Twenty-Five barons mentioned below in the security clause, or by the judgement of the majority of the same, along with the aforesaid Stephen, archbishop of Canterbury, if he can be present, and others whom he wishes to summon with him for this purpose. And if he cannot be present the business shall nevertheless proceed without him, provided that if any one or more of the aforesaid Twenty-Five barons are in such a suit they shall stand down in this particular judgement, and shall be replaced by others chosen and sworn in by the rest of the same Twenty-Five, for this case only.

56. If we have disseised or deprived Welshmen of lands, liberties or other things without lawful judgement of their peers, in England or in Wales, they are to be returned to them at once; and if a dispute arises over this it shall be settled in the March by judgement of their peers; for tenements in England according to the law in England, for tenements in Wales according to the law in Wales, for tenements in the March according to the law of the March. The Welsh are to do the same to us and ours.

57. For all those things, however, of which any Welshman has been disseised or deprived without lawful judgement of his peers by King Henry our father, or King Richard our brother, which we have in our possession or which others hold under our legal warranty, we shall have respite for the usual crusader's term; excepting those cases in which a plea was begun or inquest made on our order before we took the cross. However, when we return, or if perhaps we do not go on our pilgrimage, we will at once give them full justice in accordance with the laws of the Welsh and the aforesaid regions.

58. We will restore at once the son of Llywelyn and all the hostages from Wales and the charters delivered to us as security for peace.

59. We will treat Alexander, king of the Scots, concerning the return of his sisters and hostages and his liberties and rights in the same manner in which we will act towards our other

barons of England, unless it ought to be otherwise because of the charters which we have from William his father, formerly king of the Scots; and this shall be determined by the judgement of his peers in our court.

60. All these aforesaid customs and liberties which we have granted to be held in our realm as far as it pertains to us towards our men, shall be observed by all men of our realm, both clerk and lay, as far as it pertains to them, towards their own men.

61. Since, moreover, we have granted all the aforesaid things for God, for the reform of our realm and the better settling of the quarrel which has arisen between us and our barons, wishing these things to be enjoyed fully and undisturbed in perpetuity, we give and grant them the following security: namely, that the barons shall choose any twenty-five barons of the realm they wish, who with all their might are to observe, maintain and cause to be observed the peace and liberties which we have granted and confirmed to them by this our present charter; so that if we or our justiciar or our bailiffs or any of our servants offend against anyone in any way, or transgress any of the articles of peace or security, and the offence is indicated to four of the aforesaid twenty-five barons, those four barons shall come to us or our justiciar, if we are out of the kingdom, and shall bring it to our notice and ask that we have it redressed without delay. And if we, or our justiciar, should we be out of the kingdom, do not redress the offence within forty days from the time it was brought to the notice of us or our justiciar, should we be out of the kingdom, the aforesaid four barons shall refer the case to the rest of the twenty-five barons and those twenty-five barons with the commune of all the land shall distrain and distress us in every way they can, namely by seizing castles, lands and possessions, and in such other ways as they can, saving our person and those of our queen and of our children, until, in their judgement, amends have been made; and when it has been redressed they are to obey us as they did before. And anyone in the land who wishes may take an oath to obey the orders of the said twenty-five barons in the

execution of all the aforesaid matters, and to join with them in distressing us to the best of his ability, and we publicly and freely permit anyone who wishes to take the oath, and we will never forbid anyone to take it. Moreover we shall compel and order all those in the land who of themselves and of their own free will are unwilling to take an oath to the twenty-five barons to distrain and distress us with them, to take the oath aforesaid. And if any of the twenty-five barons dies or leaves the country or is otherwise prevented from discharging these aforesaid duties, the rest of the aforesaid barons shall on their own decision choose another in his place, who shall take the oath in the same way as the others. In all matters the execution of which is committed to those twenty-five barons, if it should happen that the twenty-five are present and disagree among themselves on anything, or if any of them who has been summoned will not or cannot come, whatever the majority of those present shall provide or order is to be taken as fixed and settled as if the whole twenty-five had agreed to it; and the aforesaid twenty-five are to swear that they will faithfully observe all the aforesaid and will do all they can to secure its observance. And we will procure nothing from anyone, either personally or through another, by which any of these concessions and liberties shall be revoked or diminished; and if any such thing is procured, it shall be null and void, and we will never use it either ourselves or through another.

62. And we have completely remitted and pardoned to all any ill will, grudge and rancour that have arisen between us and our subjects, clerk and lay, from the time of the quarrel. Moreover we have fully forgiven and completely condoned to all, clerk and lay, as far as pertains to us, all offences occasioned by the said quarrel from Easter in the sixteenth year of our reign to the conclusion of peace. And moreover we have caused letters patent of the Lord Stephen, archbishop of Canterbury, the Lord Henry, archbishop of Dublin, the aforesaid bishops and Master Pandulf to be made for them on this security and the aforesaid concessions.

63. Wherefore we wish and firmly command that the English church shall be free, and the men in our realm shall have and hold all the aforesaid liberties, rights and concessions well and peacefully, freely and quietly, fully and completely for them and their heirs of us and our heirs in all things and places for ever, as is aforesaid. Moreover an oath has been sworn, both on our part and on the part of the barons, that all these things aforesaid shall be observed in good faith and without evil intent. Witness the above-mentioned and many others. Given under our hand in the meadow which is called Runnymede between Windsor and Staines on the fifteenth day of June in the seventeenth year of our reign.

Abbreviations

(Unless otherwise indicated, the place of publication is London)

Anonymous	*Histoire des Ducs de Normandie et des Rois d'Angleterre*, ed. F. Michel (Paris, 1840).
Brut	*Brut Y Tywysogion, or the Chronicle of the Princes*, ed. J. Williams ab Ithel (Roll Ser., 1860).
Bury	'Annales Sancti Edmundi', *Memorials of St Edmund's Abbey*, ed. T. Arnold (3 vols., Rolls Ser., 1890–96).
Coggeshall	*Radulphi de Coggeshall, Chronicon Anglicanum*, ed. J. Stevenson (Rolls Ser., 1875).
Crowland	*Memoriale fratris Walteri de Coventria*, ed. W. Stubbs (2 vols., Rolls Ser., 1872–73). All references are to volume 2.
Devizes	*The Chronicle of Richard of Devizes*, ed. J. T. Appleby (1963).
Diceto	*Radulfi de Diceto Decani Londiniensis Opera Historica*, ed. W. Stubbs (2 vols., Rolls Ser., 1876).
DNB	www.oxforddnb.com (entries cited by name). For the printed text, see *The Oxford Dictionary of National*

	Biography, ed. H. C. G. Matthew and B. Harrison (60 vols., Oxford, 2004).
Dunstable	'Annales Prioratus de Dunstaplia', *Annales Monastici*, ed. H. R. Luard (5 vols., Rolls Ser., 1864–9), vol. 3.
EHD	*English Historical Documents*
EHR	*English Historical Review*
Foedera	*Foedera, conventiones, litterae*, I, i, ed. T. Rymer, A. Clarke, F. Holbrooke and J. Caley (1816).
Gervase	*The Historical Works of Gervase of Canterbury*, ed. W. Stubbs (2 vols., Rolls Ser., 1879–80).
Howden	*The Annals of Roger of Hoveden*, trans. H. T. Riley (2 vols., 1853).
HWM	*The History of William Marshal*, ed. A. J. Holden, S. Gregory and D. Crouch (3 vols., Anglo-Norman Text Soc., Occasional Publications Ser., 4–6, 2002–6).
Itinerary	T. D. Hardy, 'An Itinerary of King John', idem, *Description of the Patent Rolls in the Tower of London* (1835).
Life of St Hugh	*Magna Vita Sancti Hugonis, The Life of St Hugh of Lincoln*, ed. D. L. Douie and D. H. Farmer (2 vols., Edinburgh, 1962).
The Magna Carta Project	http://magnacarta.cmp.uea.ac.uk
Margam	'Annales de Margam', *Annales Monastici*, ed. H. R. Luard (5 vols., Rolls Ser., 1864–9), vol. 1.
Melrose	'The Chronicle of Melrose', *Church Historians of England*, vol. 4, part I, trans. J. Stevenson (1856).
Newburgh	'The History of William of Newburgh', *Church Historians of*

	England, vol. 4, part II, trans. J. Stevenson (1856).
Norgate, *Angevin Kings*	K. Norgate, *England under the Angevin Kings* (2 vols., 1887).
Norgate, Lackland	K. Norgate, John Lackland (1902).
RLC	*Rotuli Litterarum Clausarum in Turri Londiniensi asservati*, ed. T. D. Hardy (2 vols., 1833–4). All references are to volume 1.
RLP	*Rotuli Litterarum Patentium in Turri Londiniensi asservati*, ed. T. D. Hardy (1835).
Rot. Chart.	*Rotuli Chartarum in Turri Londiniensi asservati*, ed. T. D. Hardy (1837).
Rot. Ob.	*Rotuli de Oblatis et Finibus in Turri Londiniensi asservati*, ed. T. D. Hardy (1835).
Select Charters	*Select Charters and Other Illustrations of English Constitutional History*, ed. W. Stubbs and H. W. C. Davis (9th edn, Oxford, 1921).
Selected Letters	*Selected Letters of Pope Innocent III Concerning England (1198–1216)*, ed. C. R. Cheney and W. H. Semple (1953).
Wendover	*Roger of Wendover's Flowers of History*, trans. J. A. Giles (2 vols., 1849).
Worcester	'Annales Prioratus de Wigornia', *Annales Monastici*, ed. H. R. Luard (5 vols., Rolls Ser., 1864–9), vol. 4.

Notes

INTRODUCTION

1 My account of the opening of John's tomb is based on V. Green, *An Account of the Discovery of the Body of King John* (1797), 1–8. For the king's sandals and stocking, see *Berrow's Worcester Journal* (17 May 1941), 4; for his teeth, *Dundee Courier* (2 January 1923), 2. See also J. H. P. Pafford, 'King John's Tomb in Worcester Cathedral: An Account of its Opening in 1529 by John Bale', *Trans. Worcester Archaeological Soc.*, 35 (1958), 58–60; S. D. Church, 'The Care of the Royal Tombs in English Cathedrals in the Nineteenth and Twentieth Centuries: The Case of the Effigy of King John at Worcester', *Antiquaries Journal*, 89 (2009), 365–87; J. Martindale, 'The Sword on the Stone: Some Resonances of a Medieval Symbol of Power (The Tomb of King John in Worcester Cathedral)', *Anglo-Norman Studies*, 15 (1993), 199–241.

2 *DNB* Robin Hood.

1 Under Attack 1203

1 J. Gillingham, *The Angevin Empire* (2nd edn, 2001), 1–2.

2 J. Bradbury, *Philip Augustus, King of France 1180–1223* (1998), 70–1.

3 F. M. Powicke, *The Loss of Normandy* (2nd edn, Manchester, 1961), 159–62.

4 *Itinerary*; Wendover, 207.

5 Ibid., 206.

6 *Itinerary*; *HWM*, ii, 134–5; Norgate, *Lackland*, 94; Powicke, *Loss of Normandy*, 163.

7 Ibid., 161, 163–5. Powicke suggests Montfort was recovered in April, but July seems more likely.

8 J. Gillingham, *Richard I* (Yale, 1999), 301–5.

9 Norgate, *Angevin Kings*, ii, 375–8.

10 I have used the accounts in Norgate, *Angevin Kings*, ii, 411–16, and S. McGlynn, *Blood Cries Afar* (Stroud, 2011), 42–9.

11 Powicke, *Loss of Normandy*, 165–6.

12 Ibid., 164; Norgate, *Angevin Kings*, ii, 416–17.

13 *HWM*, ii, 136–7; iii, 146; Powicke, *Loss of Normandy*, 166n.

14 *HWM*, ii, 136–9.

15 Ibid., 138–41; *Itinerary*.

16 Ibid.; *HWM*, ii, 140–3.

2 The Family Empire 1120–1189

1 D. Bates, *The Normans and Empire* (Oxford, 2013), 30.

2 C. W. Hollister, *Henry I* (2001), 276–9.

3 *EHD*, ii, 296–8; Hollister, *Henry I*, 41, 278, 280, 308–9.

4 Ibid., 309–18. Cf. Gillingham, *Angevin Empire*, 10–11.

5 See J. S. Plant, 'The Tardy Adoption of the Plantagenet Surname', *Nomina*, 30 (2007), 57–84.

6 See e.g. D. Crouch, *The Reign of King Stephen* (2000).

7 W. L. Warren, *Henry II* (new edn, 2000), 31, 38; D. A. Carpenter, *The Struggle for Mastery: Britain, 1066–1284* (2003), 188–90.

8 *DNB* Henry II; *DNB* Eleanor of Aquitaine; *EHD*, ii, 386–90.

9 *DNB* Eleanor of Aquitaine. Cf. A. W. Lewis, 'The Birth and Childhood of King John: Some Revisions', *Eleanor of Aquitaine: Lord and Lady*, ed. B. Wheeler and J. C. Parsons (Basingstoke, 2002), 161, 165.

10 Ibid., 161.

11 Warren, *Henry II*, 94; N. Vincent, 'The Court of Henry II',

Henry II: New Interpretations, ed. C. Harper-Bill and N.Vincent (Woodbridge, 2007), 278–334.

12 Lewis, 'Birth and Childhood', 160–5; Warren, *Henry II*, 108–9.

13 Gillingham, *Richard I*, 28; *DNB*, Eleanor of Aquitaine.

14 Ibid.; Gillingham, *Richard I*, 39–40; Lewis, 'Birth and Childhood', 165–8.

15 *DNB* Eleanor of Aquitaine; *DNB* Henry II.

16 *DNB* Henry the Young King; M. Strickland, 'On the Instruction of a Prince: The Upbringing of Henry, the Young King', *Henry II: New Interpretations*, ed. Harper-Bill and Vincent, 184–214.

17 Norgate, *Lackland*, 2, 4–5; Gillingham, *Richard I*, 41–2.

18 Warren, *Henry II*, 72, 90.

19 Gillingham, *Richard I*, 42–7.

20 Ibid., 48–51; Warren, *Henry II*, 121–36.

21 Ibid., 138; Gillingham, *Richard I*, 50.

22 Lewis, 'Birth and Childhood', 166–9; Norgate, *Lackland*, 5.

23 *DNB* Eleanor of Aquitaine.

24 Ibid.; Gillingham, *Richard I*, 51.

25 Norgate, *Lackland*, 7–8; Gillingham, *Richard I*, 65–6.

26 Warren, *Henry II*, 584.

27 Ibid., 147–8, 608–9; Gillingham, *Richard I*, 26–7, 64–5.

28 Warren, *Henry II*, 584–7; Gillingham, *Richard I*, 69–71.

29 Ibid., 71–5; Strickland, 'On the Instruction of a Prince', 186–7.

30 *DNB* Geoffrey; Gillingham, *Richard I*, 76–7.

31 Ibid., 68, 78–9; Warren, *Henry II*, 596–7.

32 Gillingham, *Richard I*, 79.

33 Carpenter, *Struggle for Mastery*, 216.

34 See e.g. S. Duffy, *Ireland in the Middle Ages* (Basingstoke, 1996); idem, 'Henry II and England's Insular Neighbours', *Henry II: New Interpretations*, ed. Harper-Bill and Vincent, 132–3; R. R. Davies, *The First English Empire* (Oxford, 2000), 94.

35 Carpenter, *Struggle for Mastery*, 216–17; Warren, *Henry II*, 114.

36 Carpenter, *Struggle for Mastery*, 218–19.

37 S. Duffy, 'John and Ireland', *King John: New Intepretations*, ed. S. D. Church (Woodbridge, 1999), 225–8.

38 Howden, 50.

39 Duffy, 'John and Ireland', 228–9; *Expugnatio Hibernica: The Conquest of Ireland, by Giraldus Cambrensis*, ed. and trans. A. B. Scott and F. X. Martin (Dublin, 1978), 202–3; Norgate, *Lackland*, 17.

40 *Expugnatio Hibernica*, 235–45.

41 Ibid.; Duffy, 'John and Ireland', 230–2; Norgate, *Lackland*, 18; Diceto, ii, 39, says John returned on 17 December 1185.

42 Gillingham, *Richard I*, 37, 39, 77–8.

43 Ibid., 80.

44 Duffy, 'John and Ireland', 229, 233–4; Gillingham, *Richard I*, 81.

45 Warren, *Henry II*, 613–16.

46 Gillingham, *Richard I*, 66, 84. Cf. W. Burgwinkle, *Sodomy, Masculinity and Law in Medieval Literature: France and England, 1050–1230* (Cambridge, 2004), 73–82.

47 Gillingham, *Richard I*, 84–5; 96, 248n; *HWM*, i, 435; Newburgh, Book 3, Ch. 25.

48 Gillingham, *Richard I*, 84–8.

49 Ibid., 91–2, 95–8.

50 Ibid., 98–9; Warren, *Henry II*, 623–5.

51 Ibid., 626; Norgate, *Lackland*, 23; *HWM*, i, 461.

3 Refusing to Rally 1204–1205

1 As in Chapter One, I have based my account on Norgate, *Angevin Kings*, ii, 417–23, and McGlynn, *Blood Cries Afar*, 49–59 (52 for the quote).

2 McGlynn, *Blood Cries Afar*, 49–55.

3 Norgate, *Angevin Kings*, ii, 419; Powicke, *Loss of Normandy*, 255–6.

4 *Itinerary*; Wendover, 209; *Rot. Chart.*, 133b–134; Powicke, *Loss of Normandy*, 259.

5 Powicke, *Loss of Normandy*, 259–60; Coggeshall, 145.

6 Ibid.; Powicke, *Loss of Normandy*, 256–9; W. L. Warren, *King John* (new edn, Yale, 1997), 93, 97.

7 Powicke, *Loss of Normandy*, 261–4; *HWM*, ii, 146–7; Wendover, 214.

8 J. Gillingham, '*Stupor mundi:* 1204 et un obituaire de Richard Coeur de Lion depuis longtemps tombé dans l'oubli', *Plantagenêts et Capétiens: Confrontations et Héritages*, ed. M. Aurell and N.-Y. Tonnerre (Turnhout, 2006), 397; Norgate, *Lackland*, 103.

9 Coggeshall, 146.

10 N.Vincent, *Peter des Roches: An Alien in English Politics, 1205–1238* (Cambridge, 1996), 26–41.

11 Powicke, *Loss of Normandy*, 280; Warren, *King John*, 103; D. Crouch, 'Normans and Anglo-Normans: A Divided Aristocracy', *England and Normandy in the Middle Ages*, ed. D. Bates and A. Curry (1994), 51–67.

12 D. Crouch, *William Marshal: Knighthood, War and Chivalry, 1147–1219* (2nd edn, 2002), 93–4; *HWM*, ii, 144–7; iii, 147–8.

13 Powicke, *Loss of Normandy*, 109–10, 296; Anonymous, 99–100.

14 D. Danziger and J. Gillingham, *1215: The Year of Magna Carta* (2003), 51–2; J. Masschaele, 'The English Economy in the Age of Magna Carta', *Magna Carta and the England of King John* (Woodbridge, 2010), 151–67.

15 P. Latimer, 'The English Inflation of 1180–1220 Reconsidered', *Past and Present*, 171 (2001), 3–29; *PR 7 John*, xxvii–xxxii.

16 Coggeshall, 148–9; Powicke, *Loss of Normandy*, 287–9.

17 J. R. Maddicott, 'The Oath of Marlborough, 1209: Fear, Government and Popular Allegiance in the Reign of King John', *EHR*, 126 (2011), 312; Gervase, ii, 96–8; Warren, *King John*, 110–11; Coggeshall, 145–6.

18 *DNB* Ranulf de Blundeville; Powicke, *Loss of Normandy*, 167; J. C. Holt, *The Northerners: A Study in the Reign of King John* (Oxford, 1961), 205–6.

19 Ibid., 19, 205–6.

20 M. Morris, *The Norman Conquest* (2012), 121–2.

21 Holt, *Northerners*, 197.

22 T. K. Keefe, *Feudal Assessments and the Political Community under Henry II and His Sons* (Berkeley, 1981), 2–4, 24–5, 29–30; N. Barratt, 'The Revenue of King John', *EHR*, 111 (1996), 846,

850; J. R. Maddicott, *The Origins of the English Parliament, 924–1327* (Oxford, 2010), 127–8.
23 Holt, *Northerners*, 206–7; *Rot. Ob.*, 275; Coggeshall, 151.
24 Gervase, ii, 97–8.
25 Ibid.; Holt, *Northerners*, 90, 207; Warren, *King John*, 109–10; Maddicott, *Origins of the English Parliament*, 119.
26 *RLP*, 55; Warren, *King John*, 111–12.
27 *PR 7 John*, xii–xxi; Coggeshall, 154.
28 *PR 7 John*, xxi–xxv; *Itinerary*; *RLP*, 54; Gervase, ii, 98; Coggeshall, 154.
29 *HWM*, ii, 146–55.
30 Ibid., 154–63.
31 Coggeshall, 153.
32 *DNB* Hubert Walter; *HWM*, ii, 154–5; Coggeshall, 153.
33 Ibid.; Gervase, ii, 98.
34 Coggeshall, 154; Wendover, 215.

4 A Pact from Hell 1189–1194

1 Gillingham, *Richard I*, 100; *Gesta Henrici II et Ricardi I*, ed. W. Stubbs (2 vols, Rolls Ser., 1867), ii, 72, implies John met Richard later, but Newburgh, Book 3, Ch. 25, says Henry was buried 'in the presence of his sons'.
2 Gillingham, *Richard I*, 101–6.
3 Norgate, *Lackland*, 24–5.
4 Gillingham, *Richard I*, 106.
5 Norgate, *Lackland*, 6–7.
6 Ibid., 25; *DNB* Isabella of Gloucester.
7 Gillingham, *Richard I*, 109–10.
8 Ibid., 107, 109; Norgate, *Lackland*, 25.
9 Gillingham, *Richard I*, 112–16.
10 Ibid., 119–20; Norgate, *Lackland*, 26–30.
11 Gillingham, *Richard I*, 121–2; *DNB* William de Longchamp; Devizes, 9.
12 Gillingham, 121, 126; Devizes, 13–14.
13 *DNB* William de Longchamp; Newburgh, Book 4, Ch. 14; M.

Strickland, 'The "Bones of the Kingdom" and the Treason of Count John', *Culture Politique des Plantagenêt, 1154–1224*, ed. M. Aurell (Centre d'études Supérieures de Civilisation Médiévale, 2003), 147.

14 Strickland, 'Bones of the Kingdom', 147.

15 Gillingham, *Richard I*, 128–31.

16 Ibid., 131–6.

17 Ibid., 136–7; *DNB* Arthur, duke of Brittany.

18 Newburgh, Book 4, Ch. 14.

19 Ibid.

20 Ibid.; Devizes, 26 (date wrongly given as 4 March), 30.

21 Ibid., 30–31; Norgate, *Lackland*, 31.

22 Devizes, 32–3; Gillingham, *Richard I*, 227.

23 Devizes, 33–5. Devizes erroneously gives the date of the agreement as 25 April: see Ibid., 90–8; Newburgh, Book 4, Ch. 16.

24 Devizes, 29.

25 Ibid., 40–2

26 Ibid., 42–3.

27 Strickland, 'Bones of the Kingdom', 149.

28 *DNB* William de Longchamp.

29 Devizes, 45.

30 Ibid.; Norgate, *Lackland*, 39.

31 Devizes, 49–54; Howden, 245–6; Newburgh, Book 4, Ch. 18.

32 Gillingham, *Richard I*, 143–81.

33 Ibid., 123–7, 140–3.

34 Ibid., 142–3, 156–66, 223–9.

35 Ibid., 229.

36 Ibid., 119–20.

37 Above, 72

38 Newburgh, Book 4, Ch. 18; Crouch, *William Marshal*, 78–9; S. Painter, *William Marshal* (Baltimore, 1933), 93–4.

39 Devizes, 58, 60; Gillingham, *Richard I*, 229.

40 Devizes, 61.

41 Devizes, 61–2; Newburgh, Book 4, Ch. 18.

42 Devizes, 62–3.

43 Gillingham, *Richard I*, 189–90, 195, 203–8, 218–21.

44 Ibid., 222–7, 230–2.

45 Howden, 279–80; Diceto, ii, 107.

46 Newburgh, Book 4, Ch. 32.

47 Strickland, 'Bones of the Kingdom', 152; Gillingham, *Richard I*, 235–6; Gervase, i, 514.

48 Ibid., 234–6; Howden, 287; Gervase, i, 515; Strickland, 'Bones of the Kingdom', 153.

49 Gervase, i, 515; Howden, 287; Gillingham, *Richard I*, 235–6.

50 Strickland, 'Bones of the Kingdom', 152, 156.

51 Howden, 287; Strickland, 'Bones of the Kingdom', 156–7; J. T. Appleby, *England Without Richard* (1965), 110.

52 Ibid., 157; Gillingham, *Richard I*, 235, 240.

53 Ibid., 240–4; Strickland, 'Bones of the Kingdom', 158.

54 R. V. Turner and R. R. Heiser, *The Reign of Richard Lionheart* (2000), 138; Gillingham, *Richard I*, 245.

55 Howden, 298–9, 306–7; *HWM*, ii, 8–9.

56 Gillingham, *Richard I*, 245–8.

57 The regents also declared John's lands forfeit on 10 February. Strickland, 'Bones of the Kingdom', 164.

58 Ibid., 159–64.

59 Gillingham, *Richard I*, 271–3, 284–5; *HWM*, ii, 18–21.

5 Stemming the Tide 1205–1206

1 *Itinerary*; *PR 7 John*, xviii–xix; Norgate, *Lackland*, 113.

2 Coggeshall, 156; Warren, *King John*, 14, 134; Howden, 459.

3 Coggeshall, 156, 159; *Itinerary*; Warren, *King John*, 159–60.

4 C. R. Cheney, *Innocent III and England* (Stuttgart, 1976), 149; M. D. Knowles, 'The Canterbury Election of 1205–6', *EHR*, 53 (1938), 211–20; Gervase, ii, 98.

5 S. Painter, *The Reign of King John* (Baltimore, 1949), 79; Norgate, *Lackland*, 119.

6 Knowles, 'Canterbury Election', 213, 216–17.

7 Ibid., 217–18; Cheney, *Innocent III*, 148–9.

8 Gillingham, *Angevin Empire*, 30, 94; *RLP*, 53; *PR 7 John*, xx–xxi;

PR 8 John, xiv–xvi; Coggeshall, 147. Salisbury left after 7 June but had returned by 7 August. *Rot. Chart.*, 155, 157.

9 *PR 7 John*, xviii; Carpenter, *Struggle for Mastery*, 271; P. Latimer, 'Wages in Late Twelfth- and Early Thirteenth-Century England', *Haskins Society Journal*, 9 (1997), 201–5; Barratt, 'Revenue of King John', 846.

10 Carpenter, *Struggle for Mastery*, 154–5, 247; N. Barratt, 'The English Revenue of Richard I', *EHR*, 116 (2001), 649–50.

11 D. A. Carpenter, 'The Decline of the Curial Sheriff', idem, *The Reign of Henry III* (1996), 156–8; Barratt, 'Revenue of King John', 848.

12 Ibid., 839; *DNB* William de Stuteville; Holt, *Northerners*, 74, 148, 154–6.

13 Gillingham, *Richard I*, 115; Holt, *Northerners*, 148; *DNB* Walter de Gray.

14 Carpenter, *Struggle for Mastery*, 236–9.

15 Ibid., 273; J. C. Holt, *Magna Carta* (2nd edn, Cambridge, 1992), 151.

16 Carpenter, *Struggle for Mastery*, 85; Morris, *Norman Conquest*, 323–4; Painter, *Reign of King John*, 216–21.

17 Holt, *Magna Carta*, 52–4.

18 Carpenter, *Struggle for Mastery*, 202; Holt, *Magna Carta*, 52, 307; idem, *Northerners*, 177; Painter, *Reign of King John*, 220.

19 J. C. Holt, 'Feudal Society and the Family in Early Medieval England: IV. The Heiress and the Alien', *Trans. Royal Historical Soc.*, 5th ser., 35 (1985), 23–4; S. Painter, *The Reign of King John* (Baltimore, 1949), 219; *DNB* Hugh Bardolf.

20 N. Barratt, 'Finance and the Economy in the Reign of Henry II', *Henry II: New Interpretations*, ed. Harper-Bill and Vincent, 251; Barratt, 'Revenue of King John', 839, 842.

21 Crouch, *William Marshal*, 98–9; *Rot. Chart.*, 161.

22 A. A. M. Duncan, 'John King of England and the Kings of Scots', *King John: New Interpretations*, ed. Church, 255; *Itinerary*; Holt, *Magna Carta*, 305–6.

23 *History of the King's Works*, ii, 687–8; *PR 8 John*, xiii.

24 Ibid., xvi–xvii.

25 Gillingham, *Angevin Empire*, 94; *Itinerary*.
26 N.Vincent, 'A Forgotten War: England and Navarre, 1243–4', *Thirteenth Century England*, xi (2007), 116–17; Y. Renouard, *Bordeaux sous les Rois d'Angleterre* (Bordeaux, 1965), 24–7; F. Boutoulle, 'Un épisode méconnu de l'offensive d'Alphonse VIII de Castille en Gascogne: le siège de Bourg-sur-Gironde (1205-1206)', *Cahiers du Vitrezais*, 96 (2004), 33–40.
27 Wendover, 218–19. The siege is difficult to square with John's itinerary, but well attested by other chronicles: *Giraldi Cambrensis Opera*, ed. J. S. Brewer, J. F. Dimock and G. F. Warner (8 vols, Rolls Ser., 1861–91), vii, 138; Worcester, 394, says the king captured 120 knights and 2,000 sergeants.
28 Norgate, *Lackland*, 115.
29 Ibid., 115–17; Warren, *King John*, 119–20.
30 *Itinerary*; Wendover; *HWM*, ii, 166–7; *RLC*, 75.

6 Our Happy Success 1194–1202

1 Newburgh, Book 4, Ch. 34; Norgate, *Lackland*, 58.
2 Strickland, 'Bones of the Kingdom', 165–9; S. D. Church, *The Household Knights of King John* (Cambridge, 1999), 17–23.
3 Strickland, 'Bones of the Kingdom', 164; Painter, *Reign of King John*, 5.
4 Gillingham, *Richard I*, 287–90.
5 Newburgh, Book 5, Ch. 5; Howden, 355.
6 Gillingham, *Richard I*, 263–4, 297–8; Painter, *Reign of King John*, 5–6.
7 Howden, 431, 451–2; *DNB* Arthur, duke of Brittany; *Life of St Hugh*, ii, 137; Coggeshall, 99.
8 Gillingham, *Richard I*, 321–8.
9 *HWM*, ii, 92–7; J. C. Holt, 'King John and Arthur of Brittany', *Nottinghamshire Medieval Studies*, 44 (2000), 90.
10 Howden, 453; Gillingham, *Richard I*, 324, 335; *HWM*, ii, 88–91.
11 Howden, 456; *Life of St Hugh*, ii, 137–8.
12 Ibid.; Gillingham, *Richard I*, 335.
13 Howden, 456.

14 Norgate, *Lackland*, 61.
15 Ibid.; *Life of St Hugh*, ii, 146–7. This is contradicted by a charter of Eleanor of Aquitaine which John apparently witnessed at Fontevraud on 21 April, which might be thought more reliable. But if John did return to Fontevraud for that date, he would have had a hard time crossing 200 miles of territory, much of it hostile, to reach Rouen in time for his investiture on 25 April. Cf. Painter, *Reign of King John*, 9.
16 Norgate, *Lackland*, 62.
17 Coggeshall, 98; Norgate, *Lackland*, 62–4; Howden, 456–7.
18 Ibid., 457; Strickland, 'Bones of the Kingdom', 170–2; Painter, *Reign of King John*, 12–14; *PR 1 John*, xiv–xv.
19 *Itinerary*; Coggeshall, 99.
20 Ibid.; Gervase, ii, 92. Diceto, ii, 166, says 'solemnly'.
21 Wendover, 181.
22 Danziger and Gillingham, *1215*, 153–5; Howden, 459; *PR 1 John*, xv.
23 Duncan, 'John King of England and the Kings of Scots', 249–51; Howden, 459–61; *Itinerary*; Coggeshall, 100.
24 A. Richard, *Histoire des Comtes de Poitou, 778–1204* (2 vols., Paris, 1903), ii, 348–9; Howden, 461.
25 Ibid., 462; Gillingham, *Richard I*, 335.
26 J. Gillingham, 'The Meetings of the Kings of France and England, 1066–1204', *Normandy and Its Neighbours, 900–1250*, ed. D. Crouch and K. Thompson (Turnhout, 2011), 27; Howden, 462.
27 J. Gillingham, 'Doing Homage to the King of France', *Henry II: New Interpretations*, ed. Harper-Bill and Vincent, 63–84; idem, 'Meetings of the Kings of France and England', 27–8.
28 *Rot. Chart.*, 30; Gervase, ii, 92.
29 Norgate, *Lackland*, 70.
30 Vincent, *Peter des Roches*, 22–4; Howden, 463; *HWM*, ii, 122–5.
31 *Rot. Chart.*, 30. Le Vieux Lavardin, near Mézières-sous-Lavardin, is more likely than Lavardin-sur-Loir.
32 Howden, 463–4; Norgate, *Lackland*, 70–1.
33 Howden, 464; *HWM*, ii, 124–5; *Rot. Chart.*, 30; *Itinerary*; *DNB* Arthur, duke of Brittany.

34 Norgate, *Lackland*, 71–2; Gillingham, *Richard I*, 336–8.
35 Ibid., 336; *DNB* John; Warren, *King John*, 54; D. A. Carpenter, 'Abbot Ralph of Coggeshall's Account of the Last Years of King Richard and the First Years of King John', *EHR*, 113 (1998), 1219, 1224–5.
36 Norgate, *Lackland*, 72–3.
37 Coggeshall, 101–2; Duncan, 'John King of England and the Kings of Scots', 251–3.
38 Coggeshall, 103.
39 Norgate, *Lackland*, 73–4; Howden, 480–1.
40 Warren, *King John*, 64–5; Howden, 483, 487.
41 S. Painter, 'The Lords of Lusignan in the Eleventh and Twelfth Centuries', *Speculum*, 32 (1957), 43; *Rot. Chart.*, 97; Warren, *King John*, 68–9.
42 Diceto, ii, 167; Warren, *King John*, 66–7.
43 Howden, 483; *Rot. Chart.*, 97; *HWM*, ii, 98–101; *DNB* Isabella of Angoulême.
44 Howden, 483; N. Vincent, 'Isabella of Angoulême: John's Jezebel', *King John: New Interpretations*, ed. Church, 174–5.
45 Painter, 'Lords of Lusignan', 43; Warren, *King John*, 68–9.
46 *HWM*, ii, 100–1; Howden, 483; Coggeshall, 103.
47 *Itinerary*; Howden, 501–3; Coggeshall, 103; Duncan, 'John King of England and the Kings of Scots', 253.
48 Coggeshall, 103–9; Howden, 506.
49 Ibid., 516–17.
50 F. A. Cazel and S. Painter, 'The Marriage of Isabelle of Angoulême', *EHR*, 63 (1948), 85–6; Anonymous, 91; *Rot. Chart.*, 102–3.
51 *Rot. Chart.*, 102–3; Norgate, *Lackland*, 78–9; Howden, 522.
52 Ibid., 520–1, 523; Norgate, *Lackland*, 79; Warren, *King John*, 73.
53 Norgate, *Lackland*, 81–2.
54 Ibid., 82–3.
55 Ibid., 83–4; Coggeshall, 136.
56 Ibid.; Norgate, *Lackland*, 84–5.
57 Ibid., 85–6; *DNB* Arthur, duke of Brittany.

58 Norgate, *Lackland*, 86.

59 Ibid.; *Itinerary*.

60 *HWM*, ii, 104–7; Warren, *King John*, 79.

7 King versus Pope 1207–1208

1 Wendover, 219, 236.

2 Holt, *Northerners*, 152.

3 Knowles, 'Canterbury Election', 218–19; *DNB* John de Gray.

4 Maddicott, *Origins of the English Parliament*, 125; Norgate, *Lackland*, 125–6.

5 R. Bartlett, *England under the Norman and Angevin Kings, 1075–1225* (Oxford, 2000), 165–7; Carpenter, 'Abbot Ralph of Coggeshall's Account', 1222; Maddicott, *Origins of the English Parliament*, 102–4, 120–1, 418–19.

6 S. K. Mitchell, *Studies in Taxation under John and Henry III* (New Haven, 1914), 32–4; J. C. Holt, 'The Loss of Normandy and Royal Finances', *War and Government in the Middle Ages*, ed. J. Gillingham and J. C. Holt (Woodbridge, 1984), 102–4.

7 *Select Charters*, 278–9; Maddicott, *Origins of the English Parliament*, 125; Wendover, 236.

8 *PR 9 John*, xxvii–xviii.

9 Warren, *King John*, 191; *DNB* Geoffrey, archbishop of York.

10 Cheney, *Innocent III*, 149–52.

11 Wendover, 240–1. The content of this précis of John's letter is borne out by Innocent's response.

12 *Itinerary*; *Thomas Wright's Political Songs of England*, ed. P. Coss (Cambridge, 1996), 4; Anonymous, 109, 174; *History of the King's Works*, ii, 766.

13 In general, see C. R. Young, *The Royal Forests of Medieval England* (Leicester, 1979), with the quote at 22.

14 Ibid., 30; *DNB* Hugh de Neville; Warren, *King John*, 140.

15 Holt, *Northerners*, 149, 157; D. Crook, 'The Forest Eyre in the Reign of King John', *Magna Carta and the England of King John*, ed. J. S. Loengard (Woodbridge, 2010), 70–4 (cf. *PR 6 John*, 85, for 2,200 marks).

16 *PR 9 John*, xxv–xxvi; Crook, 'Forest Eyre', 75; *DNB* Hugh de Neville.

17 *Itinerary.*

18 *Selected Letters*, 86–90.

19 Cheney, *Innocent III*, 1–10.

20 H. G. Richardson, 'The Coronation in Medieval England', *Traditio*, 16 (1960), 151–61, 171–3.

21 Cheney, *Innocent III*, 152; Painter, *Reign of King John*, 171; Wendover, 240.

22 *Itinerary*; Vincent, 'Isabella of Angoulême', 194–6; *PR 9 John*, xiii.

23 Vincent, 'Isabella of Angoulême', 193, 196–7; Wendover, 206.

24 Vincent, 'Isabella of Angoulême', 196; *Itinerary.*

25 Painter, *Reign of King John*, 172; *Selected Letters*, 91–5.

26 Cheney, *Innocent III*, 300; Wendover, 245–6.

27 *PR 9 John*, xx–xxi.

28 Margam, 28.

29 *PR 9 John*, xxi–xxiii.

30 *Selected Letters*, 96–9; Cheney, *Innocent III*, 301.

31 *Itinerary.*

32 *RLP*, 78–9; Painter, *Reign of King John*, 173.

33 Ibid., 173–4; Cheney, *Innocent III*, 302.

34 Ibid., 302–7.

35 C. R. Cheney, 'King John and the Papal Interdict', *Bulletin of the John Rylands Library*, 31 (1948), 302; Wendover, 247; *RLC*, 111.

36 Warren, *King John*, 167–8.

37 Danziger and Gillingham, *1215*, 145; Painter, *Reign of King John*, 176.

38 Wendover, 247–8.

8 A Deed of Shame 1202–1203

1 *HWM*, ii, 106–113.

2 *Itinerary*; T. D. Hardy, *Description of the Patent Rolls in the Tower of London* (1835), 33–9; *RLP*, 24.

3 Wendover, 204; *HWM*, ii, 127.

4 Above, 114

5 *HWM*, ii, 120–5; Anonymous, 93–4.

6 *HWM*, ii, 124–7; *Recueil de Chroniques de Touraine*, ed. A. Salmon (Tours and Paris, 1854), 147.

7 John must have learned of des Roches' departure between 17 August, when he addressed a letter to him, and 24 August, when replacement seneschals were appointed. *RLP*, 17.

8 Norgate, *Lackland*, 87; Hardy, *Description*, 36–7; Coggeshall, 138; Powicke, *Loss of Normandy*, 154; Richard, *Histoire des Comtes de Poitou*, ii, 412.

9 *Itinerary*; above, 123–4; Powicke, *Loss of Normandy*, 313.

10 It is possible that his queen had been left at Chinon and was in danger of capture. See below, n. 19.

11 Coggeshall, 138–9; *Itinerary*; Powicke, *Loss of Normandy*, 154–5; Richard, *Histoire des Comtes de Poitou*, ii, 414–15.

12 Coggeshall, 139–41.

13 D. A. Carpenter, *The Minority of Henry III* (1990), 138.

14 J. Gillingham, '1066 and the Introduction of Chivalry into England', idem, *The English in the Twelfth Century: Imperialism, National Identity and Political Values* (Woodbridge, 2000), 209–31.

15 *RLP*, 17.

16 *Itinerary*.

17 *RLP*, 15–16, 20–3.

18 Powicke, *Loss of Normandy*, 157.

19 Why Isabella should have been at Chinon is a mystery. Either she was left there in December when John went to spend Christmas in Normandy, or else she had been sent back early in the new year. Neither scenario seems very plausible. Another problem is that John's itinerary, while it shows that he passed through Alençon, does not show the frantic dash described in *The History of William Marshal*. The *History* says the king dined with Count Robert in Alençon but did not stay there, whereas the itinerary places him in Alençon for five days. There is no easy solution. Alfred Richard believed that this episode with Isabella took place at the end of October 1202, when John rushed south to counter the invasion of Anjou by the Bretons

and William des Roches, and the king's itinerary at that point is indeed a good fit. *The History of William Marshal*, however, is explicit in placing the queen in jeopardy at the time of the revolt of the count of Alençon, an event which can be securely dated from royal writs to mid-January 1203 – a problem Richard solved by omitting all mention of the count from his narrative. A possible solution is that the two episodes were separate, and that either the Marshal or his biographer, writing many years later, confused and conflated them.

20 *HWM*, ii, 130–5; D. Power, 'The End of Angevin Normandy: The Revolt of the Count of Alençon', *Historical Research*, 74 (2001), 446.

21 *HWM*, ii, 130–1.

22 *Itinerary*; Wendover, 205.

23 *RLP*, 24; Hardy, *Description*, 34–5; Richard, *Histoire des Comtes de Poitou*, 419–20; Margam, 26. See also *Recueil de Chroniques de Touraine*, 147 *(plures in carcere mori fecit)*; A. Stimming, *Bertran de Born* (Halle, 1892), 141.

24 Strickland, 'Bones of the Kingdom', 166.

25 D. Power, 'King John and the Norman Aristocracy', *King John: New Interpretations*, ed. Church, 128–31.

26 *RLP*, 21; Powicke, *Loss of Normandy*, 229–30; D. Crouch, 'William Marshal and the Mercenariat', *Mercenaries and Paid Men: The Mercenary Identity in the Middle Ages*, ed. J. France (Leiden, 2008), 17 (for Louvrecaire); *Diplomatic Documents Preserved in the Public Record Office*, ed. P. Chaplais (HMSO, 1964), i, 140 (no. 206).

27 *Itinerary*; *HWM*, ii, 128–31.

28 Ibid.; Power, 'End of Angevin Normandy', 455n; *Catalogue des Actes de Philippe-Auguste*, ed. L. Delisle (Paris, 1856), 506 (no. 752).

29 Wendover, 205–6; M. D. Legge, 'William the Marshal and Arthur of Brittany', *Historical Research*, 55 (1982), 22.

30 Margam, 27.

31 *DNB* William de Briouze; Powicke, *Loss of Normandy*, 319–22.

32 *DNB* William de Briouze; Holt, 'King John and Arthur of Brittany', 91; Margam, 24; Powicke, *Loss of Normandy*, 319–22.

33 Legge, 'William the Marshal', 21. *RLP*, 28; *Rotuli Normanniae*, ed. T. D. Hardy (Record Comm., 1835), 35–7.

34 William Longsword witnesses John's charter to Le Bec-Hellouin on 31 March 1203 (see the forthcoming Angevin *Acta*); Holt, 'King John and Arthur of Brittany', 91–2.

35 *DNB* Peter de Maulay.

36 Powicke, *Loss of Normandy*, 325.

37 Ibid., 159–60.

38 Ibid., 311–15; Coggeshall, 145.

9 The Enemy Within? 1208–1210

1 Wendover, 248.

2 Duffy, 'John and Ireland', 234–8.

3 A large number of grants involving Ireland were made on 6 September 1199, just as John was embarking on his first campaign against Philip Augustus. Duffy, 'John and Ireland', 238.

4 Ibid., 240; C. Veach, 'King John and Royal Control in Ireland: Why William de Briouze had to be Destroyed', *EHR*, 129 (2014), 1053–4.

5 Ibid., 1057.

6 Ibid., 1057–8, 1060, 1063–4.

7 Ibid., 1062–3.

8 Ibid., 1057, 1063.

9 *DNB* William de Briouze; *DNB* Walter de Lacy; C. Veach, 'King and Magnate in Medieval Ireland: Walter de Lacy, King Richard and King John', *Irish Historical Studies*, 37 (2010), 191–2.

10 *DNB* Hugh de Lacy; *DNB* William Marshal; Veach, 'King John and Royal Control in Ireland', 1064–5.

11 Ibid., 1064, 1067; Crouch, *William Marshal*, 105–6.

12 *Rot. Chart.*, 171, 173; Veach, 'King John and Royal Control in Ireland', 1067–8; *RLP*, 77; *HWM*, ii, 184–5.

13 Ibid., ii, 190–3.

14 Veach, 'King John and Royal Control in Ireland', 1068–9; *Rot. Chart.*, 175; Worcester, 396.

15 *RLP*, 79; Veach, 'King John and Royal Control in Ireland', 1069.

16 *HWM*, ii, 188–91, 194–5.

17 Veach, 'King John and Royal Control in Ireland', 1069–70; Lacy's castle at Ludlow was restored on 19 March when he brought in William de Briouze Jr as a hostage, but it was not until Briouze Sr surrendered on 24 April that Lacy received a new charter for Meath. Ibid., 1069–72; *RLP*, 80.

18 *RLP*, 80; *RLC*, 105; *Rot. Chart.*, 175–6 shows William de Ferrers and Adam du Port were at court at this time. See Crouch, 'Complaint', 174.

19 The sheriff of Shropshire had 500 infantry and 25 mounted men. The sheriff of Gloucester presumably brought more. *RLC*, 112–13.

20 Crouch, 'Complaint', 174–5.

21 Ibid., 173–5.

22 H. Summerson, 'The 1215 Magna Carta: Clause 20, Academic Commentary', *The Magna Carta Project*. Cf. T. K. Keefe, 'Proffers for Heirs and Heiresses in the Pipe Rolls: Some Observations on Indebtedness in the Years Before the Magna Carta (1180–1212)', *Haskins Society Journal*, 5 (1993), 99–109.

23 *PR 13 John*, xxxii; Holt, *Northerners*, 170–1.

24 Holt, *Magna Carta*, 110; *PR 10 John*, xviii.

25 Ibid., xv–xvi; Holt, *Northerners*, 226–7; *DNB* Robert de Vieuxpont; J. Goodall, *The English Castle* (Yale, 2011), 164.

26 Crouch, 'Complaint', 173.

27 *DNB* Peter des Roches; Vincent, *Peter des Roches*, 58.

28 Ibid., 27, 31–3, 58–9; *DNB* Gerard d'Athée; *DNB* Hubert de Burgh; Painter, *Reign of King John*, 120–3, 206.

29 *RLP*, 80, 86; F. W. Brooks, 'William de Wrotham and the Office of Keeper of the King's Ports and Galleys', *EHR*, 40 (1925), 576–7; *Itinerary*; Gervase, ii, 101–2; *PR 9 John*, xix (where it is wrongly assumed these preparations were for Ireland).

30 Crouch, 'Complaint', 175; *RLP*, 86; *Annales Cambriae*, ed. J. Williams ab Ithel (Rolls Ser., 1860), 66.

31 *RLP*, 86.

32 J. E. Lloyd, *A History of Wales* (1911), 620–1; *Itinerary*; *PR 11 John*, xi–xii.

33 *DNB* Llywelyn ap Iorwerth.

34 *PR 11 John*, xii.

35 J. Baldwin, *The Government of Philip Augustus: Foundations of French Royal Power in the Middle Ages* (Berkeley, 1986), 199–200.

36 Cheney, *Innocent III*, 316–17; *Selected Letters*, 115–20.

37 Maddicott, 'Oath of Marlborough', 288, 291; Cheney, *Innocent III*, 318.

38 Duncan, 'John King of England and the Kings of Scots', 254–6, 259–60; *Itinerary*; *PR 11 John*, xiv.

39 Cheney, *Innocent III*, 318–19; Maddicott, 'Oath of Marlborough', 289–90.

40 Cheney, *Innocent III*, 319.

41 Ibid.; Maddicott, 'Oath of Marlborough', 286–7.

42 Ibid., 281–3, 287–8, 300–2, 316–17.

43 Ibid., 303–7, 313–14, 317.

44 Cheney, *Innocent III*, 319–20; Gervase, ii, 104.

45 Wendover, 252; Warren, *King John*, 169–70.

46 Gervase, ii, 100; Wendover, 252.

47 Crouch, *William Marshal*, 102n, 112.

48 Duncan, 'John King of England and the Kings of Scots', 261; Maddicott, 'Oath of Marlborough', 282–3, 290–1.

49 Crouch, *William Marshal*, 112–13; *HWM*, ii, 210–13; Crouch, 'Complaint', 176.

50 Duncan, 'John King of England and the Kings of Scots', 258; Veach, 'King and Magnate', 200–1; Crouch, 'Complaint', 171.

51 *PR 12 John*, xxix–xxxii.

52 Ibid., xxxii; *PR 13 John*, xiv, xvii; S. D. Church, 'The 1210 Campaign in Ireland: Evidence for a Military Revolution', *Anglo-Norman Studies*, 20 (1998), 45–57.

53 *HWM*, ii, 212–13; Crouch, 'Complaint', 176–7.

54 G. H. Orpen, *Ireland Under the Normans, 1169–1333* (4 vols., 1911–20), ii, 243–8; Worcester, 399.

55 Orpen, *Ireland Under the Normans*, ii, 251–6; S. Duffy, 'King John's Expedition to Ireland, 1210: The Evidence Reconsidered',

Irish Historical Studies, 30 (1996), 23; Crouch, 'Complaint', 177–8.

56 Orpen, *Ireland Under the Normans*, ii, 260–5.

57 Anonymous, 114–15; Crouch, 'Complaint', 177–9; Norgate, *Lackland*, 287–8.

10 Tyrannical Will 1210–1212

1 Norgate, *Lackland*, 287–8; Crouch, 'Complaint', 179.

2 Veach, 'King John and Royal Control in Ireland', 1076–7; Carpenter, *Struggle for Mastery*, 277–82; Duffy, 'King John's Expedition to Ireland', 17–20; Gervase, ii, 105.

3 R. Huscroft, *Expulsion: England's Jewish Solution* (Stroud, 2006), 11–53.

4 Ibid., 31, 41, 58.

5 H. G. Richardson, *The English Jewry under Angevin Kings* (1960), 167–72; Holt, *Northerners*, 164–5.

6 Huscroft, *Expulsion*, 59–60; Richardson, *English Jewry*, 169–70, dates the arrest to 'before Easter', but the evidence is unconvincing. John was at Bristol on several occasions in September and the first instalment of the tallage was due on 1 November.

7 D. Knowles, *The Monastic Order in England* (2nd edn, Cambridge, 1963), 367–9; C. J. Holdsworth, 'John of Forde and the Interdict', *EHR*, 78 (1963), 705–14.

8 Holt, *Northerners*, 79, 167; Bury, 23.

9 Carpenter, *Struggle for Mastery*, 44, 232–42, 273; M. T. Clanchy, 'Magna Carta and the Common Pleas', *Studies in Medieval History presented to R. H. C. Davis* (1985), 219–32.

10 *PR 12 John*, xv–xvi; Summerson, 'The 1215 Magna Carta: Clause 20, Academic Commentary', *The Magna Carta Project*.

11 Idem, 'The 1215 Magna Carta: Clause 39, Academic Commentary', *The Magna Carta Project*.

12 Lloyd, *History of Wales*, 631–2; *Brut*, 264–5.

13 Ibid., 264–7; Lloyd, *History of Wales*, 633–4.

14 *Brut*, 266–7; *Itinerary*; *PR 13 John*, xiv–xv.

15 *Brut*, 266–9; Lloyd, *History of Wales*, 632, 634–5.

16 Ibid., 635–6; *Brut*, 268–9.
17 Ibid.; Lloyd, *History of Wales*, 636; *DNB* Llwelyn ap Iorwerth.
18 *Brut*, 268–71; Lloyd, *History of Wales*, 636; Crowland, 203.
19 Cheney, *Innocent*, 322–4.
20 Ibid., 324; *Selected Letters*, 128–9.
21 A. L. Poole, *Domesday Book to Magna Carta, 1087–1216* (2nd edn, Oxford, 1955), 449–52; Norgate, *Lackland*, 163–6.
22 Above, III, 115; Baldwin, *Government of Philip Augustus*, 201–2.
23 *PR 14 John*, xix, xxiii–xxv; Barratt, 'Revenue of King John', 839, 842–3.
24 *PR 14 John*, xii; Lloyd, *History of Wales*, 637; *Brut*, 271.
25 Duncan, 'John King of England and the Kings of Scots', 261–4; Norgate, *Lackland*, 162; Bury, 19, 21.
26 *RLP*, 92; Poole, *Domesday Book*, 453–5.
27 *RLP*, 92; *RLC*, 117; *PR 14 John*, xiii–xiv.
28 *PR 14 John*, xxv–xxvi; Painter, *Reign of King John*, 262; Poole, *Domesday Book*, 455.
29 Bury, 20; *PR 14 John*, xiii.
30 *RLC*, 130; *PR 14 John*, xxi–xxii. Maddicott, 'Oath of Marlborough', 309–10.
31 *Itinerary*; *Johannis de Fordun Chronica Gentis Scotorum*, ed. W. F. Skene (2 vols., Edinburgh, 1871–2), 278–9; Bury, 20–1.
32 Ibid., 21; *Brut*, 271; Lloyd, *History of Wales*, 637–8.
33 *Itinerary*; *RLC*, 119, 131; *PR 14 John*, xv–xvi.
34 Ibid., xiv, xvi; *RLC*, 131.
35 *Itinerary*, 223; *Brut*, 270–3; Bury, 22; *PR 14 John*, xiv–xv.
36 *Brut*, 272–3; *Itinerary*, 223; Wendover, 257.

11 The Hermit's Prophecy 1212–1213

1 Wendover, 257–8.
2 Crowland, 207; Bury, 23; Dunstable, 33–4; Coggeshall, 164–5; Margam, 32; C. R. Cheney, 'The Alleged Deposition of King John', idem, *The Papacy and England, 12th–14th Centuries* (1982), XII, 100–16.
3 Crowland, 205–6; Dunstable, 33; Bury, 23–4.

4   *RLP*, 94; *RLC*, 121–2; Crowland, 207.

5   Wendover, 258; *DNB* Robert fitz Walter; Anonymous, 116–18; Painter, *Reign of King John*, 258–62.

6   Ibid., 75–6, 331–2; *DNB* Robert fitz Walter.

7   *DNB* Eustace de Vescy.

8   Holt, *Northerners*, 19–20, 83, *RLP*, 94. Painter, *Reign of King John*, 267–8.

9   *DNB* Eustace de Vescy; *DNB* Robert fitz Walter; *DNB* Saer de Quincy.

10 R. F. Treharne, 'The Franco-Welsh Treaty of Alliance in 1212', *Bulletin of the Board of Celtic Studies*, 18 (1958), 60–75; Veach, 'King and Magnate', 201. Robert fitz Walter's brother, Walter, was archdeacon of Hereford, suggesting a link with the exiled bishop of Hereford, Giles de Briouze, son of the late William. Cf. Holt, *Northerners*, 80–1.

11 Holt, *Northerners*, 82; Cheney, 326–7; Painter, *Reign of King John*, 270–2. Cf. H. G. Richardson and G. O. Sayles, *The Governance of Medieval England* (Edinburgh, 1963), 332–4.

12 *Itinerary*; Holt, *Northerners*, 83–4.

13 Norgate, *Lackland*, 170; Wendover, 258–9; Crowland, 208; Holt, 'King John and Arthur of Brittany', 94–9.

14 Crowland, 207; Holt, *Northerners*, 85–6; idem, *Magna Carta*, 211–12.

15 *HWM*, ii, 214–29; *RLC*, 122.

16 Crouch, *William Marshal*, 116–17; Dunstable, 35.

17 Cheney, *Innocent III*, 328–9; *Calendar of Documents relating to Ireland, 1171–1251* (HMSO, 1875), 73–4 (no. 448).

18 Cheney, *Innocent III*, 328–9.

19 Wendover, 261; *Itinerary*; Holt, *Northerners*, 84–6; Dunstable, 35; Crowland, 214–15; Holt, *Magna Carta*, 212–13; B. E. Harris, 'King John and the Sheriffs' Farms', *EHR*, 79 (1964), 540 (cf. *PR 16 John*, xx–xxiii).

20 N. Vincent, 'A Roll of Knights Summoned to Campaign in 1213', *Historical Research*, 66 (1993), 92–3; Lloyd, *History of Wales*, 640–1; Norgate, *Lackland*, 176.

21 Painter, *Reign of King John*, 190–2; Warren, *King John*, 202, 318. Cf. Cheney, *Innocent III*, 339–40.

22 Vincent, 'Roll of Knights', 93–4.
23 Ibid., 94; *Itinerary*; Warren, *King John*, 203; Norgate, *Lackland*, 175–6.
24 Wendover, 262; Vincent, 'Roll of Knights', 94.
25 Ibid.; Wendover, 263; Dunstable, 35; *Itinerary*.
26 Ibid.; Holt, *Northerners*, 88; Wendover, 262–3; Dunstable, 35; Crowland, 209.
27 Ibid.; *Selected Letters*, 130–7.
28 Cheney, *Innocent III*, 331.
29 Ibid., 332; Warren, *King John*, 208.
30 Cheney, *Innocent III*, 333, 338.
31 Crowland, 212; Wendover, 270; Norgate, *Lackland*, 184.
32 Ibid., 185–6; Wendover, 271–3; Poole, *Domesday Book*, 459–61; Warren, *King John*, 204–5; *HWM*, ii, 232–3.

12 Ready for Battle 1213–1214

1 J. Sumption, *The Albigensian Crusade* (1978), 156–60; N.Vincent, 'England and the Albigensian Crusade', *England and Europe in the Reign of Henry III (1216–1272)*, ed. B.Weiler and I. Rowlands (Basingstoke, 2002), 74.
2 *RLC*, 143; *Itinerary*; Norgate, *Lackland*, 186.
3 Wendover, 273; *RLC*, 164; Holt, *Northerners*, 88–9; S. Ambler 'Peacemakers and Partisans: Bishops and Political Reform in England, 1213–1268' (PhD thesis, King's College London, 2012), 24–61.
4 *Selected Letters*, 133; Cheney, *Innocent III*, 338; *RLP*, 99, 101; *RLC*, 146.
5 *Itinerary*; Coggeshall, 167; Wendover, 274–5.
6 Ibid.; Holt, *Northerners*, 89; *RLP*, 103.
7 Coggeshall, 167; Wendover, 275.
8 *Itinerary*; *RLC*, 129; Holt, *Magna Carta*, 192–3; *Rot. Ob.*, 490.
9 Ibid., 494–5; *DNB* Roger de Lacy; *DNB* John de Lacy; Holt, *Magna Carta*, 195.
10 John's income for 1212–13 is unknown because the pipe roll for that year has not survived, but from a peak of perhaps £145,000

in 1211 it fell to £72,000 in 1212, and by 1214 it had dropped to just £25,000. Barratt, 'Revenue of King John', 839.

11 Holt, *Magna Carta*, 58, 190–1.

12 Norgate, *Lackland*, 190; Crowland, 214; Cheney, *Innocent*, 345, 348–50.

13 Wendover, 291; Dunstable, 38, 40; Coggeshall, 167; *Rot. Ob.*, 501.

14 Dunstable, 40; Holt, *Northerners*, 96; *Select Charters*, 281–2; *Itinerary*.

15 *Select Charters*, 281–2; *PR 16 John*, xiv; L. W. Marvin, *The Occitan War: A Military and Political History of the Albigensian Crusade, 1209–1218* (Cambridge, 2008), 175–95; Poole, *Domesday Book*, 463–4.

16 John's writs in December show that for a time the departure date was moved to the start of January. *RLP*, 106.

17 Holt, *Magna Carta*, 193; *Itinerary*; Coggeshall, 168; J. L. Bolton, 'The English Economy in the Early Thirteenth Century', *King John: New Interpretations*, ed. Church, 34; Holt, *Northerners*, 98–100.

18 *RLP*, 111; *Foedera*, 118; Norgate, *Lackland*, 197.

19 *Itinerary*; Poole, *Domesday Book*, 466; *RLP*, 115.

20 Baldwin, *Government of Philip Augustus*, 213–14; Norgate, *Lackland*, 198; Vincent, 'England and the Albigensian Crusade', 76; *Itinerary*.

21 Wendover, 298–9; Baldwin, *Government of Philip Augustus*, 214.

22 Norgate, *Lackland*, 197; Warren, *King John*, 219, 211.

23 Ibid.; *Rot. Chart.*, 197–8; Gillingham, *Angevin Empire*, 105–6.

24 N. C. Vincent, 'King John's Diary & Itinerary', *The Magna Carta Project*; Gillingham, *Angevin Empire*, 106.

25 Ibid.; Norgate, *Lackland*, 200; Vincent, 'King John's Diary & Itinerary'.

26 Ibid.; Norgate, *Lackland*, 200–1.

27 McGlynn, *Blood Cries Afar*, 97–8.

28 Ibid., 97; Wendover, 298.

29 Ibid.; McGlynn, *Blood Cries Afar*, 99.

30 Ibid., 99–100; Vincent, 'King John's Diary & Itinerary'.

31 Warren, *King John*, 222.
32 Vincent, 'King John's Diary & Itinerary'.
33 My account of Bouvines is based on Baldwin, *Government of Philip Augustus*, 214–25; McGlynn, *Blood Cries Afar*, 102–17; J. France, *Western Warfare in the Age of the Crusades 1000–1300* (1999), 235–41.
34 Vincent, 'King John's Diary & Itinerary'; Norgate, *Lackland*, 204–6.

13 Runnymede 1214–1215

1 Vincent, *Peter des Roches*, 89–113.
2 Norgate, *Lackland*, 210; Holt, *Magna Carta*, 190.
3 *RLC*, 213; Holt, *Northerners*, 99–101; Vincent, *Peter des Roches*, 99–100, 106–8.
4 *Itinerary*; Vincent, 'King John's Diary & Itinerary'.
5 Holt, *Northerners*, 100; *Rot. Chart.*, 202; Cheney, *Innocent III*, 366.
6 Ibid., 350–2.
7 Ibid.; Danziger and Gillingham, *1215*, 144–8.
8 Cheney, *Innocent III*, 159–67; Vincent, *Peter des Roches*, 90–100.
9 Cheney, *Innocent III*, 168; Vincent, 'King John's Diary & Itinerary'.
10 Ibid.; *Select Charters*, 282–4; D. A. Carpenter, 'Archbishop Langton and Magna Carta: His Contribution, His Doubts and His Hypocrisy', *EHR*, 126 (2011), 1042–3; idem, *Magna Carta* (2015), 312.
11 Carpenter, 'Archbishop Langton', 1047–8; Holt, *Magna Carta*, 224–6. Crowland, 218, says that Henry I's charter was produced by the barons, but the matter was postponed until the new year. From John's itinerary it seems highly unlikely he had any additional meetings with them between 22 November and 6 January.
12 *Select Charters*, 116–19; *EHD*, ii, 400–2.
13 Above, 205; Carpenter, 'Archbishop Langton', 1057–8.
14 Crowland, 217–18; *EHD*, ii, 400–1; *RLC*, 178.
15 *Itinerary*; Cheney, *Innocent III*, 364; Wendover, 303–4; Anonymous, 145–6.

16 *Itinerary*; Wendover, 304–5.
17 *EHD*, iii, 310–11; Holt, *Magna Carta*, 238–9, 418–28. Crowland, 218, says John sought a truce because of 'the novelty of the business'.
18 Cheney, *Innocent III*, 367–8; Crowland, 218; Norgate, *Lackland*, 222; Wendover, 305.
19 *Itinerary*; Holt, *Northerners*, 104; Crowland, 218.
20 Ibid., 219; *Handbook of British Chronology*, ed. E. B. Fryde, D. E. Greenway; S. Porter and I. Roy (3rd edn, Cambridge, 1986), 244; Holt, *Northerners*, 111–12; *Itinerary*; Cheney, *Innocent III*, 261–3.
21 Crowland, 219; Holt, *Northerners*, 112.
22 Norgate, *Lackland*, 224; Crowland, 219.
23 C. R. Cheney, 'The Eve of Magna Carta', *Bulletin of the John Rylands Library*, 38 (1956), 313–14; Crowland, 219; Holt, *Northerners*, 106; idem, *Magna Carta*, 232.
24 *Itinerary*; Wendover, 306; Cheney, 'Eve of Magna Carta', 315, 320.
25 Ibid., 315; Wendover, 306.
26 Cheney, 'Eve of Magna Carta', 315–17; *Selected Letters*, 194–7.
27 Cheney, 'Eve of Magna Carta', 318–19.
28 Norgate, *Lackland*, 228; *Itinerary*.
29 Cheney, 'Eve of Magna Carta', 320; Holt, *Magna Carta*, 234–5, 492–3; *Foedera*, 128.
30 Cheney, 'Eve of Magna Carta', 320–1; Vincent, *Peter des Roches*, 116–17; Norgate, *Lackland*, 230.
31 Wendover, 307; Crowland, 219.
32 Wendover, 307; Norgate, *Lackland*, 230; Crowland, 221.
33 Vincent, *Peter des Roches*, 117–18.
34 Wendover, 307–8; Crowland, 220; Coggeshall, 171; Norgate, *Lackland*, 230–2; Lloyd, *History of Wales*, 643.
35 Holt, *Magna Carta*, 242; Norgate, *Lackland*, 231.
36 Ibid., 231–2; *Itinerary*; *RLP*, 142–3.
37 *Itinerary*; Holt, *Magna Carta*, 243–5.
38 Coggeshall, 172.
39 Above, 248; Holt, *Magna Carta*, 429–40 (text of the Articles in Latin); *EHD*, iii, 311–16 (English translation).
40 Articles 1–4, 17.

41 Articles 7, 32, 34–5, 39, 47.
42 Articles 12, 23, 31–2.
43 Articles 14, 18, 20–1.
44 Articles 40–2; *DNB* Gerard d'Athée.
45 Articles 8–9.
46 Articles 29–30.
47 Carpenter, 'Archbishop Langton', 1054.
48 Magna Carta, clauses 2, 14, 52–3, 57.
49 Carpenter, 'Archbishop Langton', 1041–57. Cf. Norgate, *Lackland*, 218–20, 234.
50 Magna Carta, clause 61; Holt, *Northerners*, 116–18; D. A. Carpenter, 'The Dating and Making of Magna Carta', idem, *Reign of Henry III*, 10, 14–15.
51 Ibid., 14; *Itinerary*.
52 Magna Carta, preamble.
53 Carpenter, *Magna Carta*, 366–72.

14 Fire and Sword 1215–1216

1 Holt, *Magna Carta*, 493; Coggeshall, 172; Crowland, 221.
2 Holt, *Magna Carta*, 263–6, 478–80, 490–1.
3 Ibid., 491; Magna Carta, clauses 49, 52, 55–9.
4 Holt, *Magna Carta*, 352–5, 493–5; I. Rowlands, 'The Text and Distribution of the Writ for the Publication of Magna Carta', *EHR*, 124 (2009), 1–10.
5 Holt, *Magna Carta*, 356, 359–60; idem, *Northerners*, 120; *RLP*, 143; Vincent, *Peter des Roches*, 119.
6 Holt, *Magna Carta*, 365–6, 491; *Itinerary*.
7 Norgate, *Lackland*, 237; *Itinerary*; Holt, *Northerners*, 124–5.
8 Coggeshall, 172–3; Wendover, 328; Crowland, 222.
9 Holt, *Magna Carta*, 365–6, 484–9; J. B. Smith, 'Magna Carta and the Charters of the Welsh Princes', *EHR*, 99 (1984), 345–6.
10 Holt, *Magna Carta*, 366–7, 498–9; Vincent, *Peter des Roches*, 122.
11 Crowland, 221–2; Holt, *Magna Carta*, 367, 497; Norgate, *Lackland*, 240–1.
12 Crowland, 222–3.

13 *Selected Letters*, 207–9.
14 Cheney, *Innocent III*, 379; Crowland, 223, actually says the meeting was at Staines, but Runnymede seems more likely.
15 Ibid., 223–4; Wendover, 327–8; *Itinerary*.
16 Crowland, 223–4.
17 Ibid., 224; *Itinerary*; Coggeshall, 173; Vincent, *Peter des Roches*, 124–5.
18 Crowland, 224–5.
19 I. Rowlands, 'King John, Stephen Langton and Rochester Castle, 1213–15', *Studies in Medieval History presented to R. Allen Brown,* ed. C. Harper-Bill, C. J. Holdsworth and J. L. Nelson (Woodbridge, 1989), 267–79; Coggeshall, 174–5.
20 *RLC*, 228; Coggeshall, 174; Crowland, 224–5; Warren, *King John*, 257.
21 *Itinerary*; Anonymous, 156–7; Coggeshall, 175.
22 Anonymous, 155–8; Melrose, 159; *Itinerary*.
23 Wendover, 334–6; Anonymous, 158–9; Crowland, 226; Norgate, *Lackland*, 249.
24 Coggeshall, 176; Crowland, 226.
25 Ibid.; Coggeshall, 176; Anonymous, 159–60.
26 *RLC*, 231, 238; Crowland, 227.
27 Ibid.; Wendover, 339; Anonymous, 163.
28 Ibid., 160–1; Crowland, 227; Norgate, *Lackland*, 257.
29 *Itinerary*; Wendover, 348; Coggeshall, 177.
30 Holt, *Northerners*, 131–2.
31 Norgate, *Lackland*, 256; Wendover, 348–51; Holt, *Northerners*, 50; *RLC*, 244–5; Warren, *King John*, 249. For the composition of John's army, see S. D. Church, 'The Earliest English Muster Roll, 18/19 December 1215', *Historical Research*, 67 (1994), 1–17.
32 Melrose, 161; Norgate, *Lackland*, 259–60.
33 Ibid., 261–2; Coggeshall, 177–9.
34 Ibid., 179–80; *Itinerary*; Norgate, *Lackland*, 261.
35 Coggeshall, 180; *Itinerary*.
36 Warren, *King John*, 248–9; Norgate, *Lackland*, 257, 262; Holt, *Northerners*, 134–5.
37 Coggeshall, 180–1; Norgate, *Lackland*, 264–6.

38 *RLP*, 176; *RLC*, 270; Norgate, *Lackland*, 267; Coggeshall, 181.

39 Ibid.; Anonymous, 167–8; *Itinerary*; Coggeshall, 181.

40 Ibid.; Norgate, *Lackland*, 268.

41 Dunstable, 46; J. Gillingham, 'The Anonymous of Béthune, King John and Magna Carta', *Magna Carta and the England of King John*, ed. Loengard, 36–7.

42 McGlynn, *Blood Cries Afar*, 164–5; Norgate, *Lackland*, 269–70.

43 Ibid., 271; Vincent, *Peter des Roches*, 127.

44 *Itinerary*; Holt, *Northerners*, 138; Church, *Household Knights of King John*, 97–8; Coggeshall, 182; Norgate, *Lackland*, 272; Carpenter, *Minority of Henry III*, 6.

45 Norgate, *Lackland*, 272–6.

46 *Itinerary*; *RLP*, 194.

47 Dunstable, 47; Norgate, *Lackland*, 276, 280; McGlynn, *Blood Cries Afar*, 176–7, 179–80.

48 Norgate, *Lackland*, 277; *Itinerary* (where Walton is almost certainly the hamlet outside Aylesbury, rather than Walton-on-Thames).

49 Coggeshall, 182–3; Norgate, *Lackland*, 273, 276–7; *Itinerary*.

50 Wendover, 378. John must have fled on 19 September.

51 Norgate, *Lackland*, 278–9; Crowland, 231.

52 Wendover, 376; *Itinerary*; J. C. Holt, 'King John's Disaster in the Wash', *Nottingham Mediaeval Studies*, 5 (1961), 81.

53 Coggeshall, 183; Wendover, 378.

54 *Itinerary*; Coggeshall, 183–4; Warren, *King John*, 278–85.

55 *Itinerary*; Coggeshall, 182–3; J. A. A. Goodall, 'Dover Castle and the Great Siege of 1216', *Chateau Gaillard*, 19 (2000), 91–102.

56 Coggeshall, 183; J. E. Sayers, *Papal Government and England during the Pontificate of Honorius III (1216–1227)* (Cambridge, 1984), 166–7; Carpenter, *Minority of Henry III*, 12; *The Letters and Charters of Cardinal Guala Bicchieri, Papal Legate in England, 1216–1218*, ed. N. Vincent (Canterbury and York Soc., lxxxiii, 1996), 140b.

57 Crowland, 231; S. D. Church, 'King John's Testament and the Last Days of his Reign', *EHR*, 125 (2010), 505–28.

58 Painter, *Reign of King John*, 377.

59 Coggeshall, 184; Norgate, *Lackland*, 283.

Conclusion

1   Coggeshall, 184; *A History of the County of Leicestershire*, ed. W. G. Hoskins and R. A. McKinley (London, 1954), ii, 28; Church, 'King John's Testament', 517–18; P. Draper, 'King John and St Wulfstan', *Journal of Medieval History*, 10 (1984), 41–50; Crowland, 232.

2   *HWM*, ii, 262–3; D. A. Carpenter, 'The Burial of King Henry III, the Regalia and Royal Ideology', idem, *Reign of Henry III*, 435–6. The 'celebrated monk's cowl' seems to have been introduced by Holinshed: it occurs in the second edition of his *Chronicles of England, Scotland and Ireland* (1587, vi, 195) but not the first (1577). See www.english.ox.ac.uk/holinshed. Holinshed appears to have developed the idea from D. Powel and H. Lhoyd, *The Historie of Cambria* (1584), 183–4, where the burial of Gruffudd ab Cynan ab Owain Gwynedd (d. 1200) is described in identical terms (cf. *Brut*, 254–5). Holinshed presumably knew about John's coif as a result of the opening of the king's tomb in 1529. Pafford, 'King John's Tomb', 58–60.

3   *HWM*, ii, 262–3; Crowland, 232; Coggeshall, 184; *Matthaei Parisiensis, monachi Sancti Albani, Chronica Majora*, ed. H. R. Luard (7 vols, Rolls Ser., 1867–9), ii, 669.

4   Crowland, 232.

5   *Life of St Hugh*, ii, 140–1.

6   Ibid., 142–4.

7   Ibid., 140–1.

8   Warren, *King John*, 14–15; A. Kellett, 'King John's Maundy', *History Today*, 40 (April 1990), 36.

9   J. C. Holt, 'King John', idem, *Magna Carta and Medieval Government* (1985), 95–6; D. M. Stenton, 'King John and the Courts of Justice', *Proceedings of the British Academy*, 49 (1958), 111.

10 J. C. Holt, 'The End of the Anglo-Norman Realm', idem, *Magna Carta and Medieval Government*, 23–65; idem, 'The Loss of Normandy and Royal Finances', 92–105; N. Barratt, 'The Revenues of John and Philip Augustus Revisited', *King John: New Interpretations*, ed. Church, 82–4.

11 Wendover, 206–7; Warren, *King John*, 90.
12 Gillingham, *Richard I*, 15–23.
13 Holt, 'King John', 99.
14 *HWM*, ii, 100–1.
15 Holt, 'King John', 108.
16 Holt, 'King John and Arthur of Brittany', 100–1.
17 Above, 153, 186–7, 207–8, 273; Coggeshall, 175.
18 *HWM*, ii, 126–7, 130–1.
19 Barratt, 'Revenue of King John', 855.
20 Melrose, 158.
21 Gillingham, 'Anonymous of Béthune', 29–30, 37–9.
22 Ibid., 38–9. Cf. Holt, 'King John', 108.
23 Gillingham, 'Anonymous of Béthune', 39–40; Gervase, ii, 102; Vincent, 'Isabella of Angoulême', 193–8.
24 Sayers, *Papal Government*, 168; Carpenter, *Minority of Henry III*, 12–13, 19.
25 Carpenter, *Struggle for Mastery*, 302.
26 Carpenter, *Minority of Henry III*, 21–4; idem, *Struggle for Mastery*, 307.

Bibliography

PRIMARY SOURCES

Annales Cambriae, ed. J. Williams ab Ithel (Rolls Ser., 1860).

Annales Monastici, ed. H. R. Luard (5 vols., Rolls Ser., 1864–9).

The Annals of Roger of Hoveden, trans. H. T. Riley (2 vols., 1853).

Brut Y Tywysogion, or the Chronicle of the Princes, ed. J. Williams ab Ithel (Roll Ser., 1860).

Calendar of Documents relating to Ireland, 1171–1251 (HMSO, 1875).

Catalogue des Actes de Philippe-Auguste, ed. L. Delisle (Paris, 1856).

The Chronicle of Richard of Devizes, ed. J. T. Appleby (1963).

Church Historians of England, vol. 4, trans. J. Stevenson (1856).

Diplomatic Documents Preserved in the Public Record Office, ed. P. Chaplais (HMSO, 1964).

English Historical Documents, Volume II, 1042–1189, ed. D. C. Douglas and G. W. Greenaway (1953).

English Historical Documents, Volume III, 1189–1327, ed. H. Rothwell (1975).

Expugnatio Hibernica: The Conquest of Ireland, by Giraldus Cambrensis, ed. and trans. A. B. Scott and F. X. Martin (Dublin, 1978).

Foedera, conventiones, litterae, I, i, ed. T. Rymer, A. Clarke, F. Holbrooke and J. Caley (1816).

Gesta Henrici II et Ricardi I, ed. W. Stubbs (2 vols., Rolls Ser., 1867).

Giraldi Cambrensis Opera, ed. J. S. Brewer, J. F. Dimock and G. F. Warner (8 vols., Rolls Ser., 1861–91).

Histoire des Ducs de Normandie et des Rois d'Angleterre, ed. F. Michel (Paris, 1840).

The Historical Works of Gervase of Canterbury, ed. W. Stubbs (2 vols., Rolls Ser., 1879–80).

The History of William Marshal, ed. A. J. Holden, S. Gregory and D. Crouch (3 vols., Anglo-Norman Text Soc., Occasional Publications Ser., 4–6, 2002–6).

Johannis de Fordun Chronica Gentis Scotorum, ed. W. F. Skene (2 vols., Edinburgh, 1871–72).

The Letters and Charters of Cardinal Guala Bicchieri, Papal Legate in England, 1216–1218, ed. N. Vincent (Canterbury and York Soc., lxxxiii, 1996).

Magna Vita Sancti Hugonis, The Life of St Hugh of Lincoln, ed. D. L. Douie and D. H. Farmer (2 vols., Edinburgh, 1962).

Matthaei Parisiensis, monachi Sancti Albani, Chronica Majora, ed. H. R. Luard (7 vols., Rolls Ser., 1867–9).

Memoriale fratris Walteri de Coventria, ed. W. Stubbs (2 vols., Rolls Ser., 1872–3).

Memorials of St Edmund's Abbey, ed. T. Arnold (3 vols., Rolls Ser., 1890–6).

The Oxford Dictionary of National Biography, ed. H. C. G. Matthew and B. Harrison (60 vols., Oxford, 2004).

Radulfi de Diceto Decani Londiniensis Opera Historica, ed. W. Stubbs (2 vols., Rolls Ser., 1876).

Radulphi de Coggeshall, Chronicon Anglicanum, ed. J. Stevenson (Rolls Ser., 1875).

Recueil de Chroniques de Touraine, ed. A. Salmon (Tours and Paris, 1854).

Roger of Wendover's Flowers of History, trans. J. A. Giles (2 vols., 1849).

Rotuli Chartarum in Turri Londiniensi asservati, ed. T. D. Hardy (1837).

Rotuli de Oblatis et Finibus in Turri Londiniensi asservati, ed. T. D. Hardy (1835).

Rotuli Litterarum Clausarum in Turri Londiniensi asservati, ed. T. D. Hardy (2 vols., 1833–4).

Rotuli Litterarum Patentium in Turri Londiniensi asservati, ed. T. D. Hardy (1835).

Rotuli Normanniae, ed. T. D. Hardy (Record Comm., 1835).
Select Charters and Other Illustrations of English Constitutional History, ed. W. Stubbs and H. W. C. Davis (9th edn, Oxford, 1921).
Selected Letters of Pope Innocent III Concerning England (1198–1216), ed. C. R. Cheney and W. H. Semple (1953).
Thomas Wright's Political Songs of England, ed. P. Coss (Cambridge, 1996).

SECONDARY WORKS (CITED)

Ambler, S., 'Peacemakers and Partisans: Bishops and Political Reform in England, 1213–1268' (PhD thesis, King's College London, 2012).
Appleby, J. T., *England Without Richard* (1965).
Baldwin, J., *The Government of Philip Augustus: Foundations of French Royal Power in the Middle Ages* (Berkeley, 1986).
Barratt, N., 'The Revenue of King John', *EHR*, 111 (1996).
—— 'The Revenues of John and Philip Augustus Revisited', *King John: New Interpretations*, ed. S. D. Church (Woodbridge, 1999).
—— 'The English Revenue of Richard I', *EHR*, 116 (2001).
—— 'Finance and the Economy in the Reign of Henry II', *Henry II: New Interpretations*, ed. C. Harper-Bill and N. Vincent (Woodbridge, 2007).
Bartlett, R., *England under the Norman and Angevin Kings, 1075–1225* (Oxford, 2000).
Bates, D., *The Normans and Empire* (Oxford, 2013).
Bolton, J. L., 'The English Economy in the Early Thirteenth Century', *King John: New Interpretations*, ed. S. D. Church (Woodbridge, 1999).
Boutoulle, F., 'Un épisode méconnu de l'offensive d'Alphonse VIII de Castille en Gascogne: le siège de Bourg-sur-Gironde (1205–1206)', *Cahiers du Vitrezais*, 96 (2004).
Bradbury, J., *Philip Augustus, King of France, 1180–1223* (1998).
Brooks, F. W., 'William de Wrotham and the Office of Keeper of the King's Ports and Galleys', *EHR*, 40 (1925).

Burgwinkle,W., *Sodomy, Masculinity and Law in Medieval Literature: France and England, 1050–1230* (Cambridge, 2004).

Carpenter, D. A., *The Minority of Henry III* (1990).

—— 'The Dating and Making of Magna Carta', idem, *The Reign of Henry III* (1996).

—— 'The Burial of King Henry III, the Regalia and Royal Ideology', idem, *The Reign of Henry III* (1996).

—— 'The Decline of the Curial Sheriff', idem, *The Reign of Henry III* (1996).

—— 'Abbot Ralph of Coggeshall's Account of the Last Years of King Richard and the First Years of King John', *EHR*, 113 (1998).

—— *The Struggle for Mastery: Britain 1066–1284* (2003).

—— 'Archbishop Langton and Magna Carta: His Contribution, His Doubts and His Hypocrisy', *EHR*, 126 (2011).

—— *Magna Carta* (2015).

Cazel, F. A., and Painter, S., 'The Marriage of Isabelle of Angoulême', *EHR*, 63 (1948).

Cheney, C. R., 'King John and the Papal Interdict', *Bulletin of the John Rylands Library*, 31 (1948).

—— 'The Eve of Magna Carta', *Bulletin of the John Rylands Library*, 38 (1956).

—— *Innocent III and England* (Stuttgart, 1976)

—— 'The Alleged Deposition of King John', idem, *The Papacy and England, 12th–14th Centuries* (1982).

Church, S. D.,'The Earliest English Muster Roll, 18/19 December 1215', *Historical Research*, 67 (1994).

—— 'The 1210 Campaign in Ireland: Evidence for a Military Revolution', *Anglo-Norman Studies*, 20 (1998).

—— *The Household Knights of King John* (Cambridge, 1999).

—— 'The Care of the Royal Tombs in English Cathedrals in the Nineteenth and Twentieth Centuries: The Case of the Effigy of King John at Worcester', *Antiquaries Journal*, 89 (2009).

—— 'King John's Testament and the Last Days of his Reign', *EHR*, 125 (2010).

Clanchy, M. T., 'Magna Carta and the Common Pleas', *Studies in Medieval History presented to R. H. C. Davis* (1985).

Crook, D., 'The Forest Eyre in the Reign of King John', *Magna Carta and the England of King John*, ed. J. S. Loengard (Woodbridge, 2010).

Crouch, D., 'Normans and Anglo-Normans: A Divided Aristocracy', *England and Normandy in the Middle Ages*, ed. D. Bates and A. Curry (1994).

—— *The Reign of King Stephen* (2000).

—— *William Marshal: Knighthood, War and Chivalry, 1147–1219* (2nd edn, 2002).

—— 'William Marshal and the Mercenariat', *Mercenaries and Paid Men: The Mercenary Identity in the Middle Ages*, ed. J. France (Leiden, 2008).

—— 'The Complaint of King John against William de Briouze (*c.* September 1210)', *Magna Carta and the England of King John*, ed. J. S. Loengard (Woodbridge, 2010).

Danziger, D., and Gillingham, J., *1215: The Year of Magna Carta* (2003).

Davies, R. R., *The First English Empire* (Oxford, 2000).

Draper, P., 'King John and St Wulfstan', *Journal of Medieval History*, 10 (1984).

Duffy, S., 'King John's Expedition to Ireland, 1210: The Evidence Reconsidered', *Irish Historical Studies*, 30 (1996).

—— *Ireland in the Middle Ages* (Basingstoke, 1996)

—— 'John and Ireland', *King John: New Interpretations*, ed. S. D. Church (Woodbridge, 1999).

—— 'Henry II and England's Insular Neighbours', *Henry II: New Interpretations*, ed. C. Harper-Bill and N. Vincent (Woodbridge, 2007).

Duncan, A. A. M., 'John King of England and the Kings of Scots', *King John: New Interpretations*, ed. S. D. Church (Woodbridge, 1999).

France, J., *Western Warfare in the Age of the Crusades 1000–1300* (1999).

Gillingham, J., *Richard I* (Yale, 1999).

—— '1066 and the Introduction of Chivalry into England', idem, *The English in the Twelfth Century: Imperialism, National Identity and Political Values* (Woodbridge, 2000).

—— *The Angevin Empire* (2nd edn, 2001).

—— '*Stupor mundi*: 1204 et un obituaire de Richard Coeur de Lion depuis longtemps tombé dans l'oubli', *Plantagenêts et Capétiens: Confrontations et Héritages*, ed. M. Aurell and N.-Y. Tonnerre (Turnhout, 2006).

—— 'Doing Homage to the King of France', *Henry II: New Interpretations*, ed. C. Harper-Bill and N. Vincent (Woodbridge, 2007).

—— 'The Anonymous of Béthune, King John and Magna Carta', *Magna Carta and the England of King John*, ed. J. S. Loengard (Woodbridge, 2010).

—— The Meetings of the Kings of France and England, 1066–1204', *Normandy and Its Neighbours, 900–1250*, ed. D. Crouch and K. Thompson (Turnhout, 2011).

Goodall, J. A. A., 'Dover Castle and the Great Siege of 1216', *Chateau Gaillard*, 19 (2000).

—— *The English Castle* (Yale, 2011).

Green, V., *An Account of the Discovery of the Body of King John* (1797).

Handbook of British Chronology, ed. E. B. Fryde, D. E. Greenway, S. Porter and I. Roy (3rd edn, Cambridge, 1986).

Hardy, T. D., *Description of the Patent Rolls in the Tower of London* (1835).

Harris, B. E., 'King John and the Sheriff's Farms', *EHR*, 79 (1964).

A History of the County of Leicestershire, ed. W. G. Hoskins and R. A. McKinley (1954).

The History of the King's Works: The Middle Ages, ed. H. M. Colvin (2 vols., HMSO, 1963).

Holdsworth, C. J., 'John of Forde and the Interdict', *EHR*, 78 (1963).

Hollister, C. W., *Henry I* (Yale, 2001).

Holt, J. C., *The Northerners: A Study in the Reign of King John* (Oxford, 1961).

—— 'King John's Disaster in the Wash', *Nottingham Mediaeval Studies*, 5 (1961).

—— 'The Loss of Normandy and Royal Finances', *War and Government in the Middle Ages*, ed. J. Gillingham and J. C. Holt (Woodbridge, 1984).

—— 'King John', idem, *Magna Carta and Medieval Government* (1985).

—— 'The End of the Anglo-Norman Realm', idem, *Magna Carta and Medieval Government* (1985).

—— 'Feudal Society and the Family in Early Medieval England: IV. The Heiress and the Alien', *Trans. Royal Historical Soc.*, 5th ser., 35 (1985).

—— *Magna Carta* (2nd edn, Cambridge, 1992).

—— 'King John and Arthur of Brittany', *Nottinghamshire Medieval Studies*, 44 (2000).

Huscroft, R., *Expulsion: England's Jewish Solution* (Stroud, 2006).

Keefe, T. K., *Feudal Assessments and the Political Community under Henry II and His Sons* (Berkeley, 1981).

—— 'Proffers for Heirs and Heiresses in the Pipe Rolls: Some Observations on Indebtedness in the Years Before the Magna Carta (1180–1212)', *Haskins Soc. Journal*, 5 (1993).

Kellett, A., 'King John's Maundy', *History Today*, 40 (April 1990).

Knowles, M. D., 'The Canterbury Election of 1205–6', *EHR*, 53 (1938).

—— *The Monastic Order in England* (2nd edn, Cambridge, 1963)

Latimer, P., 'Wages in Late Twelfth- and Early Thirteenth-Century England', *Haskins Soc. Journal*, 9 (1997).

—— 'The English Inflation of 1180–1220 Reconsidered', *Past and Present*, 171 (2001).

Legge, M. D., 'William the Marshal and Arthur of Brittany', *Historical Research*, 55 (1982).

Lewis, A. W., 'The Birth and Childhood of King John: Some Revisions', *Eleanor of Aquitaine: Lord and Lady*, ed. B. Wheeler and J. C. Parsons (Basingstoke, 2002).

Lloyd, J. E., *A History of Wales* (1911).

McGlynn, S., *Blood Cries Afar* (Stroud, 2011).

Maddicott, J. R., *The Origins of the English Parliament, 924–1327* (Oxford, 2010).

—— 'The Oath of Marlborough, 1209: Fear, Government and Popular Allegiance in the Reign of King John', *EHR*, 126 (2011).

Martindale, J., 'The Sword on the Stone: Some Resonances of a Medieval Symbol of Power (The Tomb of King John in Worcester Cathedral)', *Anglo-Norman Studies*, 15 (1993).

Marvin, L. W., *The Occitan War: A Military and Political History of the Albigensian Crusade, 1209–1218* (Cambridge, 2008).

Masschaele, J., 'The English Economy in the Age of Magna Carta', *Magna Carta and the England of King John*, ed. J. S. Loengard (Woodbridge, 2010).

Mitchell, S. K., *Studies in Taxation under John and Henry III* (New Haven, 1914).

Morris, M., *The Norman Conquest* (2012).

Norgate, K., *England under the Angevin Kings* (2 vols., 1887).

—— John Lackland (1902).

Orpen, G. H., *Ireland under the Normans, 1169–1333* (4 vols., 1911–20).

Pafford, J. H. P., 'King John's Tomb in Worcester Cathedral: An Account of its Opening in 1529 by John Bale', *Trans. Worcester Archaeological Soc.*, 35 (1958).

Painter, S., *William Marshal* (Baltimore, 1933).

—— *The Reign of King John* (Baltimore, 1949).

—— 'The Lords of Lusignan in the Eleventh and Twelfth Centuries', *Speculum*, 32 (1957).

Plant, J. S., 'The Tardy Adoption of the Plantagenet Surname', *Nomina*, 30 (2007).

Poole, A. L., *Domesday Book to Magna Carta, 1087–1216* (2nd edn, Oxford, 1955)

Power, D., 'King John and the Norman Aristocracy', *King John: New Interpretations*, ed. S. D. Church (Woodbridge, 1999).

—— 'The End of Angevin Normandy: The Revolt of the Count of Alençon', *Historical Research*, 74 (2001).

Powicke, F. M., *The Loss of Normandy, 1189–1204* (2nd edn, Manchester, 1961).

Renouard, Y., *Bordeaux sous les Rois d'Angleterre* (Bordeaux, 1965)

Richard, A., *Histoire des Comtes de Poitou, 778–1204* (2 vols., Paris, 1903).

Richardson, H. G., 'The Coronation in Medieval England', *Traditio*, 16 (1960).

—— *The English Jewry under Angevin Kings* (1960).

Richardson, H. G., and Sayles, G. O., *The Governance of Medieval England* (Edinburgh, 1963).

Rowlands, I., 'King John, Stephen Langton and Rochester Castle, 1213–15', *Studies in Medieval History presented to R. Allen Brown*, ed. C. Harper-Bill, C. J. Holdsworth and J. L. Nelson (Woodbridge, 1989).

—— 'The Text and Distribution of the Writ for the Publication of Magna Carta', *EHR*, 124 (2009).

Sayers, J. E., *Papal Government and England during the Pontificate of Honorius III (1216–1227)* (Cambridge, 1984).

Smith, J. B., 'Magna Carta and the Charters of the Welsh Princes', *EHR*, 99 (1984).

Stenton, D. M., 'King John and the Courts of Justice', *Proceedings of the British Academy*, 49 (1958).

Stimming, A., *Bertran de Born* (Halle, 1892).

Strickland, M., 'The "Bones of the Kingdom" and the Treason of Count John', *Culture Politique des Plantagenêt, 1154–1224*, ed. M. Aurell (Centre d'études Supérieures de Civilisation Médiévale, 2003).

—— 'On the Instruction of a Prince: The Upbringing of Henry, the Young King', *Henry II: New Interpretations*, ed. C. Harper-Bill and N. Vincent (Woodbridge, 2007).

Summerson, H., 'The 1215 Magna Carta: Clause 20, Academic Commentary', *The Magna Carta Project*.

—— 'The 1215 Magna Carta: Clause 39, Academic Commentary', *The Magna Carta Project*.

Sumption, J., *The Albigensian Crusade* (1978).

Treharne, R. F., 'The Franco-Welsh Treaty of Alliance in 1212', *Bulletin of the Board of Celtic Studies*, 18, (1958).

Turner, R. V., and Heiser, R. R., *The Reign of Richard Lionheart* (2000).

Veach, C., 'King and Magnate in Medieval Ireland: Walter de Lacy, King Richard and King John', *Irish Historical Studies*, 37 (2010).

—— 'King John and Royal Control in Ireland: Why William de Briouze had to be Destroyed', *EHR*, 129 (2014).

Vincent, N., 'A Roll of Knights Summoned to Campaign in 1213', *Historical Research*, 66 (1993).

—— *Peter des Roches: An Alien in English Politics, 1205–1238* (Cambridge, 1996).

—— 'Isabella of Angoulême: John's Jezebel', *King John: New Interpretations*, ed. S. D. Church (Woodbridge, 1999).

—— 'England and the Albigensian Crusade', *England and Europe in the Reign of Henry III (1216–1272)*, ed. B. Weiler and I. Rowlands (Basingstoke, 2002).

—— 'The Court of Henry II', *Henry II: New Interpretations*, ed. C. Harper-Bill and N. Vincent (Woodbridge, 2007).

—— 'A Forgotten War: England and Navarre, 1243–4', *Thirteenth Century England*, xi (2007).

—— 'King John's Diary & Itinerary', *The Magna Carta Project*.

Warren, W. L., *King John* (new edn, Yale, 1997).

—— *Henry II* (new edn, 2000).

Young, C. R., *The Royal Forests of Medieval England* (Leicester, 1979).

SECONDARY WORKS (CONSULTED)

Allen, M., 'Henry II and the English Coinage', *Henry II: New Interpretations*, ed. C. Harper-Bill and N. Vincent (Woodbridge, 2007).

—— 'The Quantity of Money in England, 1180–1247: New Data', *British Numismatic Journal*, 75 (2005).

Allen, R., 'The Loyal and Disloyal Servants of King John', *The Court Reconvenes: Courtly Literature Across the Disciplines*, ed. B. K. Altmann and C. W. Carroll (Cambridge, 2003).

Appleby, J. T., *John, King of England* (1958).

Aurell, M., 'Henry II and Arthurian Legend', *Henry II: New Interpretations*, ed. C. Harper-Bill and N. Vincent (Woodbridge, 2007).

Baldwin, J. W., 'Master Stephen Langton, Future Archbishop of Canterbury: The Paris Schools and Magna Carta', *EHR*, 123 (2008).

Barratt, N., 'Finance and the Economy in the Reign of Henry II', *Henry II: New Interpretations*, ed. C. Harper-Bill and N. Vincent (Woodbridge, 2007).

Beadles, A., 'The Opponents of King John: Northern Barons against the Monarch', *History Today*, 29 (May 1979).

Bradbury, J., 'Philip Augustus and King John: Personality and History', *King John: New Interpretations*, ed. S. D. Church (Woodbridge, 1999).

Carpenter, D. A., 'Justice and Jurisdiction under King John and King Henry III', *The Reign of Henry III* (1996).

—— '"In Testimonium Factorum Brevium": The Beginnings of the English Chancery Rolls', *Records, Administration and Aristocratic Society in the Anglo-Norman Realm*, ed. N. Vincent (Woodbridge, 2009).

Cheney, 'King John and the Papal Interdict', *Bulletin of the John Rylands Library*, 31 (1948).

—— 'King John's Reaction to the Interdict on England', *Trans. Royal Historical Soc.*, 4th ser., 31 (1949).

—— 'The Twenty-Five Barons of Magna Carta', *Bulletin of the John Rylands Library*, 50 (1968).

Church, S. D., 'Aspects of the English Succession, 1066–1199: The Death of the King', Anglo-Norman Studies 29 (2007).

Clanchy, M. T., *England and Its Rulers* (Oxford, 1998).

Crouch, D., 'Baronial Paranoia in King John's Reign', *Magna Carta and the England of King John*, ed. J. S. Loengard (Woodbridge, 2010).

Duffy, S., 'Henry II and England's Insular Neighbours', *Henry II: New Interpretations*, ed. C. Harper-Bill and N. Vincent (Woodbridge, 2007).

Duggan, A. J., 'Henry II, the English Church and the Papacy', *Henry II: New Interpretations*, ed. C. Harper-Bill and N. Vincent (Woodbridge, 2007).

Dunbabin, J., 'Henry II and Louis VII', *Henry II: New Interpretations*, ed. C. Harper-Bill and N. Vincent (Woodbridge, 2007).

Galbraith, V. H., 'Good Kings and Bad Kings in Medieval English History', *History*, 30 (1945).

Gillingham, J., 'Richard I, Galley-Warfare and Portsmouth: The Beginnings of a Royal Navy', *Thirteenth Century England*, vi (1997).

—— 'Historians Without Hindsight: Coggeshall, Diceto and Howden on the Early Years of John's Reign', *King John: New Interpretations* (Woodbridge, 1999).

Grant, L., *Architecture and Society in Normandy 1120–1270* (Yale, 2005)

Harper-Bill, C., 'John and the Church of Rome', *King John: New Interpretations*, ed. S. D. Church (Woodbridge, 1999).

Holden, B. W., 'The Balance of Patronage: King John and the Earl of Salisbury', *HSJ*, 8 (1996).

—— 'King John, the Braoses, and the Celtic Fringe, 1207–1216', *Albion*, 33 (2001).

Hollister, C. W., 'King John and the Historians', *Journal of British Studies*, 1 (1961).

Holt, J. C., *Robin Hood* (1982).

—— '*Ricardus Rex Anglorum et Dux Normannorum*', idem, *Magna Carta and Medieval Government* (1985).

Jolliffe, J. E. A., *Angevin Kingship* (2nd edn, 1963).

King, E., 'The Accession of Henry II', *Henry II: New Interpretations*, ed. C. Harper-Bill and N. Vincent (Woodbridge, 2007).

Latimer, P., 'Early Thirteenth-Century Prices', *King John: New Interpretations*, ed. S. D. Church (Woodbridge, 1999).

Levett, A. E., 'The Summons to a Great Council, 1213', *EHR*, 31 (1916).

Levin, C., 'A Good Prince: King John and Early Tudor Propaganda', *Sixteenth Century Journal*, 11 (1980).

Loengard, J. S., 'What Did Magna Carta Mean to Widows?', *Magna Carta and the England of King John*, ed. idem (Woodbridge, 2010).

Martindale, J., 'Eleanor of Aquitaine: The Last Years', *King John: New Interpretations*, ed. S. D. Church (Woodbridge, 1999).

—— 'Eleanor of Aquitaine', *Richard Coeur de Lion in History and Myth*, ed. J. L. Nelson (KCLMS, 1992).

Moore, A. K., 'The Loss of Normandy and the Invention of *Terre Normannorum*, 1204', *EHR*, 125 (2010).

Painter, S., 'The Houses of Lusignan and Chatellerault, 1150–1250', *Speculum*, 30 (1955).

Power, D., 'Henry, Duke of the Normans (1149/50–1189)', *Henry II: New Interpretations*, ed. C. Harper-Bill and N. Vincent (Woodbridge, 2007).

Prestwich, J. O., 'Richard Coeur de Lion: *Rex Bellicosus*', *Richard Coeur de Lion in History and Myth*, ed. J. L. Nelson (KCLMS, VII, 1992).

Reeve, M. R., and Thurlby, M., 'King John's Gloriette at Corfe Castle', *Journal of the Soc. of Architectural Historians*, 64 (2005).

Richardson, H. G., 'The Morrow of the Great Charter', *Bulletin of the John Rylands Library*, 28 (1944).

—— 'The Marriage and Coronation of Isabelle of Angoulême', *EHR*, 61 (1946).

Rowlands, I.W.,'King John and Wales', *King John: New Interpretations*, ed. S. D. Church (Woodbridge, 1999).

Spurrell, F., 'Notes on the Death of King John', *Archaeological Journal*, 38 (1881).

Stacey, R. C., 'The English Jews under Henry III', *Jews in Medieval Britain*, ed. P. Skinner (Woodbridge, 2003).

Stewart, I., 'King John's Recoinage and the Conference of Moneyers in 1208', *British Numismatic Journal*, 59 (1989).

Turner, R.V., 'The Origins of Common Pleas and King's Bench', *American Journal of Legal History*, 21 (1977).

—— 'King John in his Context: A Comparison with his Contemporaries', *Haskins Soc. Journal*, 3 (1991).

—— *King John* (1994).

—— *Eleanor of Aquitaine, Queen of France, Queen of England* (Yale, 2009).

Ullmann, W., 'Arthur's Homage to King John', *EHR*, 94 (1979).

Vincent, N.,'Henry II and the Historians', *Henry II: New Interpretations*, ed. C. Harper-Bill and N. Vincent (Woodbridge, 2007).

—— 'The Pilgrimages of the Angevin Kings of England, 1154–1272', *Pilgrimage: The English Experience from Becket to Bunyan*, ed. C. Morris and P. Roberts (Cambridge, 2002).

—— 'The Strange Case of the Missing Biographies: The Lives of the Plantagenet Kings of England, 1154–1272', *Writing Medieval Biography, 750–1250: Essays in Honour of Frank Barlow* (Woodbridge, 2006).

—— 'Stephen Langton, Archbishop of Canterbury', *Etienne Langton: prédicateur, bibliste, théologien*, ed. L.-J. Bataillon, N. Beriou, G. Dahan and R. Quinto (Turnhout, 2010).

—— *Magna Carta: A Very Short Introduction* (Oxford 2012).

Warren, M. R., 'Roger of Howden Strikes Back: Investing Arthur of Brittany with the Anglo-Norman Future', *Anglo-Norman Studies*, 21 (1999).

Warren, W. L., 'Painter's *King John* – Forty Years On', *Haskins Soc. Journal*, 1 (1989).

Webster, P., 'King John and Rouen: Royal Itineration, Kingship and the Norman "Capital"', *Society and Culture in Medieval Rouen, 911–1300*, ed. L. V. Hicks and E. Brenner (Turnhout, 2013).

Index

Bigod, Roger, earl of Norfolk
(d. 1221), 252
Binham (Norf), 205
Blanche of Castile, queen of
France (d. 1252), 116–17
Bohun, Henry de, earl of
Hereford (d. 1220), 199, 247,
272
Bolsover (Derbs), 65
Bonneville-sur-Touques
(Calvados), 13
Bonsmoulins (Orne), 37
Bordeaux (Gironde), 89, 97, 117,
158
Born, Bertran de, 131, 291
Boulogne, count of, 16, 23, 54,
112, 196–8, 212, 215, 217,
234–5
Bourg-sur-Mer (Gironde), 98
Boutavant (Eure), 123
Bouvines, battle of (1214), 234–6,
238
Brabant, duke of, 54, 235
Brackley (Northants), 247,
265
Bréauté, Falkes de (d. 1226), 195,
200
Brecon (Powys), 166, 172–3
Breton, William the, 9, 11, 155–6,
227, 231, 233
Brewer, William (d. 1226), 245
Brezolles (Eure-et-Loir), 7
Briouze, Annora de, 184
Briouze, Giles de, bp of
Hereford (d. 1215), 247,
249

Briouze, Matilda de (d. 1210),
143, 159–60, 166, 183–5, 187,
209, 284, 292
Briouze, Reginald de, 172, 184
Briouze, William de (d. 1211),
143, 156–9, 160–7, 169, 181,
183–7, 192, 209, 256–7, 284
Briouze, William de (d. 1210),
165, 172, 184, 292
Bristol, 145, 170, 182, 185–6, 189,
201, 220
Brittany, 12, 19, 24–5, 28, 98,
102–6, 124, 146–53, 155, 158,
229–30, 235, 244
Brough (Cumbria), 168
Brougham (Cumbria), 168
Brut y Tywysogion, 193–4, 201
Buckinghamshire, 86
Builth (Powys), 192
Burgh, Hubert de, 148–9, 150,
157, 170, 211, 263, 271, 280,
283, 297
Bury St Edmunds (Suff), 110,
243–4

Caen (Calvados), 27, 44, 144,
150, 153–4
Calais (Pas-de-Calais), 277
Cambridge, 198, 200, 281–2
Cambridgeshire, 267
Camville, Gerard de, 68–9
Canterbury (Kent), 62–3, 85, 136,
138, 141, 177, 210, 214, 269,
278; abp of, 20, 74, 86–8; *see
also* Becket, Thomas; Langton,
Stephen

Italy, 66, 69, 73, 78–9

Ivanhoe, 3

Jerusalem, 32, 36–7, 62, 73, 77–8
Jews, 188–90, 197, 209, 244, 251, 254
Joan, dau. of Henry II, queen of Sicily, countess of Toulouse (d. 1199), 20, 66, 196
Joan, bastard dau. of King John, princess of Wales (d. 1237), 173, 194, 203
John, king of England (1199–1216):
selective chronological survey:
birth, 19; infancy, 20–1; betrothals, 22, 61; endowed with lands (1174), 24; recognized as ruler of Ireland (1177), 31; struggle against Richard for Aquitaine (1183–4), 28–9; knighted (1185), 32; expedition to Ireland (1185), 32–3; defends Châteauroux with Richard against PA (1187), 35; forbidden from taking the cross (1188), 37; deserts Henry II to join Richard (1189), 38, 59, 100; receives county of Mortain and other lands from Richard (1189), 60, 62–3; marries Isabella of Gloucester (1189), 61, 74, 118; bears

sword at Richard's coronation, 62; swears to stay out of England (1190), 64; struggle against William Longchamp (1191), 67–72; tempted to ally with PA, dissuaded by mother (1192), 74–5; seizes Wallingford and Windsor castles (1192), 75–6; rebels against Richard in alliance with PA (1193–4), 78–84, 100, 153–4; submits to Richard (1194), 84; fights for Richard against PA (1194–8), 101–3; partially rehabilitated (1195), 102; lands seized again after rumours of treachery (1199), 103, 105–6; accession and coronation (1199), 3, 103–9, 161, 241, 287; goes to war against PA (1199), 111–113; briefly obtains custody of Arthur (1199), 113–15, 145; agrees peace with PA (1200), 115–17; called 'Soft-sword', 116, 291; divorces Isabella of Gloucester to marry Isabella of Angoulême (1200), 118–20; clash with Cistercians over tax (1200), 117, 121, 128, 130; clash with Lusignans (1200–1202), 121–5; visits Paris (1201), 122; goes to war against PA,

371

Meath (Ireland), 31, 163, 184
Meaux Abbey (Yorks), 190
Medway, river, 255, 268, 270
Melrose Abbey (Roxburghs), 274,
  294, 293
mercenaries, 10, 11, 44, 48, 79,
  89, 128, 151, 154, 170,
  199–200, 208, 252, 256
Mervent (Vendée), 228
Messina (Sicily), 66
Milford Haven (Pembs), 32
Millescu (Charente-Mar.), 226
Mirebeau (Vienne), 22, 124–5,
  144–6, 149, 151, 153, 155, 229,
  290, 292
Montauban (Tarn-et-Garonne),
  98, 290
Montbegon, Roger de (d. 1226),
  51–3, 167, 244, 273
Montfort-sur-Risle (Eure), 7
Montfort, Simon de, earl of
  Leicester (d. 1218), 204, 207,
  225, 227
Mortain (Manche), 60, 102, 161
Moulton, Thomas de (d. 1240),
  92, 167, 222–3
Mowbray, William de (d. *c.* 1224),
  93, 244
Mulgrave (Yorks), 157
Muret, battle of (1213), 225

Nantes (Loire-Atlantique),
  229–30
Navarre, king of, 73
Neville, Hugh de (d. 1234),
  133–4, 144, 153, 199, 211

New Forest, 43
Newark (Notts), 284–5
Newburgh, William of, 36, 63,
  65, 67–9, 74, 76, 79, 100, 102
Newcastle (Northumb), 19, 176,
  208
Niort (Deux-Sèvres), 97–9, 233
Norfolk, 190, 205; earl of, *see*
  Bigod, Roger
Norham (Northumb), 177, 208
Normandy, 5, 6–12, 14, 16–17,
  19, 23, 26, 28, 36–47, 55–6, 60,
  67, 79, 81, 84, 88–99, 101, 103,
  105, 110–12, 114, 122–3, 126,
  137, 144, 146, 151–9, 163, 205,
  209, 214, 231, 235, 244
Northampton, 55, 108, 176, 182,
  196, 221, 247, 259; castle, 145,
  250, 259, 264
Northamptonshire, 62, 133, 267
Northumberland, 54, 109–10,
  116, 120–1, 133, 176–7, 206–8,
  211, 221; sheriff of, *see*
  Oldcotes, Philip of
Norwich (Norf), 145; bp of, *see*
  Gray, John de
Norwich, Geoffrey of, 207, 292
Norwich, Isaac of, 189
Nottingham, 24, 68–9, 81, 83,
  145, 168, 170, 176, 198–202,
  208, 221, 238, 243, 245, 259,
  273; sheriff of, *see* Marc, Philip
Nottinghamshire, 52, 63, 134,
  208, 267

O'Toole, Peter, 17

50, 54; seals two-year truce with John (1206), 99, 126; attacks viscount of Thouars (1208), 174; conspires with king of Scots (1209), 176, 182; prepares to invade England (1213), 213; invades Flanders, fleet destroyed by English raid, 216–218; raises army to resist John's invasion, divides his forces (1214), 226–7; wins victory at Bouvines, 234–6, 238; agrees five-year truce with John, 236; offers support to English rebels (1215), 252; refuses to hear embassy from John (1216), 276

Philip of Swabia, 196

Pickering (Yorks), 145

Pipewell Abbey (Northants), 62

Pleshey (Essex), 274

Poitiers, 20, 97, 124, 235

Poitou, 23, 45, 55–8, 85, 88–9, 97–9, 103, 111, 118–19, 121, 124–6, 144–7, 151, 155, 158, 199–200, 205, 210, 213–14, 218, 220, 224–9, 232–3, 236–8, 244, 247, 250, 291

Pontefract (Yorks), 208, 222, 273; Peter of, *see* Wakefield

Ponthieu, count of, 196

Pope, 7, 18, 21, 25, 34, 65, 70, 74, 76; *see also* Honorius III; Innocent III

Portchester (Hants), 145, 279

Portsmouth (Hants), 55, 58, 60, 97, 122, 171–2, 199, 212–14, 218, 225, 238

Portugal, 118

Powys, 172–3, 192, 200

Préaux, Peter de, 44, 152

prise, 255

Prudhoe (Northumb), 206

Puiset, Hugh de, bp of Durham (d. 1195), 62, 64–5

Quincy, Saer de, earl of Winchester (d. 1219), 207, 244, 247, 252, 257, 262, 267, 272, 274

Radepont (Eure), 12, 124

Radnor (Powys), 166, 172

Ranulf, earl of Chester, 51–3, 95, 102, 192, 200, 215, 245, 252, 280, 284

Raymond of Antioch, 18

Raymond, count of Toulouse (d. 1222), 196, 218, 220, 225

Reading (Berks), 71, 238, 249

Redesdale (Northumb), 206

Reginald, abp of Canterbury-elect, 87–8, 127, 130

Rhuddlan (Denbighs), 200

Rhys ap Gruffudd, 195

Rhys Gryg, 192–3

Richard I (the Lionheart), king of England (1189–99), 110–13, 115, 128–9, 132–3, 135, 153–4, 156, 161, 167, 188, 196, 212, 276, 285, 287, 289–90, 292–3